# THE DAY THE
# REVOLUTION
# BEGAN

## HarperOne Titles by N. T. Wright

*Simply Good News*

*Surprised by Scripture*

*The Case for the Psalms*

*How God Became King*

*Simply Jesus*

*Scripture and the Authority of God*

*The Kingdom New Testament*

*After You Believe*

*Surprised by Hope*

*Simply Christian*

*The Meaning of Jesus* (with Marcus Borg)

## Other Titles by N. T. Wright

Christian Origins and the Question of God series:

*The New Testament and the People of God*

*Jesus and the Victory of God*

*The Resurrection of the Son of God*

*Paul and the Faithfulness of God*

# THE DAY THE REVOLUTION BEGAN

Reconsidering the Meaning
of Jesus's Crucifixion

## N. T. WRIGHT

HarperOne
*An Imprint of* HarperCollins*Publishers*

HarperOne

Old Testament scripture quotations are taken from New Revised Standard Version Bible (NRSV). Copyright © 1989 National Council of the Churches of Christ in the United States of America. Used by permission. All rights reserved. All New Testament scripture quotations, unless otherwise noted, are from *The Kingdom New Testament,* translated by the author, © 2011 by Nicholas Thomas Wright.

Image on page 20 is from Wikimedia Commons and is in the public domain.

HarperCollins books may be purchased for educational, business, or sales promotional use. For information, please email the Special Markets Department at SPsales@harpercollins.com.

FIRST HARPERCOLLINS PAPERBACK EDITION PUBLISHED IN 2018

Library of Congress Cataloging-in-Publication Data is available upon request.

ISBN 978-0-06-233439-8

23 24 25 26 27 LBC 12 11 10 9 8

For Leo

*Look! The Lion has won the victory!*
(Revelation 5.5)

# CONTENTS

## PART ONE: INTRODUCTION

1. A Vitally Important Scandal     3
   *Why the Cross?*
2. Wrestling with the Cross, Then and Now     19
3. The Cross in Its First-Century Setting     51


## PART TWO: "IN ACCORDANCE WITH THE BIBLE": THE STORIES OF ISRAEL

4. The Covenant of Vocation     73
5. "In All the Scriptures"     89
6. The Divine Presence and the Forgiveness of Sins     107
7. Suffering, Redemption, and Love     121


## PART THREE: THE REVOLUTIONARY RESCUE

8. New Goal, New Humanity     145
9. Jesus's Special Passover     169
10. The Story of the Rescue     195
11. Paul and the Cross     227
    *(Apart from Romans)*
12. The Death of Jesus in Paul's Letter to the Romans     263
    *The New Exodus*
13. The Death of Jesus in Paul's Letter to the Romans     295
    *Passover and Atonement*

## PART FOUR: THE REVOLUTION CONTINUES

14. Passover People                                              355
15. The Powers and the Power of Love                             383


*Acknowledgments*                                                417
*Scripture Index*                                                421
*Subject Index*                                                  427

# PART ONE

## Introduction

# I

## A Vitally Important Scandal

### *Why the Cross?*

"YOUNG HERO WINS HEARTS." Had there been newspapers in Jerusalem in the year we now call AD 33, this was the headline you would *not* have seen. When Jesus of Nazareth died the horrible death of crucifixion at the hands of the Roman army, nobody thought him a hero. Nobody was saying, as they hurriedly laid his body in a tomb, that his death had been a splendid victory, a heroic martyrdom. His movement, which had in any case been something of a ragtag group of followers, was over. Nothing had changed. Another young leader had been brutally liquidated. This was the sort of thing that Rome did best. Caesar was on his throne. Death, as usual, had the last word.

Except that in this case it didn't. As Jesus's followers looked back on that day in the light of what happened soon afterward, they came up with the shocking, scandalous, nonsensical claim that his death had launched a revolution. That something had happened that afternoon that had changed the world. That by six o'clock on that dark Friday evening the world was a different place.

Nonsensical or not, they were proven right. Whether we believe in Jesus, whether we approve of his teaching, let alone whether we like the look of the movement that still claims to follow him, we are bound to see his crucifixion as one of the pivotal moments in human history. Like the assassination of Julius Caesar around seventy years earlier, it marks the end of one era and the start of another.

And Jesus's first followers saw it as something more. They saw it as the vital moment not just in human history, but in the entire story of God and the world. Indeed, they believed it had opened a new and shocking window onto the meaning of the word "God" itself. They believed that with this event the one true God had suddenly and dramatically put into operation his plan for the rescue of the world.

They saw it as the day the revolution began.

It wasn't just that they believed Jesus had been raised from the dead. They did believe that, of course, and that too was scandalous nonsense in their day as it is in ours. But they quickly came to see his resurrection not simply as an astonishing new beginning in itself, but as *the result of what had happened three days earlier*. The resurrection was the first visible sign that the revolution was already under way. More signs would follow.

Most Christians today don't see it like this—and, in consequence, most people outside the church don't see it like that either. I understand why. Like most Christians today, I started my thinking about Jesus's death with the assumption, from what I had been taught, that the death of Jesus was all about God saving me from my "sin," so that I could "go to heaven." That, of course, can be quite a revolutionary idea for someone who's never thought of it before. But it's not quite the revolution the early Christians were talking about. In fact, that way of putting it, taken on its own, significantly distorts what Jesus's first followers were saying. They were talking about something bigger, something more dangerous, something altogether more explosive. The personal meaning is not left behind. I want to make that clear from the start. But it is contained within the larger story. And it means more, not less, as a result.

Let me put this another way. The early Christian writers used some stunning expressions of delight and gratitude when they mentioned Jesus's death. Think of Paul saying, "He loved me and gave himself for me" (Gal. 2:20), or "The Messiah died for our sins in accordance with the Bible" (1 Cor. 15:3). Think of John writing perhaps the most famous line in the New Testament, "God so loved the world, that he gave his only begotten Son" (3:16, KJV). The focus in all these cases is upon Jesus's death on the cross, not the resurrection. These must remain central in any authentic description of what the first Christians believed had happened when Jesus died. But by themselves, without paying attention to the larger elements in the picture, they can lead us into a private or even selfish way of seeing things, in which our immediate needs may seem to have been met (our needs for forgiveness in the present and salvation in the future), but without making any difference in the wider world.

Some, indeed, make a virtue of that irrelevance. This world is not our home, they say. Jesus has rescued us, and he's taking us somewhere else. But the early Christians were clear: Jesus's death made all the difference in the world, all the difference *to* the world. The revolution had begun. In this book I want to show what that means and how a fuller vision of what happened when Jesus died, rooted in the New Testament itself, can enable us to be part of that revolution. According to the book of Revelation, Jesus died in order to make us not rescued nonentities, but restored human beings with a vocation to play a vital part in God's purposes for the world. Understanding what exactly happened on that horrible Friday afternoon is a big step toward making that vocation a reality.

But whether we understand it or not, there is no denying that the sheer fact of Jesus's crucifixion and the symbol of the cross itself still carry enormous power in our world. We need to think about this for a moment before going any farther. It forces us to ask, again, the key question: Why?

## Captivated by the Cross

Someone recently drew my attention to an energetic, youthful organization calling itself the "Jesus Army." It has, of course, a website, and I confess that when I first looked at it, I was expecting trite clichés and tired slogans. Not at all. It had the feel of fresh discovery and embraced a wider variety of spiritual traditions and practical programs than I had anticipated. But at its heart it remained deeply traditional, as you can see in the posting that caught my eye. This short piece places the spotlight on the crucifixion of Jesus of Nazareth, the event that forms the subject of this book. It draws our attention to the strange, perhaps even revolutionary power that this event still appears to possess, despite all the skepticism and sneering of today's world:

> YOU can't get away from it. It's everywhere.
>
> The cross.
>
> In homes, in films, in paintings, in pop videos. Worn as an earring, on a necklace. Stitched or studded onto leather or denim. Tattooed onto skin . . .
>
> What would Coca-Cola or McDonald's give to own a symbol that millions wear around their necks every day?
>
> The cross is the universal Christian symbol, acknowledged by millions of Christians everywhere as the single visual sign of their faith.
>
> Which is weird, isn't it? Because the cross was originally a symbol of suffering and defeat. The Roman Empire killed thousands of its enemies by nailing them to wooden crosses.

It's like wearing a gibbet around your neck. Or hanging a little golden lethal injection from your necklace.

Jesus Christ was executed 2,000 years ago by the Romans. But Christians believe Jesus didn't stay dead—that Jesus beat death and rose again, beyond death's reach.

That makes the cross not a sign of death, but a sign of the end of death.

A sign of hope, a sign of possibility—for every human being.

That's why Christians wear crosses.

The Jesus Army wear and give away bright red crosses. Jesus Army member Chris, 38, says, "We give away hundreds of crosses. People like them. They glow in UV light, which makes them popular with clubbers! But all sorts of people like them and use them to help them to think about God or to pray."

"They're designed to stand out" he adds. "The cross of Jesus means we can be forgiven and can have a new start. Even death's been clobbered."

"It's worth shouting about."[1]

There's quite a lot to think about in that sharp little extract. Clearly it isn't designed as a sophisticated piece of theology, or for that matter biblical exegesis, but that's part of the point: the crucifixion of Jesus is a plain, stark fact, etched into real space and time and, even more important, into the real flesh and blood of a human being. People today, in a wide variety of ways, simply intuit that it has powerful and profound meaning for them. Others, of course, see nothing in it except an unpleasant tale from long ago.

---

1. http://jesus.org.uk/blog/streetpaper/cross-my-heart-and-hope.

Despite the predictions of people who imagined that religion in general and Christianity in particular were losing their appeal in today's world, the fact of Jesus's crucifixion and the gospel story in which we find it retain a remarkable power in late modern culture. This appeal persists even among people who don't hold any particular theory about its precise meaning or even any specific faith in Jesus or God. Why? Why does the cross of Jesus of Nazareth have this impact even today?

In 2000, the National Gallery in London put on a millennial exhibition entitled "Seeing Salvation." That was a case in point—especially remembering that European countries tend to be far more "secularized" than the United States. It consisted mostly of artists' depictions of Jesus's crucifixion. Many critics sneered. All those old paintings about someone being tortured to death! Why did we need to look at rooms full of such stuff? Fortunately, the general public ignored the critics and turned up in droves to see works of art, which, like the crucifixion itself, seem to carry a power beyond theory and beyond suspicion.

The Gallery's director, Neil McGregor, moved from that role to become director of the British Museum, a job he did with great distinction and effect for the next decade. The final piece he acquired in the latter capacity, before moving to a similar position in Berlin, was a simple but haunting cross made from fragments of a small boat. The boat, which had been carrying refugees from Eritrea and Somalia, was wrecked off the coast of the Italian island of Lampedusa, south of Sicily, on October 3, 2013. Of the 500 people on board, 349 drowned. A local craftsman, Francesco Tuccio, was deeply distressed that nothing more could have been done to save people, and he made several crosses out of fragments of the wrecked vessel. One was carried by Pope Francis at the memorial service for the survivors. The British Museum contacted Mr. Tuccio, and he made a cross especially for the museum, thanking the authorities there for drawing attention to the suffering that this small wooden object would symbolize. Why the cross rather than anything else?

Another example struck me forcibly during the 2014 season of Promenade Concerts in the Albert Hall in London. (The "Proms," as they are known, make up a major annual festival, offering world-class music cheaply to a wide audience.) On September 6, 2014, Sir Simon Rattle conducted an extraordinary performance of J. S. Bach's *St. Matthew Passion*. Not only was the music wonderfully performed, the whole thing was acted out, choreographed by the American director Peter Sellars, a professor at University of California in Los Angeles, who is noted especially for his unique contemporary stagings of classical operas and plays. In a broadcast talk during the intermission, Sellars explained that this wasn't theater; it was prayer. What he was doing, he said, related first to Bach's musical portrayal of the story of Jesus's death and then to our modern appropriation of both the story itself and Bach's interpretation. At no point did Sellars make any specifically Christian confession of faith. But it was clear throughout that he saw the story of Jesus's crucifixion as the story par excellence in which all human beings are confronted with the full darkness of human life and with the possibility, through inhabiting that story themselves, of finding a way through. Just as the world as a whole, whether Christian or not, dates itself by Jesus's birth, so the reflective world, whether Christian or not, regularly finds that the story of his death, in art, music, or literature, provides a unique focal point for the dark dilemma of human existence and also a shining light to guide us through.

We could pile up plenty of other examples, each of which would increase the volume of the question: Why? Why does this death and the story in which we find it carry this power? It seems to go well beyond any one articulate explanation, and it certainly goes way beyond the boundaries of explicit Christian faith. I think of the Jewish novelist Chaim Potok, whose artistic hero Asher Lev searches for imagery to express the pain of modern Judaism. The only thing he can find that will do—to the predictable horror of his community—is the crucifixion scene, which he paints in fresh and shocking ways. I think of the way in which the first *Harry Potter* novel ends with the disclosure that Harry had been rescued, as a young child, by the loving self-sacrifice of his mother. We could go on.

Skeptics may well continue to see the execution of Jesus as just one among thousands of crucifixions carried out by the Romans in the Middle East. But for reasons that seem to go beyond mere cultural traditions, this particular death still carries enormous evocative power. And just as in the Middle Ages many found that they could relate to that story by meditating on the "instruments of the Passion" (the scourge, the crown of thorns, the nails, and so forth), so today various human elements of the story—the cock-crow as Peter is denying that he knows Jesus, the kiss by which Judas betrays his master—have become proverbial. They seem to sum up the way in which we humans get things horribly wrong, but at the same time they do so within a larger and more powerful context of meaning.

When we come to more explicitly Christian presentations, the same point emerges all the more powerfully, especially when we notice how the cross, even though it's such a simple symbol, somehow resists being turned into a mere cliché. In Roland Joffé's award-winning 1986 movie *The Mission,* the cross in various forms haunts the whole narrative. The story begins with the death of one of the early Jesuit missionaries to the remote South American tribe of the Guarani. The tribesmen tie him to a wooden cross and send him over the vast Iguazu Falls, providing the movie with its poster image. The story ends with the massacre of the unresisting leaders, carrying the symbols of the crucifixion in procession, as the Portuguese colonial forces, bent on enslaving the natives rather than evangelizing them, close in and open fire. The meaning of the cross—especially its stark opposition to the world's ways of power—is allowed to hang like a great question mark over the entire narrative.

More explicit again are the many ways in which the cross has been described in the classics of Christian literature. In John Bunyan's famous *Pilgrim's Progress* (1678), the hero, Christian, is trudging along, weighed down with a huge burden. Eventually he comes to a place where, in Bunyan's matchless description:

> There stood a Cross, and a little below in the bottom, a sepulchre. So I saw in my Dream, that just as Christian came up with the Cross, his Burden loosed from off his shoulders, and fell from off his back, and began to tumble, and so continued to do, till it came to the mouth of the Sepulchre, where it fell in, and I saw it no more. . . .
>
> Then was Christian glad and lightsome, and said with a merry heart, *He hath given me rest by his sorrow, and life by his death.* Then he stood still awhile to look and wonder; for it was very surprizing to him, that the sight of the Cross should thus ease him of his Burden.[2]

Let me give one more example, out of thousands of possible ones, of the way in which the crucifixion of Jesus appears to carry a power that goes way beyond any attempt to rationalize it away. A Roman Catholic archbishop (I have tried to discover which one, but so far without success; the story is well known) described how three mischievous young lads decided to play a trick on the priest who was hearing confessions in their local church. They took turns going into the confessional and "confessing" all sorts of terrible sins and crimes to see how the priest would react. Two of them then made off in a hurry; but the priest stopped the third one and, as though taking him seriously, announced that he was going to impose a penance on him. The lad was to walk up to the far end of the church, toward the figure of Jesus hanging on

---

2. John Bunyan, *Pilgrim's Progress,* ed. J. M. Dent (London, 1898), 38.

the cross. He was to look Jesus in the face and to say three times, "You did all that for me, and I don't give *that* much"—snapping his fingers on the "that." The young man did it once. He did it a second time. Then he found he couldn't do it the third time, but instead dissolved into tears. He left the church a changed person. "And the reason I know that story," concluded the archbishop, "is that I was that young man."

Why? Why is this story so powerful? What kind of sense does it make to suppose that the death of one man nearly two thousand years ago, in an obscure Roman province, could have that kind of power? What sort of revolution is it that was launched on that dark and horrible afternoon?

Before we go any farther in this inquiry, let's make one thing clear. You do not have to be able to answer the question "Why?" before the cross can have this effect. Think about it. You don't have to understand music theory or acoustics to be moved by a wonderful violin solo. You don't have to understand cooking before you can enjoy a good meal. In the same way, you don't have to have a theory about why the cross is so powerful before you can be moved and changed, before you can know yourself loved and forgiven, because of Jesus's death.

Many people who have been grasped in this way couldn't begin to explain why, just as the "Jesus Army" extract doesn't attempt to explain why or how Jesus's crucifixion means that people can be forgiven. Rather, this widespread and transcultural impact highlights the prearticulate or simply nonarticulate power that people discover the cross to possess. It's like the beauty of a sunset or the power of falling in love. Trying to analyze it or explain why it's so powerful seems beside the point. People find that the story grips them; that depictions of the crucifixion are strangely compelling; that a small cross is somehow good to hold, to look at, to use as a focus for thought and perhaps prayer. Those who specialize, as I do not, in what is called "deliverance ministry" find the same thing: the cross carries a strange power through which apparent forces of evil can be defeated or held at bay. And millions have found and go on finding that simply reading the story of Jesus's death in Matthew, Mark, Luke, or John continues to console and compel, to inspire awe, love, and gratitude.

In the same way, millions around the world take part, day by day and week by week, in the simple but profound ceremony of sharing bread and wine that Jesus himself instituted less than twenty-four hours before his death. He seems to have seen it as a way for his followers to find the meaning of that death welling up inside them, transforming them, and giving them a sense of his presence and love. You don't have to have a theory in your head, all worked out in neat logical categories, for all this to happen. The question "Why?" is important. But we ask it because we observe the reality.

I found this out for myself long before I was old enough to know the words "theory" and "reality" or why I should care about the difference. Imagine, if you will, a boy of about seven years old, alone for some reason in a quiet room, finding himself overwhelmed with the sense of God's love revealed in the death of Jesus. I cannot now recall, sixty years later, what it was that reduced me to tears on that occasion. Growing up in a traditional middle-of-the-road Christian household, attending the local Anglican church (very undramatic by today's standards), I was familiar with many prayers, hymns, and passages of scripture that might suddenly have "gotten through." The old-fashioned language of the Authorized (King James) Version couldn't stifle the simple but powerful statements: "God so loved the world, that he gave his only begotten Son" (John 3:16); "God commendeth his love for us, in that, while we were yet sinners, Christ died for us" (Rom. 5:8); "The Son of God . . . loved me, and gave himself for me" (Gal. 2:20); "Neither death, nor life . . . nor any other creature, shall be able to separate us from the love of God, which is in Christ Jesus our Lord" (Rom. 8:38–39). And so on.

And, in my tradition at least, there were the great hymns, like "My Song Is Love Unknown":

*My song is love unknown,*
   *my Savior's love to me,*
*love to the loveless shown,*
   *that they might lovely be.*
*O who am I,*
*that for my sake*
*my Lord should take*
*frail flesh and die?*

*Here might I stay and sing:*
*no story so divine;*
*never was love, dear King,*
*never was grief like thine!*
*This is my Friend,*
*in whose sweet praise*
*I all my days*
*could gladly spend.[3]*

Then, less rich in either poetry or theology, but memorable nonetheless, was C. F. Alexander's well-known hymn "There Is a Green Hill Far Away":

*There is a green hill far away*
*without[4] a city wall,*
*where the dear Lord was crucified,*
*who died to save us all. . . .*

*O dearly, dearly has he loved,*
*and we must love him too,*
*and trust in his redeeming blood,*
*and try his works to do.[5]*

---

3. Lyrics by Samuel Crossman (1624–83), AMNS 63.
4. Note: "without" in the second line means "outside."
5. Lyrics by Cecil Frances Alexander (1818–95), AMNS 137.

On a different poetic plane altogether, there is John Henry Newman's majestic "Praise to the Holiest in the Height," which I knew as a hymn many years before I met it in Edward Elgar's glorious setting in *The Dream of Gerontius:*

> *O loving wisdom of our God!*
> *when all was sin and shame,*
> *a second Adam to the fight*
> *and to the rescue came.*
>
> *O wisest love! That flesh and blood,*
> *which did in Adam fail,*
> *should strive afresh against the foe,*
> *should strive and should prevail. . . .*
>
> *O generous love! That he, who smote*
> *in Man for man the foe,*
> *the double agony in Man*
> *for man should undergo.*
>
> *And in the garden secretly,*
> *and on the cross on high,*
> *should teach his brethren, and inspire*
> *to suffer and to die.*[6]

And then there was the best known of all Good Friday hymns, at least in my tradition: Isaac Watts's great meditation on Galatians 6:14, "When I Survey the Wondrous Cross":

> *When I survey the wondrous Cross*
> *on which the Prince of Glory died,*
> *my richest gain I count but loss,*
> *and pour contempt on all my pride. . . .*
>
> *Were the whole realm of nature mine,*
> *that were an offering far too small;*

---

6. Lyrics by John Henry Newman (1801–90), AMNS 117.

*love so amazing, so divine,*
*demands my soul, my life, my all.*[7]

I had sung all these and many others over and over and knew at least some by heart. The message was reinforced by the simple Anglican liturgy I heard every Sunday, in which so many prayers ended with words like "through the love of our Savior, Jesus Christ" or "through the merits and death of Jesus Christ our Lord." I would soon come to know by heart, through hearing it so often, the majestic yet intimate words of Thomas Cranmer's prayer at the heart of the Communion service:

> Almighty God, who of thy tender mercy toward mankind didst give thy Son, our Savior Jesus Christ, to suffer death upon the Cross for our redemption; who made there, by his one oblation of himself once offered, a full, perfect and sufficient sacrifice, oblation and satisfaction for the sins of the whole world.

*The love of God and the death of Jesus.* That is what it's all about. But, as with the stories I mentioned earlier, none of these hymns or prayers really explains how it "works." Cranmer's complex phrases, resonant but cumbersome, picking their cautious way through the minefields of sixteenth-century controversies, point to particular interpretations, but you'd need a crash course in medieval theology to figure out exactly what was meant. It was easier, certainly for me as a boy, to cling to the idea of a "tender mercy" that had given an extraordinary and utterly expensive "gift." The hymns were and remain wonderfully evocative rather than explanatory. Even the scriptural passages I quoted a moment ago don't really explain why we should see the death of Jesus as a divine act at all, let alone an act of love. They simply hold on to it as a reality, as *the* reality, the healing and revitalizing truth

---

7. Lyrics by Isaac Watts (1674–1748), AMNS 67.

that consoles and comforts and challenges and consoles again. *The love of God and the death of Jesus*—that combination was enough to reduce me to tears all those years ago and can still do the same today. But what exactly does it mean? How does it make sense?

Ought we even to try to fathom it out? Can we not rest in awe and wonder, as in the third verse of another classic hymn, "How Great Thou Art":

> *And when I think that God, his Son not sparing,*
> *Sent him to die, I scarce can take it in;*
> *That on the Cross, my burden gladly bearing,*
> *He bled and died to take away my sin.*[8]

It may indeed be true that we can scarcely "take it in." It may even be ultimately true, as one popular contemporary jingle has it, that "I'll never know how much it cost to see my sins upon that cross." Though since the New Testament does tell us precisely what it cost (the blood of God's own son), and since the jingle in question is as confused in theology as it is deficient in rhyme, we are not much farther ahead. But—and this is the point of writing this book—I believe it is vital that we try.

All this brings us back where we began. Granted that the story of Jesus's crucifixion as it is portrayed in the gospels and in art, music, and literature seems to have a power to move, console, and challenge people across widely different times, places, and cultures, what is it about this story, and particularly about the event itself, that carries this power? When the early Christians summarized their "good news" by saying that "the Messiah died for our sins in accordance with the Bible," what precisely did they mean? Why, in short, did Jesus die? Why would anyone suppose that his death possessed revolutionary power? And why do so many people, without holding any particular theoretical answer

---

8. Lyrics: verses 1–2, Carl Boberg (1859–1940); verses 3–4, Stuart K. Hine (1899–1989).

to those questions, find nevertheless that the cross, in story, image and song, has a power to move us at such a deep level?

The question, "Why did Jesus die?" in fact, subdivides. There is the "historical" question: Why did Pontius Pilate, egged on by the chief priests, decide to send Jesus to his death? Then there is the "theological" question: What was God hoping to achieve by Jesus's death, and why was that the appropriate method of achieving it? Underneath these there is another, even more difficult one: What did *Jesus himself* think was going on? That one is both historical (giving an account of the mind and motivation of one historical person) and theological (even if you don't believe that Jesus was the incarnate son of God, he was certainly very much in tune with Israel's scriptures and the question of their fulfillment). Or to go on walking cautiously around these questions: What deep layers of meaning are hidden in the deceptively simple phrase "for our sins"? How did people in the first century hear that kind of language, and why did the first Christians speak like that? Why did they regard it as "good news"—granted that it doesn't seem at first glance to have anything to do with the "good news" announced by Jesus himself, which was about the "kingdom of God"? What themes, images, and stories—and, not least, what themes and narratives from their Bible—did they already have in their heads that enabled them to make fresh and joyful sense of the fact that the man they had come to regard as God's anointed king had just been killed by the imperial authorities? Why did they see that not as the end of any potential Jesus-based revolution, but as its real beginning?

These questions are not, of course, new. We are only the latest in a long line of people who have wrestled with the meaning of the cross down through the years. The way we approach the questions and the problems we meet as we try to do so are inevitably shaped by these previous expositions. We therefore need to have at least a basic understanding of some key moments in the story of the church's wrestling with its foundational and revolutionary event.

# 2

———

# Wrestling with the
# Cross, Then and Now

THE QUESTION OF why the crucifixion of Jesus of Nazareth was perceived from the first to have such power is
heightened by one of the earliest writings of the New
Testament, which declares that the cross is a scandal. Or, to be
precise, it is "a scandal to Jews and folly to Gentiles" (1 Cor. 1:23).
True, Paul goes on to claim that "to those who are called" it is
the revelation of the Messiah, the unveiling of God's power and
God's wisdom. But that only intensifies the puzzle. How on earth
did something so obviously crazy or scandalous or foolish become
so central so quickly?

The very mention of crucifixion was taboo in polite Roman
circles, since it was the lowest form of capital punishment, reserved for slaves and rebels. As for the Jews, the very idea of a
crucified Messiah was scandalous. A crucified Messiah was a horrible parody of the kingdom-dreams that many were cherishing.
It immediately implied that Israel's national hope was being radically redrawn downward.

But if the Messiah's crucifixion was scandalous to Jews, it

was sheer madness to non-Jews. The early cultured despisers of Christianity had no trouble mocking the very idea of worshipping a crucified man. A famous cartoon from the Palatine in Rome, dated to some point during the first three centuries of the common era, makes the point. It reads, "Alexamenos worships his god," and features a crucified figure with a donkey's head (below).

How easy it would have been for the early Christians to tone down the fact of the cross, to highlight instead the life-giving force of the resurrection and the power of the Holy Spirit. How

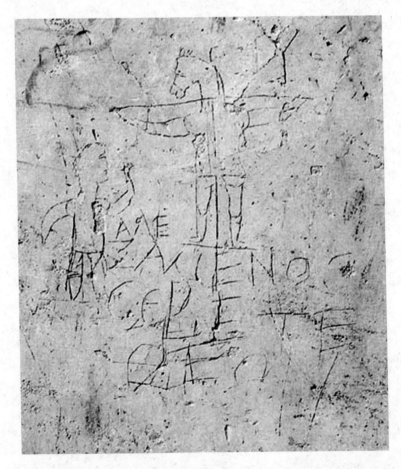

"sensible" it might have been to draw a discreet veil over the manner of Jesus's death that had preceded this sudden new life.

Some people, including some who wanted to think of themselves as followers of Jesus, took exactly that line. We can watch the process taking place in the so-called Gnostic gospels (books like the *Gospel of Thomas*). They airbrushed the cross out of the picture, redefined the resurrection as a nonbodily transformation, and reduced Jesus to being a teacher of quizzical wisdom. This has attracted enthusiastic attention from some in our own day for whom, for whatever reasons, certain presentations of the cross have become a scandal.

But over against this downplaying or mocking we also see, from the earliest documents of the New Testament right on through the first five or six centuries of church history, the resolute affirmation of the cross not as an embarrassing episode best left on the margins, but as the mysterious key to the meaning of life, God, the world, and human destiny. One of the great Christian writers of the mid-second century, Justin Martyr, wrote glowingly about the way in which the cross is the key to everything. It is the central feature of the world, he said: if you want to sail a ship, the mast will be in the shape of a cross; if you want to dig a ditch, your spade will need a cross-shaped handle. That gives us a fair indication of the way in which even those who were trying to explain the Christian faith attractively to outsiders didn't shy away from the cross, but rather celebrated it. They wallowed in it, we might say, even though they knew what the reaction would be.[1]

They did not, however, define it. Nor has the worldwide church done so at any time since—though some groups and movements have insisted on various formulations. There is wisdom in that: doctrinal definition can only go so far. Shorthand

---

1. Justin Martyr, *First Apology 55.* See the discussion in *The New Testament and the People of God* (Minneapolis: Fortress, 1992), 366f.

slogans and technical language are helpful when making sure that we are not losing sight of something vital, but they must not be mistaken for the real thing. We must bear this in mind in what follows. Once we fully grasp the biblical story and its focus on Jesus's crucifixion, we will find as a by-product that many of the puzzles that have kept theologians awake at nights and have made nonspecialists sigh with frustration can be put together in a new way.

Theology, after all, was made for the sake of the church, not the church for theology. I hope the present book will help ordinary Christians grasp, and be grasped by, the multifaceted glory of Jesus's cross, rather than getting bogged down in complex and apparently irrelevant problems. "The Word became flesh," said St. John (1:14); and Paul described the "word of the cross" as "God's power" (1 Cor. 1:18). The flesh and the power are what matter in the end, rather than the pretty patterns of our words. The point of trying to understand the cross better is not so that we can congratulate ourselves for having solved an intellectual crossword puzzle, but so that God's power and wisdom may work in us, through us, and out into the world that still regards Jesus's crucifixion as weakness and folly. Yes, there are puzzles; I shall be addressing them. But Jesus died for our sins not so that we could sort out abstract ideas, but so that we, having been put right, could become part of God's plan to put his whole world right. That is how the revolution works.

At the same time, we have to go on trying to understand. This is not an optional extra. Paul warned the church in Corinth to be little children when it came to evil, but to be grown-ups in their thinking. To go back to the example of cooking: we can all enjoy a well-prepared meal, but unless somebody in the house knows how to cook and something about balanced diets, we risk either obesity or malnutrition—or even food poisoning. The theological equivalents of those may take longer for symptoms to appear, but unless someone in the church—in each Christian

gathering, in each generation—is working on deeper understandings of foundational Christian truth, it is perilously easy for
individuals and communities to drift away from the life-giving
meaning of the gospel itself. We constantly need to press beyond
the one-line summaries and the popular slogans. The powerful
love of God is so counterintuitive that we easily scale it down in
our imagination and memory and develop ways of making ourselves immune to its ultimate and life-changing challenge. Or,
worse, we distort it and twist it until we find ourselves saying
more or less the opposite of what we ought to mean. Somebody
needs to be asking "Why?" This must of course be done humbly
and carefully, not arrogantly or scornfully. But the question must
be addressed.

The dangers of scaling things down, of domesticating or distorting the cross, face all Christians some of the time and some
Christians—especially teachers and preachers—most of the
time. Unless we are making the effort to think it all through
and understand what Jesus's first followers meant when they
said things like, "The Messiah died for our sins in accordance
with the Bible," the church as a whole will be vulnerable to the
twists and turns of different schemes of interpretation, which
can lead into various kinds of spiritual and practical dead ends,
or worse.

In some cases people can descend into endless debates about
the microscopically small details of interpretation of one or two
particular Bible passages. In others they can generate large abstract schemes full of technical jargon in order to do battle with
other large abstract schemes. At the opposite extreme from both
of those engaged positions, of course, people can reassure one
another that as long as they know God loves them, nothing else
matters that much. Well, it's certainly true that the powerful
love of God is central to every aspect of Christian faith. But
when that belief is challenged either by skeptics or by voices
within ourselves, we need to look hard not simply at relevant

biblical texts, but also at our traditional formulations of what precisely we mean by saying that Jesus "died for us." Each generation of Christians and each church in its own way needs to do this.

The task is difficult. There are different ways of probing this mystery. On the theological level, which of the "theories" or "models" do we prefer, and how does it all "work"? On the sacramental level, baptism and the Eucharist have both proved controversial; is this because they are so closely linked to Jesus's death? On the level of preaching and teaching, how can we best articulate the central gospel message, so that its impact comes from its original meaning rather than from dodgy illustrations that can easily distort the truth? And on the pastoral level, how can the truth of the cross be applied to the difficulties of real-life discipleship? The more we engage in any of these, let alone all four, the more we seem to be entering dangerous, contested territory. Things happen to distract us, to dismay us, to put us off track. I have observed this in my own work over many years and again in the writing of this book. I take this to imply that something really important is at stake. It is vital that we keep our nerve, say our prayers, and press forward.

The aim, as in all theological and biblical exploration, is not to replace love with knowledge. Rather, it is to keep love focused upon its true object. We must not make the overwhelming experience of God's love revealed in the cross of Jesus an excuse for mere muddle. As in a marriage, love doesn't stand still. A passionately devoted young couple need to learn the long-term skills of mutual understanding, not to replace love, but to deepen it. It is of course better to hold on to love (whether that of God or of a spouse), even when we are confused, than to let go because we can't understand it. But it is far better to address the confusions. It isn't only faith that seeks understanding. Love ought to do the same; not of course in order to stop loving, but so that love may grow, mature, and bear fruit.

## Models and Doctrines

So how did the story develop—the story, that is, of the ways in which the followers of Jesus have understood his death? Many books have been written on this topic alone, and I must here confine myself to a quick outline sketch. The great dogmatic disputes of the third, fourth, and fifth centuries focused on the questions of God, Jesus, and the Spirit. Their participants hammered out the official doctrines of the Trinity and the incarnation. To be sure, they all believed that Jesus had "died for their sins," and in sermons and longer writings they said many moving things about that death and what it meant. But it was never defined as such, never nailed down to one theory.

When the sixteenth-century Reformation took place, many branches of the new churches articulated their particular theories of atonement in official statements, but the great ecumenical creeds of the early centuries did not do so. They merely restated the early formula we find in 1 Corinthians 15, as, for instance, in the Nicene-Constantinopolitan Creed (381): "For us humans and for our salvation he came down from heaven, and was incarnate . . . and was crucified also for us under Pontius Pilate; he suffered and was buried." The shorter Apostles' Creed doesn't even add "for us." There is, in other words, no equivalent in atonement theology of the careful Christological formulations that emerged from the controversies over what could and couldn't be said and what should and shouldn't be said about the person of Jesus and the triune God. The rich imagery we find in, for instance, the exposition of the cross by the fourth-century bishop of Alexandria, Athanasius, is striking. But it doesn't get turned into official formulas.

Many of the early church fathers seem to assume two things in particular about the meaning of the cross, holding these two points in a more fluid combination than later theorists sometimes imagine. On the one hand, many expound some version of the idea that on the cross God in Christ won a great victory, perhaps we should say *the* great victory, over the powers of evil. This is the theme many now refer to as *Christus Victor,* the conquering Messiah. On the other hand, many of the early theologians regularly spoke of Jesus's death as somehow "in our place": he died, therefore we do not. We, with hindsight, might want to describe this as a combination of two motifs, coupled also with a third, the regular use of sacrificial imagery; but the biblical view of atonement is more than the mere heaping up of motifs or even models. These are moments in a story; and it is the story itself—a real historical story both then and now—that matters. For this I think the church fathers provide much food for thought. But, as they themselves would insist, the Bible remains central and determinative.

Detailed development of theories about what the cross achieved and how it achieved it got under way after the split between Eastern and Western Christianity (Eastern Orthodox and Roman Catholic) a thousand years ago. To put it crudely, the Eastern Orthodox churches never had "an Anselm." That alone should alert us to the possibility that some of our great controversies may have more to do with fresh interpretative schemes introduced at a later date than with the original meaning of the Bible. Anselm, archbishop of Canterbury in the eleventh century, was the first one to work out in detail what has come to be known as the "satisfaction" theory of the atonement: God's honor has been impugned by human sin and must be satisfied. (The idea that someone's honor needed to be satisfied made the sense it did within the complex codes of behavior in the High Middle Ages.) The famous alternative at the time was associated with Abelard, who pioneered the "moral example" theory: the cross shows how much God loves us and thereby gives us strong reason to love him and one another in return. Detailed research has shown that Anselm did not teach as rigid a theory as some of his followers, and that Abelard, although he put the "moral example" in the center, wanted to retain "satisfaction" as well; but the two names have been used as shorthand labels for the more simplistic versions of their positions.

Meanwhile, the Eastern churches never seem to have found it necessary to ask the kind of questions that Anselm and Abelard were addressing. On the one occasion when I had the temerity to ask a Greek Orthodox archbishop what his church taught about the cross, all he would say (with a beaming smile) in response to my repeated attempts to raise the subject from different angles was that the cross was the "prelude to the resurrection."

This emphasis on the resurrection, as opposed to the cross, is more or less the exact opposite of the theology that is implicit in the glorious settings by Johann Sebastian Bach of the crucifixion narratives of St. Matthew and St. John. Bach affirmed the resurrection, of course, and set it to music, though much less memorably than the Passion. But in his work it never seemed to play much of a role in the question of how people are saved. By the end of the *St. Matthew Passion* or the *St. John Passion,* we feel that the story is complete as it stands: the worshipper has identified with Jesus in his suffering and is somehow caught up in its deeper meaning. For the Eastern Orthodox, by contrast, the real moment is just about to begin. This is not the place to explore a two-thousand-year history of different views. I mention them here to indicate the range of belief about the crucifixion as various traditions developed.

Martin Luther and John Calvin, two of the greatest sixteenth-century Reformers, drew on many sources from the Bible and the church fathers to develop fresh ways of speaking about Jesus's death that, with hindsight, have something in common with Anselm's. Calvin in particular, however, was anxious to distinguish his view from Anselm's "satisfaction" theory, stressing instead the combination of God's justice, holiness, and love. But with this we find ourselves firmly in the sixteenth century and with its retrieval in more recent popular thinking and preaching.

## Jesus Punished, Once and for All?

Today's Western debates about the cross take place, for better and for worse, within the ongoing influence of the sixteenth-century Reformation. But, as Swiss theologian Karl Barth pointed out, the sixteenth-century Reformers never sorted out what to say about the ultimate future (for which the technical term is "eschatology"); and, as we saw, whatever we mean by "atonement" is directly related to whatever we think about God's ultimate future, particularly about what happens after death. *How* we are saved is closely linked to the question of what we are saved *for*.

This had a particularly sharp focus at the time of the Reformation. In sixteenth-century Europe, a great many people worried a lot about the doctrine of purgatory, the belief that after death faithful Christians could expect to spend time in a place of punishment and purgation where sins were finally dealt with before they might finally enter heaven. Luther's early protest was fueled by his angry rejection of the corrupt practice whereby people could buy "indulgences" that would allow relatives or friends to get out of purgatory, or at least get through it more quickly. Purgatory gripped the imagination of late medieval Europe to a degree almost impossible to imagine today. The rich, and not least the royal, often left copious sums of money to fund "chantries" in which prayers would be offered for their souls in purgatory.

Behind all this was the great heaven-and-hell scheme of Western eschatology, which we see in literary works like those of Dante and in majestic visual art like Michelangelo's Sistine Chapel frescoes. Bodily resurrection remained the official dogma, but the late medieval period more and more envisaged the ultimate promised future not as a new creation, but as the picture of "heaven" common to this day in Western Christianity, both Catholic and Protestant. Many dictionaries still define "eschatology" using the terms "death, judgment, heaven, and hell," often known as the "Four Last Things." It is possible to combine this with a belief in ultimate new creation, but most people who have been taught the traditional fourfold scheme don't even realize that this alternate schema is an option, far less that it is the *biblical* option.

The Reformers by and large rejected not only the abuses connected with purgatory (selling indulgences and the like), but the doctrine itself. In part this may have been because they saw this teaching being used as a weapon by the clerical elite to maintain social and dogmatic control. But their objections were set out in robustly theological and biblical terms. They insisted that the Christian soul went immediately to heaven after death. (Some tried to combine this with the New Testament's sense of a time lag before the ultimate new creation, teaching that the soul might in some sense "sleep" in between bodily death and bodily resurrection; but the point, again, was "no purgatory.") These issues remained unresolved and are not relevant to our present discussion, except as the context for the truly important thing. The rejection of purgatory precipitated a fresh emphasis from a new angle on an interpretation of the cross that echoed, but also differed from, that of Anselm.

Catholic apologists for the doctrine of purgatory had insisted that at the point of death the still sinful soul needed two things: further purification and further punishment. (Allowance was made for a small number of saints who would go straight to heaven, but they were assumed to be very much the exception.) The Reformers replied that the purification in question was effected not *after* death, but *by* bodily death itself (as in Rom. 6:7, where death pays all debts) and by the Spirit's present sanctifying work, putting to death the deeds of the body (as in Rom. 8:13). And they insisted, particularly, that postmortem punishment for the still sinful believer was unthinkable, *because the punishment had already been inflicted on Jesus himself in the sinner's place.* "So, therefore, there is no condemnation . . . because . . . right there in the flesh, [God] condemned sin" (Rom. 8:1–4). That punishment had already been meted out and could not be repeated. Thus the doctrine known as "penal substitution" (Jesus bearing punishment in the place of his people), though in itself a much older, indeed biblical and patristic, conception, received a new boost *and a new spin* from the Reformers' rejection of purgatory. One of the reasons it became such a hallmark of Reformation theology was that it was thus a key part of the polemic against a doctrine that lacked biblical support and had the visible propensity to generate corruption and abuse. (It is noteworthy that leading Roman theologians today, men of the stature of Karl Rahner and Joseph Ratzinger, later Pope Benedict XVI, have radically revised the doctrine, so that it bears almost no relation to what their forebears taught in the early sixteenth century.)

The Reformers did not, however, challenge the first part of the medieval doctrine, the pacification of divine wrath through the death of Jesus. Indeed, they insisted on it. (They were careful to expound it through a trinitarian theology of divine love, in other words, over against any suggestion of a "kind Jesus" pacifying an "angry God"; this too can be seen as a reaction against a tendency in medieval art and presumably theology to have a stern Father and a meek and suffering Jesus.) But they insisted on this view of Jesus's death precisely as part of their undermining of purgatory. Not only had the divine wrath been placated through the Father's own action in sending the Son; the punishment for sin had already been meted out. The more one emphasized Jesus's wrath-bearing death in the sinner's place, the less one could then ask the sinner to bear any subsequent punishment.

Luther's protest of 1517 thus kept the medieval picture of God's wrath, but insisted that this wrath was quenched by God's love through the death of Jesus. Exactly one hundred years earlier, a traveling monk called Poggio Bracchiolini discovered a previously lost manuscript of Lucretius's first-century BC masterpiece, *De Rerum Natura,* which forms an elegant, poetic exposition of the Epicureanism that would then make such an impact on Europe. Bracchiolini too was reacting against the medieval vision of an angry God. But whereas Luther kept the wrath of God and declared that the wrath had fallen on Jesus, Bracchiolini followed the ancient Epicureans in proposing that God, or the gods, were a long way away and were unconcerned with human affairs and certainly not angry about anything in our world. Both were reacting against the same medieval excess, Bracchiolini by denying it altogether and Luther by interposing Jesus and his death. Both have had a long and continuing influence in Western culture.

The other great Reformation protest was against the medieval Roman Catholic doctrine of the Mass. In particular, the Reformers objected strongly to the idea that the priest at the altar was sacrificing Jesus all over again, thus making the benefit of his atoning death available for all those who witnessed the event. (*Watching* Mass being celebrated was deemed to be as effective as actually receiving Communion, if not more so.) Here again the doctrine of penal substitution provided a strong, sharp answer: Jesus died in our place once for all, *ephapax* (as Paul puts it in Rom. 6:10); as a result, the priest could not be sacrificing Jesus again in the Mass. The Mass was thus vilified as doing blasphemous violence to the unique, one-off self-offering of Jesus by attempting to add to the "finished work of Christ" some extra "works" on the part of the congregation, or at least the celebrant. This question thus became further muddled as the specter of "justification by works" loomed up behind, enabling the Reformers to accuse their Roman opponents of not only adding to the already complete sacrifice of Christ, but also bringing their own "works" into play to supplement what Jesus had already achieved. The question of whether medieval Catholics actually taught all this is beside the point, since the Reformers certainly thought they did. As with purgatory, there is also more than a hint that there are social and cultural forces at work behind the theology as people came to reject the power exercised, through the Mass, by the clergy.

These two polemical targets—purgatory and the Mass—thus ensured that when the Reformers were developing their own ways of explaining what the death of Jesus achieved, they were understandably eager to ward off what they saw as ecclesial abuse. I am not a specialist in the sixteenth and seventeenth centuries, but it does seem to me that in general terms the Reformers and their successors were thus *trying to give biblical answers to medieval questions.* They were wrestling with the question of how the angry God of the late medieval period might be pacified, both here (through the Mass?) and hereafter (in purgatory?). To both questions, they replied: no, God's wrath was already pacified through the death of Jesus. Not only does this not need to be done again; if we were to try to do it again, we would be implying that the death of Jesus was somehow after all inadequate. (Echoes of this controversy can still be seen when exegetes tiptoe around Col. 1:24, in which Paul seems to be saying that his own sufferings are somehow completing something that was "lacking" in the Messiah's own sufferings.) They did not challenge the underlying idea that the gospel was all about pacifying divine wrath. It was simply assumed that this was the problem Paul was addressing in Romans 1:18–32 or indeed 1 Thessalonians 1:10 or 5:9.

If, of course, you are faced with the medieval questions, it is better to give them biblical answers than nonbiblical ones. But the biblical texts themselves might suggest that there were better questions to be asking, which are actually screened out by concentrating on the wrong ones. As I have sometimes remarked in reading the gospels, it is possible to check all the correct boxes, but still end up with the wrong result, like a child doing a connect-the-dots puzzle who doesn't realize the significance of the numbers and ends up with an elephant instead of a donkey; or perhaps, writing from Scotland, I should say a Saltire instead of a Union Jack.

I should also add that these last two or three paragraphs, taken by themselves, could give a very lopsided view of the Reformers.

Luther and his colleagues were energetic biblical expositors, excited about the New Testament message of the grace and love of God, which they had not heard taught in the days of their youth. In particular, they went back again and again to grace, love, faith, hope, freedom, and joy as the ultimate reasons for everything, and certainly the ultimate reasons for their own excitement and energy. That, for them, was what it was all about. However, in their insistence on certain particular ways of understanding the biblical teaching on Jesus's death, the two factors I have highlighted—purgatory and the Mass—remained extremely influential. Even when they were gazing in gratitude on the cross as the effective sign of God's love, these concerns and the need to consolidate a Reformation in which abuses would not return to a half-taught church remained powerful.

In thus giving (as it seems to me) the right answers to the wrong questions, the Reformers failed to challenge the larger heaven-and-hell framework itself (which Eastern theologians challenge to this day) or to think through what new creation and resurrection would actually mean or how they might come about. Of course, the great Reformers had a strong agenda for the reformation of society as well as theology. A good deal of their energies went into the attempts to create new kinds of Christian societies within European cities, like Calvin's Geneva, and even countries, like Cromwell's Britain. But the underlying eschatological framework remained in place.

I have often reflected that if the Reformers had focused on Ephesians rather than Romans or Galatians, the entire history of Western Europe would have been different. In Ephesians 1:10 the divine purpose is to sum up, in the Messiah, all things in heaven and on earth. Romans 8 makes the same point, but the key passage, 8:18–24, has routinely been bracketed out, since it has been assumed that Paul's talk in that chapter about "inheritance" and "glorification" is simply a roundabout way of speaking of "going to heaven." That vision of a nonbodily ultimate "heaven" is a direct legacy of Plato and of those like the philosopher and bi-ographer Plutarch, a younger contemporary of St. Paul, who interpreted Plato for his own day. It is Plutarch, not the New Testament (despite what one sometimes hears!), who suggested that humans in the present life are "exiled" from their true "home" in "heaven." That vision of the future—an ultimate glory that has left behind the present world of space, time, and matter—sets the context for what, as we shall see, is a basically paganized vision of how one might attain such a future: a transaction in which God's wrath was poured out against his son rather than against sinful humans.

In particular, the churches of the Reformation, including my own, have often not known what to do with Easter itself. Conservatives have said that Jesus was bodily raised, while liberals have denied it, but neither group has seen the bodily resurrection as the launching of God's new creation within the present world order. And with that failure many other things have been lost as well. I have written about this elsewhere, particularly in *Surprised by Hope*. Once we say that the aim of God's saving plan is the new heaven and new earth, with resurrection bodies for his redeemed people, then the means by which we are brought to that goal, leaving sin and death behind, must be rethought as well. Atonement (how humans are rescued from their plight and restored to their intended place within the loving and creative purposes of God) must dovetail with eschatology (what God ultimately intends for the world and for humans). And if we rethink our eschatology, as I have been trying to do over the last decade or two, we must rethink our view of atonement as well. In fact, the two go together very closely in the New Testament: the cross was the moment when something *happened* as a result of which the world became a different place, inaugurating God's future plan. The revolution began then and there; Jesus's resurrection was the first sign that it was indeed under way. That is what the present book is about.

The unresolved theological problems of the sixteenth century were made worse, in my view, by the collusion of the Western churches with the eighteenth-century Enlightenment. Many Christians in the seventeenth and eighteenth centuries still held to a robust resurrection hope. That, indeed, formed part of the postmillennial "Puritan hope," reflecting a mood of cultural optimism as well as spiritual hope. But by the nineteenth century the notion of "going home to heaven" had all but taken over. The essential Epicureanism of the Enlightenment insisted on a great gulf between earth and heaven. Many devout Christians accepted that unbiblical cosmology, opting for a detached spirituality (a heavenly-mindedness with a questionable earthly use) and an escapist eschatology (leaving the world and going to heaven). Over the course of the nineteenth and twentieth centuries, on both sides of the Atlantic, this has taken us back once more to the medieval heaven-and-hell eschatology, which has radically conditioned both soteriology ("How are we saved for that goal?") and missiology ("How should the church set forward God's work of salvation?").

True, the doctrine of purgatory was not so popular outside Roman circles in the nineteenth century. But "penal substitution," which had been emphasized partly in order to ward off that idea, then found a new home in the Western piety that focused not on God's kingdom coming on earth as in heaven, but on *my* sin, *my* heavenly (that is, nonworldly) salvation, and of course *my* Savior. This, indeed, presses a particular question upon us: if many of our contemporary ideas about what was achieved on the cross belong with a nineteenth-century view of "sinners" being "saved" and "going to heaven," what might the cross mean for the earlier view in which the gospel is transforming the whole world? That is a question for the historians, though since my own view of the cross as the start of a revolution has a lot in common with those earlier beliefs, I will be giving my own answer in due course.

Another problem emerges in the eighteenth century and is still with us powerfully today. I have written about this in *Evil and the Justice of God*. When much European culture in the eighteenth century was embracing Deism and then Epicureanism, a radical split emerged between personal sin, which stopped people going to heaven, and actual evil in the world, including human wrongdoing, violence, war, and so on, but also what has been called "natural evil," earthquakes, tsunamis, and the rest. "Atonement theologies" then addressed the former (how can our sins be forgiven so we can go to heaven?), while the latter was called the "problem of evil," to be addressed quite separately from any meaning given to the cross of Jesus by philosophical arguments designed to explain or even justify God's providence. The two became radically divided from one another, and questions about the meaning of Jesus's death were related to the former rather than the latter. The revolution that began on Good Friday—whose first fruit was the socially as well as theologically explosive event of the resurrection—seemed to be pushed to one side.

One unexpected result of this, therefore, as I suggested in that earlier book, is that it has been tacitly assumed that the cross has nothing to do with social and political evil. Such "evil" was then to be addressed in (apparently) nontheological ways. After the terrible events of September 11, 2001, Western leaders united in declaring that there was "evil" at large in the world and that they and their allies were going to deal with it—basically by dropping bombs on it. That proposal was not only politically naive and disastrous, not only philosophically shallow; it was also theologically naive or even, one might say, heretical. It was trying to "deal with evil" all by itself, with no reference to any belief that this might be God's job. (This is an analogy to the Reformers' protest against what they saw as the Roman tendency to add to the unique sacrifice of Christ, whether in purgatory or in the Mass.)

In Christian theology it is God who deals with evil, and he does this on the cross. Any other "dealing with evil" must be seen in the light of that. This is of course very difficult to work out on the ground. For that we would need a freshly thought through theological analysis of international politics in the postmodern age of global empire, on the one hand, and terrorism, on the other. There are no easy or glib solutions. But just as we must (I believe) restore the biblical vision of God's ultimate future and reconceive atonement in relation to that—the task of Part Three of the present book—so we must restore the biblical analysis of evil and see the cross as addressing it all, not just part of it.

## Scandalous—For the Wrong Reasons?

If a quick tour of two thousand years of church history leaves us somewhat confused about the meaning of the cross, we will not be surprised that there is plenty of confusion in our own day as well. When, as I mentioned earlier, the National Gallery opened its 2000 exhibition "Seeing Salvation" and the skeptics sneered, the standard Christian response might have been, "Well, he died for our sins." But that, for many today, just makes it worse. Skeptics come back with more scorn. "Sin" itself is out of date, they say. It's just a projection of anxieties or childhood phobias. To land our "sins" onto a dead first-century Jew is not just ridiculous; it's disgusting. To suggest that some god projected our "sins" onto that man is even worse: it's a sort of cosmic child abuse, a nightmare fantasy that grows out of—or might actually lead to!—real human abuses in today's world. We can do without that nonsense.

The angry scorn of the skeptics gets extra traction from the fact that some have found the sign of the cross to be a symbol of fear. The horrible dark history of "Christian" persecution of people of other faiths, particularly Jewish people, has left a stain on what should be a symbol of hope and welcome. I remember being shocked, as a young man, to read about Jews who had escaped from persecution in supposedly "Christian" cultures in eastern Europe and who then, upon arriving in America, saw on street corners the sign of the cross, which they had come to fear and loathe. Those of us who grew up with crosses in our churches and all around us and with no anti-Jewish ideas in our heads have to face the fact that our central symbol has often been horribly abused. It has been used as a sign of a military might or of a dominant culture determined to stamp out all rivals. The emperor Constantine, facing a crucial battle, saw a vision of the cross in the sky and was told, "In this sign you will conquer." The Ku Klux Klan burns crosses, claiming to bring the light of the Christian gospel into dark places. The fact that such nonsense is a scandalous denial of the early Christian meaning of the cross doesn't make it any better.

It isn't just those outside the Christian faith who have found the cross a symbol of fear. Many inside the church too have shrunk back from one particular interpretation that, in some form or other, has dominated much Western Christianity over the last half millennium. One recent hymn puts it like this:

> And on the cross, when Jesus died,
> The wrath of God was satisfied—

(This makes it sound like hunger that is satisfied by a good meal.) The line of thought goes like this, usually based on a particular arrangement of biblical texts:

a. All humans sinned, causing God to be angry and to want to kill them, to burn them forever in "hell."

b. Jesus somehow got in the way and took the punishment instead (it helped, it seems, that he was innocent—oh, and that he was God's own son too).

c. We are in the clear after all, heading for "heaven" instead (provided, of course, we believe it).

Many preachers and teachers put it much more subtly than this, but this is still the story people hear. This is the story they *expect* to hear. In some churches, if you don't tell this story more or less in this way, people will say that you aren't "preaching the gospel."

The natural reaction to this from many who have grown up hearing this message and feeling they *had* to believe it (if they didn't, they would go to hell) is that its picture of God is abhorrent. This God, such people instinctively feel, is a bloodthirsty tyrant. If there is a God, we must hope and pray that he (or she, or it) isn't like that at all. So they react in one of a number of predictable ways. Some people reject the whole thing as a horrible nonsense. Others, puzzled, go back to their Bibles and to the great teachers of the early church, and there they find all sorts of other things being said about the cross, for instance, that it was the means by which God's rescuing love won the ultimate victory over all the forces of darkness. Or they find early writers urging Christians to imitate the self-giving love of Jesus, and they seize upon that as the "answer": the cross, they say, wasn't about God punishing sin; it was about Jesus giving us the ultimate example of love. Thus many different interpretations have arisen, affecting the ways in which people have been taught the Bible and the Christian faith. This has been a recipe for confusion.

This confusion, as I shall be suggesting, gets in the way of what is arguably the most important thing. The New Testament insists, in book after book, that when Jesus of Nazareth died on the cross, *something happened as a result of which the world is a different place.* And the early Christians insisted that when people are caught up in the meaning of the cross, they become *part of* this difference. You wouldn't necessarily guess this from many of the debates and reactions that I've just sketched or, sadly, from the way many Christians and many churches have sometimes behaved. But it's what the first Christians thought, said, and taught. Jesus's crucifixion was the day the revolution began.

In particular, they seem to have interpreted Jesus's crucifixion within a much bigger—and perhaps more dangerous—story than simply the question of whether people go to "heaven" or "hell." That question, in fact—to the astonishment of many people—is not what the New Testament is about. The New Testament, with the story of Jesus's crucifixion at its center, is about God's kingdom coming *on earth as in heaven*. This is, after all, what Jesus taught his followers to pray. That is a rather obvious piece of evidence, though people regularly ignore it in practice. However, it points us in the direction I shall be following as we try to figure out what exactly happened on the cross and why it launched a revolution that continues to this day.

Confusions about the cross have come in many shapes and forms, but the one most Western Christians are familiar with today has to do with violence. Today's global population is more aware of violence, its scale, and its nature than any previous generation. But now, among the unintended consequences of the technological revolution, the twentieth and early twenty-first centuries have offered two remarkable things. First, humans have devised ways of killing one another on an industrial scale. Second, the nastiest details about such horrors are now transmitted instantaneously around the world through social media. Apart from those directly involved either in war or torture, most people in earlier generations never really faced the disgusting actualities of raw violence. We all now know not only *that* it has happened and is happening, but what it looks like and sounds like. And even if we don't watch the relevant news bulletins, the movie industry has made an entire art form, new and dark, out of the graphic depiction of every kind of violence.

This seems to have been a kind of signature tune for the twentieth century, in which truly appalling acts of violence became defining moments for global culture. The mere names "Auschwitz" and "Hiroshima" say it all. It remains to be seen whether September 11, 2001, will become a defining moment of the same kind for the twenty-first century or whether it will be overtaken by other yet more terrible crimes. But the point is this. The present generation has gazed with justified revulsion upon the whole late modern culture of violence and death; *and it has noticed worrying signs of the same culture in some expressions of Christianity.* Many have pointed out that traditional expressions of belief about Jesus's crucifixion sometimes mirror all too closely language that has been used to justify violence.

Putting it like that is deliberately vague. Things haven't been helped by the tendency in some quarters first to regard the Bible as a book of "moral examples" and then to express shock and alarm when a significant number of the stories, particularly but not exclusively in the Old Testament, display various characters behaving extremely badly. The book of Judges provides several examples (Jephthah and his daughter, for a start), but there are many others. Often it seems to be the women who come off worst: a daughter killed, a concubine raped and murdered, a slave girl treated as a substitute wife and then sent packing with her child. In fact, of course, the Bible was not written as a collection of "moral examples" in the first place. The stories are regularly told in quite a sophisticated way, nudging alert readers into seeing serious and complex underlying patterns and narratives that warn against simplistic readings and that, indeed, encourage them to draw conclusions beyond anything stated on the surface of the text.

But this both does and doesn't help. People naturally ask: Does the Bible justify violence? And, in particular: Is the death of Jesus a supreme example of the God of the Bible using violence—violence, it seems, against his own son!—as a way of achieving his purposes? (I once heard that argument made explicitly in the 1970s by some who wanted to use violence to oppose South African *apartheid;* they were saying, in effect, if God could do it, so can we.) Even supposing those purposes are ultimately loving and aimed at rescuing people, is this an appropriate way for the one true God to behave?

These questions come to a head when some preachers and teachers present the meaning of the cross in relation to punishment. Here we have to be careful. There are many ways of talking about the "punishment of sin" and how that might relate to the event of Jesus's death. At least one of those ways is clearly taught in the Bible, but it means something significantly different from what many people suppose—many, that is, of those who teach it and many who oppose it. But another way in which the cross has been interpreted in connection with "punishment" has been very popular in some quarters. In this view, God hates sinners so much that he is determined to punish them, but Jesus more or less happens to get in the way and take the death blow on their behalf, so they are somehow spared. It would (I think) be difficult to find a work of serious theology in any tradition that puts the matter as baldly as that. Theologians will almost always say, "But of course this was because of God's love for us." But at a popular level, in sermons and talks to young people, enthusiastic preachers will often throw caution to the winds and use illustrations or explanatory stories that fall into this trap.

The day after I wrote that last sentence I received an e-mail that included a link to a short video claiming to sum up the gospel in a way that, I was told, I would find refreshing. It would build up my faith. Intrigued, I watched it. It was well put together, with clever sequences and plenty of hi-tech touches. But at the center of the message was a line that made my blood run cold. The video had described how we all mess up our lives, how we all do things that spoil God's world, and so on. Then said the narrator, "Someone has to die," and it turned out, of course, to be Jesus. That sums up the problem. What kind of "good news" is that? What kind of *God* are we talking about once we say that sort of thing? If God wants to forgive us, why can't he just forgive us? (Heinrich Heine famously suggested God would indeed forgive us, since after all that was his job.) Why does "someone have to die"? Why *death*? Why would that help? And could it just be "someone," anyone? Did it have to be God's own son? How does it all *work*?

The danger with this kind of popular teaching—and examples of it are not hard to come by—is that ultimately we end up rewriting one of the most famous verses in the Bible. I already quoted the King James Version of John 3:16: "God so loved the world, that he gave his only begotten Son." Look at the two verbs: God so *loved* the world that he *gave* his son. The trouble with the popular version I have described is that it can easily be heard as saying, instead, that God so *hated* the world, that he *killed* his only son. And that doesn't sound like good news at all. If we arrive at that conclusion, we know that we have not just made a trivial mistake that could easily be corrected, but a major blunder. We have portrayed God not as the generous Creator, the loving Father, but as an angry despot. That idea belongs not in the biblical picture of God, but with pagan beliefs.

There are many reasons, most of them good ones, why people want to reject the picture of God-the-angry-despot. (Among the bad reasons for wanting to get rid of it is the lazy idea that God, if such a being exists at all, is like an indulgent elderly relative who doesn't want to spoil people's fun and so never gets angry about anything. As has often been pointed out, this is mere sentimentalism. If there is a God, and if he does not hate injustice, child prostitution, genocide, and a lot of other things as well, then he is not a good God.) Page after page of the New Testament insists, as we have already glimpsed, that what happens in the death of Jesus happens because of the *love* of God. But the problem with the "angry despot" picture of God is not solved by simply producing a few texts that say the opposite. Most preachers who *in fact* offer this picture will always say, if challenged, that God did what he did because of "love." It's just that it doesn't *look like that* or *sound like that* to anyone trying to make sense of what's just been said. It is easy for a preacher to deny the "angry despot" picture in theory, but to reinforce it in practice. Talk to people who attend those churches. They know.

But the problems don't stop there. Many people have pointed out that the idea of an angry, bullying deity who has to be appeased, to be bought off, to have his wrathful way with someone even if it isn't the right person fits uncomfortably well with the way many human authority figures actually behave: tyrants, rulers, bosses, sometimes tragically also fathers, within families older men in general. Sometimes, of course, clergy. People who have grown up in a family with a violent, perhaps drunken, father or who have been abused one way or another by people in authority hear someone in a pulpit telling the story of the angry God, and they think, "*I know that character, and I hate him.*" It doesn't do any good to tell people in that state of mind that this angry God is really a loving God in disguise. "*If that's love,*" they think," *then I don't want it.*" They have quite possibly been told by an abuser how much he "loves" them. You cannot rescue someone from the scars of an abusive upbringing by replaying the same narrative on a cosmic scale and mouthing the word "love" as you do so.

Now, as I say, there are many ways of speaking of the death of Jesus in relation to the punishment of sin. At least one of those ways is biblical. We shall come to that, and when we do we will find that the entire setting undermines any suggestion of the angry, bullying God. There is a different story, one that we need to think through in fresh ways. But even as we say that, we must face the other challenge to any such account of the meaning of the cross.

Some will say that a story in which God uses violence to redeem the world might serve as an excuse for those who want to believe, presumably on quite other grounds, that "redemptive violence" is the way the world is rescued from its various ills. I mentioned a moment ago an example of this argument from the 1970s, but it goes on today. Critics have found it easy to point out that some versions of the "punishment" view of Jesus's death seem to be entrenched in the same communities, in parts of America, where a harsh penal regime, including the death penalty, is not only the norm, but is held up as a fine example of how to deal with crime and social unrest. In some of the same communities one might find the belief that when things go wrong in the wider world, the best thing to do is to use more violence there as well, dropping bombs on faraway towns and villages or sending drones to take out designated targets.

My point here is not that some ways of addressing global terrorism are more morally justified or more effective than others. These are complex issues. Easy "solutions" are bound to be oversimplifications. I want to say simply this: that many have observed an apparent connection between ways in which people have described the meaning of Jesus's death and ways in which others have seen fit to try to "solve" problems in the world. If God needs to punish, then perhaps we do as well. If God solves problems by using violence, maybe he wants us to do so too. However, the shift if not toward pacifism itself, then at least toward a strict limitation on military responses to global problems in certain sectors of public opinion in the Western world as a whole over the last century, has caused some in the churches to suggest views of the death of Jesus in which divine punishment plays no role at all. Some have even suggested that the connection between divine punishment and Jesus's death is a comparatively modern invention, though in truth we can find the same theme stated (in a different context, as I shall show) in the Bible itself. We also find it in the early church fathers, and we should note that many of them were strongly opposed to the death penalty at a time when it was taken for granted in the violent world of the Roman Empire. We should not too quickly assume that theories of atonement are directly reflected in or reflective of social practice.

All this points to the complexity of recent debates about the meaning of Jesus's crucifixion, about the "Why?" that haunts the whole subject. If certain "punishment" models of atonement are perceived to license abusive or aggressive behavior, whether in families or between nations, does that mean we should rule them out of order, even if they seem to be sanctioned by some passages of scripture? Or—to look at things from the other end of the telescope—if such models of atonement are deemed after all to be central to scripture and to the preaching of the gospel itself, so that to soft-pedal such ideas would be to give up on an element of vital spiritual power, ought we instead to regard the sort of objections I have described as a diabolical trick to distract the church from its core message? Sadly, these questions often get bundled up with other ones, including ones about cultural, political, and social problems. At that point, clear-headed fresh readings of scripture can be seen receding over the horizon.

But if you take the first line—that "punishment" models of atonement are to be ruled out because of their horrible view of God or their equally horrible social consequences—what are the alternatives? Traditionally there have been two, both with strong claims to some kind of biblical basis.

First, as we saw earlier, there is the remarkable and paradoxical idea that on the cross Jesus won a victory—or at least God won a victory through Jesus—over the shadowy "powers" that had usurped his rule over the world. That idea was popular in some quarters during the first few Christian centuries. Many thinkers in the second half of the twentieth century and up to the present day have advocated some version of this, partly as a way of warding off what they see as those dangerous ideas about punishment. But this simply pushes the question around the circle rather than answering it directly. What or who are these "powers"? Why would someone's death—anyone's death, the Messiah's death, the death of the Son of God himself—why would such an event defeat these "powers"? Why would that be a revelation of divine *love*? And—perhaps the most pressing question of all—if these "powers" have been defeated, why does evil still appear to carry on as before, to reign unchecked? Did anything actually *happen* on the cross that made a real difference in the world, and if so what account can we give of it? Has the revolution really begun, or is it all wishful thinking?

Second, there's another idea that comes through prominently in the Bible that many have advocated as the "real meaning" of Jesus's death. In this view, on the cross Jesus offered the supreme example of love, the ultimate display of what love will do. He thus transformed the world by offering a uniquely powerful example, a pattern for others to imitate. Now, of course, the New Testament does indeed insist on this line of thought. Jesus's death is regularly appealed to as the gold standard of "love." In John's gospel, Jesus commands his followers to love one another and declares, "No one has a love greater than this, to lay down your life for your friends" (15:13). The First Letter of John insists on the same point, as do Paul and many other early writers.

But this too runs into problems. Unless there was a *reason* for Jesus to die, and perhaps even a reason for him to die that particular and horrible kind of death, it is hard to see how this death could actually be an example of love. If Bill's dearest friend falls into a fast-flowing river and Bill leaps in to try to save him, risking his own life in the process, that would indeed provide an example of love (as well as heroic courage) for anyone who witnesses the event or hears about it. But if Fred, wishing to show his dearest friend how much he loves him, leaps into a fast-flowing river when the friend is standing safely beside him on the bank, that would demonstrate neither love nor courage, but meaningless folly.

My point is this: unless Jesus's death *achieved* something—something that urgently needed to be done and that couldn't be done in any other way—then it cannot serve as a moral example. The "exemplary" meaning must always depend on something prior. As John puts it: "Love consists in this: not that we loved God, but that he loved us and sent his son to be *the sacrifice that would atone for our sins.* Beloved, if that's how God loved us, we ought to love one another in the same way" (1 John 4:10–11). John does not expect his readers to offer themselves as the sacrifice to atone for one another's sins. That has already been done. They are expected to *copy* the self-sacrificial love through which Jesus did something unique, something that urgently needed doing. So our question presses: What was that "something"?

At this point other questions have come into the contemporary discussion. First, as we have seen, the wars and genocides of the last century have generated a new kind of Christian pacifism in which all violence is to be rejected outright, including the apparent violence of some traditional atonement theories (God using violence against Jesus, and so on). Second, at the same time and perhaps with similar motivation, many have embraced the previously unthinkable idea that the suffering of the cross is the suffering not only of the Son, but also of the Father. Others, again, have reacted by proposing new versions of the old idea that though the "human" Jesus suffered on the cross, the "divine" Jesus did not. Whether that makes any sense is difficult to say. These questions demonstrate rather sharply something that is always going to be true: whatever we say about the cross will sooner or later involve us in discussions of the Trinity and the incarnation in the questions of who God really is and who Jesus really was and is.

Having mentioned earlier the ways in which Western hymnody has struggled to articulate the meaning of the cross, I note that at least one recent writer has expressed this new emphasis memorably:

> And when human hearts are breaking
> Under sorrow's iron rod,
> Then they find that self-same aching
> Deep within the heart of God.[2]

---

2. Timothy Rees, "God Is Love, Let Heaven Adore Him."

Perhaps it all depends what you mean by "love" and by the love of God in particular. But to explore this any further we must go back to the primary evidence: the remarkably varied picture of the cross we find in the New Testament itself. What might happen if, instead of an ultimate vision of saved souls going to heaven, we were to start with the eschatology of Ephesians 1:10, with God's plan to sum up all things in heaven and earth in the Messiah? What if, instead of a disembodied "heaven," we were to focus on the biblical vision of "new heavens and new earth," with that renewal and that fusion of the two created spheres taking place in and through Jesus himself? What if, instead of the bare "going to heaven," we were to embrace (along with theologians like John Calvin) the biblical vocation of being the "royal priesthood"? What would happen if we thought through the ongoing cross-shaped implications, writ large as they are in the New Testament, of the once-for-all event of Jesus's death? What difference might that make to our view of salvation—including once more its philosophical and political dimensions? How, in other words, does the cross fit into the larger biblical narrative of new creation? What would happen if, instead of seeing the resurrection (both of Jesus and of ourselves) as a kind of happy addition to an otherwise complete view of salvation, we saw it as part of its very heart?

# 3

## The Cross in Its First-Century Setting

To UNDERSTAND ANY event in history, you must put it firmly *into* that history and not rest content with what later generations have said about it. That is certainly true of the crucifixion of Jesus, and unless we allow first-century contexts and insights to surround the event, we can be sure we shall fail to grasp its original meaning.

There are three very different contexts in which the crucifixion finds its meaning—or perhaps we should say its meanings, plural, since, as we shall see, these different contexts all provide quite different angles of vision, and within each one there are further variations. I shall be arguing later on that among Jesus's followers there quickly emerged a complex but coherent central core of meaning. But we cannot and must not short-circuit the discussion. Before we get to the heart of it, we must go the long way around.

Historically speaking, the widest context of meaning is the Greco-Roman world of late antiquity, the world in which (according to Luke) a decree from Caesar Augustus sent Joseph and

Mary to Bethlehem, and the world in which Augustus's successor, Tiberius, sent Pontius Pilate to govern Judaea. It was Roman soldiers who nailed Jesus to his cross. What did their world look like? How might it help us understand that crucifixion?

★ ★ ★

The first and greatest Greek epic begins with the word "wrath": *Mēnin aeide, thea, Pēlēiadeō Achilēos,* "The wrath sing, goddess, of Peleus's son Achilles." The word *mēnis,* found here in the first line of Homer's *Iliad,* is frequent from Homer on, designating a wrath both human, as here, and divine: sulky wrath, vengeful wrath, a wrath sometimes appeased by sacrifice and sometimes merely overtaken, as in the case of Achilles, by a greater wrath over a different matter. The whole *Iliad* is about wrath: the revenge of the Greeks for Paris's snatching of Helen and the multiple secondary revenges and feuds both princely and petty among both Greeks and Trojans—and also among the gods and goddesses who watch the whole show from Mt. Olympus and regularly come down to interfere on this side or that. Lingering jealousy, ancient spite, offense easily taken but less easily averted: this is the constant theme of the world's first great poem. If you wanted "salvation," it meant being rescued from that kind of thing. All this was still true several centuries later when people went out from the Jewish into the pagan world with the news of a different lord, a different empire, a different salvation—and perhaps also a different wrath.

When we turn to the Roman equivalent of Homer, we find a striking parallel. Virgil's great epic, the *Aeneid,* begins not with wrath, but with arms: *Arma virumque cano,* "I sing of arms and the man." Virgil can also write poems of great pastoral beauty, just as Homer gives us wonderfully rich natural imagery. *But it is no accident that the greatest and best-known poems of pagan antiquity begin with the words "wrath" and "arms."* That was the world everyone knew, even if they reacted against it: war and violence, and the human and divine rage that smoldered or flamed beneath them. Wrath and arms! With the gods themselves sharing in the wrath and urging on the violence, what escape could there be? And—we cannot help commenting already—is it not against this world of wrath and arms and its all too apparent reflection in various theories or models of "atonement" that so much recent theology and popular opinion has reacted?

Readers of the New Testament might want to say, and in a more nuanced fashion, that we believe in a different sort of wrath, a different kind of battle, and indeed a very different vision of God and of salvation. Yes, indeed. But it is within the world of the Greeks and the Romans that Jesus was crucified; and it was within that same world that the originally Jewish message about Jesus received its wider airing and, arguably, its early shaping.

The world of wrath and arms helps to explain why anyone would want to execute a fellow human being in so brutal a fashion. A brief reminder of what crucifixion entailed—necessary sooner or later in this book—will make the point, lest we take for granted or gloss over what was actually involved in the event whose meaning we are discussing.

Few readers of this book are likely to have seen, except on screen, the kind of violence that was common in the first century. Even those who watch Mel Gibson's *The Passion of the Christ* might either screen out the gratuitous horror of it all or be so overwhelmed by the physical brutality as to miss the point that such a death was designed to degrade as well as kill. Crucifixion was one of the central ways in which authorities in the ancient world set out quite deliberately to show subject peoples who was in charge and to break the spirit of any resistance.

Crucifixion was, after all, one of the most horrible fates that humans could devise. That isn't a modern overstatement. It was the considered opinion of the Roman orator Cicero and the Jewish historian Josephus, two men who had seen plenty of crucifixions, and also another who knew what he was talking about, the church father Origen. Cicero refers to crucifixion as *crudel-*

*issimum taeterrimumque supplicium,* the "most cruel and terrifying penalty" (*In Verrem* 2.5.165). Josephus speaks of a Jewish protest against the "most pitiable of deaths," *thanatōn ton oiktiston* (*Jewish War* 7.202f.). Origen refers to it as *mors turpissima crucis,* the "most shameful form of death, namely, the cross" (*Commentary on Matthew* 27.22).

The point is often made but bears repetition: we in the modern West, who wear jeweled crosses around our necks, stamp them on Bibles and prayer books, and carry them in cheerful processions, need regularly to be reminded that the very word "cross" was a word you would most likely not utter in polite society. The thought of it would not only put you off your dinner; it could give you sleepless nights. And if you had actually seen a crucifixion or two, as many in the Roman world would have, your sleep itself would have been invaded by nightmares as the memories came flooding back unbidden, memories of humans half alive and half dead, lingering on perhaps for days on end, covered in blood and flies, nibbled by rats, pecked at by crows, with weeping but helpless relatives still keeping watch, and with hostile or mocking crowds adding their insults to the terrible injuries. All this explains Cicero's statement that everything to do with crucifixion, including the word *crux* itself,

> should be far removed not only from the person of a
> Roman citizen but from his thoughts, his eyes, and his
> ears. For it is not only the actual occurrence of these
> things, or the endurance of them, but liability to them,
> the expectation, indeed the very mention of them,
> that is unworthy of a Roman citizen and a free man.
> (*In Verrem* 16)

The horrible personal and physical aspects of crucifixion were matched by the social, communal, and political meaning. This is important not just as the "context" for our understanding of the Jesus's execution (as though the barbaric practice were just a dark backdrop to a theology produced from somewhere else), but as part of the very stuff of the theology itself. We might already have figured this out from the careful placing of Philippians 2.8b, *thanatou de staurou,* "even the death of the cross," at the dead center of the poem that some think antedates Paul himself. As we shall see later, the first half of that poem is a downward journey, down to the lowest place to which a human being could sink with regard to pain or shame, personal fate or public perception. This was precisely the point. Those who crucified people did so because it was the sharpest and nastiest way of asserting their own absolute power and guaranteeing their victim's absolute degradation. The early Christians did not suppose that Jesus might in principle have died in one of a number of ways (being stoned, killed in battle, assassinated with a dagger in a crowd, or whatever). Reading backward in the light of the subsequent events, they interpreted the crucifixion as part of the strange, dark divine plan in which the shame and horror were part of the intended meaning. Jesus, they believed, had gone to the lowest point possible for a human being, never mind a Jew, never mind one whose followers had hoped he was the coming king.

So how had crucifixion come to be used in this way? The early history of the practice is lost in the mists of the pre-Roman world. The first historians, Herodotus and Thucydides, mention the execution of people on poles and trees, though it isn't always clear whether this was simply hanging or impaling, both of which would have resulted in a much quicker death. Recent scholarly work has surveyed the evidence from the entire ancient world and has stressed that part of the point of crucifixion itself, as opposed to impaling or hanging, was that the victim was often able to see, to speak, to cry out in pain or protest for hours or even days. In some cases it was even possible for a victim to be rescued, to be brought down from the cross in time to recover. Part of the point of crucifixion, then, was precisely the lingering, extended process, which added to the horror as well as the pain. Seneca describes it as a long-drawn-out affair, in which the victim would be "wasting away in pain, dying limb by limb, letting out his life drop by drop . . . fastened to the accursed tree, long sickly, already deformed, swelling with ugly tumors on chest and shoulders, and drawing the breath of life amid long-drawn-out agony" (*Epistle* 101.12–14).

People could be affixed to crosses with ropes, but nails seem to have been more common. Indeed, the nails that might be retrieved after a crucifixion were sometimes used in magical or medicinal potions, suggesting that some may have regarded the whole event as possessing, at some prearticulate level, a kind of dark potency. This is perhaps related to the indescribable lusts of those who gave the order to crucify and particularly of those who carried it out, who on occasion—as Josephus tells us—became so hardened to the practice that they experimented for fun with different positions and modes. Here too we touch on something that may be more germane than sometimes imagined to the quest for a fuller meaning of Jesus's crucifixion. Imagine the Roman soldiers, battle-hardened yet battle-weary, trying to police a small overheated nation with ridiculous beliefs and ambitions, in which sporadic terrorism hinted at an insatiable desire for revolt and independence. We who know about Guantanamo Bay and Abu Ghraib should not find it impossible to imagine something of the mind-set of an execution squad outside Jerusalem. Nor should we find it difficult to suppose that, in a world where raw emotion and raw religion got horribly mixed up, all sorts of meanings might be given to an event of this kind.

The Romans, then, didn't invent crucifixion. (Some have suggested that it was practiced in ancient Carthage; certainly it predates the rise and the imperial brutality of Rome.) But they quickly made it their own, and it became the "death of choice" for two categories of undesirables in particular: slaves and rebels—and of course especially slaves who were also rebels or rebel leaders whom the Romans wanted to display as no better than slaves.

Having mentioned Mel Gibson's *The Passion of the Christ,* we might note another spectacular historical movie, *Spartacus.* The real-life Spartacus, who led a major slave revolt, met his end about a hundred years before Jesus. Many died in the final battle, but six thousand of his followers were crucified all along the 130 or so miles of the Appian Way from Rome to Capua (inland from Naples), making it roughly one cross every forty yards (Appian, *Civil Wars* 1.120).

Crucifying people beside busy roads or by the entrance to a city was of course designed to make a statement and issue a warning. People with business on those highways would walk past these terrible spectacles every day, and we may presume that many slaves who might have toyed with the idea of running away or joining the revolt would look, shudder, and decide that even their present miserable life was better than that. No doubt the authorities would often tell themselves that this was the only language such people understood. And, though there is evidence of friends or relatives taking away a corpse for burial, the more usual outcome was that the remains would stay there for several days and nights, becoming food for vultures and vermin, until (as with Jezebel in 2 Kings 9:21–37) there was nothing much left to bury. Nobody who had witnessed such a horror would be likely to regard such a death as "noble." The point was emphasized by the harsh and degrading physical treatment that preceded crucifixion itself. The routine whipping and scourging were designed partly to weaken the victim and prevent a struggle, but also as part of the total public humiliation.

Two particular details about Roman crucifixions are of special interest to us in this book. First, it would not be much of an exaggeration to say that Jesus of Nazareth grew up under the shadow of the cross. (Crucifixion, by the way, was not a punishment used by the Jews, except for the Hasmonean monarch Alexander Jannaeus, who in 88 BC had eight hundred Pharisees crucified for resisting his rule. The incident is mentioned with horror in the

Qumran commentary on the book of Nahum.) Immediately after the death of Herod the Great in 4 BC there was a serious attempt at revolt in Galilee led by Judas ben Hezekiah. Josephus describes this as the most serious incident of its kind between Pompey's conquest of Palestine in 63 BC and the fall of the Temple in AD 70 (Josephus *Apion* 1.34; *Antiquities* 17.271f.; *War* 2.56). Varus, the Roman general in charge in the province of Syria at the time, did what the Romans did best: he crushed the rebellion brutally and crucified around two thousand of the rebels. The Galilee of Jesus's boyhood, then, knew all about Roman crosses (*Antiquities* 17.286–98; *War* 2.66–79).

When I was growing up, all the local towns and villages had their own war memorials from World Wars I and II. I knew many families (including my own) who had lost one, two, or more members in those conflicts, and we solemnly remembered them year after year. In ancient Galilee, even without stone memorials to the rebels who had died, the towns and villages in which Jesus announced God's kingdom would have had similar memories of people known, loved, and lost to Roman brutality. When he told his followers to pick up their own crosses and follow him, they would not have heard this as a metaphor.

The next time that Roman crosses littered the landscape Jesus knew so well came two generations later. The Roman general Vespasian and his son Titus closed in on Jerusalem at the end of the war of AD 66–70. As they overran the surrounding countryside and laid siege to the holy city itself, they crucified so many Jews outside the walls that they ran out of timber and had to fetch some from farther afield. Josephus says that he walked past these crucifixions and, finding three of his friends among them, had them taken down from their crosses. One survived; the others died, their corpses rotting and providing food for the birds and the dogs.

The crucifixion of Jesus of Nazareth, most likely in AD 33, is poised historically in between these two large-scale crucifixions. Nobody in that world would have been able to hear the word "cross" or be reminded of someone dying in that way without feeling instinctively the horror and shame of the whole thing. So too Saul of Tarsus, traveling the Roman world, must have seen plenty of crosses in his time: plenty of blood, plenty of rotting flesh, plenty of carrion and vermin picking over squirming carcasses. He must have known in his gut, more perhaps than we ever can, why the "word of the cross" was shocking, scandalous, and foolish beyond all measure. All of this needs to be in our minds and imaginations if we are even to glimpse, let alone understand, why that "word" was so utterly revolutionary.

The second point of special interest for us is the way in which the Romans sometimes used crucifixion as a way of mocking a victim with social or political pretensions. "You want to be high and lifted up?" they said in effect. "All right, we'll give you 'high and lifted up.'" Crucifixion thus meant not only killing by slow torture, not only shaming, not only issuing a warning, but also parodying the ambitions of the uppity rebels. They wanted to move up the social scale? Let them be lifted up above the common herd, then—on a cross! When the emperor Galba was governor of his native Spain, a man condemned to crucifixion objected that he was a Roman citizen. Galba's response was to make his cross higher than before and to have it painted white, signifying his high social status. When Pilate had "The King of the Jews" written on a placard above Jesus's head, that's the kind of message he intended to send—not only about Jesus, but about the Jews in general: "This is what we think of your kind."

I have said enough here, I trust, to bring to mind the violence and sheer nastiness of the world ruled by the Romans. And also the irony. Augustus, the first great Roman emperor, solemnly announced that he had brought peace and prosperity throughout Rome's wide domains. He set up the *Ara Pacis* ("Altar of Peace") in Rome, with stately, dignified carvings of himself and his pious family. At the same time, his lieutenants throughout his empire were making sure, in their bloody and brutal way, that the locals stayed "peaceful" and knew who was in charge. Augustus's projected vision of tranquil peace was perched on top of a world of horror and violence. Wrath and arms continued to dominate classical culture.

All this helps us to understand the symbolic meanings of a crucifixion in that world. The early Christians very quickly gave Jesus's cross meanings that were deep, rich, and revolutionary, but this was done in the teeth of the meanings that the cross already possessed. It already had a *social* meaning: "We are superior, and you are vastly inferior." It had a *political* meaning: "We're in charge here, and you and your nation count for nothing." It therefore had a *theological* or *religious* meaning: the goddess Roma and Caesar, the son of a god, were superior to any and all local gods. As Jesus of Nazareth hung dying that Friday afternoon, all those meanings would have been deeply intuited and understood not only by the Roman soldiers, but by the weeping women at the foot of the cross and the disgraced disciples behind their locked doors. Unless we grasp and hang on to not only the physical horror of the cross, but also its multiple symbolic meanings in late antiquity, we will fail to understand why the early preaching of the cross was what it was. We will fail too to understand the questions the historian and theologian must ask: How and why did the cross so quickly acquire a radically different symbolic meaning? And what precisely did that revolutionary meaning say about God, the world, Israel, and the human race?

All this means that when we are attempting to understand the crucifixion of Jesus, to think the early Christians' thoughts after them, we are entering a dark and dangerous area. We should not expect to be able to "capture" this theme, to summarize it in an easy slogan. The early Christians' shorthand summaries point beyond themselves into areas with which the thought of our own day, including contemporary Christian thought, is not nearly as familiar as it should be. Just as the resurrection of Jesus cannot be fitted into any other worldview, but must be either rejected altogether or allowed to reshape existing worldviews around itself, so the cross itself demands the rethinking of categories. We cannot capture it; to be Christian means, among other things, that it has captured us. If we make it our own too easily, fitting it into the theories and preachers' illustrations that explain it all neatly, we will have shrunk it, reduced it to a size that we can manage and perhaps manipulate. The aim of the present book is to do the opposite: to point to new visions more robustly biblical and more deeply revolutionary of what the cross meant to the first Christians and even to Jesus himself.

Within the world of Greece and Rome there is a remarkable feature that some have seen as helping to explain how the cross of Jesus so quickly acquired its specific meaning, that Jesus died "for us," "for our sins," and so on. The idea of someone *dying for* someone else, so familiar from Christian statements of the gospel, is far more clearly visible in ancient pagan literature than in ancient Jewish literature. (It is, in fact, hardly there at all in ancient Israel, though the exceptions are important too, as we shall see.) No fewer than six of Euripides's plays have this as a major theme. Ancient legends abound in which people sacrificed either themselves, a favorite daughter, or a special animal in order to gain divine favor or to ward off divine vengeance.

This theme comes to astonishing expression in a writing roughly contemporary with St. Paul. Lucan is describing the Roman civil war of the previous century between Julius Caesar and Pompey. Like many historians of the period, he puts speeches into the mouths of his characters, and among his characters there are few to match the nobility of Cato. This is what Lucan's Cato says as he offers his own life in the struggle for justice and redemption:

> Would it were possible for me, condemned by the powers of heaven and hell, to be the scapegoat for the nation! As hordes of foemen bore down Decius when he had

offered his life, so may both armies pierce this body, may
the savages from the Rhine aim their weapons at me;
may I be transfixed by every spear, and may I stand between and intercept every blow dealt in this way! Let my
blood redeem the nations, and my death pay the whole
penalty incurred by the corruption of Rome. . . . Aim
your swords at me alone, at me who fight a losing battle
for despised law and justice. My blood, mine only, will
bring peace to the people of Italy and end their suffering;
the would-be tyrant need wage no war, once I am gone.
(*Civil War* 2.306–19)

Other examples abound. Plato, Aristotle, the Stoics, and many
others speak of dying for the law, for one's country, one's friends,
one's family, even for the emperor. Horace's well-known *Dulce et
decorum est pro patria mori* ("Sweet and fitting it is to die for one's
country"; *Odes* 3.2.13) merely sums up what many had said and
believed. When Caiaphas counsels the Sanhedrin in John 11:50
that one man should die for the people rather than have the whole
nation perish, the obvious echoes of this sentiment are found in
ancient pagan literature, not in the Hebrew scriptures and only
infrequently in the postbiblical Jewish writings.

What are we to make of this? Are we to say, with some (like
the great scholar Martin Hengel, in his book *The Atonement,*
which lays out the evidence far more fully than we have done)
that all this functioned as a kind of preparation for the gospel in
the non-Jewish world? Are we to suppose that the Maccabean
and other Jewish texts (see below) that do envisage people giving
their lives for the nation are borrowing from pagan sources rather
than relying on their own scriptures? Or what? Or is there a difference, and if so in what does it consist? Are we to suggest that
the objection often raised to certain would-be Christian theories
of the atonement, that they look like bloodthirsty paganism, has
a certain justification? If so, how can we articulate what has to be

said without providing that hostage to critical fortune?

Of course, the analogies only go so far. The people who died on behalf of others in the pagan writings were dying what would be seen as a "noble death." Nobody in the ancient world would have said that about crucifixion. The idea of *that* kind of death having some special significance would have been—as Paul knew only too well—sheer nonsense within the pagan world. There is an obvious mismatch as well as obvious echoes. As we consider how the message about Jesus of Nazareth would be heard within the wider world of Paul's day, both elements are important.

## Within the Jewish World

The second context of meaning within which we have to place the death of Jesus is that of the early Jewish world. Between the fall of Babylon in 539 BC and the failure of the bar-Kochba revolt in 135 there were many movements and many strands of thought, many changes of foreign regime and many attempts at new expressions of the Jewish way of life. I have written about this at length elsewhere (especially in Part III of *The New Testament and the People of God*), and there is no point going over that ground again. In any case, we shall be looking at the actual biblical material in Part Two, since the early Christians insisted that Jesus's death should be interpreted "in accordance with the Bible." But before we get to that point there are three things to be noted as of considerable importance.

First, Jews of the first century, like a great many Jews in the twenty-first century, organized their lives around the major festivals and holy days. Among the festivals, incomparably the greatest was Passover, which commemorated the time when, in the book of Exodus, Israel's God had acted dramatically to break the power of Pharaoh of Egypt and to set free his previously enslaved people. The whole story is important and was and is rehearsed in detail every Passover: the slavery, the hardship, the plagues on Pharaoh and his nation, the judgment on the firstborn of Egypt (and the protection of the Israelites through the blood of the Passover lambs), the crossing of the Red Sea, the journey in the wilderness, the giving of the law (the Torah) on Mt. Sinai, and the construction of the tabernacle. We have every reason to suppose that when the Jewish people celebrated Passover year after year they thought of it as the freedom festival that not only looked back to the original act of liberation, but ahead to another great act of liberation, especially when the people once more felt themselves enslaved or oppressed. And the point for our purposes is this: Jesus himself chose Passover as the moment to do what he had to do, and the first Christians looked back to Passover as one of the main interpretative lenses for understanding his death.

Second, however, a great many Jews of the first century sharpened their hope for a fresh act of divine liberation in the light of the book of Daniel and similar writings. Here (in Dan. 9) they found assurance that the "exile" had not consisted merely of the seventy years in Babylon, but was continuing to their day in a different form, that of continuing pagan oppression. All the great prophets of the exile had insisted that Israel's disaster (including the destruction of the Temple and the consequent sense of being excluded from the divine Presence) was the result of Israel's own idolatry and sin. If and when, therefore, a fresh act of deliverance were to undo this long exile, it would be a divine act of "forgiveness of sins." The great annual holy day at which confession of sin was made and forgiveness was available was the Day of Atonement. This had little in common with Passover, except that both took place in the Jerusalem Temple (after which the Passover meal was then eaten in private homes). But since, in the time of Jesus, many Jews were looking for a great event that would be *both* a "new Passover" *and* the "forgiveness of sins," it is possible to see that the two might somehow be combined. Jeremiah had spoken of a "new covenant" in which sins would be forgiven (Jer. 31:31–

34). All this generates a framework of potential meaning within which the actions of Jesus himself and the perceptions of his first followers could find fertile soil.

Third, we should not imagine that any first-century Jews outside the Christian movement were carrying in their heads anything like the complex constructions that Jesus's first followers quickly developed to talk about his death. Some were hoping for a Messiah or at least a prophetic leader who would point the way out of Israel's present troubles, but nobody, as far as we can tell, thought that such a figure would suffer. Equally, some thought that a time of terrible suffering was to come, a time through which Israel would be delivered, but nobody connected this with a potential Messiah. Likewise, some picked up the texts that spoke of Israel's God himself coming back in a whole new way, as promised in Isaiah 52, to judge the world and deliver his people. But nobody connected that with either the possibility of a Messiah or the likelihood of intense suffering. There was no template of expectations out of which, granted the crucifixion of Jesus, one might have anticipated the sophisticated range of interpretation that the early Christian movement in fact produced, understanding the death of Jesus as a messianic victory and connecting it with the long-awaited divine return. For that we must look elsewhere.

The larger picture of how Jews were reading their scriptures and how Jesus's followers came to reread them in the light of his death and resurrection are topics to which we must return in the next part of the book. For the moment we must glance, in conclusion, at the world of the first Christians themselves.

## Approaching the New Testament

Here, perhaps to our surprise, we find a bewildering range of material. We do not always stop to acknowledge the extraordinary explosion of new ideas and new understandings of old ones that occurred in the first fifty years of the faith. Turning the pages of the early Christian writings sometimes seems like turning the tube of a kaleidoscope: the same colors and shapes, but in constantly shifting combinations and patterns. Nothing in the ancient world, whether Jewish or non-Jewish, prepares us for the sudden flurry of themes and images that tumble over one another as the early Christians tried to express and interpret what had just happened to Jesus, the world, and themselves. Simply to set these out one by one will show what I mean. Each one will be explored further in Part Three, but it is important here to note them, if only because, though all readers of the New Testament realize how significant it all is, it is surprisingly difficult to give a coherent account of what is going on. I think this is in part because, as we saw in the previous chapter, many theologians and preachers have homed in on one part of the question only and have not succeeded in integrating the rest. I will not offer a comprehensive treatment either. But I hope that my later argument will go some way to revealing a deeper coherence among these early Christian writings than is sometimes imagined.

The New Testament meets us with complex and puzzling information about the cross in both outline and detail. Many have struggled to fit together what the four gospels present (a story of Jesus announcing God's kingdom and then going to his death) with what the letters appear to present (a story of God acting through the death of Jesus to save sinners). Within the gospels themselves, many have found it difficult to see how Jesus's kingdom announcement and his approaching death somehow belong together. The early Christian writings refer in complex ways to Israel's scriptures, and they formulate this into a rule ("The Messiah died for our sins in accordance with the Bible"), but it is difficult to see how their use of scripture worked even in their own minds, and especially in relation to the crucifixion: Was it a matter of individual "proof-texts," or the whole narrative structure of scripture, or what? There are many particular passages that have challenged and puzzled commentators, not least the famous poem of Philippians 2:6–11, whose mention of the crucifixion forms a "hinge" at the middle. And there are many incidents in the gospels (such as the Last Supper) and many strands of meaning in the letters (such as the frequent reference to sacrifice) that have either defied explanation or been given an overly simple reading that clearly does not plumb the depths. If this is how the "early Christian" context of meaning for understanding Jesus's death appears, we are in for a difficult time.

In particular, there has been little agreement on the meaning of sacrifice in Jesus's world. Since both he and many of his earliest followers used the language of sacrifice in relation to his death (remarkable enough in itself, in that the Jews did not believe in human sacrifice), it will be important to clarify some at least of the meaning that seems to have been attached to the ritual slaughter of animals in the Temple. This is harder than some might imagine. The old sense, that the animals were suffering a kind of transferred death penalty so that the worshippers who had brought the animals might be spared, simply will not do, for reasons that will become apparent. Only when we have gotten our minds into the world of first-century Jewish Temple theology will we even begin to make sense of it all.

The actual material in the New Testament thus presents us with a smaller scale but no less sharp version of the problem we met in the previous chapter. The crucifixion of Jesus seems to have generated a wide range of interpretation not only over the last two thousand years, but even over the first century or so of church life. What sense can we make of it all? And what use will this be to the world or the church or the individuals within either in the next generation? This book is written to try to answer those questions.

Before we plunge into the second part of the book, in which I shall sketch out the way in which I think the first Christians understood and appropriated their ancient scriptural heritage, I want simply to state where the argument is going. Every part of this will be filled out in the course of the later exposition.

First, it seems clear to me that once we replace the common vision of Christian hope ("going to heaven") with the biblical vision of "new heavens and new earth," there will be direct consequences for how we understand both the human problem and the divine solution. Second, in the usual model, what stops us from "going to heaven" is sin, and sin is dealt with (somehow) on the cross. In the biblical model, what stops us from being genuine humans (bearing the divine image, acting as the "royal priesthood") is not only sin, but the idolatry that underlies it. The idols have gained power, the power humans ought to be exercising in God's world; idolatrous humans have handed it over to them. What is required, for God's new world and for renewed humans within it is for the power of the idols to be broken. Since sin, the consequence of idolatry, is what keeps humans in thrall to the nongods of the world, dealing with sin has a more profound effect than simply releasing humans to go to heaven. It releases humans from the grip of the idols, so they can worship the living God and be renewed according to his image.

All this is very abstract, but in the Bible it becomes startlingly concrete. In the Bible, God's plan to deal with sin, and so to break the power of idols and bring new creation to his world, is focused on the people of Israel. In the New Testament, this focus is narrowed to Israel's representative, the Messiah. He stands in for Israel and so fulfills the divine plan to restore creation itself. That is the very short version of the story we shall be telling for the rest of this book—the revolutionary story in which all Jesus's followers are caught up.

There is one final note of introduction before we proceed. In the English language the work of dealing with sin is commonly spoken of as "atonement." Because this word occurs in many passages in English translations of the Bible, it is easy to imagine that it carries a single and obvious meaning. It does not. Like many theological terms, it is shorthand. Some people say "atonement" when they mean "what Jesus achieved on the cross." But in the Bible it extends farther than this to include, for instance, in Romans 8 or the whole Letter to the Hebrews, the work of Jesus the Messiah not only in his crucifixion, but also in his resurrection and particularly in his ascension, where (we are told) he continually offers intercession to the Father on behalf of his people. And if "atonement" can thus be, as it were, extended forward, it can also be extended backward. The book of Revelation speaks mysteriously of the Lamb "slain from the foundation of the world" (13:8, KJV). Whatever that means, the four gospels certainly present Jesus throughout his public career and as far back as the prophecies given before his birth as the one who would "save his people from their sins."

Because of all this, I shall use the word "atonement" sparingly as my argument proceeds. These larger questions are extremely important, but I want to try to maintain the focus on the ultimate question, the question that has to do with the launch of the revolution. By six in the evening on the first Good Friday, according to the early Christians, the world was a different place. What was different? Why was it different? And how might that revolutionary difference challenge us today, summoning us to our own vocation as followers of the shameful, scandalous crucified Jesus?

# PART TWO

# "In Accordance with the Bible"

## The Stories of Israel

# 4

---

# The Covenant of Vocation

T HERE IS AN old cliché from the Boy Scout movement in which three Scouts report that they had helped an old lady across the road. "Why did it take three of you?" asks the Scoutmaster. "Because," they explain, "she didn't want to go."

Sometimes you meet the opposite problem: the right destination but the wrong treatment. A few days before I was drafting this chapter, the newspapers reported a story about a teenage girl who for some years had been suffering a strange and debilitating illness whose symptoms included frequent headaches, blurry vision, and sudden weight gain. Her own doctor had come up with various diagnoses, including the suggestion that the girl might be allergic to cheese. Eventually the mother, frustrated and worried, took the girl to a different clinic for further tests. Suddenly the true diagnosis came to light: she was suffering from a brain tumor. At once, with a mixture of anger and relief, the girl was sent to the specialist to start the appropriate treatment. Addressing the wrong problem wasn't getting anywhere.

Many theories about what the cross achieved, including some of the most popular and vocal, have made both of these mistakes. They have insisted, like the Boy Scouts with the old lady, that the human race really needed help to go to "heaven," when all along the New Testament was insisting that the divine plan was "to sum up . . . everything in heaven and on earth" in the Messiah. And they have insisted on a particular diagnosis of the human plight and have treated that rather than the real disease.

These two mistakes have reinforced one another. In most popular Christianity, "heaven" (and "fellowship with God" in the present) is the goal, and "sin" (bad behavior, deserving punishment) is the problem. A Platonized goal and a moralizing diagnosis—and together they lead, as I have been suggesting, to a paganized "solution" in which an angry divinity is pacified by human sacrifice. The zealous theological Boy Scouts have gotten it wrong. Humans are made not for "heaven," but for the new heavens and new earth. And the equally zealous theological doctors have produced the wrong diagnosis. The human problem is not so much "sin" seen as the breaking of moral codes—though that, to be sure, is part of it, just as the headaches and blurry vision really were part of the medical problem—but rather idolatry and the distortion of genuine humanness it produces. These two mistakes go together, reinforcing the basic heaven-and-earth dualism that continues to haunt Western theology. They lead some to suppose that the human problem has to do, after all, with our "earthly" and "bodily" selves and that our ultimate aim is for our "souls" to escape this body and find rest in an existence outside space, time, and matter altogether. I have argued elsewhere, and will continue here, that this is highly misleading. The "goal" is not "heaven," but a renewed human vocation within God's renewed creation. This is what every biblical book from Genesis on is pointing toward.

In particular, much thinking and preaching about the cross has assumed a tradition that, in the seventeenth century, came to be known by some as the "covenant of works." This idea, enshrined in the famous 1646 Westminster Confession, is central to much popular belief. Here we must be careful. There are many varieties of Protestantism, and even many varieties of "Reformed" doctrine within that larger category. Some of the varieties have seen the same problems that I see here and have responded in ways not too far, though still different, from what I am recommending. Some of those who agree with me in wanting to avoid those problems have used the phrase "covenant of works" in a way significantly different from the view I am opposing. Laying all that out would be a task for another time, and I shall try to avoid getting tangled up in all this by referring to the view I am opposing as the "works contract."

The "works contract" functions in the popular mind like this. God told his human creatures to keep a moral code; their continuing life in the Garden of Eden depended on their keeping that code perfectly. Failure would incur the punishment of death. This was then repeated in the case of Israel with a sharpened-up moral code, Mosaic law. The result was the same. Humans were therefore heading for hell rather than heaven. Finally, however, Jesus obeyed this moral law perfectly and in his death paid the penalty on behalf of the rest of the human race. The overarching arrangement (the "works contract") between God and humans remained the same, but Jesus had done what was required. Those who avail themselves of this achievement by believing in him and so benefiting from his accomplishment go to heaven, where they enjoy eternal fellowship with God; those who don't, don't. The "works contract" remains intact throughout.

This scheme is regularly explained by reference to the first three chapters of Paul's Letter to the Romans. There, one of the key technical terms is "righteousness," in Greek *dikaiosynē*. For many centuries in many traditions, "righteousness" has been understood as the moral status we would have if only we had kept the "works contract" perfectly, and then (by various explanations) as the status we can have by faith because, despite our moral failure, Jesus has taken the punishment and so provided the "righteousness" as a gift ("the righteousness of Christ").

The problem—to put it bluntly—is that this is not what Romans is all about. I shall come back to this passage in the final chapter in Part Three of this book, but for the moment let me say this. Such a view of the relationship between God and humans is a travesty. It is indeed unbiblical. It insists on taking us to a goal very different from the one held out in scripture. It ignores, in particular, the actual meaning of Israel's scriptures, both in themselves and as they were read by the earliest Christians. And it insists on a diagnosis of the human plight that is, ironically, trivial compared with the real thing. Left to itself, this theory would launch a revolution very different from the one the New Testament has in mind.

What the Bible offers is not a "works contract," but a covenant of *vocation*. The vocation in question is that of being a genuine human being, with genuinely human tasks to perform as part of the Creator's purpose for his world. The main task of this vocation is "image-bearing," reflecting the Creator's wise stewardship into the world and reflecting the praises of all creation back to its maker. Those who do so are the "royal priesthood," the "kingdom of priests," the people who are called to stand at the dangerous but exhilarating point where heaven and earth meet. In saying this I am echoing what many theologians (including John Calvin, the founder of all "Reformed" theologies) have said before me. This is not surprising, because it is all there in the Bible. But this is not the story that normally comes through in popular preaching and teaching.

Within this narrative, creation itself is understood as a kind of Temple, a heaven-and-earth duality, where humans function as the "image-bearers" in the cosmic Temple, part of earth yet reflecting the life and love of heaven. This is how creation was designed to function and flourish: under the stewardship of the image-bearers. Humans are called not just to keep certain moral standards in the present and to enjoy God's presence here and hereafter, but to celebrate, worship, procreate, and take responsibility within the rich, vivid developing life of creation. According to Genesis, that is what humans were made for.

The diagnosis of the human plight is then not simply that humans have broken God's moral law, offending and insulting the Creator, whose image they bear—though that is true as well. This lawbreaking is a symptom of a much more serious disease. Morality is important, but it isn't the whole story. Called to responsibility and authority within and over the creation, humans have turned their vocation upside down, giving worship and allegiance to forces and powers within creation itself. The name for this is idolatry. The result is slavery and finally death. It isn't just that humans do wrong things and so incur punishment. This is one element of the larger problem, which isn't so much about a punishment that might seem almost arbitrary, perhaps even draconian; it is, rather, about direct consequences. When we worship and serve forces within the creation (the creation for which we were supposed to be responsible!), we hand over our power to other forces only too happy to usurp our position. We humans have thus, by abrogating our own vocation, handed our power and authority to nondivine and nonhuman forces, which have then run rampant, spoiling human lives, ravaging the beautiful creation, and doing their best to turn God's world into a hell (and hence into a place from which people might want to escape). As I indicated earlier, some of these "forces" are familiar (money, sex, power). Some are less familiar in the popular mind, not least the sense of a dark, accusing "power" standing behind all the rest.

## Called to the Royal Priesthood

I am suggesting that in the Bible humans are created in order to live as worshipping stewards within God's heaven-and-earth reality, rather than as beings who, by moral perfection, qualify to leave "earth" and go to "heaven" instead. This vision of the human vocation comes into focus in the book of Revelation:

> Glory to the one who loved us, and freed us from our
> sins by his blood, and *made us a kingdom, priests to his God
> and father*—glory and power be to him forever and ever.
> Amen. (1:5–6)

> *You are worthy to take the scroll;*
> *You are worthy to open its seals;*
> *For you were slaughtered and with your own blood*
> *You purchased a people for God,*
> *From every tribe and tongue,*
> *From every people and nation,*
> *And made them a kingdom and priests to our God*
> *And they will reign on the earth.* (5:9–10)

> Blessed and holy is the one who has a share in the first
> resurrection! The second death has no power over them.
> They will be *priests to God and the Messiah, and they will
> reign with him* for a thousand years. (20:6)

The third passage repeats the vocation ("royal priesthood"), but not the means by which it is achieved (the Messiah's death); but the first two are quite clear. The death of Jesus, "freeing us from our sins" and "purchasing a people for God," was not simply aimed at rescuing humans from "hell," so that they could go to "heaven" instead—which is the picture most Christians have when they think about Jesus's death. The great scene at the end of the book is the joining together of the "new heavens and new earth." Being there in the presence of God and the Lamb will give back to the redeemed the role marked out for them from the beginning in Genesis and reaffirmed as Israel's vocation in the book of Exodus. There God promises his newly rescued people that they will be his "treasured possession," "a priestly kingdom and a holy nation" (19:5–6). The priestly vocation consists of summing up the praises of creation before the Creator; the royal vocation, in turn, means reflecting God's wisdom and justice into the world. This is a direct outworking of Genesis 1:26–28, where humans are created in the divine image. The book of Revelation picks up this theme exactly where Israel's scriptures left off. It says—shockingly, of course—that the ancient vocation had been renewed in a new and revolutionary way through the death of the Messiah. Once we get the goal right (the new creation, not just "heaven") and the human problem properly diagnosed (idolatry and the corruption of vocation, not just "sin"), the larger biblical vision of Jesus's death begins to come into view.

A short aside may be needed at this point. Some readers may feel anxious about both elements of the vocation I am describing, the "royal" bit and the "priestly" bit. Let me say a word about each.

For many people, not least those who got rid of monarchs in the eighteenth century, the very idea of kings or queens seems outdated, antiquated, unnecessary, and quite possibly abusive. People often ask me why I continue to talk about the "kingdom of God" when kingdoms in general have been such a disaster, making a few people rich and proud and a great many people poor and downtrodden. My normal answer is that things were like that in the first century too, if anything worse (think of Herod; think of Caesar!), but that Jesus went on talking about *God* becoming king anyway. Why did he do that?

Answer: Because the perversion of human rule is just that, a perversion. We ought not to let the perversion rob us of the good news; and the good news is not only that God is sorting out the world, but that his rule is a different kind of rule entirely from those that give monarchs a bad name. Prophetic passages such as Isaiah 11 and psalms such as Psalm 72 demonstrate that when God is faced with the corruption of monarchy, he promises not to abolish monarchy, but to send a true king to rule with utter justice, making the poor and needy his constant priority. The human vocation to share that role, that task, is framed within the true justice and mercy of God himself.

So too with "priesthood." This word makes many people think of corrupt hierarchies, organizing "religion" for their own purposes and threatening dire, and indeed "divine," punishments for any who step out of line. Again, the abuse does not invalidate the proper use. The notion of priesthood, admittedly now often exposed as a cloak for selfish wrongdoing, is another vital part of being human. We humans are called to stand at the intersection of heaven and earth, holding together in our hearts, our praises, and our urgent intercessions the loving wisdom of the creator God and the terrible torments of his battered world. The Bible knows perfectly well that this priestly vocation can be corrupted and often has been. But once more it proposes not abolition, but full and complete cleansing. The Coming One "will purify the descendants of Levi and refine them like gold and silver, until they present offerings to YHWH in righteousness" (Mal. 3:3). This ancient Jewish promise points ahead to the ultimate "priesthood" of Jesus himself.

We should not be surprised, then, that horrible abuses have spoiled our sense of both the royal and the priestly vocations. That is what we should expect. The remarkable thing is that the Creator, having made the world to work in this way—with humans functioning like the "image" in a temple, standing between heaven and earth and acting on behalf of each in relation to the other—has not abandoned the project. Yes, it gets distorted again and again. But it remains the way the world was supposed to work—and the way in which, through the gospel, it will work once more. The powers that have stolen the worshipping hearts of the world and that have in consequence usurped the human rule over the world would like nothing better than for humans to think only of escaping the world rather than taking back their priestly and royal vocations.

## Communities of Reconciled Worshippers

Those passages from the book of Revelation are not the only places in the New Testament where the result of Jesus's death is described as a renewal of vocation. Two famous Pauline passages point the same way. In the first, 2 Corinthians 5:21, the natural reading has been obscured and overlaid by generations who have seen in it the regular "works contract" idea. But the wider context of 2 Corinthians 5–6, in which Paul is explaining the nature of apostolic ministry and locating it within his fresh reading of Isaiah 49 (one of his favorite passages), indicates that his train of thought is the same as that of Revelation: the death of Jesus, reconciling people to God, generates the renewal of their human vocation.

In this carefully constructed passage, Paul says the same thing three times, developing it to a climax. In each case he first says something about Jesus's death and then something about the "ministry of reconciliation" to which people are called as a result:

> God reconciled us to himself through the Messiah, *and he gave us the ministry of reconciliation. (5:18)*

> God was reconciling the world to himself in the Messiah, not counting their trespasses against them, *and entrusting us with the message of reconciliation. (5:19)*

> The Messiah did not know sin, but God made him to be sin on our behalf, *so that in him we might embody God's faithfulness to the covenant. (5:21)*

The translation of the last clause is controversial. The word I have translated with the phrase "faithfulness to the covenant" is the word often rendered "righteousness"—the word regularly used within the kind of "works contract" I have described (Christ takes our sins, we take his "righteousness," in the sense of his moral achievements). But, as I and others have argued at length elsewhere, this is misleading. What Paul is talking about is the same thing that occupies him from the end of chapter 2 of 2 Corinthians to the end of chapter 7: the nature of his apostolic ministry. V. 21 is an additional statement, exactly in line with the two others immediately above, of the way in which *the Messiah's reconciling death results in a new human vocation.* Here Paul is speaking specifically of his "apostolic" vocation. The point would easily apply too to all those who are "in Christ," but that isn't his principal subject here. He is explaining why he does what he does and why his suffering—of which the Corinthians were ashamed—is a necessary part of the deal.

Paul sees himself standing at the cutting edge of the revolution. The death of Jesus has opened up a whole new world, and he is part of the team leading the way into unexplored territory. He is not only to *announce,* but also to *embody* the faithfulness of the creator God to his covenant and his world. He is thinking of Isaiah's vision of Israel's "servant" vocation and quoting from one of his favorite chapters, Isaiah 49: "I listened to you when the time was right; I came to your aid on the day of salvation" (2 Cor. 6:2, quoting Isa. 49:8). The remainder of that verse in Isaiah goes on, "I have kept you and given you as a covenant to the people." Paul is not summarizing the "works contract" (Jesus takes our sin, and we take his "righteousness"). He is doing what Revelation is doing: celebrating the fact that Jesus's reconciling death sets people free to take up their true vocation. The Messiah's death gives to him, and by extension to all who follow Jesus, the vocation to be part of the ongoing divine plan, the covenant purpose for the whole world.

Something similar is visible in Galatians 3:13. "The Messiah redeemed us from the curse of the law," writes Paul, "by becoming a curse on our behalf." This is not a statement of an abstract works-based atonement theology, though it is often snatched out of context and made to play that role. Many sermons have been preached about how the "curse of the law" (seen as the threatening moral code) is removed by the death of Jesus. Some have even supposed that Paul was regarding Israel's law itself as a bad thing that had no business pronouncing this "curse" and that Jesus's death had showed this up. But this has nothing to do with Paul's meaning. He does not go on—as such sermons regularly have—to say, "The Messiah became a curse for us *so that we might be freed from sin and go to heaven,*" or anything like it. He says in v. 14 that the Messiah bore the curse of the law, "so that the blessing of Abraham could flow through to the nations in King Jesus—and so that we might receive the promise of the spirit, through faith."

Paul is not saying that the Messiah's death rescues people from hell. Nor is he saying that it brings humans back into fellowship with God. These are important, but they are not the point he is making. Galatians 3 as a whole is about how God's promises to Abraham always envisaged a worldwide family and how the gospel events have brought that into reality. The death of Jesus launched the revolution; it got rid of the roadblock between the divine promises and the nations for whom they were intended. And it opened the way for the Spirit to be poured out to equip God's people for their tasks. Once again, the biblical view of what was achieved through Jesus's death has to do with the restoration of the human vocation, of Israel's vocation, of the larger divine purpose for the world.

Something similar is also going on—though the passage is one of Paul's densest—in Romans 5:17. In a grand sweep of biblical story, he is contrasting the effects of Adam's trespass with the effects of the Messiah's work. Here if anywhere, we might suppose, we would be dealing with a "works contract" in which Jesus's performance of the duties that Adam failed to perform would be credited to his people. But no. The "obedience" of Jesus is important in this passage, but not for that reason. What Paul has in mind is, once more, a covenant of *vocation:*

> For if, by the trespass of the one, death reigned through
> that one, how much more will those who receive the
> abundance of grace, and of the gift of covenant member-
> ship, of "being in the right," reign in life through the
> one man Jesus the Messiah.

They will *reign in life*! The word "reign" is a royal word, from the Greek root *basileus* (as in "king" or "kingdom"). Traditional readings might have led us to expect the conclusion that through the work of the Messiah those who receive his gift will escape death, will find "salvation." That is true (provided we understand "salvation" in the way Paul does), but it is not the particular truth he is emphasizing, either here or in chapter 8, where he expands the point. What Paul is saying is that the gospel, through which people receive the divine gift, *reconstitutes them as genuine humans, as those who share the "reign" of the Messiah.*

Once we grasp this, it plays back into our understanding of the earlier part of the verse and, with it, the analysis of the "problem" throughout Romans 5. Here is the point. When humans sinned, they abdicated their vocation to "rule" in the way that they, as image-bearers, were supposed to. They gave away their authority to the powers of the world, which meant ultimately to death itself. Thus, in the climactic conclusion in v. 21, Paul declares that "sin reigned in death." Sin is *the human failure of vocation,* with all that this entails. When we sin, we abuse our calling, our privileges, and our possibilities. Our thoughts, words, and actions have consequences. They were meant to. That is what being image-bearers is all about. Sin risks replacing good consequences with damaging ones. Turning away from the source of life, we invite death to fill the vacuum. *Both these elements, sin and death, need to be dealt with on the cross.* The whole New Testament and Paul in particular declare that this is what was achieved. That is why the cross launches the revolution.

Most people suppose that when Paul explains what is wrong

with the human race, he focuses on "sin." This is wrong. What he says about "sin" in Romans 1–2 is secondary to what he says about idolatry. The primary human failure is a failure of *worship.* In Romans 1:18–25, "ungodliness" precedes "injustice": those who worship that which is not God will inevitably produce distortions in the world. The point of "injustice" is not just that it means "wrong behavior" (for which the perpetrator would be culpable), but that it means *introducing powerful rogue elements into God's world.* Like a foolish businessman who appoints to the board friends without the company's best interests at heart, we have handed over control to forces that will destroy us and thwart our original purpose.

Consider how this works out. God is known, Paul explains, through the things that he made. The priestly calling of all humans was then to honor God, to thank and praise him. Instead, however, humans "swapped the glory of the immortal God for the likeness of the image of mortal humans—and of birds, animals, and reptiles" (Rom. 1:23). This results from a still more fundamental "exchange": "They swapped God's truth for a lie, and worshipped and served the creature rather than the creator, who is blessed forever" (1:25). Paul here echoes the ancient Israelite insistence on worshipping the true God rather than idols. That is primary. Sin does indeed have dire consequences: "People who do things like that deserve death" (1:32). But his point is much wider than the fate of the human beings in question, important though that is (as 2:1–16 makes clear). Paul's concern is that the Creator's whole plan is put in jeopardy by the failure of humans to *worship him alone.* Only through that worship will they be sustained and fruitful in their vocation to look after his world.

"Idolatry," of course, covers a lot more than simply the manufacture and adoration of actual physical images. It happens whenever we place anything in the created order above the Creator himself. When humans worship parts of creation or forces within creation, they *give away their power* to those aspects of the created order, which will then come to rule over them. "Sin," for Paul, is therefore not simply the breaking of moral codes, though it can be recognized in that way. It is, far more deeply, the missing of the mark of genuine humanness through the failure of worship or rather through worshipping idols rather than the true God. That action, to say it again, hands over to lifeless "forces" or "powers" the authority that should have belonged to the humans in the first place. The problem is not just that humans have misbehaved and need punishing. The problem is that their idolatry, coming to expression in sin, has resulted in slavery for themselves and for the whole creation.

The Bible, then, offers an analysis of the human plight different from the one normally imagined. "Sin" is not just bad in itself. It is the telltale symptom of a deeper problem, and the biblical story addresses that deeper problem; it includes the "sin" problem but goes much farther. The problem is that *humans were made for a particular vocation, which they have rejected; that this rejection involves a turning away from the living God to worship idols; that this results in giving to the idols—"forces" within the creation—a power over humans and the world that was rightfully that of genuine humans;* and that this leads to a *slavery,* which is ultimately the rule of death itself, the corruption and destruction of the good world made by the Creator.

It ought to be clear from all this that the reason "sin" leads to "death" is not at all (as is often supposed) that "death" is an arbitrary and somewhat draconian punishment for miscellaneous moral shortcomings. The link is deeper than that. The distinction I am making is like the distinction between the ticket you will get if you are caught driving too fast and the crash that will happen if you drive too fast around a sharp bend on a wet road. The ticket is arbitrary, an imposition with no organic link to the offense. The crash is intrinsic, the direct consequence of the behavior. In the same way, death is the *intrinsic result* of sin, not simply an arbitrary punishment. When humans fail in their image-bearing vocation, the problem is not just that they face punishment. The problem is that the "powers" seize control, and the Creator's plan for his creation cannot go ahead as intended.

All this comes into much sharper focus when we see it displayed in the biblical story of Israel. This is the story to which Paul is referring when, quoting the early formula, he reminds the Corinthians that "the Messiah died for our sins in accordance with the Bible." This story is what Luke's Jesus has in mind when (in 24:27) he begins with Moses and the prophets and sets out the way that all the scriptures point forward to the "things about himself" that have just taken place. The great story of Israel's scriptures is more complex and many-sided than any brief summary can indicate, and these complexities matter. The New Testament reaffirms the ancient biblical narrative of vocation—Israel's vocation, the human vocation itself—and insists that this has been fulfilled in Jesus and, through Jesus, in his people. The early Christians are therefore drawing on Israel's scriptures to form their dense, compact statements about the meaning of Jesus's death. We must therefore set out this biblical story at somewhat more length.

# 5

## "In All the Scriptures"

W E  H A V E  S E E N how the New Testament writers claim that through the death of Jesus the original human vocation has been reestablished, so that redeemed humans are now seen as the "royal priesthood" or "a kingdom of priests." When the early Christians say this kind of thing, they are not only retrieving the inner meaning of Genesis 1–2, claiming that the original project of creation is now at last back on track. They are also retrieving, from one specific point of view, the vocation of Israel:

> You have seen what I did to the Egyptians, and how I bore you on eagles' wings and brought you to myself. Now therefore, if you obey my voice and keep my covenant, you shall be my treasured possession out of all the peoples. Indeed, the whole earth is mine, but you shall be for me a priestly kingdom and a holy nation. (Exod. 19:4–6)

This vocation generates the remarkable vision found in various sections of Isaiah:

*It is too light a thing that you should be my servant*
   *to raise up the tribes of Jacob*
   *and to restore the survivors of Israel;*
*I will give you as a light to the nations,*
   *that my salvation may reach to the ends of the earth. . . .*
*Kings shall see and stand up,*
   *princes, and they shall prostrate themselves,*
*Because of YHWH, who is faithful,*
   *the Holy One of Israel, who has chosen you. (49:6–7)*

*Arise, shine; for your light has come,*
   *and the glory of YHWH has risen upon you.*
*For darkness shall cover the earth,*
   *and thick darkness the peoples;*
*but YHWH will arise upon you,*
   *and his glory will appear over you.*
*Nations shall come to your light,*
   *and kings to the brightness of your dawn. (60:1–3)*

Passages like these, though striking, do not stand alone. They are telltale signs of a much deeper set of themes. And this set of themes, sometimes awakened by reference to these passages, are central to what the New Testament says about Jesus's death and its effects.

If you read quickly through Israel's scriptures—what Christians came to call the "Old Covenant" or the "Old Testament"—you will discover that, contrary to some popular suppositions, they tell a single great story. But this story is strangely inconclusive. It seems to be pointing toward, but not finding, an appropriate ending. The Hebrew Bible is arranged so that the books of Chronicles come last. In the traditions that shaped most modern translations, including English Bibles, Chronicles comes after Kings, and the collection ends with the prophets, the last of which is Malachi. But whether it's Chronicles or Malachi, a quick read through leaves us straining forward, wondering what's going to happen next.

Actually, you get the same effect if you read quickly through the Pentateuch, the "Five Books," which stand at the head of Israel's scriptures. Deuteronomy, the fifth of the Five Books, does not conclude with a "happily ever after" vision of the future, but rather with a challenging prospect, a mixture of warning and hope. Yet the great opening sequence of the Bible—the creation of heaven and earth and man and woman; the call of Abraham; the slavery in Egypt and the subsequent Exodus; the journey to the land of promise—all this seems to indicate that ancient Israel, at least in the view of those who compiled and edited the scriptures, was playing a critical role in a great drama, the drama of the Creator himself and his creation. But the drama wasn't over yet. At the end of Deuteronomy, Israel is warned about rebellion, exile, and death. At the end of Chronicles, the exile was still continuing. At the end of Malachi, God was promising to come back and sort everything out, but it hadn't happened yet. One cannot imagine Shakespeare playing this trick, working his way through the stages of a plot and then stopping in the middle without tying the narrative strands together and reaching a resolution.

## Israel and Adam

In particular, the scriptures tell the story of how Israel went into *exile*. In a sense, the whole story is about little else. The larger story, in which there is a single great "exile" in Babylon, is shot through at point after point with other "exiles," which lead the eye up to the eventual one. Abraham goes down into Egypt and nearly gets into deep trouble. So does his son Isaac. Isaac's younger son, Jacob, escaping his brother's anger, runs away and stays in the land of his ancestors fourteen years before returning to the territory God had promised to Abraham. Jacob's family goes into Egypt to escape a famine, and the Israelites remain there for four centuries, ending up as slaves, before the dramatic events of

Passover and Exodus through which they are set free and led at last to their promised land.

Once there, they struggle for survival and independence. Even when that is briefly attained under the kingship of David, an internal rebellion forces David himself to flee into exile before returning to resume his throne. Then, after the kingdom is divided into "north" (with its own non-Davidic kings) and "south" (still under Davidic rule), the northern tribes are captured by the Assyrians and taken away, never to return. The southern tribes—Benjamin, Judah, and those Levites who live among them—are left. But they too eventually succumb to the might of Babylon, and most of them are taken there as captives. The Temple is destroyed. According to Ezekiel, this is made possible because YHWH himself has abandoned it to its fate, following the shocking behavior of priests and people alike. The Babylonian captivity is what is normally referred to as "*the* exile."

What follows is in a way the most puzzling moment of all. After two generations, some of the exiles in Babylon return to their land. They rebuild the Temple. But they do not regain their independence, except for a few brief periods. They continue to tell and retell their own story as one of continuing "slavery." There is a strong, widespread sense that the great prophecies about a glorious return (Isaiah and Ezekiel in particular) have not been fulfilled. The prophets of what we think of as the postexilic period (Haggai, Zechariah, Malachi) warn that all is not well. In particular, they suggest that, though the exiles themselves (or some of them) had returned, YHWH himself had not, despite the promises of Isaiah 52, Ezekiel 43, and elsewhere. Malachi promises that he *will* return, but he seems not to have done so yet. Fresh divine action would be needed to undo the present slavery, to complete the story, to put all things right at last.

Into this puzzling situation, the book of Daniel (now generally reckoned to have reached final form in the second century BC) introduces a new note. Jeremiah had said that the exile would last for seventy years; but now it seems that the real, deeper "exile" of continuing slavery to foreign powers would last for a much longer period: seventy *weeks of years,* that is, seventy times seven (9:24). Nearly five hundred years of exile! Well, the slavery in Egypt had been nearly that long; perhaps this too would be within the great divine plan . . . But the story was still unfinished. It was still in search of an ending. That is why, throughout this period, one of the great themes of Jewish thought, writing, and life was *hope:* a hope born of the faith that because Israel's God was the creator of the whole world he would—he must!—take action sooner or later to put everything right.

Anyone used to reading books about the "atonement" might well ask at this point, "What has this ancient story, with all of its twists and turns and dark mysteries, got to do with Jesus's death and the meaning it had for his first followers?" Even when Jewish writers contemporary with the New Testament invoke themes and passages from Israel's scriptures, they do not normally see them within this larger narrative. But from the New Testament's point of view, the story was what mattered—and the story had come into sudden, explosive, revolutionary focus through the death and resurrection of Jesus himself. As in many stories and dramas, the shocking ending suddenly made everything that had gone before make sense. The ending meant what it meant in the light of the previous story, but you wouldn't have told the story quite like this if you didn't know the ending. One of my main arguments in the present book is that only when we see Jesus's death in its proper connection to this entire narrative, can we begin to resolve the questions we want to ask about what the early Christians actually meant.

When the early Christians wrote about Jesus's death, they used what are often seen as different models or metaphors. These include "redemption," a metaphor from the slave market; "justification," a metaphor from the law court; and "sacrifice," a metaphor well known from the Temple. People often suggest

that these don't really fit together; they are simply different pic-
torial ways of getting at the central truth. I think this represents
a failure to see what it means that Jesus's death was *in accordance
with the Bible*.

What look to us like detached images actually mean what they
mean in relation to one another *within this story*. Take them out
of this story, and you will put them into a different one, most
likely some version of the abstract "works contract" in which sinful human beings are heading for either hell or heaven. Only
when we give full early Christian weight to the phrase "in accordance with the Bible" will we discover the full early Christian
meaning of the phrase "for our sins." And this means renounc-
ing the Platonized views of salvation, the moralizing reduction
of the human plight, and ultimately the paganized views of how
salvation is accomplished. The first blunts the leading edge of the
revolution. The second treats one part of the problem as if it were
the whole thing. The third produces a distorted parody of the
true biblical picture.

The clue to a solution comes, as so often, right at the start. *The
story of Israel and its land is set in deliberate parallel to the story of Adam
and Eve in the garden.* Of course, we may well suppose that it was
conceived and written the other way around; that is, whoever
put the first few chapters of Genesis together in the way we now
read them presumably had the longer story of Israel in mind. The
stories are designed to interpret one another. Read the story of
Adam and Eve and you see, close up, the stark meaning of the
much longer story of Israel. Read the full story of Israel and you
see, worked out in great and tragic detail, what the plight of the
human race really meant.

The stories are not, however, designed simply to stand in parallel, the one as a mere "example" of the other. Genesis introduces
the story of Abraham and his family in terms that make it clear
that this family is supposed to be *the means by which the problem of
the human race would itself be resolved*. Here's how the story of Gen-

esis 1–12 works. God called Abraham and Sarah to reverse and undo the problem of Adam and Eve. This was how the original purpose would get back on track. The promised land was to be the new Eden. This can be shown clearly from both the original texts themselves and the way the story was retrieved in many later Jewish as well as Christian writings.

Three things follow at once. First, the promised land would be the place of *life,* as opposed to death. This comes out with great emphasis toward the end of Deuteronomy (30:15–20), resonating back all the way to Genesis 3:22–24, where Adam and Eve are expelled from the garden and barred from having access to the Tree of Life. The life given and then lost at the beginning is to be restored in the end. "Life" in the land will be the answer to the "death" of expulsion from the garden.

Second, the land would eventually become the place of *divine Presence.* The original heaven-and-earth creation was meant to function as a dwelling not only for the humans, but for the creator God himself. Creation as a whole was a kind of Temple, with humans, the divine "image," placed at its heart. The tabernacle in the wilderness and then ultimately the Temple in Jerusalem were each to be a creation-in-miniature, a "microcosmos," a place where God would dwell in the midst of his people as a sign of his eventual intention to renew and restore creation itself, flooding it with his powerful Presence. (This ultimate purpose is taken for granted in many biblical texts, but emerges into view in such passages as Num. 14:21; Ps. 72:19; Isa. 11:9; and Hab. 2:14.) When we read Genesis and Exodus together, the construction of the tabernacle toward the end of Exodus and the role of Aaron the high priest within it can be seen as a renewal or restoration of the original creation. In the "little world" of the sacred tent, close up and divinely personal, the story echoes the original creation. Heaven and earth belong together. God himself is mysteriously present. Humans, bearing the divine image, play their priestly role at the center.

Third, there are signs within Israel's scriptures that the land itself was seen as an advance signpost for something much greater. "Ask of me," says God to his anointed king, "and I will make the nations your heritage, and the ends of the earth your possession" (Ps. 2:8). This explicit expansion of the "promised land" to include the entire world is repeated, at more length, in Psalms 72 and 89, and prophetic passages like Isaiah 11 fill in the picture with a visionary sketch of creation renewed. Other psalms and other prophetic writings insist that the divine purpose is eventually to bring the whole world under the rescuing and rehumanizing rule of Israel's God. Once again, the scriptural vision is not of human souls "going to heaven," but of a promised new creation for which the promised land is a sign and symbol.

Every single element in this (to us) increasingly complex picture is important if we are to get inside the minds of the first followers of Jesus and understand what they meant when they spoke of Jesus's death being "in accordance with the Bible" and "for our sins." If we fail to grasp how all this fits together, how the whole framework functions *as* a whole, it isn't just that we will reduce our view of Jesus's death to inadequate shorthands and slogans. We will put it into a different framework. And that alternate framework, invented to fill the gap left by the original one, will impart to central phrases like "for our sins" a meaning subtly but importantly different from the original one. We will, in fact, de-biblicize the story. We will de-Judaize it. We will paganize it.

So what happens when we read the story of Adam and Eve and then the story of Israel in parallel, on the one hand, and in sequence, on the other? In both cases the promise of life is exchanged for the reality of death, and for the same reason. The early humans rejected the Creator's call and command; Israel rejected the much-amplified call and commands of the covenant God. Faced with the tragedy and terror of exile, the great prophets struggled for meaning. The pagan hordes had triumphed over

Israel, trampled upon the holy places, and taken the chosen people off to Babylon (the "Babel" where, in Genesis 11, human arrogance had reached its full height). What sense could be made of that? The prophets' central insight, exactly in line with Deuteronomy, was to see the exile as a kind of living death. But this could not be the end of the story, or chaos would indeed have come again. Somehow—and the greatest of the prophets struggled in prayer and poetry to bring this insight to birth—just as the Creator chose the covenant people to be the means of rescuing the human race, so now, with the chosen people themselves in need of rescue, God might do the same thing again. He might act in a new way to call from within exilic Israel a remnant, perhaps even a remnant of one, through whom he would deliver Israel. How that deliverance would be accomplished remained obscure. That it would have to happen was the conviction born of the prophetic belief. If Israel's God was indeed the world's creator, he was under a solemn obligation to bring it to pass. He would, despite all, be faithful to his covenant, to his purposes for creation itself. The early Christians believed that this was what had just happened in and through Israel's Messiah, Jesus.

So why would this whole story lead to the idea of a coming climactic moment of "forgiveness of sins"? Why would Paul or anyone else suggest that when God dealt with sins this would be "in accordance with the Bible"? To answer those questions we need to retrieve and develop our earlier discussion of "sin" and show what it meant within this larger story.

## "Sin" and "Exile" in a Biblical Framework

The word "sin" is not only sad and ugly as it stands; it is much misunderstood. In Western culture it has come to be associated, rightly or wrongly, with a killjoy, finger-wagging, holier-than-thou moralism, with a fussy, nit-picking concentration on small personal misdemeanors that ignore major injustice and oppression. Talk about "sin" is regularly associated with a dualistic rejection of the "world," with a smug "otherworldly" pietism, and with a severe story line that cheerfully sends most of the human race into everlasting fire. There are of course many preachers and teachers who have spoken wisely and biblically about "sin." It remains an enormously important topic.

But what I have just described is *how a great many people,* both inside and outside the church, *perceive the language of "sin."* One of the reasons some former "insiders" are now "outsiders" is because they have reacted against such perceived teaching. There was a time when the people who worried about "sin" were impenitent wrongdoers. Today, the wrongdoers aren't worried any more. The people banging on about "sin" are those who think it's someone else's problem. Over the last generation or so, therefore, the Western world, including the church, has found the language of "sin" sorely inadequate, not least because, as Jesus said about the Pharisees, it often cleans up things on the surface while hiding a deep rottenness within. But we haven't yet decided what to put in its place.

Some critics have suggested, with a certain amount of justification, that the whole point of talking about "sin" was really a way of controlling people. Sin talk is a power game, people have said; it is the moral equivalent of an overly fussy "health and safety" culture. It is designed to quench free spirits and to play a safety-first game with other people's lives. It reflects an outdated and probably neurotic refusal to embrace the random indeterminacy of life and the radical freedom for which humans are born.

Some in the churches, fearful of moral anarchy, have tried to cling to the old rules. Others have switched attention to newer, more fashionable issues, still thumping the pulpit, but now warning against fossil fuels rather than fornication. The older "sins" have been replaced by newer ones; the fierce energy of earlier moralisms has been transferred now to issues like ecology, feminism, and international debt. Others again have thrown over the whole idea, so that self-righteousness—the idea that "our way of life" is superior to "theirs"—is the only "sin" left. (This, of course, produces an infinite regress in which we congratulate ourselves because we are not self-congratulatory.)

We cannot here go into the question of how we got into this muddle. Far more important for our present purposes is to see how to get out of it. Fortunately, the answer lies close at hand, and it offers a direct route to what the early Christians meant when they said that the Messiah had died "for our sins in accordance with the Bible."

As always, words mean what they mean within the larger story that is being told. In this case, the word "sin" means what it means *within the story the Bible is telling.* Taking it out of that context generates the difficulties just outlined. Actually, the Bible has several different words for sin: "wickedness," "transgression," and other terms for inappropriate or illegal behavior. These words all converge on the idea we sketched in the previous chapter: that humans were made for a purpose, that Israel was made for a purpose, and that humans and Israel alike have turned aside from that purpose, distorted the vision, and abused their vocation.

The normal Greek word for "sin," namely *hamartia,* means "missing the mark": shooting at a target and failing to hit it. This is subtly but importantly different from being given a long and fussy list of things you must and mustn't do and failing to observe them all. In the story the Bible is telling, humans were created for a purpose, and Israel was called for a purpose, and the purpose was not simply "to keep the rules," "to be with God," or "to go to heaven," as you might suppose from innumerable books, sermons, hymns, and prayers. Humans were made to be "image-bearers," to reflect the praises of creation back to the Creator and to reflect the Creator's wise and loving stewardship into the world. Israel was called to be the royal priesthood, to worship God and reflect his rescuing wisdom into the world.

In the Bible, "sin"—for which there are various words in He-brew—is the outworking of a prior disease, a prior disobedience: a failure of *worship*. Humans are made to worship the God who created them in his own image and so to be sustained and re-newed in that image-bearing capacity. Like many scholars today, I understand the idea of the "image," as in Genesis 1:26–28, to mean that humans are designed to function like angled mirrors. We are created in order to reflect the worship of all creation back to the Creator and by that same means to reflect the wise sover-eignty of the Creator into the world. *Human beings, worshipping their Creator, were thus the intended key to the proper flourishing of the world.* "Worship" was and is a matter of gazing with delight, gratitude, and love at the creator God and expressing his praise in wise, articulate speech. Those who do this are formed by this activity to become the generous, humble stewards through whom God's creative and sustaining love is let loose into the world. That was how things were meant to be. The purpose of the cross is to take us back, from where we presently are, to that intended goal.

Because, of course, we have all failed in this vocation. When humans turn from worshipping the one God to worshipping any-thing else instead, anything within the created order, the problem is not just that they "do wrong things," distorting their human minds, bodies, hearts, and everything else, though of course that is true as well. In addition—and this is vital for grasping the meaning of Jesus's crucifixion—they give to whatever idol they are worshipping the power and authority that they, the humans, were supposed to be exercising in the first place. Worshipping things other than the one true God and distorting our human behavior in consequence is the very essence of "sin": the Greek word for "sin" in the New Testament means, as we saw, not just "doing wrong things," but "missing the target." The target is a wise, full human life of worship and stewardship. Idolatry and sin are, in the last analysis, a failure of *responsibility*. They are a way of declining the divine summons to reflect God's image. They constitute an insult, an affront, to the loving, wise Creator himself. The Great Playwright has composed a drama and written a wonderful part especially for us to play; and, like a spoiled and silly child, we have torn up the script and smirked our way through a self-serving but ultimately self-destructive plot of our own.

As we know in other walks of life, when people duck out of their assigned responsibilities, someone else will take them over instead, and no good will come of it. When humans sin, they *hand to nondivine forces a power and authority that those forces were never supposed to have.* And that is why, if God's plan is to rescue and restore his whole creation, with humans as the active agents in the middle of it, "sins" have to be dealt with. That is the only way by which the nondivine forces that usurp the human role in the world will lose their power. They will be starved of the oxygen that keeps them alive, that turns them from ordinary parts of God's creation into distorted and dangerous monsters.

You can see this in the obvious examples: money, sex, and power itself. Like fire, these "forces" are good servants but bad masters. Not for nothing were they treated as gods and goddesses in the ancient world—as indeed many people treat them today (though without using that language), sacrificing to them and obeying their every command. These "powers" need to be overcome not so that we can live disembodied lives in which they play no part, but so that we can live fully human lives in which they make their contribution as and when appropriate. They stop being demons when they stop being gods. But behind all specific "powers" or "forces" many Jewish and Christian thinkers have recognized a darker, more nebulous power that drives ordinary people to do horrible things. It is not surprising that many liberal-minded Western thinkers who had stopped believing in the old medieval caricatures of the "devil" found themselves reaching for very similar language by the end of the twentieth century. The horrors of that century, never mind our own so far, are hard to explain simply as the sum total of foolish human behavior.

Sometimes the Bible refers to this dark force simply as "sin" (singular) as opposed to the "sins" (plural) that humans commit when they behave in a less than fully human fashion. Sometimes it uses the semipersonal language of "the satan" (a Hebrew term that means "the accuser," the one who lures people into error and then blames them for it). But the point is this. The reason we commit "sins" is because, to some extent at least, we are failing to worship the one true God and are worshipping instead some feature or force within the created order. When we do that, we are abdicating our responsibilities, handing to the "powers" in question the genuine human authority that ought to be ours. And that is the somewhat more complex, but fully coherent, scenario that has to be addressed if God's new creation, the promised "new heavens and new earth," is going to come at last. The early Christian writings leave us in no doubt: if we reduce the problem to "our wrong behavior" and try to explain the cross simply as the divine answer to that, we will never get to the heart of the matter. Nor, in fact, will we fully understand how the cross dealt with sin itself.

To recap, then, humans were made to be "vicegerents." That is, they were to act on God's behalf within his world. But that is only possible and can only escape serious and dangerous distortion when worship precedes action. Only those who are worshipping the Creator will be humble enough to be entrusted with his stewardship. That is the "covenant of vocation." (The word "covenant" is not used explicitly at that point, but it sums up neatly the sense of divine purpose in which human creatures are summoned to play their part.) *That is what is lost when humans decide to rebel and take orders instead from within the world itself.* That is why, in the developed view within Israel's traditions, the basic "sin" is actually idolatry, worshipping and serving anything in the place of the one true God. And, since humans are made for the life that comes from God and God alone, to worship that which is not God is to fall in love with death.

Here is the fundamental truth that generates the inner logic of 1 Corinthians 15 and many other passages in which Paul and other early Christians are explaining the meaning of Jesus's death and resurrection. We have all too often imagined "sin" as the breaking of arbitrary commandments and "death" as the severe penalty inflicted by an unblinking divine Justice on all who fail to toe the line. We have then tried to insert Jesus and his death into this picture, so that an unblinking divine Justice kills him instead. This doesn't look good. More important still, it doesn't look *biblical*. It is not "in accordance with the Bible." It may invoke a few odd proof-texts, but it snatches them out of the much larger context of Israel's scriptures as a whole. They mean something different as a result.

So what happens if we understand the human vocation as bearing God's image, of reflecting God's wise authority into the world and the glad praises of creation back to God? What happens if we see "sin" in *that* context?

Within that story, "sin" becomes the refusal of humans to play their part in God's purposes for creation as a whole. It is a *vocational* failure as much as what we call a *moral* failure. This vocational failure, choosing to worship the creature rather than the Creator, is the choice of death over life. This is why "sin" and "death" are so inextricably intertwined in biblical thinking. The former is not the breaking of arbitrary rules; the latter is not the inflicting of arbitrary punishment. To be sure, they can often be spoken of, not least in the prophets, as a legal code to which appropriate penalties are attached. That is a natural way, on the surface, to refer to the whole sorry state of affairs. But deep down underneath there is nothing arbitrary about sin or death. Choose the one, and you choose the other. Worship idols, and you'll go into exile. Obey the serpent's voice, and you will forfeit the right to the Tree of Life. You can't have it both ways.

When, therefore, the biblical writers see the story of Israel as Adam and Eve writ large, they are making the same point on a grand, historical scale. Despite repeated warnings, Israel as a whole commits apostasy, worships idols, and copies the lifestyles of the non-Israelite nations all around. The result, predicted in Leviticus 26 and Deuteronomy 28, is exile. Genesis 3 is inscribed into the pages of history. Again and again Isaiah, Jeremiah, and Ezekiel insist on the point: exile has come about because of *sin,* the sin that fundamentally consists in and then grows out of idolatry. The people's sins have been stacked up higher and higher, and they have finally paid the price. Exile is therefore to be understood as a kind of corporate national *death.* Leaving the land is leaving the garden; leaving the ruined Temple means being debarred from the Tree of Life. Israel is, after all, no better than the pagan nations.

This is made abundantly, embarrassingly clear in Deuteronomy 32, the great "Song of Moses," predicting the ways in which Israel would spurn the covenant God and behave like the nations all around. (It is significant for understanding the first century that both the apostle Paul and the historian Josephus seem to have thought that Deuteronomy 32 was coming true in their own day.) If, therefore, exile is eventually undone—whatever precisely that will mean—this will be *both* a "forgiveness of sins" *and* a new life the other side of death—*and* the restoration of the life-giving divine Presence. A resurrection, in fact. Ezekiel 37 makes exactly this point, using resurrection as a glorious, if somewhat lurid, picture for Israel's rescue from Babylon.

Nor is this simply a metaphor or a type that would point forward, like a signpost, to something quite different. (A signpost may offer a symbol of a particular building, perhaps a hospital or a restaurant. The symbol doesn't need to look at all like what you will see when you arrive at the destination. By itself, the signpost will give you neither medication nor food; but it will point you in the right direction. That is how many Christians have seen the biblical story of exile and the promise of restoration: a truthful signpost, but a signpost to something essentially different.) Western culture has been so wedded to the platonic idea that God's purpose for humans is to leave this world and go to "heaven" to be with him—as opposed to the biblical idea that God's purpose for humans is to reflect the praises of creation back to him and to reflect his image in the world, so that ultimately heaven and earth will be one—that many who hear and understand the point I have been making will still try to see it as an "illustration" rather than as *part of the story in which Jesus and his followers were still living.*

Such people, perhaps the most frustrating of dialogue partners, will at once insist on "translating" the Israel-specific historical and biblical context into an abstract idea, as though Israel itself were simply an example of something else rather than the people through whom the divine project of restoration was to be taken forward. Such readers will then have to create a new context for Jesus and his death. It will only be "in accordance with the Bible" in a thin, twisted sense. The new context will distort what the Bible itself—both Old and New Testaments—actually says. This has happened time and again. But if we keep our nerve, we may perhaps be able to get things straight at last.

If exile is the result of Israel's sin, and if this exile is therefore to be understood as death, it is not simply that Israel happens to have done on a grand scale what the human race, symbolized in Adam and Eve, had done all along. Israel—the people called by God for the unique role in his purposes—could never be merely an example, even a large-scale example, of *something else.* Israel's idolatry and exile, Israel's sin and death are seen in Israel's scriptures themselves not just as the quintessence, but also as the radical deepening of the human plight. It is as if the lifeboat sent to rescue drowning sailors from a stricken ship has itself been submerged under a giant wave before it has reached those in need of it.

But the project continues nonetheless. When the early Christian formula says that Jesus's death happened "in accordance with the Bible," it really does mean, as Jesus himself indicated in Luke

24, that the single great narrative had now come forward to its long-awaited goal. Somehow, *Israel's sins must be dealt with so that the project of global restoration—including dealing with the sins of the world in general—can go forward.* The larger biblical narrative indicated that the fate of humankind as a whole was hanging upon the rescue operation that had been launched in the family of Abraham, but that was now itself, it seemed, in peril. What was then required, in both the focused personal sense and the national and cosmic sense, was the "forgiveness of sins." This would take the form of the real return from exile, which would have its full effect not only in Israel, but in the whole world.

This is more or less exactly the point of Isaiah 40–55. But when we get to those chapters, we find another vital theme awaiting us. Exile will be undone, sins will be forgiven, and new life will be offered to the world—through the personal Presence and the powerful rescuing action of Israel's God himself. This belief stands at the heart of the early Christian understanding of Jesus's death. To explore this theme and to show how it belongs with this idea of the forgiveness of sins, we will need another chapter.

# 6

## The Divine Presence and the Forgiveness of Sins

I N THE BIBLE, the idea of God's personal Presence forms itself into a story. The short form of the story goes like this. The Creator is present with his human creatures in the original creation, "walking in the garden at the time of the evening breeze" (Gen. 3:8). Some later texts speak of God hiding from sinful humanity, but in the fateful opening scene it was the humans who were trying, unsuccessfully, to hide. In the aftermath, God seems to be a brooding onlooker, grieving over the wickedness of the human creatures, drowning the world in a flood from which one family is rescued to restart the project and finally disrupting the arrogant building of the Tower of Babel. Then, in Genesis 12, God calls Abraham and appears to him on various occasions. Abraham builds shrines and worships God there. Already there is a sense, fitful but nonetheless powerful, of the challenging, vocation-renewing divine Presence in the land of promise.

The theme continues. Jacob, running away into exile, has a vision of a ladder between heaven and earth, with God standing at the top; Jacob names the place Bethel, the "house of God," and it eventually becomes another such shrine. But the God who called Abraham makes himself known in a new way through the Exodus, revealing the divine name (the mysterious "I AM WHO I AM" of Exod. 3:13–15 and 6:2), declaring the law (Exod. 20), and above all, despite the people's shocking idolatry with the golden calf, coming to dwell with them in the tabernacle in the wilderness, and leading them to the promised land. As we saw, the tabernacle was designed as a miniature heaven-and-earth, a "little world" in which God and his people would meet. It would be a miniature Eden. Now, however, it would be placed under strict conditions, because of the danger of rebellious humans bringing their polluted lives into direct contact with the holy God himself.

## Presence and Glory

One item of furniture in the tabernacle becomes important in the New Testament, and we must glance at it briefly here. The "ark of the covenant" was a special box containing, among other things, the tablets of the law that constituted the covenant between God and Israel. Much as a new householder might place the title deed, insurance certificates, and other vital documents in a fireproof safe or the rulers and elders of a city might keep its founding and guiding charter in an official chest, so God's people were to keep in this box those things that spoke of and symbolized the union of God and Israel and hence the purposes that God had *for* Israel.

This was above all the place of meeting: according to Exodus 25:17–22, the lid of the ark was where God would meet with his people. This lid (*kappōreth;* in Greek *hilastērion*), with its carved angels at either end, then played an important role in one strand of early Christian interpretation of the cross. God's intention to meet in this way with his people provided the context for the whole sacrificial system. The glad offerings of worship, the necessary offerings for purification (since nothing impure could approach the divine Presence), and the equally necessary offerings for sins all make this point. When this furniture and these sacrifices are referred to in the New Testament, they must be seen within the larger story of God and tabernacle (or Temple), which is itself part of the larger story of God, Israel, and the world.

When the Israelites finally entered the promised land, conquered it, and occupied it, the tabernacle was placed in a shrine at Shiloh until it was captured by the Philistines (another "exile" of sorts). David then brought it back, intending to build a permanent shrine in his new capital, Jerusalem. This became the subject of one of the most significant brief conversations in the Old Testament. The prophet Nathan, responding to David's proposal to build God a "house," declared that God would instead build David a "house." This was an important passage for some Jews in the time of Jesus, and it was extremely important for the early Christians as they reflected on the meaning of Jesus's life, death, and resurrection:

> YHWH declares to you that YHWH will build you a
> house. When your days are fulfilled and you lie down
> with your ancestors, I will raise up your seed after you,
> who shall come forth from your body, and I will estab-
> lish his kingdom. He shall build a house for my name,
> and I will establish the throne of his kingdom forever.
> I will be a father to him, and he shall be a son to me.
> (2 Sam. 7:11–14, slightly altered)

The point is, of course, a pun on "house." David asks permission to construct a *building,* but God promises him a *family.* Has God, speaking through Nathan, changed the subject? Is it just a verbal trick? No. First, because David's son Solomon will be responsible for constructing the Temple in Jerusalem; and, second, because David's ultimate son will be, in a tantalizingly special yet unspecific sense, God's own son. In the shimmering possibilities of later readings, particularly the early Christian readings generated by Jesus's resurrection (where "I will raise up your seed" suddenly took on a meaning never before imagined), the building that Solomon would construct was only a signpost to the ultimate divine answer to David's request. If there is to be a place where the living God will dwell forever among his people, *it will not be in a building of bricks and mortar; it will be in and as a human being, the ultimate son of David.* Somehow everything that might be thought and celebrated about the Temple and about God's intention of dwelling with his people would come into a new world of meaning when David's projected "house" turned out to be a human being.

The great royal psalms, such as Psalms 2, 72, and 132, celebrate this promise. Psalm 89, intriguingly, likewise celebrates the promise, but questions rather sharply why it isn't being fulfilled as expected. We can imagine devout Jews through to Jesus's day and beyond singing and praying those ancient prayers in the hope that one day deliverance would come, one day a true king would come, one day the living God would call the whole world to account and come back to live forever with his people. *How* he would do this, when and where and through whom he would do it remained frustratingly indistinct. *That* he would do it was the scriptural promise.

When Solomon built the Temple and dedicated it with great pomp, splendor, and the sacrifice of thousands of animals, the divine Glory did indeed come to dwell in it. The magnificent scene is described in 1 Kings 8, which comments that the priests were unable to stand before the glorious divine Presence (v. 11). This description resonates with what had happened when the tabernacle was constructed and dedicated in the wilderness (Exod. 40). The creator of the world had deigned to take up residence in *this* building in fulfillment of the promises made to *this* royal house. Here was the spot where heaven touched earth, where a "little world" came into being as a sign of the ultimate intention that the divine Glory would fill the whole earth (Ps. 72:19). Indeed, in the later vision of the prophet Isaiah, the angels surrounding the divine Presence sang that the whole earth was already full of his glory (6:3). We are not told of other occasions when the divine Glory was so clearly visible in Solomon's Temple. But the building remained the focus of prayer, sacrifice, and pilgrimage for the great festivals up to the time when the Babylonians destroyed it in 587 BC. Even after that, devout Jews might pray toward its location. That, according to Daniel 6:10, is what Daniel did in his room in Babylon, perhaps reflecting Solomon's prayer in 1 Kings 8:46–53.

The destruction of the Temple was only possible, according to Ezekiel, because the glorious divine Presence had finally abandoned it to its fate. Ezekiel provides a graphic description, in chapters 10 and 11, of the divine Glory—whirling wheels and all—leaving the Temple, alighting briefly on the Mount of Olives, and then taking off for an unknown destination. The Glory had departed. It was only a matter of time before the Temple would be destroyed.

But it is to Ezekiel, toward the end of his book in chapter 43, that we owe one of the fullest descriptions of the divine Glory returning to a rebuilt Temple, once God had thoroughly cleansed and purified his people. This is where the promise of "resurrection," the promised restoration after the "death" of exile, fits in. And that leads us back once more to Isaiah 40–55, where the prophet declares that the Glory of YHWH will be revealed once more and all flesh shall see it, because sins have been forgiven, the people have been pardoned; the exile will be over, Babylon will be destroyed, the ancient covenant will be renewed, and creation itself will flourish as always intended. Once again we note that this is the passage in which we find, in chapters 52 and 53, the most striking of all biblical images about one person suffering and dying on behalf of the many. All this—the rich combination of story and promise, of Glory and Temple, of exile and restoration—would be in the front of people's minds during the

Second Temple period, that is, between the late fifth century BC and the late first century AD.

Throughout that period, though the Temple was rebuilt and the sacrifices regularly offered until AD 70, when the Romans destroyed it once and for all, nobody ever suggested that the divine Presence had actually returned in power and glory. Like all holy places, the Temple undoubtedly retained a strong sense of memory, of "presence" in that sense. It does to this day, which is why devout Jews pray fervently at the Western Wall, often scribbling prayers, folding them up, and pushing them into the cracks between the massive, ancient stones. But they do not suppose that the divine Glory, which the later rabbis referred to as the *Shekinah*, the "tabernacling Presence" of God, is there in the same way as in Exodus 40, 1 Kings 8, Isaiah's vision, or the promises of Ezekiel 43 or Isaiah 40 and 52. Isaiah spoke, after all, of the sentinels on Jerusalem's walls lifting up their voices and singing for joy, because "in plain sight they see the return of YHWH to Zion" (52:8). That never happened. The postexilic prophets—Haggai, Zechariah, and Malachi—insisted that it *would* happen, but it hadn't yet.

Centuries later, the rabbis looked back on this period and produced a list, with a sense of gloomy resignation, of all the ways in which the Second Temple was deficient in comparison with the First Temple. Notable on the list of what was missing in the Second Temple was the *Shekinah* itself, the glorious divine Presence. In Jesus's day, the hope was alive that the Glory would return at last. But nobody knew exactly what that would mean, how it would happen, or what it would look like.

To these questions the New Testament writers offer an answer that is so explosive, so unexpected, so revolutionary, that it has remained entirely off the radar for most modern readers, including modern Christian readers. To take the most obvious example, the Gospel of John says: "The Word became flesh, and lived among us. We gazed upon his glory, glory like that of the father's only son, full of grace and truth" (1:14). The word for "lived" here is *eskēnosen,* "tabernacled," "pitched his tent." John is saying that in Jesus the new tabernacle, the new Temple, has been built, and the divine Glory has returned at last. The "Word" who was and is God has become flesh. The vehicle of this glory is the "father's only son": picking up 2 Samuel 7 and the related psalms, the evangelist is declaring that the ancient promises and the long-awaited hopes have been fulfilled in this Messiah, this Jesus, this Davidic son of God. Through this Jesus we glimpse that the very phrase "son of God," like the tabernacle itself, was a building designed for God himself to dwell in. Readers are invited to see the creative Word through whom all things were made coming as a human being and, as Isaiah had promised, unveiling the divine Glory before all the nations. Once we understand the image-bearing purpose of human beings, this is perhaps not so hard to imagine as some have supposed. As John's gospel progresses, we come to realize that the moment when that Glory is fully unveiled is the moment when Jesus is crucified. This is part of John's dramatic and revolutionary theology of the cross.

We should note what all this means. Modern Christians need to be reminded regularly that Jews in this period did not perceive themselves to be living within a story of an angry moralistic God who threatened people that he would send them to hell if they displeased him. Nor were they hoping that, if somehow they could make things all right, they would go to a place called "heaven" and be with God forever. Some ancient pagans thought like that; most ancient Jews did not.

They were hoping, longing, and praying for what the prophets had sketched, what the Psalms had sung, what the ancient promises to the patriarchs had held out in prospect: not rescue *from* the present world, but rescue and renewal *within* the present world. Israel's fortunes would plunge to a low ebb, and then lower, down to the very depths; but there would come a time when God would return in person to do a new thing. Through this new thing not only would Israel itself be rescued from the "death" of exile, the inevitable result of idolatry and sin, but the nations of the world would somehow be brought into the new creation the creator God was planning. And one of the central, vital ways of expressing this entire hope—rescue from exile, the rebuilding of the Temple, the return of YHWH himself—was to speak of the "forgiveness of sins." Exile was the result of sin. As many biblical writers insisted (one thinks, for a start, of Deuteronomy, Isaiah, Jeremiah, Daniel, and the Psalms), if exile was to be undone, sin would have to be forgiven.

This can be seen in many places, but one striking example is found in Lamentations, the poetic quintessence of the theme of exile as a result of sin. Line after line indicates the direct connection: Israel's sin is the cause of exile. Then at last, after the brief note of consolation in chapter 3, we find the sudden promise toward the end of chapter 4:

> *The punishment of your iniquity, O daughter Zion, is*
> *    accomplished,*
> *    he will keep you in exile no longer. (4:22)*

This is exactly in line with the promise of Isaiah 40:1–2:

> *Comfort, O comfort my people, says your God.*
> *Speak tenderly to Jerusalem,*
> *    and cry to her*
> *that she has served her term,*
> *    that her penalty is paid,*
> *that she has received from YHWH's hand*
> *    double for all her sins.*

Israel's God comes as a warrior king who will defeat the idols of Babylon and set his people free and also as the gentle shepherd who will lead his flock and give special care to the mother sheep with their lambs (40:3–11). All these promises are finally made good in the Servant Songs, particularly the fourth and final one (52:13–53:12). This is where Israel's sins are finally dealt with.

The same is true of Jeremiah 31, a collection of oracles predicting the joyful return of the exiles. Wave upon wave of poetry declares and celebrates the powerful love of YHWH, as a result of which sins will be forgiven, exile will be undone, Jerusalem will be rebuilt, and so on. At the heart of this there will be a "new covenant":

> The days are surely coming, says YHWH, when I will make a new covenant with the house of Israel and the house of Judah. It will not be like the covenant that I made with their ancestors when I took them by the hand to bring them out of the land of Egypt—a covenant that they broke, though I was their husband, says YHWH. But this is the covenant that I will make with the house of Israel after those days, says YHWH: I will put my law within them, and I will write it on their hearts; and I will be their God, and they shall be my people. No longer shall they teach one another, or say to each other, "Know YHWH," for they shall all know me, from the least of them to the greatest, says YHWH; *for I will forgive their iniquity, and remember their sin no more.* (31:31–34)

The "forgiveness of sins" was a huge, life-changing, world-changing reality, long promised and long awaited. It was the fulfillment of Israel's hopes for restoration, coupled with the sense that when Israel was restored, this would somehow generate a new day for the whole human race. It is startling to reflect on just how diminished the average modern Western Christian vision of "hope," of "inheritance," or indeed of "forgiveness" itself has become. We have exchanged the glory of God for a mess of spiritualized, individualistic, and moralistic pottage. And in the middle of it we have radically distorted the meaning of the central gospel message: that, in accordance with the Bible, sins are forgiven through the Messiah's death. We have domesticated the revolution.

Three additional elements in this picture demand our attention. First, Isaiah declared that when Israel's God returned, he would come back as king. That will conclude the present chapter, leaving the second and third for the following one, which are simply summarized here. The second theme is the belief that the final redemption might be achieved not merely in a context of intense sufferings for the people, but actually *by means of* that suffering. But throughout it all, third, the overwhelming theme would be that the "forgiveness of sins," the "end of exile," and all that went with them would be the dramatic expression of the divine covenant *love*.

Each of these three elements is to be found within the varied pre-Christian expressions of Jewish hope. Each then played a large part in the early Christian understanding of what actually happened on the cross. Together they form the heart of that extraordinary event and of its continuing effects to this day and beyond.

## Kingdom of God

The famous oracle in Isaiah 52:7 pictures the messengers of good news hurrying to Jerusalem with the news that Babylon was overthrown and that the glorious divine Presence was returning at last. Their message can be summed up in one swift slogan: "Your God reigns!" This idea of Israel's God as the world's rightful king echoes across much of Israel's scriptures, invoked particularly in the Psalms. Israel's God, the creator of the world, rules the world with justice, and in the end he will act to put that justice into effect once and for all.

This was, of course, a statement of faith, said or sung as often as not in the teeth of apparent evidence to the contrary. Imagine singing Psalm 98, celebrating YHWH's powerful and justice-bringing reign, or Psalm 46, celebrating YHWH's strong defense of Jerusalem, when foreign armies were invading and Israel seemed powerless to resist. As many generations discovered, invoking the royal power of the one true God was itself an act of resistance, perhaps in some settings the most important act of resistance available.

Throughout its history, the people of Israel had to learn that God was well capable of acting in human affairs in a variety of ways, some of which would involve his people as active agents within his purposes and some of which would not. But the important thing was the faith in God's sovereign right and power, a faith that was regularly expressed as hope in the face of adversity: the faith that Israel's God was already, by right, the one true king of the world and that one day this kingship would be established forever. In Isaiah 52 the point is clear: Babylon, the greatest superpower of the day, was going to fall quite suddenly, and those held captive under its power would be freed. The dark power would be overthrown, the people's sins forgiven, the exile undone, and the glorious Presence unveiled. All this is kingdom-of-God language, summed up in the excited shout "Your God reigns!"

This event would be, above all, a "new Exodus." To this day Jews keep the festival of Passover, as did their ancestors in Jesus's time. Passover looks back in story and festival to the great act of promise-fulfilling liberation in which God overthrew Pharaoh and his armies, set his people free, and came to dwell in their midst. That event, like the new one Isaiah promised, was celebrated as a sign of God's universal kingship (Exod. 15:18).

There is, however, a difference between the original Exodus and the new one promised by the prophets. The original Exodus had nothing to do with the forgiveness of sins; the slavery in Egypt was never seen as a result of Israel's sins. The Babylonian exile, however, was seen in exactly that way. Thus two themes combined into a new, complex reality. The "new Exodus," freeing Israel from foreign oppression, would also be the "forgiveness of sins," the real return from exile. This sets the stage exactly for the claims made by the early Christians about what Jesus's death had accomplished. Forgiveness of sins and the overthrow of the enslaving power would belong exactly together. Both would form part of the core meaning of the coming of God's kingdom on earth as in heaven.

The same complex but coherent point emerges from that other great source of kingdom themes of political defiance and resistance: the book of Daniel. The book as a whole, despite remarkable shifts in genre and tone, has a constant theme: Israel's God is sovereign over the nations of the world, and one day he will set his people free forever from pagan oppression. This theme is expressed in various ways, but among the passages that seem to have been important in the first century and that were given a fresh reading by Jesus and his first followers are chapters 2, 7, and 9.

In chapter 2 Daniel interprets King Nebuchadnezzar's dream in which a statue composed of different metals is smashed to pieces by a stone. The statue is a symbol for a succession of world empires; the stone represents the coming messianic kingdom set up by God. This theme is repeated in the vision of the monsters in chapter 7, in which "one like a son of man" is exalted to sit beside the "Ancient of Days" and given kingdom, power, and authority. Again, the monsters are obviously the pagan empires, and the "one like a son of man," at least in the finished form of the book, is the messianic kingdom. (This created a puzzle for later Jewish thinkers. What might it mean to have the Messiah sitting beside God and sharing his authority?)

Then, in chapter 9, a passage we have already noted, Daniel is given a vision of a very extended "exile" and its eventual conclusion. After the "seventy weeks of years," sins will be dealt with once and for all. This will be the time "to finish the transgression, to put an end to sin, and to atone for iniquity, to bring in everlasting righteousness, to seal both vision and prophet, and to anoint a most holy one" (9:24). The passage goes on, alarmingly, to warn that within the same sequence of events the holy city itself will be destroyed and the Temple desecrated with a desolating "abomination."

Readers in the second century BC would have had no difficulty identifying the latter events with the time when the Syrians had desecrated the Temple in 167 BC. Readers in the first century AD, including the early Christians, would naturally see Rome rather than Syria as the invading empire. And all this has to do with the coming multifaceted reality of the end of exile, the forgiveness of sins, the renewal of the covenant, the victory over the pagan power, the unveiling of the divine Glory, and now especially the putting into effect of the divine kingship.

The kingship or "kingdom" of God was, of course, a major theme of Jesus's own public proclamation. He related it directly to his own work. Both he and those who later told his story linked it directly and dynamically to his own death. This alone would justify paying close attention to the theme of God's kingdom in a book on the meaning of the cross, and we shall return to this in the next part of the book. But it is also important to notice that the idea of God being king played a large part in the revolutionary movements of the first century, movements already active around the time of Jesus's birth and even more so in the years leading up to the Roman-Jewish war of the late 60s. The idea of Jesus himself as the king, the king who attained his ultimate royal status through being killed, belongs exactly on the map of first-century resistance movements, drawing as they did on scriptural themes, and particularly on Daniel, for a revolutionary theology in which Israel's God was to "finish transgression, put an end to sin, atone for iniquity," and thereby to win the ultimate victory over the powers of evil. If we are searching for the historical context in which the early Christians were to say that the Messiah "died for our sins in accordance with the Bible," this would be no bad place to start.

To develop this further would demand that we examine the two other themes mentioned a moment ago: the relation of Israel's suffering to the coming kingdom and the revelation of divine love, covenant faithfulness, underneath the entire picture. For this we need a new chapter.

# 7

## Suffering, Redemption, and Love

THE BOOK OF DANIEL bears witness to a recurring theme found in some parts of scripture and then in some post-biblical Jewish literature. When Israel's God finally acted to accomplish the long-awaited end of exile—which, as we saw, meant the forgiveness of the sins that had caused the exile in the first place—this would come about through a time of intense suffering, either for the people as a whole or for a particular group within the people. This theme was highlighted over a century ago by Albert Schweitzer as part of what he called an "apocalyptic" understanding of Jesus's vision of the coming kingdom. Subsequent scholarship has drastically modified some of Schweitzer's proposals, but I am convinced that this part of his theme should still be regarded as central and important.

We should note at the outset, however, that we do not find in pre-Christian Jewish literature any suggestion of a coming *Messiah* who would die for the sins of the nation or the world. Some Jews (not all) expected a coming king, but such a figure would follow his ancestor David in winning military victories that would set Israel free. Some Jews (not all) believed that deliverance would come through suffering, but such suffering would not be undergone by the Messiah himself. It would be hard for a Second Temple Jew to read key passages like Psalm 2 or Psalm 110 without envisaging the Messiah as a military conqueror. This is all the more striking in that the early Christians continued to invoke just those passages, shorn of their explicit violence, in their interpretation of Jesus and what he had accomplished.

It is important, then, to detach the pre-Christian Jewish notion of a coming Messiah from the notion of suffering. Albert Schweitzer, as I mentioned a moment ago, popularized the idea that the long-awaited new age would come about through a period of intense suffering, which came to be termed the "messianic woes." The phrase "messianic woes" by itself, however, is imprecise and potentially misleading. Schweitzer was referring to a visible reality: that from quite early on in the writing of the books that became Israel's scriptures, some prophets and psalmists seemed to come back regularly to this idea of great suffering as the prelude to the coming deliverance. This suffering would, however, only be "messianic" in the loose sense that it might immediately precede the "messianic age." Sometimes Israel's scriptures refer to the suffering that results from Israel's idolatry and sin. Sometimes, however, as in many of the psalms, it is suffering inflicted on God's people, or perhaps on an individual, despite their innocence. The night gets darker, the pain still more intense, and then the new day will dawn. All this comes to a head in passages like Daniel 12:1: "There shall be a time of anguish, such as has never occurred since nations first came into existence. But at that time your people shall be delivered."

This is then seen in some of the classic "suffering" psalms, like Psalm 22, which begins with the experience of desolation, shame, and suffering:

> *My God, my God, why have you forsaken me?*
> 　*Why are you so far from helping me, from the words of my*
> 　　*groaning?*
> *O my God, I cry by day, but you do not answer;*
> 　*and by night, but find no rest. . . .*
> *But I am a worm, and not human;*
> 　*scorned by others, and despised by the people.*
> *All who see me mock at me;*
> 　*they make mouths at me, they shake their heads. . . .*
> *For dogs are all around me;*
> 　*a company of evildoers encircles me.*
> *My hands and feet have shriveled;*
> *I can count all my bones.*
> *They stare and gloat over me;*
> *they divide my clothes among themselves,*
> 　*and for my clothing they cast lots. . . . (22:1–2, 6–7, 16–18)*

And then, in a dramatic change, the mood suddenly gives way to a shout of triumph:

> *I will tell of your name to my brothers and sisters;*
> 　*in the midst of the congregation I will praise you;*
> *You who fear YHWH, praise him!*
> 　*All you offspring of Jacob, glorify him;*
> 　*stand in awe of him, all you offspring of Israel! . . .*
> *All the ends of the earth shall remember*
> 　*and turn to YHWH;*
> *And all the families of the nations*
> 　*shall worship before him.*
> *For dominion [malkuth, "kingdom"] belongs to YHWH,*
> 　*And he rules over the nations. (22:22–23, 27–28)*

This theme receives full, detailed, and highly personal expression in the Servant Songs in Isaiah:

*The sovereign YHWH has opened my ear,*
  *and I was not rebellious,*
  *I did not turn backward.*
*I gave my back to those who struck me,*
  *and my cheeks to those who pulled out the beard;*
*I did not hide my face*
  *from insult and spitting. (50:5–6)*

*He was despised and rejected by others;*
  *a man of suffering and acquainted with infirmity;*
*and as one from whom others hide their faces*
  *he was despised, and we held him of no account.*
*Surely he has borne our infirmities*
  *and carried our diseases;*
*yet we accounted him stricken,*
  *struck down by God, and afflicted. . . .*
*He was oppressed, and he was afflicted,*
  *yet he did not open his mouth;*
*like a lamb that is led to the slaughter,*
  *and like a sheep that before its shearers is silent,*
  *so he did not open his mouth.*
*By a perversion of justice he was taken away.*
  *Who could have imagined his future?*
*For he was cut off from the land of the living,*
  *stricken for the transgression of my people.*
*They made his grave with the wicked*
  *and his tomb with the rich,*
*although he had done no violence,*
  *and there was no deceit in his mouth. (53:3–4, 7–9)*

And the "servant" goes on to "divide the spoil with the strong" (v. 12): this is clearly a *victory* as well as the forgiveness of sins, and following 52:7–12 we should have no difficulty in seeing the latter as the key to the former. In any case, as far as I can tell, within Israel's scriptures it is only in Isaiah 53 that the intense suffering is the *means,* and not simply the *context,* of the expected deliverance, of the forgiveness of sins. This is all the more striking in view of what we saw earlier, that such an idea—one person suffering to redeem many—was widespread in the ancient *non*-Jewish world, turning up in Homer, Euripides, and many other famous non-Jewish writers as well as in reported speeches from heroes in battle. Did the great poet who penned Isaiah 53 intend to allude to that pagan tradition? It seems unlikely.

When we read Isaiah 40–55 as a whole, we find that the motif of redemptive suffering in chapter 53 is new. Up to this point in the poem there is the promise of redemption *from* suffering, on the one hand, and the strange vocation of suffering for the "servant," on the other. But only in the final poem (52:13–53:12) are the two brought together. When this happens, as in many great poems and indeed other art forms, we realize that the new thing has grown organically out of the varied elements of the poem as a whole, so that its meaning is not isolated, a strange new idea sitting by itself, but rather is held in place by the major themes of the surrounding chapters.

This observation will be all the more important when we consider the striking ways in which Isaiah 53, above all other passages, is used in the New Testament as the scriptural clue to the meaning of Jesus's death. It is not a proof-text taken out of the context of either Isaiah 40–55 as a whole (or 40–66 as a whole) or the entire larger narrative of Israel we have been considering. It is simultaneously a quintessential summing up of the plight of Israel and the promise of deliverance, on the one hand, and, on the other hand, a unique new statement of the hope that this plight and this promise would somehow dovetail together. The "servant" represents Israel's plight ("You are my servant, Israel, in whom I will be glorified"; Isa. 49:3); but then the "servant" becomes not simply a personification of the people as a whole, but a different figure, one who would stand over against the rest of the people, even over against any righteous remnant (since in 50:10

those who "fear YHWH" are those who "obey the voice of his servant"). Like many puzzling poems, this one keeps many of its secrets hidden, teasing subsequent generations to ferret them out. And that, of course, is what many early Christians thought they could do with this passage in relation to Jesus.

The problem comes, I think, when the central thrust of Isaiah 53—that *this* suffering was the *means,* not merely the *occasion,* of the forgiveness of sins and all that went with it—is taken out of the context, both literary and historical, in which it is found and made to serve a different narrative. At that moment, I suggest—and this is one of the main arguments of the present book—those who read the text in this new way are in imminent danger of exchanging the ancient Israelite covenantal context of the notion of redemptive suffering for a very different context, namely, a pagan one. And however much a generous reading of the ancient non-Jewish world may discern in it several true signposts pointing toward what in retrospect turns out to be true, that is no excuse for exchanging the full biblical truth for the damaged signpost.

This dilemma emerges in the two contexts in postbiblical Jewish literature where the theme of Isaiah 53—of suffering as the means, not merely the occasion, of forgiveness and restoration—is invoked. These reflect the time of intense suffering in the 160s BC, when the small and struggling Jewish nation was overrun by the energetically paganizing Syrians. Those who died in that struggle were hailed as martyrs, and in the retelling of their stories we find passages that might be echoing Isaiah 53 or might be echoing the pagan stories of vicarious death. Here is the seventh of seven brothers confronting Antiochus Epiphanes not only with warnings of divine punishment, but also with a claim about the redemptive value of the martyrs' sufferings:

We are suffering because of our own sins. And if our living Lord is angry for a little while, to rebuke and

discipline us, he will again be reconciled with his own
servants. . . . I, like my brothers, give up body and life
for the laws of our ancestors, appealing to God to show
mercy soon to our nation and by trials and plagues to
make you confess that he alone is God, and through
me and my brothers to bring to an end the wrath of the
Almighty that has justly fallen on our whole nation.
(2 Macc. 7:32–33, 37–38)

The implicit echo of Isaiah 53 is not the only biblical allusion
here. The "trials and plagues" that this young martyr invokes
upon the pagan tyrant send us back to the story of Moses and
Pharaoh, in which God inflicted "plagues" on the Egyptians as
the prelude to the dramatic rescue of Israel from slavery. That,
presumably, is part of the point. When Israel is enslaved and suffering, what is required is a *new* Exodus. The Maccabean martyrs
look back to the first Exodus in order to suggest that it is time
for a second one. But this new Exodus will have to do something
extra, something the first one had not. It will have to deal with
the sins (v. 32) because of which the Jewish people are suffering.
The new Passover, if and when it comes, will also have to be the
ultimate and exile-ending "dealing with sins." This martyr at
least is claiming that his own suffering will be part of that. Perhaps, he suggests, it will complete that process.

The way the book of 2 Maccabees is constructed suggests that
this was what the writer intended to say. Right after this horrible scene of torture and death, Judas Maccabeus and his followers begin their surprisingly successful revolt against Antiochus
Epiphanes. This leads to the establishment of the Maccabean (or
"Hasmonean") family as rulers of the independent kingdom of
Judaea for the next century and more. This was the more remarkable in that, though they were a priestly family (1 Macc.
2:1), there is little evidence that they were Zadokites, that is,
from the high-priestly family itself; and, naturally, if as priests

they were descended from Aaron, they could not claim to be descendants of David. They nevertheless functioned as priest-kings, in fact, as a "royal priesthood." Our earlier discussion of the renewed human vocation, as in Revelation 1, 5, and 20 and other parts of the New Testament, comes suddenly into new focus as a matter of history, not simply of literary imagination: here, through the suffering of the martyrs, the defeat of the pagans, and the cleansing the Temple is a kingdom of priests! The claim of the seventh brother in 2 Maccabees 7 emphasizes the first point. The victory and the cleansing came because the suffering of the martyrs *somehow brought to an end the sufferings of the people as a whole, which had been caused by their sins.* Now the victory over the pagans could begin.

I do not suppose that the author of Revelation was consciously alluding to the Hasmonean priest-kings. Nor do I imagine that 1 Peter 2:9, which also invokes Exodus 19:6, had in mind the claims of that dynasty, which by the middle of the first century AD had passed into ignominious history, having failed to prevent the Roman invasion, the rise of Herod, and many other ills. But the parallel does indicate the ways in which the larger implicit story of Israel, anchored in the ancient scriptures, could be brought back to life not just in theory but also in concrete practice. The hundred-year reign of the Maccabean priest-kings may be seen as a distant cousin of the thousand-year reign of the Messiah's people, the "reigning priesthood," in Revelation 20:6.

The theoretical basis for the claims made by 2 Maccabees about the effect of the martyrs' sufferings is explained in a revealing passage that has some additional similarities to early Christian reflection. The terrible sufferings that the Jews endured during the period of Syrian domination, says the writer, had a particular purpose. They were designed in order to allow the Jewish people to experience their necessary punishment in advance, in the present time, rather than having to wait, along with the other nations, for the final day of judgment:

I urge those who read this book not to be depressed
by such calamities, but to recognize that these punishments were designed not to destroy but to discipline
our people. In fact, it is a sign of great kindness not to
let the impious alone for long, but to punish them immediately. For in the case of the other nations the Lord
waits patiently to punish them until they have reached
the full measure of their sins; but he does not deal in this
way with us, in order that he may not take vengeance
on us afterward when our sins have reached their height.
Therefore he never withdraws his mercy from us. Although he disciplines us with calamities, he does not
forsake his own people. (6:12–16)

The writer does not *quite* put it the way one might have expected, granted what the seventh brother says later on. We might,
looking back from the latter's speech in chapter 7, have expected
the writer to say in chapter 6 that the sins of the Jewish people had
reached their height and that the martyrs were somehow exhausting the vengeance that had resulted. He draws back from that
idea, but the thought is not far away. As we shall see, this is close
to what Paul says in Romans 5–8.

The suffering and death of the Maccabean martyrs and their
potential redemptive significance are discussed in more detail in
*4 Maccabees*, where the language of ransom and sacrifice becomes
prominent. The book is drawing into Israel's traditions philosophical ideas from elsewhere and indeed frames itself as a philosophical
treatise extolling the exemplary virtues of the martyrs. This may
mean that the author does indeed have the famous non-Jewish traditions about "dying for others" in mind. In setting up these Jewish heroes, he is saying that the Jews too can show evidence of the
kind of noble behavior much vaunted in the non-Jewish world.
Nevertheless, the language used here still carries the overtones of
the Jewish cult, through which the land is purified:

> At this time it is fitting for me to praise for their virtues those who, with their mother, died for the sake of nobility and goodness, but I would also call them blessed for the honor in which they are held. All people, even their torturers, marveled at their courage and endurance, and they became the cause of the downfall of tyranny over their nation. By their endurance they conquered the tyrant, and thus their native land was purified through them. (1:10–11)

This is then developed in the story of Eleazar. Having exhorted the "children of Abraham" to "die nobly for [their] religion" (6:22), he then addresses God in an explicit prayer of self-sacrifice:

> You know, O God, that though I might have saved myself, I am dying in burning torments for the sake of the law. Be merciful to your people, and let our punishment suffice for them. Make my blood their purification, and take my life in exchange for theirs. (6:27–29)

When it comes to the seven brothers, the account follows that in 2 Maccabees in outline, though the final speech of the seventh brother is not so explicitly redemptive as the earlier version; he merely calls on God to be merciful to the nation, while warning the tyrant that God will take vengeance on him here and in the hereafter (12:17). But when the writer sums up what the martyrdom means, the redemptive note emerges again, and this time more fully:

> These, then, who have been consecrated for the sake of God, are honored, not only with this honor, but also by the fact that because of them our enemies did not rule over our nation, the tyrant was punished, and the homeland purified—they having become, as it were, a ransom for the sin of our nation. And through the blood of those devout ones and their death as an atoning sacrifice [*hilastērion*], divine Providence preserved Israel that previously had been mistreated. (17:20–22)

This is perhaps the clearest passage in which the redemptive and sacrificial traditions of Israel are drawn together with the ancient pagan idea of the noble death through which others are spared. We do not need to assess in what proportion these very different traditions are present here. Suffice it to note that at precisely the point where a Jewish writer is drawing explicitly on pagan philosophical traditions and doing his best to present a story of Jewish martyrdom as a story of human virtue, especially courage and nobility, these themes come suddenly into prominence. Was that the reason, one might wonder, why some of the early Christians said some things about Jesus's death that strike us, at least at first glance, as very similar? Or were they following a subtly different interpretative line?

In any case, the point is clear. Within the larger Jewish hope, there are signs that some people at least, under pressure of intense suffering and persecution, reached for ways of interpreting that experience not only as something *through which* God's people might pass to deliverance, but as something *because of which* that deliverance would come about. The extent to which they were consciously drawing on Isaiah 53 or were consciously imitating ancient non-Jewish sources can be debated. The point for our present purposes is that the idea of redemptive suffering, though certainly not associated with messianic expectation, was clearly available in the Jewish world of Jesus's day. I have given the two well-known examples, from the books of the Maccabees. One might also adduce a line or two from the writings found at Qumran. But the matter is not in dispute.

## Divine Faithfulness and Covenant Love

One theme that is constantly emphasized in Isaiah 40–66 but noticeably lacking in the Maccabean writings is the final strand of meaning to be considered here. When the creator God redeems his covenant people, this will be the result of his *faithful love*.

The normal objection to theories of atonement and redemption that focus on divine *anger* is that this seems to run contrary to the deepest themes of the New Testament. Now, of course, divine anger at human rebellion and particularly at the rebellion of the chosen people features prominently throughout Israel's scriptures. Similar notes are struck in the New Testament, not least in the teaching of Jesus himself. And suggestion that "sin" does not make God angry (a frequent idea in modern thought as a reaction against the caricatures of an ill-tempered deity) needs to be treated with disdain. When God looks at sin, what he sees is what a violin maker would see if the player were to use his lovely creation as a tennis racquet. But here is the difference. In many expressions of pagan religion, the humans have to try to pacify the angry deity. But that's not how it happens in Israel's scriptures. The biblical promises of redemption have to do with God himself acting because of his unchanging, unshakeable love for his people.

This theme runs like a scarlet thread through the scriptures, going back at least to Deuteronomy:

> You are a people holy to YHWH your God; YHWH your God has chosen you out of all the peoples on earth to be his people, his treasured possession.
>
> It was not because you were more numerous than any other people that YHWH set his heart on you and chose you—for you were the fewest of all peoples. It was because YHWH loved you and kept the oath that he swore to your ancestors, that YHWH has brought you out with almighty hand, and redeemed you from the house of slavery, from the hand of Pharaoh king of Egypt. Know therefore that YHWH your God is God, the faithful God who maintains covenant loyalty with those who love him and keep his commandments, to a thousand generations. (Deut. 7:6–9)

Although heaven and the heaven of heavens belong to
YHWH your God, the earth with all that is in it, yet
YHWH set his heart in love on your ancestors alone and
chose you, their descendants after them, out of all the people, as it is today. . . . He is your praise; he is your God,
who has done for you these great and awesome things that
your own eyes have seen. (Deut. 10:14–15, 21; cf. 4:37)

*Do not fear, for I have redeemed you;*
  *I have called you by name, you are mine. . . .*
*For I am YHWH your God,*
  *the Holy One of Israel, your Savior.*
*I give Egypt as your ransom,*
  *Ethiopia and Seba in exchange for you.*
*Because you are precious in my sight,*
  *and honored, and I love you,*
*I give people in return for you,*
  *nations in exchange for your life. (Isa. 43:1, 3–4)*

*For he said, "Surely they are my people,*
  *children who will not deal falsely";*
*And he became their savior*
  *in all their distress.*
*It was no messenger or angel,*
  *but his presence that saved them;*
*in his love and in his pity he redeemed them;*
  *he lifted them up and carried them all the days of old. (Isa.*
    *63:8–9)*

*I have loved you with an everlasting love;*
  *therefore I have continued my faithfulness to you. (Jer. 31:3)*

*The steadfast love of YHWH never ceases,*
  *his mercies never come to an end;*
*they are new every morning;*
  *great is your faithfulness. (Lam. 3:22–23)*

> *When Israel was a child, I loved him,*
> *and out of Egypt I called my son. (Hos. 11:1)*

These texts are just a small sample, generated as much by the concordance as anything else, of a theme that runs throughout the scriptures. Equally important, if not more so, are the sustained expositions of the way in which the powerful new work of rescuing Israel from exile, of the new Exodus and all that would go with it, are the direct result of the unbreakable covenant commitment of YHWH to his people. Whether words like "love" occur, passages like these convey the reality with poetic power:

> *See, the sovereign YHWH comes with might,*
> *and his arm rules for him;*
> *his reward is with him,*
> *and his recompense before him.*
> *He will feed his flock like a shepherd;*
> *he will gather the lambs in his arms,*
> *and carry them in his bosom,*
> *and gently lead the mother sheep. (Isa. 40:10–11)*

> *But you, Israel, my servant,*
> *Jacob, whom I have chosen,*
> *the offspring of Abraham, my friend;*
> *you whom I took from the ends of the earth,*
> *and called from its farthest corners,*
> *saying to you, "You are my servant,*
> *I have chosen you and not cast you off";*
> *do not fear, for I am with you,*
> *do not be afraid, for I am your God;*
> *I will strengthen you, I will help you,*
> *I will uphold you with my victorious right hand. (Isa. 41:8–10)*

It is out of this context that there emerges a new promise: the covenant love that YHWH has for Israel is to be extended to the nations.

> *I am YHWH, I have called you in righteousness,*
>> *I have taken you by the hand and kept you;*
> *I have given you as a covenant to the people,*
>> *a light to the nations,*
>>> *to open the eyes that are blind,*
> *to bring out the prisoners from the dungeon,*
>> *from the prison those who sit in darkness. (Isa. 42:6–7)*

In other words, non-Jewish peoples too are to have their own Exodus! This is revolutionary indeed, and it transforms the exclusive note of the earlier passages about the divine love. It now appears that this love is not only the divine love *for* Israel, but the divine love *through* Israel, resulting in the worldwide appeal of Isaiah 55:

> *Ho, everyone who thirsts,*
>> *come to the waters;*
> *and you that have no money,*
>> *come, buy and eat!*
> *Come, buy wine and milk*
>> *without money and without price. . . .*
> *Incline your ear, and come to me;*
>> *listen, so that you may live.*
> *I will make with you an everlasting covenant,*
>> *my steadfast, sure love for David. (55:1–3)*

On the way to that conclusion, the message comes from one angle after another and always with the reassurance of the powerful and unshakeable divine love:

> *Sing for joy, O heavens, and exult, O earth;*
>> *break forth, O mountains, into singing!*
> *For YHWH has comforted his people,*
>> *and will have compassion on his suffering ones.*
> *But Zion said, "YHWH has forsaken me,*
>> *my Lord has forgotten me."*

*Can a woman forget her nursing child,*
*or show no compassion for the child of her womb?*
*Even these may forget,*
*yet I will not forget you.*
*See, I have inscribed you on the palms of my hands;*
*your walls are continually before me. (49:13–16)*

*For YHWH will comfort Zion;*
*he will comfort all her waste places,*
*and will make her wilderness like Eden,*
*her desert like the garden of YHWH;*
*joy and gladness will be found in her,*
*thanksgiving and the voice of song. (51:3)*

This message of divine comfort, extending from the opening of the poem in 40:1 through 52:9 ("For YHWH has comforted his people, he has redeemed Jerusalem"), crescendos to the very passage where the "servant" is "despised and rejected by others" (53:3). It is flatly impossible, reading this passage in its wider context, to see it as anything other than the strange and shocking outworking of the powerful divine covenant love. Thus, immediately after chapter 53 itself, where the death of the "servant" is seen as the ultimate punishment of Israel's sins, we find the covenant gloriously reaffirmed: sins are now forgiven, exile is over, and YHWH and his people are bonded together forever:

*For your Maker is your husband,*
*YHWH of hosts is his name;*
*the Holy One of Israel is your Redeemer,*
*the God of the whole earth he is called.*
*For YHWH has called you*
*like a wife forsaken and grieved in spirit,*
*like the wife of a man's youth when she is cast off,*
*says your God.*
*For a brief moment I abandoned you,*

*but with great compassion I will gather you.*
*In overflowing wrath for a moment*
  *I hid my face from you,*
*but with everlasting love I will have compassion on you,*
    *says YHWH, your Redeemer. . . .*
*For the mountains may depart*
  *and the hills be removed,*
*But my steadfast love shall not depart from you,*
  *and my covenant of peace shall not be removed,*
    *Says YHWH, who has compassion on you. (54:5–10)*

We should not miss the contrast with the ancient non-Jewish sources that spoke of the noble death on behalf of others. In those cases, it was always the human beings involved who were managing to turn away wrath, danger, malevolence, or sheer bad fortune. In Isaiah—and, we might add, Deuteronomy, the Psalms, Jeremiah, and many other places—the rescue has been accomplished by Israel's God himself. It was his initiative, his accomplishment. It was his love.

## Redemption and Forgiveness of Sins

Is it possible to see all these themes as fitting together into a single whole? Probably not—at least within the limitations of Israel's scriptures themselves. No one book or writer gathers together all the ideas I have sketched in this short summary. Isaiah and some of the Psalms come as close as any. But my point has been to trace briefly the rich materials through which Jews of the Second Temple period could, and sometimes did, reflect on the puzzles of their continuing exile, on the challenge of their ongoing but unfinished story, and on the question of how and when the promised resolution would appear. From all this, three themes emerge that are of particular relevance for our overall study.

First, these ancient writings constantly insist that what God's people in the Second Temple period needed was, from one point of view, the "end of exile," and from another point of view, the "forgiveness of sins." Israel's sins were responsible for exile, so forgiveness and "return" would be the inside and the outside of the same thing. When, in the New Testament, we meet the gospel summary in which the Messiah "died for our sins in accordance with the Bible," this is the natural home base of such language. Something has happened through which exile has been undone. The sins that caused exile in the first place have been dealt with once and for all, forever. This is part of the clue to the revolutionary vision of what happened on the cross.

Second, this great and long-awaited event would be the ultimate new Exodus, the final great Passover. The victory over Babylon recapitulates the victory over Egypt. Images of Exodus crowd into passage after passage, so that even though in one text we may be dealing with Babylon, in another Syria, or in another ultimately with Rome, memories of the ancient slavery in Egypt are never far away. When we put these themes together—forgiveness of sins and end of exile, on the one hand, and Passover and Exodus, on the other, we find a composite notion of complete redemption transcending anything that Passover had meant before, transcending also anything that could be conveyed by the Day of Atonement on its own. When, in the New Testament, we find a strong emphasis on one particular set of Passover events fused together inextricably with the notions of dealing with sin, return from exile, and of course the kingdom of God and other related ideas, this combination of ideas provides the natural context of meaning.

Third, the Passover context contributes, through its dramatic theme of the rescuing and guiding Presence of YHWH himself, the sense that the redemption, when it comes, will come through the personal, powerful work of Israel's God himself. The Maccabean literature may indeed flirt with the possibility, borrowed from the non-Jewish themes of the "noble death" on behalf of others, that the martyrs may somehow have taken upon themselves the divine wrath. But the only biblical passage that might be read in that way—Isaiah 53—forms the climax of a matchless poem whose overall theme is the powerful and unchangeable love of the one God. When we find, in the New Testament, a repeated emphasis on the love of God as the driving agent for this great act of forgiveness and new Exodus—when the early Christians said things like, "God so loved the world that he gave his son," or "The son of God loved me and gave himself for me," or "Nothing in all creation shall be able to separate us from the love of God in the Messiah"—then we should be in no doubt that they were intending to draw on this entire narrative, focused particularly on Isaiah and Daniel.

This brings to the fore more sharply than before some key theological questions. How, in Isaiah, can the shameful, cruel, and unjust death of the "servant" be a revelation of the divine love for Israel? And who is this "servant," anyway? This last question has kept scholars up at night for many generations. That indeterminacy seems to me quite deliberate. As I said before, like many poets and other writers, whoever wrote Isaiah 40–55 did not want to make it too easy, did not want to foreclose on options. This is not the place to reopen an old, vexed, and many-sided question. But two brief points may be made in concluding this already overlong chapter.

First, it really does look as though the sequence of Servant Songs (42:1–9; 49:1–7 [or possibly 1–12]; 50:4–9; 52:13–53:12) carries at the least overtones of the "royal" passages in the first part of the book (9:2–7; 11:1–10) and the similar, presumably messianic, passages in the later parts (61:1–4; 63:1–6). There is a well-known fluidity between the nation and its royal representative: the king holds the key to the destiny of the people. (That too is an old and difficult question, but some sort of "royal representation" makes a great deal of sense in the texts and the world of the time.) The "servant," then, is some kind of "anointed" figure through whose work YHWH will bring justice to Israel and the nations, reminding us of Psalms such as 2 and 72. The shock of discovering that this royal "servant" was called, as part of his obedient vocation, to die an unjust and shameful death is almost too much, and perhaps it was for the prophet as well, or at least for his anticipated readers. But this is where the poem seems to point. The themes of the divine kingdom, the divine victory, and the divine forgiveness of sins all converge on this point. Thus, if the "servant" is the coming king through whom God's redemptive purposes will be accomplished, one can at least imagine the possibility that his horrible death might be seen—with help, perhaps, from some of the Psalms—as a vocational necessity. David, already anointed but not yet recognized as the coming king, had to go to battle against Goliath; he was one man representing the whole people. Similarly, this "servant" has to take upon himself the consequences of the people's age-old sins.

But at least David defeated Goliath and killed him! How can the *death* of a hypothetically royal servant be part of the overwhelming loving purposes of Israel's God? Here the second point comes in. The powerful action of YHWH is spoken of in this poem as the divine "arm":

> *See, the sovereign YHWH comes with might,*
>    *and his arm rules for him. (40:10)*

> *Awake, awake, put on strength,*
>    *O arm of YHWH:*
> *Awake, as in days of old,*
>    *the generations of long ago!*
> *Was it not you who cut Rahab in pieces,*
>    *who pierced the dragon?*
> *Was it not you who dried up the sea,*
>    *the waters of the great deep;*
> *who made the depths of the sea a way*
>    *for the redeemed to cross over? (51:9–10)*

> *YHWH has bared his holy arm*
> > *before the eyes of all the nations;*
> *and all the ends of the earth shall see*
> > *the salvation of our God. (52:10)*

Finally, it seems, the "arm" of YHWH is revealed—in the person and in the fate of the "servant" himself:

> *Who has believed what we have heard?*
> > *And to whom has the arm of YHWH been revealed?*
> *For he grew up before him like a young plant,*
> > *and like a root out of dry ground. (53:1–2)*

The only way this seems to make sense is if somehow, having been anointed with YHWH's own spirit (42:1), the "servant" is now somehow *embodying* the powerful, redeeming love of Israel's God himself. Like many other questions thrown up by the turbulent ocean of this mighty poem, this is not something on which we can be dogmatic. It is as though the prophet is pointing into the dark, hardly able to believe what he finds himself saying. But he claims to know three things: first, that redemption will come through the work of YHWH's anointed; second, that it will involve intense suffering and death, through which the exile-causing sins of Israel would at last be dealt with; and third, that this achievement will be the work of YHWH himself. As the later passages put it:

> *YHWH saw it, and it displeased him*
> > *that there was no justice.*
> *He saw that there was no one,*
> > *and was appalled that there was no one to intervene;*
> *so his own arm brought him victory,*
> > *and his righteousness upheld him. (59:15–16)*

> *I looked, but there was no helper;*
> > *I stared, but there was no one to sustain me;*

*so my own arm brought me victory,*
   *and my wrath sustained me. . . .*
*It was no messenger or angel*
   *but his presence that saved them;*
*in his love and in his pity he redeemed them;*
   *he lifted them up and carried them all the days of old. (63:5, 9)*

It would be impossible to scoop up all the passages we have looked at in this part of the book and turn them by some alchemy into the theology of the New Testament. Nothing in the Second Temple world encourages us to suppose that Jews before the time of Jesus were composing the kind of fresh construct we discover among the early Christians. But when we find those early Christians saying that "the Messiah died for our sins in accordance with the Bible" and telling the story of the Passover-time death of Jesus both to make that point and to sustain the freshly narrated world in which they themselves were living, we should be in no doubt that these were the themes they intended to evoke. These were the narratives they saw rushing together into a new, decisive, revolutionary dénouement. This is the context in which they glimpsed the nonplatonic goal of salvation and declared, in Jewish rather than pagan terms, that this goal had been won. By the evening of the first Good Friday, sins had been dealt with and the powers defeated in fulfillment of the ancient divine promise. The Messiah had died for sins in accordance with the Bible.

We now turn, therefore, to the key early Christian texts in which this revolutionary message was spelled out.

# PART THREE

# The Revolutionary Rescue

# 8

## New Goal, New Humanity

THE TWO DISCIPLES who met the risen Jesus, without recognizing him, on the road to Emmaus said plaintively, "We were hoping that he was going to redeem Israel" (Luke 24:21). When Jesus, still incognito, began to explain to them what was going on, he was not saying, in effect, "You've got it wrong. Forget all that stuff about redeeming Israel. I've had a better idea." No. In fact he said, "This is what *had* to happen: the Messiah had to suffer, and then come into his glory!" After that, "He began with Moses, and with all the prophets, and explained to them the things about himself throughout the whole Bible" (24:26–27). His answer was, to be sure, a radical redefinition of the "redemption of Israel." It brought the entire expectation into a new focus, namely, his own unique role. The story of the Bible as a whole, he insisted, had been rushing forward toward the events of his own death and resurrection. The recent happenings were to be seen as fulfillment, not simply as a shocking turn of events.

But to redefine is not to abandon. Many Jews of Jesus's day had been praying and pondering what it might mean for God to fulfill his ancient promises at long last. There was no single template. Many groups, many teachers, many would-be prophets offered different interpretations. Jesus's particular redefinition (and Luke's showcasing of that redefinition) belongs on that map, even though it transforms it beyond anything previously imagined. The hope of Israel, expressed variously in the Torah, Prophets, and Psalms, was not for a rescue operation that would snatch Israel (or humans or the faithful) *from* the world, but for a rescue operation that would be *for* the world, an operation through which redeemed humans would play once more the role for which they were designed. It was the hope for a renewed world in which justice and mercy would reign forever. Jesus was explaining not that this hope had been abandoned in favor of "saved souls going to heaven," but that this hope for new creation had been fulfilled in a shockingly unexpected way. The revolution had already taken place. By the evening of that Friday, had they but known it, the world had changed.

From our point of view, as we read this story, it all involves a double redefinition. First, there is indeed a radical redefinition of the Jewish hope of rescue from pagan oppression, of a new justice and peace for the world, of the ultimate return of YHWH to his Temple. Once you put the crucifixion and resurrection of Israel's Messiah in the middle of that story and make it the new focus, everything looks different. Second, the Christian world has for so long clung to and taught a meaning of "redemption" that involves "saved souls going to heaven" that it takes quite an effort of the imagination to come to terms with the New Testament's message, that what we are promised in the gospel is the kingdom of God coming "on earth as in heaven"; or, to put it another way, for all things in heaven and on earth to be summed up in the Messiah; or, to put it yet another way, "new heavens and a new earth, in which justice will be at home" (2 Pet. 3:13). Once we learn, with the puzzled disciples on that extraordinary evening, to grasp the way the ancient biblical hope was redefined around Jesus himself, then we are bound to embrace the far more radical revision of our own "Christian" cultural expectations concerning "heaven." And once we do that, we are forced into two more major questions that hover over the present part of the book.

The two questions are as follows. First, what is the calling of humans in this promised new world? Second, granted human failure ("sin"), how are humans to be rescued so that they can fulfill that calling?

The common view has been that the ultimate state ("heaven") is a place where "good" people end up, so that human life is gauged in relation to moral achievement or lack thereof. This sets up a "works contract" in the sense we outlined earlier. Then, this usual view goes on, humans all fail the moral test and so need to be rescued, and this is the effect of Jesus's death. This leads, in some very popular schemes of thought, to a view of "salvation" in which the "punishment" for moral failure is meted out elsewhere while the "moral achievement" that was lacking in everyone else is supplied by Jesus himself. Some versions of this, I have suggested, are closer to the pagan idea of an angry deity being pacified by a human death than they are to anything in either Israel's scriptures or the New Testament.

In other words, in much popular modern Christian thought we have made a three-layered mistake. We have *Platonized* our eschatology (substituting "souls going to heaven" for the promised new creation) and have therefore *moralized* our anthropology (substituting a qualifying examination of moral performance for the biblical notion of the human vocation), with the result that we have *paganized* our soteriology, our understanding of "salvation" (substituting the idea of "God killing Jesus to satisfy his wrath" for the genuinely biblical notions we are about to explore).

This is a fairly drastic set of charges. Some will no doubt accuse me of caricature, but long experience of what people in churches think they have been taught suggests otherwise. Others will perhaps accuse me of pulling the house down on top of myself, denying things that are basic to the faith. However, it seems to me—and I hope the rest of the book will demonstrate this—that, once the new way of looking at things is grasped, all that was best in the old way will be retained, but in a new framework through which it loses its frankly unbiblical elements. The new creation will indeed be "heavenly," possessing in complete measure that heaven/earth overlap we sense fitfully in prayer, in scripture study, in the sacraments, and in working for God's kingdom in the world. The human vocation certainly includes a strong and nonnegotiable moral element, which is enhanced rather than eliminated when placed within the larger category of the "image-bearing" *vocation*. And the means of salvation, as we shall see throughout this part of the book, does indeed involve the death of Jesus as the *representative* and then the *substitute* for his people, though not in the sense that many have understood those rather abstract categories.

At the heart of it all is the achievement of Jesus as the true human being who, as the "image," is the ultimate embodiment (or "incarnation") of the creator God. His death, the climax of his work of inaugurating God's kingdom on earth as in heaven, was the victory over the destructive powers let loose into the world not simply through human wrongdoing, the breaking of moral codes, but through the human failure to be image-bearers, to worship the Creator and reflect his wise stewardship into the world (and, to be sure, breaking any moral codes that might be around, but this is not the focus). And the reason his death had this effect was that, as the representative and substitute in the senses we shall explore in due course, he achieved the "forgiveness of sins" in the sense long promised by Israel's prophets. Once we step away from Platonizing, moralizing, and paganizing schemes of thought and back into the world of Israel's scriptures ("The Messiah died for our sins in accordance with the Bible"), this all makes sense, though it is a different kind of sense from what many Christians imagine.

With that, we are ready to return to Luke's story. When we left it a moment ago, the two disciples were on the road to Emmaus with the risen Jesus, who was offering a radical redefinition of Israel's hope and explaining that this hope had, in fact, been accomplished through his death and resurrection. But when we look at the whole sweep of Luke's two books, the gospel and Acts, we see the same kind of redefinition going on throughout. The hope of Israel is not abandoned: it is affirmed, but, as with many other Jewish groups of the time, the early Christians saw this affirmation as involving a redefinition around actual people, particularly of course Jesus himself.

The redefinition begins, however, not with Jesus, but with John the Baptist. Zechariah, John's father, produces a hymn of praise to Israel's God. We cannot suppose that Luke has set this out so graphically for the purpose of saying that Zechariah was misguided, that Israel had hoped for the wrong thing. On the contrary, the old man has glimpsed a strange fulfillment:

> *Blessed be the Lord, Israel's God!*
> *He's come to his people and bought them their freedom.*
> *He's raised up a horn of salvation for us*
> *In David's house, the house of his servant,*
> *Just as he promised, through the mouths of his prophets,*
> *The holy ones, speaking from ages of old:*
> *Salvation from our enemies, rescue from hatred,*
> *Mercy to our ancestors, keeping his holy covenant.*
> *He swore an oath to Abraham our father,*
> *To give us deliverance from fear and from foes,*
> *So we might worship him, holy and righteous,*
> *Before his face to the end of our days. (1:68–75)*

This large-scale vision of national redemption then focuses specifically on the vocation of the baby John:

> *You, child, will be called the prophet of the Highest One.*
> *Go ahead of the Lord, preparing his way,*
> *Letting his people know of salvation,*
> *Through the forgiveness of all their sins. (1:76–77)*

There we have it again: "forgiveness of sins" is one of the key ways of referring to the fulfillment of the ancient promises, promises whose practical outworking would not be "going to heaven," but rather the great, long-awaited national deliverance. *That is the goal toward which the notion of "forgiveness of sins" and "in accordance with the Bible" are pointing.* And in the New Testament, exactly as in some strands of Israel's scriptures themselves, this goal will extend not only to the Jews, but also to the whole world. The shorter poem that Luke ascribes to Simeon, greeting the boy Jesus in the Temple, makes this clear:

> *These eyes of mine have seen your salvation,*
> *Which you made ready in the presence of all peoples:*
> *A light for revelation to the nations,*
> *And glory for your people Israel. (2:30–32)*

To return from the start of Luke's gospel to its close, we witness exactly this transition happening as Jesus addresses the disciples. As the Psalms and prophets had made clear all along, the fulfillment of Israel's hopes is the means by which the nations of the world are to be welcomed into the people of the one true God:

> Then he said to them, "This is what I was talking to you about when I was still with you. Everything written about me in the law of Moses, and in the prophets and the Psalms, had to be fulfilled." Then he opened their minds to understand the Bible.
>
> "This is what is written," he said. "The Messiah must suffer and rise from the dead on the third day, and in his name repentance, for the forgiveness of sins, must be announced to all the nations, beginning from Jerusalem. You are the witnesses for all this. Now look: I'm sending upon you what my father has promised. But stay in the city until you are clothed with power from on high." (24:44–49)

"Forgiveness of sins," in other words, is to be seen *both* as the summary of the redemptive blessings promised to Israel *and* as the key blessing that will enable non-Jews to be welcomed into the one family. As Deuteronomy 30, Jeremiah 31, Daniel 9, and many other passages had indicated, "forgiveness of sins" was the key thing that Israel needed for the long years of desolation to be over at last. And if the non-Jewish nations were to escape from their slavery to idolatry and all that went with it, "forgiveness of sins" would summarize what it meant for them to leave that past behind—for, in the words of the Psalm, the "princes of the people" to "gather as the people of the God of Abraham" (47:9). This would become one of the main foundations of Paul's argument for the equal status, in the Messiah's family, of believing Gentiles alongside believing Jews. The latter, turning back as Deuteronomy had indicated to their true God, were experiencing through the Messiah's death and resurrection the "forgiveness of sins" in the ancient biblical sense of the long-awaited covenant renewal and "end of exile." The former, turning from their idols to serve the living God, were experiencing the "forgiveness of sins" through the divine amnesty that all along had been aimed at their full inclusion.

It is noticeable how, in the early preaching reported in the book of Acts, this notion of "forgiveness of sins" is highlighted as the key thing that will result from believing the good news about Jesus. Peter urged the crowds on the day of Pentecost: "Turn back ["Return," in other words, "Repent," as in Deut. 30:2]! Be baptized . . . in the name of Jesus the Messiah, so that your sins can be forgiven and you will receive the gift of the holy spirit" (2:38). John's baptism had been aimed at the same things, repentance and the "forgiveness of sins" (Luke 3:3). Now, baptism in the name of Jesus the Messiah had the aim of bestowing the blessing of covenant renewal. The message is reinforced in the next chapter of Acts, with explicit evocation both of the promises in Deuteronomy and the prophets and of the larger hope for the renewal of all things:

This is how God has fulfilled what he promised through the mouth of all the prophets, that his Messiah would suffer. So now repent, and turn back, so that your sins may be blotted out, so that times of refreshment may come from the presence of the Lord, and so that he will send you Jesus, the one he chose and appointed to be his Messiah. He must be received in heaven, you see, until the time which God spoke about through the mouth of his holy prophets from ancient days, the time when God will restore all things. Moses said, "The Lord your God will raise up for you a prophet like me, one from among your own brothers; whatever he says to you, you must pay attention to him. And everyone who does not listen to that prophet will be cut off from the people." All the prophets who have spoken, from Samuel and his successors, spoke about these days too. You are the children of the prophets, the children of the covenant which God established with your ancestors when he said to Abraham, "In your seed shall all the families of the earth be blessed," When God raised up his servant he sent him to you first, to bless you by turning each of you away from your wicked deeds." (3:18–26)

That last phrase should allay any puzzled suspicions that might have been arising over the last page or two, suspicions that the phrase "forgiveness of sins" was now being used in a purely technical sense (to mean simply "end of exile") without any reference to actual wicked deeds. Far from it. This is not an either/or. My point is rather that in the early preaching—and it is very interesting that Luke, writing (we assume) at least a generation or more after the events, does not attempt here to inject any more developed "atonement theology" into the picture—we find the goal of God's rescue operation so firmly and explicitly anchored in the biblical narrative and prophecies. This is what "for our sins in accordance with the Bible" actually meant: that the scriptural narrative of the restoration of Israel and then the welcome of the non-Jews into this restored people (though this is not yet in view in Acts 2–3) had been launched through the death and resurrection of Jesus, and that the single-phrase summary of all this, operating at both the large, national scale and the small, personal level, was the "forgiveness of sins."

Of course, there was one particular "sin" for which, in the early chapters of Acts, repentance would be required: the rejection by the Jewish leaders of Jesus as Messiah. That, presumably, is why the chief priests and Sadducees accused the apostles of "trying to bring this man's blood on [them]" (5:28). Peter's response is to repeat, briefly, the point made earlier. The underlying thrust of what he says is not simply, "We know about Jesus, so we have to go on talking about him," but "What has happened through Jesus and the Spirit is the fulfillment of Israel's prophecies"; in other words, the court cannot accuse the disciples of being disloyal to Israel's ancestral traditions:

> The God of our ancestors raised Jesus, after you had laid
> violent hands on him and hanged him on a tree. God
> exalted him to his right hand as leader and savior, to
> give repentance to Israel and forgiveness of sins. We are
> witnesses of these things, and so is the holy spirit, which
> God gave to those who obey him. (5:30–32)

Once again, therefore, we have the statement of the goal of the gospel: the new world in which "forgiveness of sins" has released Israel from its bondage. Here, as throughout Acts, we begin to see the way in which this theme enfolds within itself the idea of the renewed human vocation. "We are witnesses," equipped with the Holy Spirit to play an active role in the new divine purposes.

The next time "forgiveness" is mentioned in Acts it comes in the wider context of the welcome of non-Jews. When Peter goes to the house of Cornelius in Acts 10, the summary of his gospel announcement, which in other ways stays very close to the passages we have just looked at, adds the note of final judgment. This appears to be seen by Luke as an important part of the message to non-Jews. And now the "everyone" clearly takes in these non-Jews too:

> He commanded us to announce to the people, and to
> bear testimony, that he is the one appointed by God to
> be judge of the living and the dead. All the prophets give
> their witness: he is the one! Everyone who believes in
> him receives forgiveness of sins through his name. (10:
> 41–42; see also 17:31)

The final mention of this theme in Acts is in the sermon of Paul in Pisidian Antioch:

> Let it be known to you, my brothers and sisters, that
> forgiveness of sins is announced through him, and that
> everything from which you were unable to be set right
> by the law of Moses, by him everyone who believes is set
> right. (13:38–39)

This leads directly to the point at which the gospel opens up explicitly, still exactly in fulfillment of scripture, to include the whole world (13:46–47). Paul and Barnabas, faced with angry rejection of their message by many of the Jews, declare that to deny this good news is to judge oneself "unworthy of the life of God's new age." They therefore turn to the Gentiles and quote Isaiah 49:6: "I have set you for a light to the nations, so that you can be salvation-bringers to the end of the earth."

Where does all this take us? To a fresh understanding of what I have called the "goal" of the gospel through a fresh understanding of the early Christian use of the phrase "forgiveness of sins" (which obviously relates directly to the early gospel formula "The Messiah died *for our sins*"). The goal is not for people "to go to heaven when they die." That is never mentioned in

Acts. The whole book of Acts assumes, first, that God's kingdom has already been well and truly launched through the death and resurrection of Jesus (1:6; 8:12; 19:8; 20:25; 28:23, 31); second, that this kingdom will be fully and finally established when Jesus returns (1:11; 3:21); and, third, that in this final new world all God's people will be raised to new bodily life (4:2; 24:15, 21; 26:23). The book has not one word to say about people "going to heaven"—except, of course, for Jesus himself in 1:9–11, and his "ascension" has nothing to do with the popular image of people "dying and going to heaven" and everything to do with his enthronement and the commencement of his worldwide reign (as in 1 Cor. 15:25). "Forgiveness of sins" belongs, in Acts, within a narrative different from the one most people imagine today. The purpose of forgiving sin, there as elsewhere, is to enable people to become fully functioning, fully image-bearing human beings within God's world, already now, completely in the age to come.

Nor is the heart of the gospel described in Acts as the message that sin separates people from God and grace restores that relationship, though no doubt Peter and the rest would have agreed that that was true as well. They knew Isaiah 59:2 ("Your iniquities have been barriers between you and your God, and your sins have hidden his face from you so that he does not hear") as well as we do, but the early Christians did not explain the message of the gospel in those terms. They did not propose that God had set up, through Jesus, a kind of spiritual mechanism whereby anyone at any time could repent, be assured of God's forgiveness, and experience the loving presence of God in a new way. Once again, I do not think any early Christians would have denied that this was true, but it is interesting that they didn't put it like that. These are all meanings that belong in the much later world of modern Western piety. They are important, but they do not give us the original, and larger, biblical picture.

No. If we are to be faithful to the biblical overtones of "forgiveness of sins," we must insist that all such meanings are *included within something much larger,* something far more revolutionary. It is this larger reality that really matters. The smaller reality—that I, as a sinner, need to know the forgiving love of God in my own life—is vital for each person, one by one. But, as history shows, that reality can all too easily be understood within the Platonized version of the gospel in which the whole emphasis falls on a detached spirituality in the present and a detached future salvation in which the created order is abandoned altogether.

Once again, that is how to domesticate the revolution. The larger reality is that *something has happened within the actual world of space, time, and matter, as a result of which everything is different.* By six o'clock on the Friday evening Jesus died, something had changed, and changed radically. Heaven and earth were brought together, creating the cosmic "new temple": "God was reconciling the world to himself in the Messiah" (2 Cor. 5:19).

This was totally unexpected. No Jews prior to Jesus were walking around with this kind of messianic narrative in their heads. But when the resurrection compelled the disciples to rethink their original and natural reaction to the death of Jesus—a reaction we see graphically portrayed in Luke's picture of the two on the road to Emmaus—we find them grappling with the fresh belief that these events were seen as the dramatic, unexpected, but nevertheless appropriate fulfillment of the ancient prophecies and therefore as the events through which *the long-awaited new age was being ushered in at last.* This was not about inventing a new kind of religion. It had nothing to do with getting rid of the earthbound hopes of the ancient Jews and embracing a "spiritual" reality instead. It was far more revolutionary. It was about the kingdom of God coming "on earth as in heaven."

Within that new reality, the "forgiveness of sins" was neither simply a personal experience nor a moral command, though it was of course to be felt as the former and obeyed as the latter. It was the name for a new state of being, a new world, the world of resurrection, resurrection itself being the archetypal forgiveness-of-sins moment, the moment when the prison door is flung open, indicating that the jailor has already been overpowered. As Paul said, if the Messiah is not raised, "your faith is pointless, and you are still in your sins" (1 Cor. 15:17).

"Forgiveness of sins," for the first disciples, was now to be seen as *a fact about the way the world was,* a fact rooted in the one-off accomplishment of Jesus's death, then revealed in his resurrection, and then put to work through the Spirit in the transformed lives of his followers. Forgiveness of sins became another way of saying "Passover" or "new Exodus." Or, as in Isaiah 54–55, following hard on the heels of the kingdom announcement of chapter 52 and the "servant's" work in chapter 53, it would come to mean "new covenant" and "new creation." The gospel was the announcement of this new reality.

This new reality—hard to perceive except by faith in Jesus's death-defeating resurrection, as all the early Christians knew well—was designed to come to ultimate fruition in the eventual new creation, the "new heavens and new earth." I have written about this at length elsewhere (notably in *Surprised by Hope*), and we do not need to repeat or labor the point. Ephesians 1:10 says it all: God's plan was to unite all things in the Messiah, things in heaven and on earth.

The final scene in Revelation (chaps. 21–22) spells it out: the new heavens and new earth function as the ultimate Temple, the new world in which God will wipe away all tears from all eyes. First Corinthians 15 describes the accomplishment of this final reality under the image of the messianic battle: Jesus, having already conquered sin and death, will reign until these and all other enemies are totally destroyed. Romans 8 describes it as the birth of the new creation from the womb of the old, weaving into that great metaphor a powerful allusion to the events of the Exodus, so that creation itself will have its own "Exodus" at last, being set free from its slavery to corruption and sharing the freedom that comes when God's children are glorified. That is the ultimate hope.

All of this is the "goal" of God's rescue operation accomplished through Jesus. All of this is in direct fulfillment of the ancient hopes of Israel: it is all "according to the Bible"—though it was quite unexpected. Nobody had read Israel's scriptures like this before, but the events concerning Jesus left his followers with no choice. What had happened could have no other meaning. And all of this can be summed up in the phrase "forgiveness of sins." None of it has to do with redeemed souls leaving the world of space, time, and matter for something better. All of it has to do with the strange, unanticipated fulfillment of the hope of Israel.

"Forgiveness of sins," then, is an altogether *bigger* reality than we have imagined. It is (to use the fashionable language) "cosmic." When individuals share in it, experiencing for themselves the glorious relief of knowing themselves to be forgiven, they are, whether they realize it or not, learning to sing one of the "inside parts" within the much larger symphonic chorus of new creation. The alto line (if that's what our part is) matters. The harmony needs it. But if you only had the altos singing their line, you wouldn't have much idea of what the music as a whole was supposed to mean. That is the kind of problem we have faced in the Western church as we have labored under the Platonized vision of the goal of salvation.

As we saw briefly above, one of the key problems about the idea of a platonic "disembodied heaven" is that it generates the wrong view of what human life ought to be in the present time as an anticipation, or even a qualification, for that destiny. The idea of "heaven" carries with it in the popular mind and even in many well-taught Christian minds the notion that this is where "good people" go, while "bad people" go somewhere else. This, of course, quickly gets modified by standard teachings of the gospel: we are all "bad people," so that if anyone "goes to heaven," it must be because our badness has somehow been dealt with and, in some traditions, because someone else's "goodness" has somehow been "reckoned to our account."

But the problem with this entire way of looking at things is that *the idea of moral behavior as the qualification for "heaven" is itself a distortion.* As we saw above, we have Platonized our eschatology—our vision of the ultimate end—and, to match, have "moralized" our anthropology, our sense of what humans are and what they are meant to be. This has worked its way into traditions of Christian ethics, and I have argued elsewhere (in my book *Virtue Reborn,* whose American title is *After You Believe*) that we need to replace this with the biblical vocation of human beings, which is to be image-bearers, God's "royal priesthood."

Being priests *includes* "moral behavior" as a central component. But, as with "forgiveness," it points to a much larger reality: a human vocation to an active, involved role within God's future world, anticipated by an equivalent active, involved role within God's present creation. Of course, once this is in place, we need to make the same moves as before. We all fail in this vocation; Jesus fulfills Israel's vocation as the rescuing Royal Priest; his death (as it says in Rev. 5:9–10) ransoms us so that we can be "a kingdom and priests" as always intended. And once we get that clear, we will find that what we believe about the ultimate goal and what we believe about the human vocation here and hereafter will have quite an effect on what we believe about the way in which the death of Jesus rescues humans and the world from disaster. Our view of "salvation," after all, is tied in closely to our view of the human possibility and plight, and that in turn is tied in closely to our view of our final destiny. Adjust one, and we must adjust them all.

Here again the book of Acts comes to our aid. It does not use the phrase "royal priesthood," but it describes the reality to which that phrase points. Acts describes what happens to human beings who are learning to live within God's new world: they *worship* and they *witness.* The first corresponds to the "priesthood" theme, the second to the "royal" theme. Both, as we shall presently show, are closely related to the hope and vocation of Israel. Here is how it begins:

So when the apostles came together, they put this question to Jesus.

"Master," they said, "is this the time when you are going to restore the kingdom to Israel?"

"It's not your business to know about times and dates." He replied. "The father has placed all that under his own direct authority. What will happen, though, is that you will receive power when the holy spirit comes upon you. Then you will be my witnesses in Jerusalem, in all Judaea and Samaria, and to the very ends of the earth." (1:6–8)

Here we see, concentrated at one point, *both* the continuity of the church's mission with the ancient hope of Israel *and* the way in which that hope is now transformed. (All this is exactly in line, of course, with the passages in Luke 24 that we looked at earlier.) What might it look like for the "kingdom" to be "restored to Israel"?

## The Cross-Shaped Kingdom

Many Jews of the period, faced with that question, would have said three things at least. *First,* Israel must be set free from the domination of pagan overlords. *Second,* Israel's God, perhaps through the agency of his Messiah, would become the ruler of the whole world, bringing to birth a new reign of justice and peace. *Third,* God's own Presence would come to dwell with his people, enabling them to worship him fully and truly. There might be much more, of course: plenty of prophecies to be explored, plenty of promises to be prayed into fulfillment. But these three things would be a start. *And the book of Acts is the story of how these three things in particular came into being.*

Acts describes what it looked like when, "in accordance with the Bible," a people whose watchword was the "forgiveness of sins" went out into all the world to announce the kingdom of God and the sovereignty of Jesus—which is what, at the end of the book, Paul was doing in Rome itself (28:31). But the way in which this was done bore little relation to any pre-Christian Jewish dreams of how Israel was to be liberated, the powers were to be overthrown, and the true worship of God was to be reinstated. Acts insists that the long-awaited liberation had happened through Jesus and the Spirit, that the powers had been overthrown by the power of the cross and the word of God, and that the powerful Presence of the living God had been unveiled not in the Jerusalem Temple, but in the community of believers.

How easy it has been for the later church, not least the Western church of the last three or four hundred years, to imagine that this redefinition of the hope of the kingdom was a "spiritualization," a move away from "worldly" reality into a "heavenly" dimension. How easy it has been for some to suppose that Luke has in mind a *postponement* of the kingdom, so that Jesus's answer to his followers is not, as I have suggested, a kind of "Yes, but in a way different from what you were thinking," but rather a "No, not yet, but you have a job to do in the meantime." Of course, the ultimate kingdom is yet to come. Luke makes that very clear: Jesus will return to judge and restore all things (Acts 1:11; 3:31; 17:31). But, just as Jesus had said at the Last Supper, the events of his death and resurrection really were going to usher in the new day, the reality of the kingdom (Luke 22:18). If comparatively modern readings of Luke and Acts have shrunk the meaning of the "kingdom" simply to the final return of Jesus, that is our modern problem, not Luke's.

Take the three kingdom symbols in reverse order. *First,* the restoration of true worship. Acts describes the new-Temple reality of the coming together of heaven and earth, just as Ephesians 1:10 said: Jesus, the risen human being, is taken up into heaven, thereby joining together in his own person the two spheres of God's good creation. (A major problem must be faced at this point, which I have addressed in chapter 7 of *Surprised by Hope*. We have often fondly supposed that in the ancient world people imagined "heaven" as a location within ordinary cosmology, somewhere "up there," and we project onto that supposition the great divide between divine and human habitations proposed by the ancient Epicureans and their modern successors. Once we realize that "heaven" means "God's space," that "earth" means "our space," and that these two, made from the start to overlap and interlock, did so fully and finally in Jesus, the problems disappear. As always in Christian theology, we have to start with Jesus and reconfigure our ideas around him, rather than trying to fit him into our existing worldviews.) But if heaven and earth are already joined in the ascension, with part of "earth"—the human body of Jesus—now fully and thoroughly at home in "heaven," then they are joined again in the opposite direction, as it were, in Acts 2, when the powerful wind of the divine Spirit comes upon the disciples. *This is one of the New Testament equivalents of the filling of the tabernacle with the cloud and fire or of Solomon's Temple with the glorious divine Presence.*

Here is the foundation of the belief that with Jesus and the Spirit a new creation has come into being. Instead of the "microcosmos" of the Jerusalem Temple, Jesus himself and his Spirit-filled people constitute the new Temple, the start of the new world. Only by dwelling in and living out of this new reality could it make any sense for the first disciples to speak as they did of the ways in which the kingdom was in the most important sense already present, even though in another sense, with Herod and Caesar still on their thrones, it was also obviously future. The first followers of Jesus were thereby constituted as new-Temple people, which is why of course most of the controversies in the book of Acts focus on temples: the charges against Stephen (and his answer to them) in chapters 6–7 and Paul's clashes with the local cult (Acts 14), with the temples in Athens and Ephesus (chaps. 17–19), and then with the Temple in Jerusalem itself (21:28–29; 24:6; 25:8).

And the new life of this new community was itself anchored in worship, declaring "the powerful things God has done" (2:11), establishing a new pattern of life centered upon "the teaching of the apostles and the common life," "the breaking of bread and the prayers" (2:42), a life that, to begin with at least, tried to hold together the ancient Temple and the ordinary domestic sphere:

> Day by day they were all together attending the Temple.
> They broke bread in their various houses, and ate their
> food with glad and sincere hearts, praising God and
> standing in favor with all the people. (2:46–47)

Many of the subsequent scenes in Acts focus upon the new life of worship and the ways in which, through this new pattern of life, the apostles found themselves standing, priestlike, at the uncomfortable intersection of heaven and earth, drawing both together in scripture-based worship and intercession and indeed in danger and martyrdom. Scenes like Acts 4:24–31 make the point well enough. Another graphic example is provided by Stephen's witnessing of Jesus's standing at the right hand of God and then joining with Jesus's own intercession by praying for his murderers (7:56–60). These are essentially *priestly* scenes. Acts tells the story of the early church as the story of the powerful personal Presence and the reconstituted worship of Israel's God, the world's creator.

*Second,* then, there is the hope for the worldwide rule of this God. Out of worship and prayer there grows witness; and the "witness" is not simply about people saying, "I've had this experience; perhaps you might like it too," but about people announcing that a new state of affairs has come into being. This too begins from the day of Pentecost, as we have seen, when the disciples announced to the startled crowds that the ancient prophecies had been fulfilled, that "forgiveness of sins" had *happened as an event in real space and time,* and that the whole world was now called to order in the name of its creator and restorer. To announce Jesus as Israel's Messiah is to say that this is now happening and "forgiveness of sins" is the key to it all. This witness continues through the many different scenes of gospel announcement: Philip to the Ethiopian eunuch in Acts 8, Peter to Cornelius in Acts 10, and so on. It reaches a first decisive climax in chapter 12, when Herod Agrippa I begins a serious attack on the church but is forestalled, first by Peter's angelic release from prison and then by his own sudden death. Luke's comment makes the position clear: Herod died, "but God's word grew and multiplied" (Acts 12:24). Here is the vital note of *kingdom:* the kingdoms of the world turn out to be, in ultimate terms, powerless against the kingdom of God. They can persecute and kill Jesus's followers, but this—as other New Testament writers were quick to emphasize, following Jesus himself—only strengthened the kingdom of God, since that kingdom was accomplished precisely through Jesus's death and then implemented through the suffering of his followers.

Thus, throughout Paul's career, we find him living boldly in the faith that Jesus is Lord and that the local and international rulers and magistrates are ultimately under his command. This, indeed, is part of the foundation of Paul's mission to the Gentiles: the "powers" that had ruled the pagan world had been overthrown, defeated on the cross, as he hints in 1 Corinthians 2:8 and states clearly in Colossians 2:13–15, so now people who had formerly been enslaved could be summoned to allegiance to the new, liberating rule of Israel's Messiah.

That did not prevent Paul from being beaten, driven out of town, imprisoned, or even stoned. That isn't how the kingdom works, as Jesus himself repeatedly warned (or promised!). The last great narrative sequence in Acts, Paul's trials, his journey to Rome and the shipwreck, and his final arrival, is told in such a way as to highlight the paradoxical nature of the kingdom: the powers of the world, whether they are corrupt magistrates, casually brutal soldiers, incompetent sailors, storms at sea, or even deadly serpents, cannot prevent Paul from arriving in Rome and, though under house arrest, announcing the kingdom of God and teaching about Jesus as Lord "with all boldness, and with no one stopping him" (28:31).

All this, I suggest, is Luke's way of saying that with the death, resurrection, and exaltation of Israel's Messiah and with the powerful gift of the Spirit, God's world has been renewed, the kingdom has been inaugurated, and those who believe in Jesus and who are indwelt by the Spirit are now formed as a royal priesthood, who in their worship and their witness are carrying forward the work of the kingdom. The decisive victory against the powers has already been won. The revolution has already begun.

*Third,* therefore, after worship (acclaiming the returned and reigning God of Israel) and witness (announcing to the world its rightful and rescuing Lord), there is the hope that Israel will be rescued from pagan rule. One might imagine that this had been left behind in the flurry of events taking place on a different plane, but it is important to see that this is not so. When Jesus himself, Israel's Messiah, was raised from the dead, Israel-in-person was set free from death and, with that, from the ultimate weapon of every tyrant, the ultimate exile imposed by every Babylon. In the excitement of the Gentile mission, the reflex for ancient Israel is not forgotten. The death of Jesus, going ahead of Israel into the mouth of the pagan lion, has created a breathing space in which Peter can urge his hearers, "Let God rescue you from this wicked generation" (Acts 2:40). "The whole house of Israel must know this for a fact: God has made him Lord and Messiah" (2:36). Thousands of Jews, including a great many priests, believed this message and became part of the renewed community (2:41, 47; 4:4; 5:14; 6:7; 11:24; 21:21). We should be in no doubt that Luke, like most other early Christian writers, saw the messianic community focused on Jesus as the liberated, redeemed people, those in and for whom the long-awaited promise of rescue from pagan overlords had been fulfilled.

Luke has thus inscribed into history the truth spoken of in the formulas of Revelation 1, 5, and 20, which we studied in chapter 4. The other New Testament writers make the same point in different ways. What has happened to Jesus's followers? They do not simply have some new, exciting ideas to share with people who are interested in such things. They are not telling people that they have discovered a way whereby anyone can escape the wicked world and "go to heaven" instead. They are functioning as the worshipping, witnessing people of God: as the "priestly kingdom" of Exodus 19, as the "servant" of Isaiah 49, as the people who, in one psalm after another, worship the God of Israel and discover in doing so that he is also the God of all the earth.

How has this come about? The whole early church answers: through the death, resurrection, and ascension of Israel's Messiah and through the power of the Spirit. But when we look at this narrative sequence we discover, again and again, that though the resurrection, ascension, and Spirit are vital for the whole thing to work in the way it must, none of these is even thinkable unless a meaning is given to the death of Jesus, a meaning far greater than simply that it is the prelude to these other events.

"With your own blood you purchased a people for God," sang the group around the throne in Revelation 5, "and made them a kingdom and priests to our God, and they will reign on the earth" (vv. 9–10). This was always the goal of the great act of redemption. The earliest Christians held on tightly to the creational monotheism of ancient Israel, to the scriptural narratives of slavery and Exodus, of exile and restoration, of the destruction and rebuilding of the Temple, and of the ultimate renewal of creation itself. They believed that all these things had now come to pass, albeit in ways they had never imagined. They believed themselves to be living in the long-promised new world in which God was sovereign in a new way, in which Jesus had already been enthroned as Lord. They found themselves called to live and act as worshippers and witnesses, as the royal priesthood. And they believed that all this had happened, had been made not only possible but actual, because of what happened when Jesus of Nazareth died on the cross. By six in the evening on the 14<sup>th</sup> of Nisan AD 33 it was accomplished, even though that accomplishment would remain unrecognized—unimagined!—for three days, and even though it would take a lot longer than that to begin taking visible effect.

Only if we keep in mind this larger narrative—the triple hope of Israel and the new vocation of the royal priests—can we be sure that we are interpreting Jesus's death in the same way that the early Christians did. Only in this way can we keep our fingers on the actual pulse of the original revolution.

With that, we are ready to plunge into the early texts that describe and interpret the central event.

# 9

---

# Jesus's Special Passover

S O HOW DID the first Christians interpret the death of Jesus? What did they say about it, what did they mean, and how did they arrive at that view? This brings us at last to the heart of our investigation. I have insisted that we cannot jump straight in with the normal Western assumptions about what "dying for our sins" or even "in accordance with the Bible" might actually mean. We need to go back, as we have now done, and investigate, first, the set of first-century Jewish assumptions within which those phrases meant what they meant and, second, how the very first Christians went about putting this new vision into practice.

But, having done all that, we must return to the underlying question. Already by the time of Paul, the early Christians believed that something had happened on the cross itself, something of earth-shattering meaning and implication, something as a result of which the world was now a different place. A revolution had been launched. We must remind ourselves that for a full account of "atonement"—as we have seen, more of a complex word than we often recall—we need to speak of resurrection, ascension, the Spirit, the life of faith, the ultimate resurrection of the dead, and the renewal of all things. But we must still insist that it is proper, necessary, and vital to ask: By six o'clock on the first Good Friday evening, what had changed and how had that happened? That is the task to which we must now give attention.

Right away we meet something very peculiar. You might suppose that if Christian theologians were going to trace the meaning of Jesus's death, they would begin with Jesus himself. Mostly, they do not. I possess many books on the "atonement." Few give much attention to the gospels. None, as far as I recall, starts with Jesus himself. They may sooner or later highlight one famous saying, Mark 10:45 ("The son of man . . . came to be the servant, to give his life 'as a ransom for many'"), but they do not normally go much beyond that. They seldom if ever link the meaning of Jesus's death with Jesus's announcement of God's kingdom coming "on earth as in heaven." They seldom highlight the fact that Jesus chose to go to Jerusalem and (so it seems) force some kind of a showdown with the authorities not on the Day of Atonement, not at the Festival of Tabernacles, the Festival of Dedication, or any other special day on the sacred calendar, laden with meaning as they were, but at Passover.

Discussions of Jesus's last Passover have tended to focus narrowly on the words he reportedly said at the Last Supper. These are important, and we shall return to them. But it is the larger context that makes all the difference. And that context is routinely ignored in treatments of early "atonement" theology. I regard all this as very strange. In what follows I shall not only try to remedy this remarkable deficiency. I shall make Jesus's choice of Passover and all that it meant central to my whole case.

We had better say something at the outset about the broad reliability of the gospels. I shall presuppose here the longer and more complicated arguments I have set out elsewhere in favor of taking the gospel accounts of Jesus's public career as substantially historical. This has been a major storm center in the study of early Christianity, and now is not the time to open the issues once more. Fortunately, nothing major will hinge on this, since almost all scholars, however skeptical, will agree that Jesus did indeed go to Jerusalem and die at Passover time; that in the course of his public career he did indeed declare that through his work Israel's God was becoming king in a new way; that this theme, signaled by the placard on the cross, formed part of the first public perception of any "meaning" that his death might have; and that Jesus undoubtedly said various things about the kingdom coming through suffering. Some such sayings were no doubt cryptic at the time, and we too may find them opaque. But these points, widely agreed upon, form a solid platform.

If it is true that Jesus's own view of his forthcoming death has been largely ignored in studies of atonement, one might nevertheless suppose that theologians would be eager to learn about early Christian views of how his death "worked" by reading Matthew, Mark, Luke, and John. But this too has not been a major strand in studies of the "atonement." Theologians and preachers might refer not only to Mark 10:45, but also John 3:16 ("God so loved the world . . .") and a few other texts. But they do not usually engage in deep or detailed reflection as to how the actual story told by the four evangelists in their different ways might contribute to an understanding of the theological meaning of Jesus's crucifixion. Sometimes, indeed, it is suggested that some of the evangelists may not have held any particular view on the matter. For a long time it was fashionable to say this about Luke, though as we shall see this is very strange, since in fact Luke gives to the cross as strong and important a meaning as anyone else.

The problem, I think, is once again that if we assume the regular Platonized "goal" of the divine rescue operation—the idea that what matters is how sinful souls get saved and go to "heaven"— then it does indeed appear that the evangelists and even Jesus himself had comparatively little to say on the subject. One might have thought that this would already have caused theologians and others in the church to question some basic assumptions. Perhaps, they might have thought, it is our view of salvation that is mistaken. This, by and large, has not happened. There are naturally many exceptions, but for the most part people studying and writing about "atonement" have treated the four gospels simply as the "backstory." True, the gospels inject some scriptural material into the narrative of the crucifixion itself, but apart from that they say (so it has been thought) very little about how this particular death was to be understood as the event through which salvation came to the world. Again, I propose to approach the matter differently and to discern in all four evangelists, in their different ways, vital themes that contribute to the overall construction.

Another aside is appropriate here. It has been fashionable in some quarters to place other early accounts of the life of Jesus alongside the four we find in the New Testament. Thus the so-called *Gospel of Thomas* and other similar documents have been compared with and sometimes privileged over Matthew, Mark, Luke, and John. This, to be sure, is part of a natural reaction against the way in which an insecure church has tried to defend its embattled position by heavy-handedly insisting on the canonical scriptures. But the move to "other gospels" is more than simply reactive. It emerges not least from the philosophy of the Enlightenment; it has often been noted that Gnosticism, the ancient philosophy expressed in some at least of these "other gospels," has clear echoes both in the idea of "enlightenment" itself and in some of the specific ways that cultural project has worked its way through the Western world of the last two or three centuries. And here is the point: since *Thomas* and most of the other documents in that group do not mention Jesus's crucifixion, and since those that do mention it give it a wildly different interpretation, the question has been raised as to whether those interpretations represent earlier views and the canonical gospels a later one.

Sometimes the material commonly known as Q (parallel traditions in Matthew and Luke, but not in Mark) has been cited here too. Q, by definition, does not have a Passion narrative, since at that point Matthew, Mark, and Luke closely overlap, and some have therefore suggested that Q might be a document reflecting a version of early Jesus faith in which Jesus's death was irrelevant. Such a suggestion represents a failure of logic as well as history. The fact that Mark overlaps with Matthew and Luke in the story of Jesus's death can hardly be used to say that, therefore, a hypothetical document consisting of only the overlaps of Matthew and Luke either knew or cared nothing about Jesus's death.

When it comes to history, we must take very seriously what Paul says in 1 Corinthians 15:11, that the tradition that begins by saying, "The Messiah died for our sins in accordance with the Bible," was the universal proclamation of all early Christians. The Corinthians knew of teachers other than Paul, perhaps in some respects opposed to Paul. Paul could not have said what he said had he expected the Corinthians to come back and say, "But, Paul, what about those Thomas Christians? What about those Q Christians? They don't seem to bother about Jesus's death." No, Paul is saying: "Whether it was from me or them, that was the way we announced it, and that was the way you believed."

## Resurrection

Where, then, must we begin as we look at the gospels for interpretation of Jesus's death? The first thing to realize is that the crucifixion, by itself, carried no "meaning" whatever other than the depressingly normal one. Roman "justice" was once again doing what it did best, stamping out any sign of dissent. The Romans (we remind ourselves) crucified tens of thousands of young Jews over the course of the first century. It was a horribly familiar event. Nobody—neither Jesus's followers, nor his mother, nor Pontius Pilate, nor the mocking crowds—were saying to themselves, as evening drew on and Jesus's body was taken down from the cross for burial, "So he died for our sins!" Nobody was saying "All this has happened in accordance with the Bible!" Nobody, as far as our evidence goes, had been expecting Israel's Messiah to die for the sins of the world. Nobody, on the evening of Jesus's crucifixion, had any idea that a revolutionary event had just taken place.

True, Matthew and Mark both record that the centurion in charge of the execution muttered something about Jesus really being "son of God." (In Luke, he declares that Jesus was "in the right," innocent, thus agreeing with what one of the brigands alongside Jesus had said moments before; 23:47, 41.) In the centurion's world, the phrase "son of God" referred of course to Tiberius Caesar. The levels of irony detected by the gospel writers, and perhaps intended by the centurion himself, are profound, but they do not approach anything like the early Christian confession of faith.

No. Despite Jesus's repeated attempts to warn his followers of what was going to happen and even to explain to them something of what it would mean, his sudden arrest, trial, and execution came as a horrible shock that by itself carried no explanation, no hidden and perhaps consoling meaning. As we have seen, some people in the ancient Jewish world were hoping and praying for a Messiah. Jesus's followers had even concluded that he was the one, despite the fact that he hadn't been doing what many had expected a Messiah would do (leading the fight against the occupying pagan forces, for a start). But nobody thought a Messiah, even if one should appear, would die a horrible death at the hands of those same pagan forces.

In the same way, as we noted in the previous part of the book, some people in the ancient Jewish world had pondered the fate of the martyrs of former generations. Perhaps, some had dared to suggest, their sufferings, torture, and horrible deaths would function within a strange, dark divine plan according to which the sufferings of the few would be the means of rescue for the many. But there is no evidence that anybody supposed such a suffering figure could be the Messiah. The elements of later Christian interpretation were to hand, but they required a new impetus in order to rush together into a new configuration. On the evening of the first

Good Friday, nobody was coming up with anything that would look like even the first stirrings of an "atonement theology."

The first impetus for such a thing came, by all accounts, on the third day after Jesus's execution. Just as his followers had not at all been expecting him to be crucified, so, after his crucifixion, they were certainly not anticipating that he would be bodily raised from the dead. The shock, the initial incomprehension, the lingering doubts, and the breathless excitement of the stories at the end of all four gospels convey perfectly both what seems to have happened and the fact that nobody was expecting it.

In the languages of the day, "resurrection" didn't mean "going to heaven"; it didn't mean that Jesus, or perhaps his "soul," had "survived" in some nonbodily sense. That was precisely what it did *not* mean. There were words to denote that kind of non-bodily postmortem survival. Many people in many cultures would have found it quite normal to envisage such a survival for someone recently dead. The word 'resurrection' was different. It meant a new bodily life after a period of being bodily dead. Many first-century Jews believed in "the resurrection of the body" in this sense. But for them it was to be a great final event in which all God's people would be raised from the dead in the end. It would be the launching point of God's new world, his new creation, the "age to come." It would happen to *all* God's people in the *end,* not to one person, inconveniently and out of sequence (as it were) in the middle of history, with all the muddle and mess of the world still going on around it. As I and others have argued in detail elsewhere, the only way we can make sense of the first century is to say that Jesus's first followers really did believe he had been bodily raised from the dead and that this meant that God's "new age" had somehow begun.

The only way we can make sense of that belief is to say that they were not deluded or deceived, but were telling the truth, even though it was a truth for which the world was unready: that Jesus really was fully and bodily alive again, indeed more fully and more bodily alive than before. He had gone through death and out the other side, and his body itself was the start of the new creation. This wasn't a matter of "resuscitation," but of a new, transformed kind of body. And—though this takes more explanation, to which I alluded in the previous chapter—this new body seemed to be equally at home in the two interlocking dimensions of created reality, what the Bible calls "heaven" and "earth," that is, God's space and our space. All of this and much more is given with the extraordinary and totally unexpected event of Jesus's resurrection.

*And with the resurrection we find the beginnings of the interpretation of the crucifixion.* The cross meant what it meant in the light of what happened next.

Everybody in that world, just like everybody in our world, knew that dead people don't just come back to life, let alone reappear in a new, transformed body. Something must have happened to make that possible. If the prison door is standing open, someone must have unlocked it, perhaps overpowering the guards in the process. Something about Jesus's death seems to have had that effect. According to Luke, Jesus himself began this process of interpretation when he explained to the puzzled disciples on the road to Emmaus that his death had not been simply a horrible accident, a tragic mistake, but had been the strange fulfillment of *the long narrative of Israel's scriptures.* And within that narrative we find, as we shall discover step by step, the deep meaning of the claim that his death was "for our sins." The *formula* in which the early Christians summarized their basic belief ("The Messiah died for our sins in accordance with the Bible") is rooted in the *story* of what actually happened.

The resurrection of Jesus did not immediately generate anything like an "atonement theology." The resurrection stories in all four gospels and the similar passage at the start of Acts are full of dense and fascinating interpretation of what has just happened, but none of them even begins to offer any interpretation of Jesus's death itself—with the important exception, as we saw in the previous part, that Luke's Jesus explains that it was necessary for the Messiah to suffer as part of the divine plan (24:26). But neither Luke's Jesus nor anyone else explains why this might have been so.

Nor, as we have seen, is any explanation of that sort forthcoming in the book of Acts. This is all the more striking not only because Acts was certainly produced after Paul had written all his letters (imagine the temptation to include a scene or two in which Paul or someone else expounds some of the theology of the letters), but also because, as we shall see, Luke himself did believe in quite a sophisticated understanding of the cross, which he has woven into the narrative rather than letting it appear as a formula. It looks for all the world as though the specific belief that "the Messiah died *for our sins*," though it was the centerpiece of the commonly agreed formula by the early 50s, was not immediately deduced from the fact that after his death Jesus had been raised to new life.

Only once we have probed into the explicit meanings that *were* given, very soon though not immediately, can we even guess at the stages by which those explicit meanings emerged. Certainly the resurrection convinced Jesus's disciples that he really was Israel's Messiah, despite his shameful death. They quickly discerned that any new meaning to be found would be found in the scriptures. But how they began that quest is another matter.

Nor, when it came, did the interpretation of Jesus's death focus solely on the dark hours of that first Friday. The flurry of events from the resurrection on, up to and including the gift of the Spirit, all meant what they meant in relation to one another. In particular, as the Letter to the Hebrews makes clear, if Jesus's death was to be understood as in some sense a "sacrifice," then its meaning would not be complete with his death by itself. As we saw earlier, in the ancient Hebrew scriptures the death of the sacrificial animal was not the heart of the ritual; it was only the preliminary event. What mattered was that the blood, symbolizing the life that would "cover" all impurities of whatever sort, would then be presented on the altar. For Hebrews, that happened not at Jesus's death, but after his resurrection and ascension. And even when, as in Paul and indeed the gospels, a great deal of emphasis is placed on what actually happened theologically as well as historically when Jesus was executed, the full meaning can only be understood in relation to what was then to happen in the life and through the work of his followers. The transformed and transforming human lives they were to lead in the power of the Spirit were in themselves part of the "meaning" of the event. But it still makes sense—to return to the point yet again—to inquire how the first generation of Christians understood the death itself.

## Why Did Jesus Choose Passover?

There are certain things we know about Jesus's death beyond any reasonable historical doubt. First, he was executed by the Romans in the way normally reserved for rebels, slaves, and others whom the Romans wanted not merely to dispatch, but also to disgrace. Second, the Roman executioners displayed a notice above Jesus's head on the cross. Normal practice was to state, in such a fashion, the crime for which the victim was being executed. In Jesus's case they wrote it in all three relevant languages; they wanted to leave no doubt. The multilingual notice read "Jesus of Nazareth, King of the Jews."

What does this prove? Perhaps it was just a case of mistaken identity. Perhaps, some have thought, Jesus was a harmless teacher who just happened to be in the wrong place at the wrong time when the Roman soldiers were looking to make a point. Perhaps he never saw himself as a "king." Perhaps the whole thing was a setup. That suggestion falls foul of another secure historical datum: that during his brief public career Jesus of Nazareth had spoken continually about the "kingdom of God" and had linked that powerful and implicitly revolutionary theme with his own work and teaching.

Though modern expositors both inside and outside the church have found it remarkably difficult to connect what Jesus meant by "God's kingdom" with the ancient Jewish expectations, on the one hand, or with his imminent death, on the other, it seems to me that the connections work extremely well in both directions. Jesus was certainly declaring that this was the time for Israel's God to "become king" in ways toward which the ancient prophecies in the Psalms, Isaiah, Daniel, and elsewhere would be the obvious signposts. This would inevitably appear (and could easily be portrayed as) revolutionary and was bound to attract attention from the nervous imperial forces. However much Jesus was redrawing the "kingdom" expectations around his own innovative and vocational reading of those scriptures, so that he was more often the target of hostility from groups with rival Jewish agendas than he was the object of suspicion from the official rulers such as Herod and the Roman governor, it was still these expectations that he was invoking. One way or another, it makes historical sense to say that, "Jesus announced God's kingdom and died as a would-be Messiah." Everything we know about Jesus inclines me to say that he was as aware of this link as we are *and that he understood it vocationally within his own web of prayerful, scriptural reflection.*

It is of course difficult to get inside anybody's sense of vocation. Human hearts and their imaginative capacities are deep and mysterious. But when a person makes a habit of saying certain things and then at an ideal and opportune moment takes decisive action that, though dangerous, makes exactly the point to which he or she had been referring, we are on reasonably safe ground. And at the heart of what we securely know about Jesus's death is the time of year at which it took place. It happened at Passover time, and it seems clear that this was deliberate on Jesus's part. He chose, for his final and fateful symbolic confrontation with Jerusalem and its authorities, the moment when all his fellow Jews were busy celebrating the Exodus from Egypt and praying that God would do again, only on a grander scale, what he had done all those years ago.

It makes sense. To announce God's kingdom is to announce that God is at last overthrowing the dark powers that enslave his people. To announce God's kingdom is to say that this is the time for God to reconstitute his people, rescuing them and regrouping them for new life and new tasks. To announce God's kingdom is to say that, as in Isaiah 52:7–12, God himself is coming back to display his Glory in person and in power. Each of these three themes can be shown to be characteristic of Jesus's public teaching and activity, his healings (particularly the exorcisms), his celebrations with outcasts and "sinners," his call of the Twelve (as an obvious sign of reconstituting the people Israel around himself), and his telling of stories that seemed to have an obvious reference to what God was doing as a way of explaining what he himself was doing. To be sure, a lot of this was oblique, and necessarily so. We must not try to short-circuit the historical investigation, pass by the Jewish context and the messianic overtones, and jump straight into a picture of Jesus "claiming to be God." Many theologians and preachers have tried that; it leaves vital questions unasked, let alone unanswered, and it all too easily collapses into a different narrative altogether. When, however, we put the bits of the puzzle back together, the overtones of Isaiah 52 are clear at numerous points, especially when Jesus himself is making his final journey to Jerusalem and telling stories about the master who comes back—an obvious allusion to the much-anticipated return of Israel's God after the long years of exile.

In any case, what matters for our purposes is that *Jesus chose Passover* to do what had to be done and indeed to suffer what had to be suffered. This alone already tells us that he had in mind a highly dramatic and story-laden climax to his public career: this, it seems, was how he believed Israel's God would become king. With Passover as the context and his repeated clashes with hostile forces both human and nonhuman during his public career, there is every reason to suppose that he saw the task as paralleling the liberation of Israel from Egypt, an event preceded by clashes with Pharaoh and his entourage and by the "plagues" visited on Egypt.

We do not need to propose exact typological matches for elements in the Exodus narrative and elements in Jesus's work and teaching. Indeed, to do so might be to miss the point. What matters is that the *entire* Passover context made sense of the *entire* event that Jesus envisaged as he went up to Jerusalem for that final visit. Passover said, "Freedom—now!" and "Kingdom—now!"

This seems to be exactly what Jesus wanted to convey or, better, what Jesus *believed would happen*. He was not, after all, offering a new theory for people to get their minds around. He was announcing that something was happening and that it would happen immediately, an event through which freedom and kingdom would become realities in a whole new way. He was launching a revolution.

What he did in Jerusalem brings all this into sharp focus. By itself, his dramatic action in the Temple might have various interpretations, as it has had in much subsequent discussion. Where people have tried to turn Jesus's one-off kingdom movement into a "religion," it has been seen as an attempt to clean up the "religious" establishment, to oppose commercialism, and so forth. This is all very worthy and no doubt necessary from time to time; but it has almost nothing to do with a one-off new Passover, a unique Exodus moment.

When we put Jesus's Temple action (Mark 11:12–18) into a Passover context, however, it suddenly carries the memory of Moses's confrontation with Pharaoh. This echo is heightened when we add in material (Mark 13:1–31 and elsewhere) in which language about the imminent fall of the Temple awakens biblical echoes of the fall of Babylon. More particularly, what Jesus did in the Temple, interpreted (as seems most likely) as a Jeremiah-like symbolic prediction of its forthcoming destruction, must have had to do in some way with his aim of declaring that Israel's God, returning to his people at last, had found the Temple sadly wanting and was establishing something different instead.

This in turn points back once more to the Exodus. Moses had told Pharaoh all along that the point of the Israelites leaving Egypt was ultimately in order to worship their God (Exod. 3:12, 18; 4:23; 5:1–3; 7:16; 8:1, 20;9:1, 13; 10:3, 24–26). The climax of the book of Exodus is not the giving of the law in chapter 20, but the construction of the tabernacle, the "microcosm" or "little world" that symbolized the new creation, the place where heaven and earth would come together as always intended. If Jesus did and said things that pointed to a "new Exodus," many in his day would have understood this to mean some kind of renewal or even replacement of the present Temple. Those who wrote the Dead Sea Scrolls, for instance, believed that the present Temple hierarchy was irredeemably corrupt and that they themselves constituted the true Temple, the place where Israel's God was now at home and was to be worshipped and served. Such things were indeed thinkable at the time, even if it was extremely dangerous to attempt to put them into practice.

Did Jesus believe something like that? All the signs are that he did—and that he connected this too to Passover.

The other key action of that week was Jesus's organizing and celebrating a strange meal with his followers, and this seems to be central to his own interpretation of the events that were rapidly unfolding. I have made the point elsewhere, but it bears repeating: when Jesus wanted to explain to his followers what his forthcoming death was all about, he did not give them a theory, a model, a metaphor, or any other such thing; he gave them a *meal,* a Passover meal—or at least what they seem to have thought was a Passover-meal, though it turned out to be significantly different. Instead of looking back fifteen hundred years or so to the great event of the Exodus from Egypt—though that inevitably remained in the forefront of everyone's minds on that day—he turned the meal around so that its primary significance looked *forward* to what was going to happen the next day. And already, before we try to understand any of the words that Jesus is reported to have said on that occasion, we know beyond any reasonable historical doubt that Jesus saw his approaching death in connection with *the coming of the kingdom*.

He seems to have believed, somehow, that what was going to happen would confront and defeat the dark powers with which he had been waging a running battle for the last few years. Just as Israel's God overcame the power of Egypt and even the myth-laden power of the Red Sea, so, Jesus believed, God would use the upcoming event to overthrow all the dark powers that had kept not only Israel but also the whole human race in captivity. This would be the ultimate freedom moment. "Let me tell you," he said to his friends as they shared the cup at the meal, "from now on I won't drink from the fruit of the vine until the kingdom of God comes" (Luke 22:18; Matt. 26:29 has a slightly longer version of the same saying). The evangelists, writing much later, clearly believed that this prediction had come true. The victory had been won. Something was about to happen through which, as was fitting for an ultimate Passover, God would overthrow all the powers of the world and liberate his people from them once and for all.

I therefore regard it as a fixed point in understanding Jesus's death that Jesus himself understood what was about to happen to him in connection with Israel's ancient Passover tradition and that this was linked directly to his beliefs about the launch of God's kingdom. The royal power of God had already been displayed, close up and dramatically, in his public career. But Jesus believed that through his death this royal power would win the decisive victory through which not just Israel but also the whole world would be liberated: ransomed, healed, restored, forgiven.

The Passover and Exodus themes cluster together in an almost bewildering and overdetermined fashion: the fulfillment of ancient promises, the liberation from slavery, the crossing of the Red Sea, the coming of God himself in the pillar of cloud and fire, the promise of inheritance. All these, in parables, healings, promises, and warnings, formed part of Jesus's public proclamation and private teaching. Now they gathered to a greatness.

Up to this point, it might appear that the theological significance with which Jesus was investing his death was simply about a great, freedom-bringing victory. That, indeed, is the overarching significance of the evidence, all the way from his initial kingdom announcement after his baptism through to his dark words about the imminent kingdom at the final meal. But how would this victory be won? What had to happen for the dark powers to be defeated?

Here we come a step closer to the heart not only of Jesus's own vocational vision, but of the whole New Testament picture of what actually happened, theologically speaking, on the first Good Friday. I have stressed that Jesus chose Passover as the moment for his final dramatic symbolic actions—including the death he believed he would suffer. He did not choose one of the other festivals. In particular, he did not choose the great and somber Day of Atonement. However, as we saw in Part Two, by the time of Jesus the long story of Israel had reached a point where two things ran together, at least potentially. The victory over the powers would be won *by Jesus dealing with the people's sins.*

Recall how the narrative now worked. Israel had been in "continuing exile," according to Daniel 9 and many later texts, ever since the Babylonian destruction. Renewal, reform, and even revolution had taken place, but the plight was still a reality, visibly underlined at Passover time in Jerusalem by the presence of Roman soldiers and the Roman governor himself, up from his normal residence in the port city of Caesarea to keep a personal eye on things during the notoriously dangerous freedom festival.

But the analysis of that extended plight was that Israel was still "in its sins." That had been the view of Isaiah, Jeremiah, Ezekiel, and Daniel—to say nothing of Ezra and Nehemiah, both of whom continued after the supposed "return from exile" to lament Israel's sins and its consequent unredeemed, enslaved state. Thus, as long as Israel was still in bondage to hostile powers, what was needed was a new Exodus; but, because the cause of that bondage was Israel's sins, what had to happen was for those sins to be dealt with. This combination of themes—the Passover victory, on the one hand, and the exile-ending "forgiveness of sins," on the other—would then become characteristic of many strands in the New Testament.

My argument in this book is that the combination goes right back to the Last Supper itself, the interpretative grid that Jesus himself chose and structured. And on this basis I will suggest that we can see at last how to rescue the central elements of early Christian "atonement" theology from their own pagan captivity. At the center of the whole picture we do not find a wrathful God bent on killing someone, demanding blood. Instead, we find the image—I use the word advisedly—of the covenant-keeping God who takes the full force of sin onto himself.

This, I suggest, goes some way toward explaining the remarkable power that, as we saw at the start of this book, the story still retains. And it retains it *as story* more than as theory—especially when the various theories are detached from this story, not least from the ancient Jewish story in which it belongs, and relocated in different stories, images, illustrations, and the like, where their central themes can be subtly transformed to carry significantly different meanings. It retains its power particularly *as acted story,* as Jesus's followers to this day "do this in memory of him." But that brings us to the "words of institution." This is where the theme of "end of exile" nests within and interprets the larger theme of the kingdom-bringing Passover.

The words over the bread resonate out in several directions. "This is my body, which is given for you" (Luke 22:19; Matt. 26:26 and Mark 14:22 lack "which is given for you"; 1 Cor. 11:24 reads "which is for you"). It misses the point to ask whether Jesus is identifying himself with the crisp unleavened bread of the traditional meal or with the Passover lamb itself, or both, or something more. Enacted symbolism doesn't work in that either/or way. The point is that a Passover meal focused on all the events of the original occasion; that the food eaten year after year linked the worshippers to that original event; and that, in particular, the bread that symbolized the hasty escape from Egypt and the lamb whose blood was daubed on the doorposts of the houses spoke of the complex, hurried, but symbol-laden actions through which the Israelites were to understand that their God was delivering them in person, rescuing them from slavery and sending them off on the journey to their promised inheritance. Eating the Passover said: it happened, once for all, and we are part of the people to whom it happened. Jesus's words over the bread transformed this, so that it now said: the new Passover *is about to happen,* and those who share this meal thereafter will be constituted as *the people for whom it had happened* and through whom it will happen in the wider world.

So too with the cup. "This cup," said Jesus, "is the new covenant, in my blood which is shed for you." That, at least, is Luke's version of the saying (22:20). Matthew's version reads, "This is my blood of the covenant, which is poured out for many for the forgiveness of sins" (26:28). Mark simply has "This is my blood of the covenant, which is poured out for many" (14:24). Paul, discussing problems with the Eucharist in Corinth, quotes Jesus as saying, "This cup is the new covenant in my blood. Whenever you drink it, do this as a memorial of me" (1 Cor. 11:25).

There are numerous ways of interpreting the subtle variations between accounts. These are made more complicated still by the fact that many good early manuscripts give slightly different wording here and there. This is easily explained: scribes who could remember not only what the other gospels had said, but also the ways in which the saying was repeated in regular worship would naturally slip in or perhaps omit this or that word or phrase. Fortunately for our purposes this does not affect the point. Perhaps the best comment is that, given the subsequent events of that same night (not to mention the quantity of food and drink that had already been consumed), it isn't surprising to find various slightly different versions already current among Jesus's earliest followers. These were strange and surprising words, sprung on them without warning at a moment of tension and excitement. What matters is that within the overarching Passover theme of the meal, the whole occasion, and the events that would happen the next day, Jesus insisted that this new Passover would perform its freedom-bringing victory by means of the long-awaited final undoing of exile. "Forgiveness of sins" would be the means by which the ultimate Passover would come about. We shall presently explain this link: it has to do with the analysis we have already offered of "sin" in relation to the human vocation.

How, then, would the "forgiveness of sins" itself come about? The mention of "blood" indicates a sacrificial interpretation of Jesus's death. This would, of course, be scandalous, since no good Jew would dream of drinking blood. One might recall the early story of King David refusing to "drink the blood" of his three mighty colleagues who went to get him a drink from the well at Bethlehem (2 Sam. 23:17): there it is clearly a metaphor indicating that, had he drunk the well water, David would have been profiting from the fact that the three had risked their lives to get it for him. But the mention of "blood" right beside "covenant" strongly suggests that the primary meaning has to do with the covenant renewal spoken of in Jeremiah 31, which refers to the original covenant ceremony in Exodus 24:3–8.

There, the sacrifices are offered and the blood put into basins. Half is thrown on the altar; the other half is thrown on the people, with the words, "See the blood of the covenant that YHWH has made with you in accordance with all these words"—the "words" in question being, of course, the words of the Torah. Again, we do not need here to probe further. The central meaning ought to be clear. Jesus had spoken and acted throughout his public career as if he believed it was his vocation to be the agent of the great renewal, the great new-covenant moment that had been promised ever since Deuteronomy 30 and referred to one way or another in many prophecies and psalms. It should be no surprise that, as he saw his career drawing to its shocking end, he would speak explicitly about this moment of covenant renewal. What is startling is that he would associate it so directly with his own death, that he would refer to his own blood as if it were like the sacrificial blood of the animals in Exodus 24. (Once again we note that this reference to sacrifice carries no suggestion that the animals were somehow being "punished" in the place of the Israelites. Nor, therefore, does Jesus's reference to "blood" at this point carry such a meaning. We must not look for the right answer in the wrong place. To do so will make it the wrong answer.)

Thus far, we are on solid historical ground. Jesus chose Passover for his final kingdom moment, because Passover always was a kingdom moment, and this was to be the ultimate one, the real victory over the powers of evil. And Jesus, through his words with the cup, interpreted this new Passover, this intended new Exodus, as the covenant renewal that would bring about the real "return from exile," the ultimate "forgiveness of sins." The two go together. Releasing people from their sins and from the effects of those sins would be the means whereby the victory would be won. But this brings us to the last question in this chain. In what sense and by what means would Jesus's death effect "forgiveness of sins"?

The answer must lie—can only lie—in Jesus's own creative reinterpretation of Israel's scriptures. Here the historical ground is less certain. We know for sure that the early church interpreted Jesus's death as having been "in accordance with the Bible," so of course it is likely that in retelling the story of his death his early followers echoed the scriptures that, they believed, had thereby been fulfilled. But this doesn't mean that we are left with no trails to follow to the intention of Jesus himself. There are lines that converge and produce a highly probable scenario.

For a start, there are the passages we surveyed earlier that, taken together, contribute to the strand of thought summarized by Albert Schweitzer as "messianic woes." Texts all the way from the eighth-century BC prophet Hosea through to the writings found at Qumran testify to a belief that final redemption would come through a time of suffering. Some texts, as we saw, imagined that this might be focused on a small group. One text, Isaiah 52:13–53:12, stated quite specifically that it would be focused on one person, the "servant" who would do for Israel what Israel could not do for itself and would thereby do for the world what (as in 49:6, perhaps echoed in 52:13) Israel had been called to do for the world. An earlier generation of scholars, seeing the damage done by decontextualized notions of vicarious suffering (paganized notions, as I am suggesting), tried to eliminate Isaiah 53 from consideration of Jesus's vocation. I and many others, however, have remained convinced (and have argued in considerable detail) that this passage of Isaiah, *seen in its full and proper context of the coming of the kingdom, the return of YHWH, and the renewal of both covenant and creation,* was at the very heart of Jesus's understanding of how his vocation would be fulfilled. He would go ahead of his people and take upon himself the suffering that would otherwise fall upon them.

As we shall see in the next chapter, this theme is drawn out in particular by Luke—despite the popular impression that he has no atonement theology to speak of. But we can trace it back to Jesus himself through a number of incidents and sayings that, as far as we know, are unprecedented in the Jewish world prior to Jesus and that the early church, apart from the evangelists who report them, developed no further. There is the saying about the hen and the chicks (Luke 13:34): Jesus is longing to gather the chicks under his wings, to protect them like a mother hen, but they are refusing. There is the saying about the green tree and the dry one (Luke 23:31): Jesus is the green tree, innocent of the violent revolutionary dreams because of which the wrath of Rome will fall upon the Jewish people, but all around him are the young firebrands, zealous for revolt and so like dry sticks for the coming conflagration. This is not how the church from Paul on discerned or described or theorized about the meaning of Jesus's death. These hints seem to have stayed in the tradition despite—or perhaps because of—being without precedent and without subsequent development.

Then there is the incident in the garden at the time of Jesus's arrest. Jesus wanted three of his friends in particular to watch and pray with him, in case they would "come into the trial" (Luke 22:40). Here we are close to Schweitzer's theme, that the "trial" or the "tribulation" was coming upon Israel, a time of intense suffering crashing in like a tidal wave, and Jesus was determined that his followers should not suffer it with him. This might easily have happened: close associates of someone regarded as a revolutionary leader would expect to be rounded up and dealt with in the first century just as in the twenty-first. Somehow, in the dark and mayhem of that terrible night, that theme of the "tribulation" was remembered, as was the saying reported by John (18:8) in which Jesus insists that if it is him they have come to arrest, the others should be allowed to leave.

Skeptics can of course quibble about any element in such a reconstruction (as one can about any reconstruction of motive for any figure of history). But once we grant the solid evidence in the middle of the picture from Jesus's choice of Passover on, fragments like these can be seen as forming a coherent and even plausible picture of the way Jesus had construed his own vocation, perhaps from as far back as his baptism by John, when the voice from heaven ("This is my son, my beloved one; I am delighted with him," Matt. 3:17) drew together the royal vocation of Psalm 2:7 ("You are my son; today I have begotten you") and the "servant" vocation from Isaiah 42:1 ("Here is my servant, whom I uphold, my chosen, in whom my soul delights"). Even if that too were to be deemed a later idea read back into the texts, one would still have to explain why anyone in the early church would begin to think down those lines if the seeds of such beliefs were not already present in things that Jesus himself said and did.

Behind all this there stands one feature of the gospel portrait of Jesus that is often noted, but not so often brought into this specific discussion. The impression made by Jesus on one person after another, one village after another, one community after another, seems to have been constant. Wherever he went, he was celebrating the arrival of God's kingdom, as often as not by partying with people who would normally be excluded because of their apparently shady moral background. Wherever he went, he healed people of all kinds of diseases, including particularly the strange inner corruption associated with the presence of dark nonhuman forces. (However we want to interpret this, there should be no question that Jesus was an effective exorcist. Only so can we explain the charges hurled at him that he was himself in league with the dark powers—a charge which the early church certainly did not invent.) And, wherever he went, Jesus was offering *forgiveness of sins,* which we have now learned to recognize both as something one might normally get on an individual basis by going to the Temple and as shorthand for the larger blessing of covenant renewal, return from exile, and so on.

In all of this and much, much more, Jesus comes across—the portrait is remarkably coherent even through four very different presentations—as a man of powerful compassion or, as we might say, compassionate power. The word "love" is grossly overused in contemporary English and can so easily collapse into sentimentalism, not least in pious portraits of Jesus. But when we read a complex chapter in which Jesus sidesteps a tricky political issue, rebukes his followers for stopping children coming near him, and rebukes them again for arguing about who would be the greatest among them; then find Jesus welcoming children, hugging them, and blessing them; and then see him in dialogue with a sincere but misguided inquirer, looking hard at the man and loving him (Mark 10:16, 21), we find the portrait utterly convincing.

When Jesus then says, at the end of the rebuke to the ambitious disciples, "The son of man didn't come to be waited on; he came to be the servant, to give his life 'as a ransom for many,'" the sense it makes is the sense already present in the narrative as a whole, both in Mark 10 and throughout the gospels. This was not simply a theological principle superimposed onto a historical scenario that might or might not have sustained it. It was the key to everything Jesus was, did, and said. When John says, at the start of the long passage leading up to Jesus's death, that now, having always loved his people, Jesus "loved them right through to the end" (13:1), John is summarizing one of his own major themes. But nobody who reads through the gospel portraits feels this summary to be jarring, to clash with what we have seen of Jesus in the four accounts. It makes sense. It rings true. We bring it back to the frantic scramble of narrative that leads from the upper room to Gethsemane, to the high priest's house, to Pilate's tribunal, and to the horrid hill called Golgotha, and we find ourselves saying, with Paul, "The son of God loved me and gave himself for me" (Gal. 2:20), or, with John, "He had always loved his own people in the world; now he loved them right through to the end" (13:1).

This, then, is what we find about Jesus himself. He announces God's kingdom coming on earth as in heaven. The obvious symbol for this is Passover, and Jesus chooses Passover as the moment to state in symbol and word that Israel's God is now at last rescuing his people from the dark powers that had oppressed them, powers for which the occupying military force was just an outward sign. The "blood of the covenant," as in Exodus 24:8, seems to be a reinterpretation of the blood of the Passover lamb, in line with Jesus's claim that he was launching the *new* covenant of Jeremiah 31:31. The reason this new Passover can be seen as the defeat of the powers, however—despite the obvious fact that it took place through Jesus's death at the hands of the occupying forces, hardly the sign of a dramatic victory!—is that the same event, Jesus's death, was to be seen as the inauguration of Jeremiah's new covenant, the covenant in which sins would be forgiven and thus, of course, exile would be undone at last.

The covenant renewal itself is explained by the principle of the *representative substitute,* namely, that the "servant," the quintessential Israelite, takes upon himself the fate of the nation, of the world, of "the many." And this principle itself is not something other than the faithful love that, as a human being, Jesus showed again and again when he touched the leper, or the unclean woman, or the corpse on the pallet. When, again in John, Jesus says, "No one has greater love than this, than to lay down your life for your friends" (15:13), this does not seem like a new point. It merely sums up the way he had been all along. Theories of atonement do not need to be superimposed on an abstract narrative about Jesus, as has so often been attempted. They grow out of the real-life Jesus stories we already have. It is astonishing that the four gospels have been so underused in "atonement theology."

It was only with hindsight that Jesus's first followers realized what had been going on in that last dramatic week, in the Last Supper and on the cross. In particular, it was only with hindsight that they came to recognize that the central element in Passover, the central fact of the kingdom announcement in Isaiah 52:7 ("Your God reigns!"), was the personal and glorious presence of Israel's God and that they had all unknowingly been witnessing this very thing. John says this quite explicitly (the divine Glory is unveiled throughout Jesus's career, but especially on the cross), but the other three gospel writers say it too in their own ways, as of course does Paul. And it is this element, finally, that ties the ends together and gives to the whole event the only sense it can ultimately have. Take this away, and we are left once more with a paganized doctrine in which one man decides to throw himself on the wheel so that it may turn at last in the opposite direction.

That was Schweitzer's image. It is powerful and has its own point to make. But it can all too easily suggest a merely human Jesus doing his best, through heroic misunderstanding, to force the hand of the God of Israel. We may suspect that the early Christians did not have particularly good language to say what they wanted to say at this point, and we certainly don't have good language for it either. But if we are talking about Passover and new Exodus; if we are talking about covenant renewal and the forgiveness of sins, which in Isaiah goes with the return of the glorious divine Presence; if we are talking about the Isaianic "servant" who seems, strangely, to be the embodiment of the "arm of YHWH"; if, at street level, we are talking about someone who was known for a remarkable yet remarkably familiar combination of power, wisdom, and above all compassion—then it makes sense to look to Paul once more for a summary of what the story is all about. Take this element away and, as with Schweitzer's image, the whole thing can collapse into another sort of paganism. Put it back, and the answer to the question, "What happened on Good Friday?" is simple, though fathomless in its implications: "God was reconciling the world to himself in the Messiah" (2 Cor. 5:19).

There is much more to say, of course. Are we then talking about a suffering God? What about the cry of dereliction, indicating Jesus's sense that God had abandoned him on the cross? We shall return to those. But the overwhelming *historical* impression from the gospels as a whole is of a human being doing what Israel's God had said *he* would do, of a human being embodying, incarnating what Israel's God had said he would be across page after page in Israel's scriptures. The new Passover happened because the pillar of cloud and fire—though now in a strange and haunting form, the likeness of a battered and crushed human being—had come back to deliver the people. The covenant was renewed because of the blood that symbolized the utter commitment of God to his people, the lifeblood that spoke of divine protection, of God's self-giving love. Paul, in Acts 20:28, speaks of "the church of God, which he purchased with his very own blood." Forgiveness happened because the "arm of YHWH" was "wounded for our transgressions, crushed for our iniquities" (Isa. 53:5). The cross became the encoded symbol as well as the actual outworking of the dying, and hence the undying, love of Israel's God.

# 10

## The Story of the Rescue

THE BRITISH ARE noted for their sense of irony, often applied particularly to themselves. Self-deprecating humor is, at least in theory, our stock in trade. One current example is a brilliant and rightly popular BBC sitcom called *W1A*, which is the postal code for the headquarters of the BBC itself. The satire, created by people who themselves work for the organization they are sending up, is often telling as well as very funny. In one now famous episode, while a middle-aged broadcasting executive is trying to figure out how to solve a particular problem about a program, he is being badgered by a young, sassy eager beaver of a PR agent who has her own agendas. The man keeps trying to explain to her that she doesn't understand the question, and she keeps trying to explain to him how her proposals are going to solve everything and make the program a roaring success.

Eventually, exasperated, he turns on her. "You're just not listening!"

Back comes the answer, pitch-perfect for the character: "I totally am listening! What it is—you guys aren't saying the right stuff!"

I was reminded of that moment when reflecting on the ways in which the four gospels have routinely been ignored by people trying to construct a vision of the atonement, trying to understand the meaning of Jesus's death. The long tradition of in-house church discussions about such things, swapping theories and schemes for how precisely to understand what happened on Good Friday, has emerged—especially in popular culture—from a world where it was assumed, as we saw earlier, that the point of Christianity was how to go to heaven granted that we are all sinners deserving hell. That is the agenda: How do we get to that goal?

The four gospels have very little to say about this topic. Almost nobody talks about "going to heaven." When Jesus talks about the "kingdom of heaven," he doesn't mean a place called "heaven," but the rule of "heaven," that is, God's reign, coming to birth *on earth*. Almost nobody in the gospels warns about "going to hell." The dire warnings in the four gospels are mostly directed toward an imminent *this*-worldly disaster, namely, the fall of Jerusalem and other events connected with that. There are occasional sayings that go beyond that, such as Matthew 10:28 and its parallel in Luke 12:4–5, but this dimension seems to be taken for granted rather than made central. And despite a wealth of detail in the buildup to Jesus's death, so much detail in fact that the gospels have sometimes been described as "Passion narratives with extended introductions," the four writers do not seem particularly concerned with building into their accounts any kind of answer to the expected question of how this death somehow enables sinners to be forgiven and to go to heaven after all.

One can imagine a conversation between the four evangelists who wrote the gospels and a group of "evangelists" in our modern sense who are used to preaching sermons week by week that explain exactly how the cross deals with the problems of "sin" and "hell." The four ancient writers are shaking their heads and trying to retell the story they all wrote: of how Jesus launched the kingdom of God on earth as in heaven and how his execution was actually the key, decisive moment in that accomplishment. The modern evangelists come right back with their theories, diagrams, and homely illustrations. The ancient writers eventually explode: "You're just not listening!" "Yes, we are," reply the modern preachers (who are, after all, committed to "believing in the Bible"), "but you guys just aren't saying the right stuff!"

Of course, modern readers and preachers have invented ways of making them say the "right stuff" despite what is actually on the page. We have become adept at picking out a verse here and a phrase there that will fit into our schemes even if it means ignoring the context. Thus, as we have seen, Mark 10:45 ("The son of man . . . came . . . to give his life 'as a ransom for many'") is taken as warrant for invoking Isaiah 53, *which is then itself read in the decontextualized way I described earlier.* John 19:30, the last shout of Jesus from the cross, is sometimes translated "It is finished" or "It's all done!" This is then turned into a statement about a bill being paid or an account being settled to fit in with a particular atonement theology rather than being allowed to make John's point, which is the completion of Jesus's vocation in parallel with the completion of creation itself in Genesis 2:2 (see also John 17:4).

One hears less often the quotation of Jesus's words over the cup at the Last Supper, even though the idea of Jesus's blood being shed "for the forgiveness of sins" might be thought relevant to the "normal" story. Perhaps the problem there is that preachers in the Protestant or evangelical tradition have sometimes been anxious about any focus on the Last Supper, lest they find themselves being drawn into a more sacramental world of meaning than they had intended.

In any case, when people preach or teach about the "meaning of the cross" in modern Western churches, they seldom if ever consider taking seriously the larger stories the four evangelists are telling—stories about the kingdom, the Temple (including Jesus's supposed threat to destroy it), Pontius Pilate, Jesus's followers, or the mocking crowds at the foot of the cross. Part of my purpose in this book is to persuade people who normally talk over the evangelists because they don't seem to be "saying the right stuff" to be quiet for a bit and listen to the story (and the stories, plural) they are actually telling. The present chapter is not trying to provide an exhaustive account of all that—as if that would be possible within a single volume—but to offer some clues as to the direction these four great books are taking us as they move toward their own answers to the question, "What exactly happened on the first Good Friday?"

The question, "What exactly happened?" is of course ambiguous. At one level the answer is relatively clear: betrayal, arrest, nighttime hearings, rough Roman justice, violence, beating, weeping, death, burial. But the question underneath that (as with almost all narratives, we should always be alert for the "underneath" bit, the probing of motives and meanings) is: What was going on in regard to God and the world? What did this mean for the fulfillment (or the failure) of Jesus's hopes, of his kingdom announcement? How does this event either complete his work or destroy it? Had Jesus been intending to continue preaching, healing, and teaching for several more years, only to find himself caught in the wrong place at the wrong time, or was this horrible end somehow envisaged within his own vocational awareness? And, whatever answer we give to that, what can we say about the divine intention and indeed the divine accomplishment?

This is the same double set of questions and answers that we find if we ask, "Why did Jesus die?" You can give historical reasons: the chief priests were angry because of what he did in the Temple; the Romans were suspicious that he might be some kind of rebel leader; the Pharisees hated him because his kingdom vision clashed at several points with their own. Or, still within historical reasons, you could say that Jesus died because his followers failed to defend him, and one of them actually betrayed him to the authorities. The question "Why," even at the historical level, can get quite complicated. But we can also ask the theological "Why?" What was the *divine* reason? Already in Acts we find the strange combination: God meant it, but you (the Jewish leaders) were wicked in carrying it out by handing Jesus over to the pagans (2:23; 4:27–28). And here is the point: the Western church, looking for the "theological" answer to the question "Why?" ("How did Jesus's death mean that sins could be forgiven so we could go to heaven?"), has largely ignored the historical answer, and indeed the historical questions. They have been regarded as irrelevant circumstantial details.

But are they? The answer, clearly, is no. The historical questions and answers are the place to go if we want to find the theological answer. If we cannot see it there, that might be an indication that we are trying to answer the wrong question. If the gospels do not seem to be "saying the right stuff," maybe it is our idea of the "right stuff" that needs adjusting.

The main theme that makes this point graphically is the relationship, which we have already noted in relation to Jesus's own understanding of his vocation, between the proclamation of the kingdom, on the one hand, and the crucifixion, on the other. In much reading, teaching, preaching, and indeed scholarship, these have appeared to be almost contradictory: the positive message and moment of the kingdom program followed by the negative and disastrous moment of the cross. Alternately, if the cross is given a positive value ("He died for our sins so we could go to heaven"), then what was the "kingdom" theme all about? But in all four gospels the two themes clearly belong together. They explain one another. The kingdom comes through Jesus's entire work, which finds its intended fulfillment in his shameful death. The cross is the cross of the "king of the Jews." Our traditions, including our traditions of atonement theology, have separated themes that belonged inextricably together.

## Listening to the Evangelists

In particular, all four gospels tell the story of Jesus as one of *Israel's God returning at last*. This theme, so often ignored in the past, has come to the fore in recent scholarly analysis. When Mark opens his gospel by lining up John the Baptist with the prophetic messengers of Malachi 3 and Isaiah 40, the point is that those messengers are preparing the way not simply for a coming Messiah, but for YHWH himself. When John opens his gospel with multiple echoes of Genesis and Exodus, bringing the prologue to its climax in v. 14 with the Word becoming flesh and revealing the divine Glory and in v. 18 with the unveiling of the otherwise unseen Father through the divine Son, he is setting the stage for his readers to understand that Jesus is not simply "son of God" in the sense of the Davidic king of Psalm 2, 2 Samuel 7, and so on. John's Jesus is the living embodiment of the one creator God, Israel's covenant God. The messianic language of the divine "Son" is discerned as the perfect vehicle (going back, we may suppose, to Jesus himself) to express this. When Matthew has the angel tell Joseph that the child to be born will be "Emmanuel," "God with us," and then finishes his gospel with Jesus himself telling his followers that *he* will be "with them always," alert readers know that the entire story ought to be read with this in mind. Luke's birth narratives are still more explicit, designating the child in Mary's womb as the "Holy One" who will be "God's son" (Luke 1:35). When Luke's gospel nears its climax, the coming of Jesus to Jerusalem is clearly to be seen as the moment when, at last, Israel's God is "visiting his people," that is, coming back in person to judge and to rescue (19:44). There is much more that could be said to fill in this picture. But this will suffice for our present purposes.

We should not then be surprised when all four gospels tell the story of Jesus in such a way as to draw out, repeatedly, his sense of compassion and love, which we have already noted as a striking feature. This was by no means necessarily the case for prophetic or would-be messianic figures in the Second Temple Jewish world. We do not know as much as we would like to about the leaders, including the would-be Messiahs, whom we meet briefly in the pages of Josephus or indeed about Simon bar-Kochba, who led the final failed revolt almost exactly a hundred years after Jesus's public career. But we do not get the impression from them of a character such as we find in the stories about Jesus. Nor, for that matter, does John the Baptist come over as the sort of person who might claim to have a heart that was "gentle, not arrogant" or to offer his followers "the rest they deeply need" (Matt. 11:29).

This is one place where the long traditions of displaying a romantic or sentimental Jesus figure have let us down. We are so used to the soppy picture of "gentle Jesus, meek and mild" and to the reaction that such a picture provokes, stressing Jesus's occasional sternness and warnings against the Pharisees and others, that we have perhaps failed to notice how strange it is to have a major public figure who is treading a dangerous line between affirming ancient traditions and criticizing current abuses and who is known at the same time for a deeply caring approach to people of all sorts, especially those in distress. The reason for highlighting this here is not simply that it is an important and easily overlooked feature of the gospels, but that for all four evangelists this deliberately and explicitly constructs a picture of Jesus's death not in terms of an angry father lashing out at an innocent and defenseless son, but in terms of someone *embodying the love of God himself,* acting as the personal expression of that love all the way to his death.

If more attention had been paid to this feature, which is built into the narrative rather than being stuck in from the side by means of one or two scriptural quotations or allusions or the odd authorial "aside," some of the more disturbing and unbiblical features of would-be "atonement" theology—and the social and cultural spinoffs that have sometimes accompanied them—

could have been avoided. John, as we saw, opens his account of the events leading up to Jesus's death by stressing that this was the completion of Jesus's constant love (13:1). But this does not stand alone. For John, it draws out and makes explicit what has been implicit in passage after passage as Jesus transforms the lives of people of all sorts; biblical imagery, such as that of the "good shepherd," also makes the same point.

The balancing element in the portrait of Jesus in all the gospels is the constant buildup of hostility toward him, his message, and his accomplishments. I have argued elsewhere (against some worrying trends in contemporary thinking that want to make the story of Jesus stand all by itself without historical context) that all four canonical gospels are careful to link the story of Jesus to the larger story of Israel, going back to prophetic traditions (Mark 1; Luke 1–2), Abraham (Matthew 1), Adam (Luke 3), and the creation itself (John 1). But this does not at all mean, as some have absurdly imagined, that the evangelists are simply envisaging the story of Israel as a kind of "progressive revelation," a smooth crescendo, a steady development, at the end of which Jesus simply emerges as the final fulfilment. The story of Israel was never seen like that, not even in the thoroughly positive retellings such as, for instance, Psalm 105 (and in any case that is accompanied at once by Psalm 106, which brings out the dark side all too obviously). Matching the story of the chosen people stride for stride and sometimes indeed overwhelming that story in darkness and misery is the long story of evil.

Evil comes in many forms in Israel's scriptures. It is seen graphically in the total wickedness of the generations before and after the flood and then in the crazy arrogance at Babel. But, after the call of Abraham, we are never given the impression that "evil" only exists outside Abraham's family. Abraham himself appears deeply flawed, as do all his successors, not least Jacob, whose new name, "Israel," becomes the designation for his family ever after. Moses begins his public life with a premeditated murder. The books of Joshua and Judges do not spare the reputation of the new nation. Even the greatest kings, such as David, Solomon, Hezekiah, and Josiah, all have serious and damaging flaws. The priesthood is no better. As for the prophets—well, for every prophet who seems genuinely to want to listen for and then announce the true word of YHWH, there seem to be hundreds who will say what people, especially rulers, want to hear. The exile itself, as we have seen, indicates the ultimate failure of Israel and its results. "Evil" is not an occasional blip on the radar or a problem that can be pushed to one side or blamed on other nations. It is universal. According to Israel's own scriptures, evil is just as much in evidence in Israel as anywhere else.

The four gospels see this same disease converging at one point. Matthew's opening sequence includes Herod's scheme to kill Jesus while still a baby and the consequent flight into Egypt. Mark has Pharisees and Herodians plotting against Jesus from early on; Luke has Jesus's fellow citizens in Nazareth wanting to throw him off a cliff. John's Jesus is a marked man from as early as the Temple incident in chapter 2 and the healing on the Sabbath in chapter 5. There is no "Galilean springtime" to correspond to the nineteenth-century fantasy of a happy, early ministry for Jesus before the storm clouds gathered. The storm clouds were there from the start. This is all part of the "why" to which the gospels are giving their answer. Jesus's announcement of God's kingdom did not check the boxes his fellow Jews were expecting. His very birth was perceived as a threat to the (insecure) ruling elite. His actions connected with the holy place (the Temple), the holy law (the Torah), and the holy day (the Sabbath) were perceived as dangerous and subversive, for the very good reason that they were. Nor was the opposition confined to rulers and official bodies. From early on the Pharisees, a populist pressure group aiming at rigorously applying the ancestral traditions as part of their own hopes for the long-awaited new age, were opposed to Jesus's announcement of the kingdom. This is hardly surprising.

Here an analogy may help. Those of us who live in Scotland are getting used to politicians campaigning for independence. Now suppose you belonged to a political party agitating for that goal, but then another party arose saying they were launching their own independence movement, but they didn't consider the national dress (the kilt), the symbolic national food and drink (haggis and whisky), or the national musical instrument (the bagpipes) to be of any importance. Suppose such a new party seemed to be gaining widespread support. Your reaction would be a combination of jealousy and righteous indignation ("Who do they think they are?"). That is what happened in Jesus's case. He was talking about the kingdom of God, but he was appearing to ignore all the things that marked the Jews out as God's people! Behind this we can sense, as in the reaction of the synagogue congregation in Nazareth and elsewhere, a settled resistance to this new kingdom teaching and a determination not to be taken in with Jesus's talk of peace, reconciliation, turning the other cheek, going the second mile, and so on. That wasn't what they wanted or expected. When Jesus warned Jerusalem of the things that would come upon the city because they had refused the way of peace (Luke 19:42), we have a sense that the implacable hostility to his proposed new way of being God's people had reached its height at last. That, indeed, is the point that all the evangelists are making, not by adding a slogan or even a scriptural reference to their narrative, but by the substance of the narrative itself. This was how evil was gathering itself together, drawing itself up to its full height, so that Jesus's death, when it came, would be causally and not (as it were) merely theologically linked to the tidal wave of evil.

All this is focused particularly in what we can only describe as Jesus's long-running battle with the unseen (though sometimes very vocal) forces of evil. It is striking that, apart from one or two incidents in Acts, most of the early Christian references to exorcisms and the problem they were addressing are found in Matthew, Mark, and Luke. Nor were the hostile forces whom Jesus thus encountered simply corrupting and destroying the unfortunate humans in whom they appeared to have taken up residence. They were, it seems, bent on unmasking Jesus and thereby placing him and his kingdom mission in grave danger; one of them remarks, "I know who you are: you're God's Holy One!" (Mark 1:24). In the evangelists' portrait of Jesus as he is faced with this kind of opposition, we have a sense that all the varied evil in the world is somehow closing in. And just as time after time Jesus expels the demon and heals the afflicted person, so the evangelists are saying that as evil closes in, literally, for the kill, Jesus will perform one final great act of deliverance in which at last his true identity will be disclosed. This time the "exorcism" will displace forever the iron grip that the unseen and nebulous, but very powerful, quasi-personal force of evil has not only on Israel, but on the whole world. *This, in other words, is how the evangelists explain that Jesus has won the unique victory over the powers of evil: not by superimposing the notion of victory upon the narrative, but by allowing it to emerge and reach its climax from within the narrative itself.*

Once we recognize that the four gospels are telling not only the story of God's kingdom being inaugurated, but also the story of how evil draws itself up to its height so that it can then be defeated by the Messiah, we recognize that this emerges not only in the four gospels themselves (and also in Paul, as we shall see), but also in the Acts of the Apostles. In Acts 4, Peter and John are hauled in front of the chief priests and elders because of the lame man they had healed and the preaching about Jesus that had followed. Those in charge give the apostles a lecture and warn them against continuing to speak in Jesus's name, which of course makes little or no impact on Peter and John. They return to their own people and report what has happened, and the whole company prays together, invoking Psalm 2:

*Why did the nations fly into a rage*
*And why did the peoples think empty thoughts?*

*The kings of the earth arose*
*And the rulers gathered themselves together*
*Against the Lord and against his anointed Messiah.* (4:26, quoting
    *Ps. 2:1–2*)

The psalm continues by declaring that God has established his
Messiah, who will then judge the world and call all rulers to
account—a passage well known and often expounded in various
other Jewish traditions of the period. The whole psalm is clearly
in mind at this point. And here it has acquired a particular significance. Evil—in the persons of Herod and Pilate—has gathered itself together, as the psalm always said it would, and God in
response has raised up his true king, who will bring justice to the
whole world. This will happen not least through the strange healing ministry that comes by the powerful name of Jesus:

> So now, Master, look on their threats; and grant that we,
> your servants, may speak your word with all boldness,
> while you stretch out your hand for healing, so that signs
> and wonders may come about through the name of your
> holy child Jesus. (4:29–30)

The same point—of evil gathering itself together and then
being overthrown—comes out clearly in the striking parallel between the challenges and claims made by the satan in the temptation narratives in Matthew 4 and Luke 4 and the mocking of Jesus
on the cross: "If you're God's son . . ." (Matt, 27:40; 4:3, 6; Luke
4:3, 9). We are clearly meant to hear, in the crucifixion scene, the
earlier whispered voice in Jesus's head now turning into a public
mockery from the chief priests and other bystanders. Jesus had spoken of an initial victory over the "strong man," because of which
he was now enabled to plunder his house—referring presumably
to an initial victory in the battle with the satan, resulting in the
exorcisms in his subsequent public career (Matt. 12:29). Now the
battle is resumed and comes to a head. "This is your hour," he says

to the soldiers coming to arrest him. "Your moment has come at last, and so has the power of darkness" (Luke 22:53).

Directly linked to this is the claim of the satan to possess all authority over the kingdoms of the world, implicit in Matthew 4:9 and explicit in Luke 4:6, and then explicitly reversed in Matthew 28:18, where all authority in heaven and on earth is claimed by Jesus himself. *Something has happened to dethrone the satan and to enthrone Jesus in its place.* The story the gospels think they are telling is the story of how that had happened.

John, interestingly, has no stories of exorcisms—just as he does not mention other well-known features of Jesus's life, such as Jesus's baptism (though he mentions John the Baptist's comment about the Spirit descending on Jesus) or the Last Supper (where he highlights the foot washing, but does not mention the bread or the cup). But, as many commentators have seen the meaning of the baptism and the Last Supper diffused throughout the whole gospel, so we would be correct to see the meaning of Jesus's exorcisms both diffused across John's narrative and then coming to a new and particular focus as Jesus goes to the cross. From chapter 12 through to chapter 19 it becomes more and more explicit: the "ruler of this world" (shades of the satan in Luke 4:6) is being thrown out, so that now people of every ethnic background will be welcome to come to Jesus (12:31–32). But as the story progresses, it becomes increasingly clear that the "ruler of this world" is a more complicated figure than we might have imagined. As Jesus prepares to leave the upper room, he knows that the "ruler of the world is coming" to get him (14:30). The satan has, after all, entered into Judas (13:2), making him "the accuser" par excellence, the one through whose work the great accusation that arises in horrid shouts from all human history is now going to be presented against Jesus. And, as a result of Judas's actions, the forces of empire will range themselves against Jesus, leading to the showdown in chapters 18–19. That is part of the inner dynamic of the story John is telling.

Jesus then assures his followers that the Spirit he will send to them will enable them not only to withstand the pressure they will face, but also to call the world to account (16:8–11). But the so-called Farewell Discourses (chaps. 13–17) are full too of the coming confrontation, full, therefore, also of the meaning that that confrontation will carry. Just as (in the argument I presented in the previous chapter) Jesus gave to his disciples his own interpretation of his forthcoming death in the form of a meal, so John gives his own interpretation in the form of the discourses he sets at that same meal. And when, finally, the soldiers close in and Jesus is hurried off to the high priest's house and then to Pontius Pilate, John's readers already know, in outline at least, what this all means.

This is not simply the "narrative background" to a death whose meaning is determined by an abstract scheme concocted elsewhere, in supposed readings either of Paul in the first century or of the later theologians in the traditions of the church. For John, this story *is* the "meaning," because the whole point about Jesus's death, at the climax of a book that began explicitly with the story of the creation of the good world and of the way in which the darkness cannot overcome the light, is that here at last Jesus is confronting the "ruler of the world" in the person of Pontius Pilate. The light is shining in the darkness, and the darkness cannot quench it—though it will look for a while as though it has done just that. And as John allows the narrative to unfold, weaving in all kinds of extra strands as he does so, readers are invited to understand Jesus's death in terms of the victory he had predicted in chapter 12 and also in terms of the love John had highlighted at the start of chapter 13. "No one has a love greater than this, to lay down your life for your friends" (15:13); and this, John has signaled in a thousand different narrative clues, is what Jesus is doing. Victory and love, both growing from the story itself: that is John's interpretation of the cross.

All four gospels, of course, bring the story to its climax at Passover. I have already explored the ways in which Jesus himself seems clearly to have chosen that moment as the appropriate and meaning-laden time to do what had to be done. It is John who makes the connection most explicit when he identifies Jesus as the Passover lamb (1:29, 36; 19:36). But here we see the transition from Passover as victory to Passover as dealing with sin: the lamb is "the one who takes away the world's sin" (1:29). As in the introductory word in Matthew 1:21, where the child is to be called "Jesus" ("YHWH saves") because, explains the angel, "he is the one who will save his people from their sins," so here the theme of "exile undone at last," joined as always with the theme of "YHWH returning at last," comes within the larger theme of the true Passover. Echoing the combination of themes that Jesus himself drew together, the evangelists in their different ways saw the great victory over the powers of evil being won by means of taking away sin.

This same combination—of the great victory over the powers of darkness, won by the overcoming of sin and therefore exile—is at the heart of the frequent allusions in the gospels to Jesus as the "son of man." This is not the place for any detailed exposition of this much-discussed phrase. It echoes, often explicitly and sometimes implicitly, the scenario in Daniel 7, in which a sequence of four monsters culminates in the "little horn" that grows out of the fourth and final one; whereupon the scene changes to the divine throne room, in which judgment is pronounced and "one like a son of man" is brought to the Ancient One and seated beside him in judgment. To this figure is given "dominion and glory and kingship, that all peoples, nations, and languages should serve him" (7:14). The horn is silenced, the monsters are condemned, and the kingdom of God, exercised through the human figure, is inaugurated at last.

Josephus tells us that, in the first century, an oracle in Israel's scriptures propelled the Jews to war against the Romans: it seems clear that he has the book of Daniel in mind. Daniel 2 contains

the messianic prophecy of the "stone" that will smash the idolatrous statue and become, in its turn, a great mountain. Daniel
9 contains the prophecy about the extended exile, at the end of
which "an anointed one shall be cut off" (v. 26), though this will
be the time "to finish the transgression, to put an end to sin, and
to atone for iniquity" (v. 24). Put these together with Daniel 7,
and the composite picture seems clearly to be the one that all four
evangelists are offering. Jesus is the true Messiah, whose inaugurated rule will overthrow the rule of the powers of the world. It
will, in other words, be the new Passover, though seen now in
the lurid colors of mythological metaphor. But it will achieve this
by putting an end to sin, which as we have frequently seen means
the ending of exile and the return of YHWH.

We have said enough to make it clear that for all four evangelists the meaning of Jesus's death is found in the big picture
of the narrative they are telling, moving as it does from Jesus's
kingdom-inaugurating work to his crucifixion, with "King of
the Jews" written above his head. They are all, in their different ways, highlighting this combination of kingdom and cross.
Luke says several times, in one way or another, that Jesus has been
the one through whom God's liberation of Israel has taken place,
even if not in the form that people at the time were expecting or
necessarily wanting. And I have suggested that within this overall
theme of the cross as the kingdom-bringing victory we see nesting the secondary but vital theme of the "forgiveness of sins," a
strand highlighted by Jesus himself on regular occasions, causing
controversy for obvious reasons.

## Representative Substitution

What I now want to suggest is that, within this larger picture,
the evangelists have also explained *how* this "forgiveness of sins,"
this "return from exile," comes about. It comes about because the

one will stand in for the many. It comes about because Jesus dies, innocently, bearing the punishment that he himself had marked out for his fellow Jews as a whole. It comes about because from the beginning Jesus was redefining the nature of the kingdom with regard to radical self-giving and self-denial, and it looks as though that was never simply an ethical demand but, at its heart, a personal vocation. It comes about because throughout his public career Jesus was redefining power itself, and his violent death was the ultimate demonstration-in-practice of that redefinition. These last four sentences have summarized some strands from John, Luke, Matthew, and Mark, and we must set out each one slightly more fully. (Each one, of course, could be expanded into a whole chapter at least. My aim here is to sketch, not to fill in all the details.)

For John, Caiaphas the high priest declares the truth, even though for him it was merely a political ploy. "Let one man die for the people, rather than the whole nation being wiped out" (11:50). John comments that Caiaphas, being high priest that year, was inspired to prophesy, even though he himself would not have seen it like that. This meant, said John, "that Jesus would die for the nation; and not only for the nation, but to gather into one the scattered children of God" (11:51–52).

This hints at the truth then articulated from another angle in chapter 12. When some Greeks come looking for Jesus, Jesus comments that when he has been "lifted up from the earth," he will "draw all people" to himself (12:32). Once the "ruler of the world" has been "cast out," then those held captive under his reign will be free. This line of thought makes sense on the assumption, rooted in Israel's scriptures, that what God does at last for Israel will have worldwide repercussions. This is the deep theological root of the Gentile mission, hitherto impossible, but now, with the defeat of the dark power, an open possibility. The servant will die for the nation, but will thereby do for the world what Israel was called to do but could not do, setting the nations free from their ancient bondage so that they can now join the single People of God. The same train of thought is visible in the First Letter of John: "The Righteous One, Jesus the Messiah . . . is the sacrifice which atones for our sins—and not ours only, either, but those of the whole world" (2:1–2). It stands behind passage after passage in Paul.

Coming back from John's letter to his gospel, there are hints and signs at various points that Jesus is taking upon himself the fate of others. John has woven this personal exchange into the larger narrative of Jesus's victory over the "ruler of the world." Thus, at the start of chapter 8, the crowd is ready to stone the adulterous woman; at the end of chapter 8 it is Jesus himself whom they want to stone. When the soldiers arrest Jesus, he insists that they let his companions go (18:8; John explains this with a reference to what Jesus had said in 17:12 about not losing any of the people the Father had given him). And all this takes place under the larger theme expressed in a striking biblical image:

> Just as Moses lifted up the snake in the desert, in the
> same way the son of man must be lifted up, so that
> everyone who believes in him may share in the life of
> God's new age. (3:14–15)

The reference is to Numbers 21:4–9, where the Israelites are being struck down by fiery serpents in response to their persistent grumbling against Moses. Moses is commanded to make a serpent of bronze and put it on a pole; anyone who was bitten by the serpents could look on it and so live. The bronze serpent thus became the sign of both the problem and God's solution to the problem. The assumptions and mythological echoes that surround both the ancient story and the way John has Jesus allude to it are not our concern. What matters is that here too we are to see the underlying problem being dealt with. The sin and death that have afflicted humankind in general are to be drawn together to one point in Jesus's going to the cross, so that all may gaze upon that event and come to realize that *their* snakebites, their sin and death, have been dealt with. And this leads directly into the best-known Johannine statement of the meaning of the entire story: "This, you see, is how much God loved the world: enough to give his only, special son, so that everyone who believes in him should not be lost but should share in the life of God's new age" (3:16). Thus for John the larger victory is achieved by means of the intimate and personal exchange in which the one dies on behalf of the many.

In Luke's gospel this is expressed in several sharply personal scenes that likewise explain the *means* through which the *goal* of the kingdom is realized. Jesus is accused of crimes that Luke's readers know he has not committed, but that are characteristic of the many revolutionary groups around at the time (23:2). He is thus to die the death of the brigand, the revolutionary, *in place of rebel Israel as a whole*. This is captured in the way Luke somewhat belabors his explanation of the "exchange" of Barabbas for Jesus:

> "Take him away!" they shouted out all together. "Release Barabbas for us!" (Barabbas had been thrown into prison because of an uprising that had taken place in the city, and for murder.) . . . Pilate gave his verdict that their request should be granted. He released the man they asked for, the one who'd been thrown into prison because of rebellion and murder, and gave Jesus over to their demands. (23:18–19, 24–25)

In case we missed the point, Luke says it again, this time through the strange conversation between the two brigands crucified alongside Jesus:

> One of the bad characters who was hanging there began to insult him. "Aren't you the Messiah?" he said. "Rescue yourself—and us, too!"

But the other one told him off. "Don't you fear God?"
he said. "You're sharing the same fate that he is! In our
case it's fair enough; we're getting exactly what we asked
for. But this fellow hasn't done anything out of order."
(23:39–41)

This time Luke takes the whole question a giant step forward.
Jesus is dying the death that others deserved and he did not. The
man who has seen that strange but powerful truth then turns to
Jesus himself:

"Jesus," he went on, "remember me when you finally
become king." (23:42)

This in turn elicits the famous response from Jesus, promising
him, as he had promised the disciples at the Last Supper, that the
kingdom would be arriving sooner than anyone had expected,
because Jesus's death would bring it about. "Paradise" here is not,
of course, the final resting place of either Jesus or the man asking the question. Nor does Jesus's "kingdom" consist in people
"going to heaven after they die," though this passage has often
been mistakenly read that way. Luke is most emphatic, in his
gospel and then over and over again in Acts, that the ultimate
destination of God's people is the resurrection. But "paradise,"
the interim state, the blissful garden of refreshment prior to that
final destination, will be won that very day for all who trust in
Jesus, because through his death, the innocent dying the death
of the guilty, the sovereign rule of God will come to birth in a
whole new way, with results as personal and intimate as they are
cosmic and global:

"I'm telling you the truth," replied Jesus, "you'll be with
me in paradise, this very day." (23:42–43)

This sequence of thought comes to its conclusion when the
centurion at the foot of the cross, watching Jesus die, insists like

the others that Jesus was innocent, was "in the right" (23:47). Against those who have insisted that Luke has no theological interpretation of the cross—because he does not include a "formulaic" or "dogmatic" statement like Mark 10:45!—we must insist that for Luke the cross does two things in particular. First, it is the means by which the powers of darkness (note again 22:53) are defeated, so that God's kingdom, his newly minted sovereign rule over the world, can at last begin. Second, this is accomplished because the innocent Jesus is dying the death of the guilty. In fact, though Luke does not have the "ransom" saying, he does include, on the lips of Jesus, a clear reference to Isaiah 53:

> Let me tell you this: when the Bible says, "He was reckoned with the lawless," it must find its fulfillment in me. Yes: everything about me must reach its goal. (22:37, quoting Isa. 53:12)

In the light of this, one can only wonder at the real agendas behind the attempts to deny Luke a theological understanding of the crucifixion.

The idea that Jesus was identifying with his fellow Jews as they faced imminent judgment is in fact inscribed into the larger narrative of Luke's gospel as a whole. Particularly from chapter 9 on, Jesus is constantly warning his people of the great disaster that is hanging over their heads. His message about God's kingdom is offering a different way, but their determination to resist the way of peace that he is advocating will lead to nothing but ruin. Yes, he says, Pilate had instigated a massacre of Galilean pilgrims in the Temple, but that event was not unique: "Unless you repent, you will all be destroyed in the same way." Eighteen people had indeed been killed when the tower in Siloam collapsed: "Unless you repent, you will all be destroyed in the same way" (13:1–5). *In the same way.* What does this mean?

Jesus is not here speaking of people ending up in "hell" (Gehenna?) after their death. That too is a reality not to be forgotten, though Jesus does not often speak of it (an exception, as we saw, is 12:5). He is speaking, rather, of Roman troops and falling buildings within Jerusalem, as he is again in the climactic warnings in 19:42–4, in his symbolic action in the Temple (19:45–46), and in his interpretation of that action in the following two chapters. Judgment is coming upon God's people as upon the tenants in the vineyard for their refusal to pay attention not just to a string of prophetic messengers, but to the owner's son himself (20:9–19). But the climax of that parable tells its own story. The owner's son, Jesus himself, will indeed be killed—and Luke has told the story in such a way as to say that in this large-scale scenario as well as the smaller ones with Barabbas and the dying brigand Jesus will take upon himself the death he had prophesied for the impenitent nation. Somehow, as in the dense and paradoxical summaries in the book of Acts, the wickedness of the people's rejection of his message will converge with the overarching saving plan of Israel's God, so that the death Jesus dies will be the death he had predicted for them.

That convergence itself speaks volumes for Luke's theology of the cross. Suddenly, reflecting on this, we find ourselves at the end of Romans 5: evil has focused itself onto one place, but where sin abounded grace super-abounded. Jesus would be like the mother hen, trying to protect the chicks at the cost of her own life (13:34). He would be the green tree, unready for the fire, but going ahead to meet the fate that was only too appropriate for the dry twigs all around him (23:31). What Luke is saying, through the whole narrative rather than through any dogma imposed upon it from outside, is that in historical reality as well as in theological interpretation the one bore the sins of the many.

We can, if we like, use the old formulas, provided we realize that they are merely shorthand for this kind of narrative. Jesus *represents* his people, as Israel's Messiah, and so he and he alone can appropriately be their *substitute*. And it is through that substitution, both national (as in the gospel as a whole) and personal (as in the exchanges in chap. 23), that the larger reality comes about. Jesus, by taking upon himself the weight of Israel's sins and thereby of the world's sins, dies under the accumulated force of evil, *so that now at last the kingdom can come in its fullness.* He had anticipated this in his public career. Now, through his royal, representative, and substitutionary death he "comes into his glory" (24:26), that is, his newly inaugurated rule over the whole world.

Matthew would not, I think, dissent from any of the above, though he has not made this theme so prominent. But what we see in Matthew, again not totally different from what we find in Luke except perhaps in emphasis, is the way the original kingdom agenda already foreshadowed the meaning of the cross. Matthew, like the others, understands the whole of Jesus's career, including his royal death, in relation to the coming of God's kingdom "on earth as in heaven." But it is perhaps Matthew who most explicitly summarizes what that kingdom looks like, how it is that God now intends to establish what we might call "theocracy" in Israel and the world.

What will it look like, when Israel's God (as opposed to any other god) becomes king? It will not be a matter of soldiers and police imposing the divine will on people by brute force. It will be through a different kind of power altogether:

> Blessings on the poor in spirit! The kingdom of heaven is yours.
>
> Blessings on the mourners! You're going to be comforted.
>
> Blessings on the meek! You're going to inherit the earth.
>
> Blessings on people who hunger and thirst for God's justice! You're going to be satisfied.
>
> Blessings on the merciful! You'll receive mercy yourselves.
>
> Blessings on the pure in heart! You will see God.

Blessings on the peacemakers! You'll be called God's children.

Blessings on people who are persecuted because of God's way! The kingdom of heaven belongs to you.

Blessings on you, when people slander you and persecute you, and say all kinds of wicked things about you falsely because of me! Celebrate and rejoice: there's a great reward for you in heaven. That's how they persecuted the prophets who went before you. (5:3–12)

This famous passage (the Beatitudes, or "Blessings") is usually read as though it is simply a promise of blessing *to* the people thus described. But a moment's thought will reveal that though this is obviously true, it is actually the second-order truth. What matters is that these are the kind of people *through* whom the kingdom will be launched. We should beware too of the usual trap of misunderstanding "heaven" here. The "kingdom of heaven" is Matthew's way of saying "kingdom of God," and as Matthew himself makes clear in both the Lord's prayer (6:10) and the final claim of the risen Jesus (28:18) God's kingdom is not a place called "heaven," detached from "earth," but *the rule of heaven coming to birth on earth.* Thus the "great reward in heaven" promised in v. 12 does not mean that people will get that reward when they "go to heaven." It means that a great reward is stored up safely in God's Presence until the time of its unveiling on earth.

In any case, the key thing about so many of these "blessings" is that they demonstrate the way in which God's kingdom will actually be put into operation: *through* the poor in spirit, the mourners, the meek, the justice-hungry people, the merciful, the pure in heart, the peacemakers, the people who are prepared to face persecution and slander because of their commitment to the way Jesus is pioneering. Some of these characteristics are more obviously "active"—the justice-hungry people, the merciful, the peacemakers—but the entire package is what matters. God's sovereign rule will come to birth through people like this. They will learn to be the salt of the earth, the light of the world (5:13–16). They will learn the way of forgiveness and reconciliation (5:21–26), the way of purity (5:27–32), the way of truthfulness (5:33–27). And, in particular, as chapter 5 comes to its climax, they will learn the way of nonviolence, the way of love for enemies and prayer for persecutors (5:38–48). They will turn the other cheek; they will go the second mile; they will allow someone to strip them of both shirt and cloak. And they will thereby demonstrate that they truly are children of their Father in heaven (5:39, 41, 40, 45).

Among the dozens of other things that Matthew is saying in his gospel, it seems beyond doubt that he is highlighting the point that the kingdom agenda set out in chapter 5 is not simply an outline for a bracing ethic for Jesus's followers to attempt; it is the dramatic outline of Jesus's own vocation. He would stand there unresisting as people slapped him and mocked him. He would be compelled by the Roman soldiers to carry his burden all the way to Golgotha. He would find his clothes stripped off him and divided up. And, as he died, one of those very soldiers would declare that he really was the son of God (26:67; 27:30–32, 35, 54). These echoes cannot be accidental. They express part at least of what Matthew wants to say about both the kingdom and the cross.

Jesus's suffering and death are indeed, for Matthew, the means through which God is becoming king, through which "all authority" is being given to Jesus himself. This will set the pattern not just for a "new ethic," though it will be that, but for a new kind of behavior, a new lifestyle, *through which the saving rule of God will be brought to bear upon the world.* And it will come about through Jesus's unique kingdom vocation, through his taking upon himself the scorn, malevolence, and hatred of the world, in order to do what, in the last analysis, only Emmanuel himself can do. The long story of Israel, sketched by Matthew in terms of the genealogy from Abraham to David, through the exile, to the Messiah, has come to its fulfillment. This is how the saving plan of Israel's God has been put into effect. Israel has borne the fate of the world; the Messiah has borne the fate of Israel; through his death the Herods and Pilates of the world are called to account; and the reign of God—characterized still by those Beatitudes as they are lived out in the lives of Jesus's followers—has come to birth.

Mark, finally, is the one evangelist normally credited with an explicit "atonement theology"—mostly on the basis of one verse, often taken right out of context. When we put it back in its place, it does indeed offer a striking interpretation of the death that Jesus is going to suffer in Jerusalem. But it does so as part of a much larger whole. Once again the pattern of that larger whole and of the specific focus of the verse in question support the argument I am making throughout. Jesus's death is seen, right across the New Testament, not as rescuing people *from* the world so that they can avoid "hell" and go to "heaven," but as a powerful revolution—that is, a revolution full of a new sort of power—*within* the world itself.

Here is the passage in question. James and John have presented their request (in the parallel in Matthew, they get their mother to do it for them). They want to sit on either side of Jesus, one on his right and the other on his left, when Jesus is "there in all [his] glory" (Mark 10:37)—in other words, when Jesus becomes king in Jerusalem, having overthrown all the earthly powers that stand in his way. They are still living within a straightforwardly first-century Jewish picture of the coming "kingdom of God," which Jesus's redefinitions throughout the story have done nothing to change. They are expecting Jesus to be installed as king (perhaps after some great battle?), at which point he will need not only a "right-hand man," but also a "left-hand man." He will need loyal, trusted colleagues who will share a measure of his authority, and no doubt also reap the appropriate rewards.

We may suspect that this was (among other things) something of a power play. Peter, presented in all the gospels as Jesus's closest associate, had a brother, Andrew, and they might be supposed to be the natural people to occupy the positions of greatest responsibility in any coming kingdom. James and John are getting in first.

But all this jockeying for position misses the point entirely. First, the kingdom is not going to come the way they expect. Jesus has a baptism with which to be baptized (10:38), an allusion it seems to the suffering he will experience for which his baptism at the start of the gospel story was an advance signpost. He also has a "cup" to drink, an allusion to the vocation, which comes into sharp focus in the later scene in the Garden of Gethsemane (14:36); he must drain to the dregs the "cup of the wrath of God" so that his people won't have to drink it (see particularly Jer. 25:15–17; 49:12; 51:7; Lam. 4:21). It is striking that though "baptism" is associated with Jesus's death in one or two passages in the New Testament (Romans 8 and Colossians 2 come to mind), the idea of the "cup" seems to belong only to the traditions about Jesus we find in the gospels.

In any case, James and John appear to interpret these cryptic warnings as applying to a great coming battle or struggle, and they assure him that they can share that too. Jesus admits that they may indeed face great suffering themselves (10:39). But, as the irony in the passage mounts higher and higher, Jesus warns them that sitting at his right and his left "in his glory" is not his to grant. Those positions have already been assigned (10:40). Only as Mark's story reaches its grisly end do readers realize what is meant. James and John have been asking for the places at Jesus's right and left so as to accompany him *as he completes the glorious work of bringing in God's kingdom,* defeating all the powers that have held the human race captive. But those places are reserved for the two who are crucified alongside him as he hangs there with "King of the Jews" above his head.

Can this really be Mark's meaning? Emphatically, yes. Here is how it works out. Jesus's death accomplishes God's kingdom, *be-*

*cause he is giving his life in the place of sinners, as "a ransom for many."* Jesus explains this by describing two radically different sorts of power:

> You know how it is in the pagan nations. Think how their so-called rulers act. They lord it over their subjects. The high and mighty ones boss the rest around. But that's not how it's going to be with you. Anyone who wants to be great among you must become your servant. Anyone who wants to be first must be everyone's slave. Don't you see? The son of man didn't come to be waited on. He came to be the servant, to give his life "as a ransom for many." (10:42–45)

Here we see the full integration of what have seemed to subsequent generations to be two key elements of the meaning of Jesus's crucifixion. A new sort of power will be let loose upon the world, and it will be the power of self-giving love. This is the heart of the revolution that was launched on Good Friday. You cannot defeat the usual sort of power by the usual sort of means. If one force overcomes another, it is still "force" that wins. Rather, at the heart of the victory of God over all the powers of the world there lies self-giving love, which, in obedience to the ancient prophetic vocation, will give its life "as a ransom for many." Exactly as in Isaiah 53, to which that phrase alludes, the death of the one on behalf of the many will be the key by which the powers are overthrown, the kingdom of God ushered in (with the glorious divine Presence seen in plain sight by the watchmen on Jerusalem's walls), the covenant renewed, and creation itself restored to its original purpose.

Mark 10:35–45 contains within itself more or less the whole of the New Testament's complex but coherent vision of how Jesus's death, completing his vocation as Israel's Messiah, overthrew the dark powers that had enslaved the world by coming to take the place of sinners. The new Passover was accomplished by the new exile-ending "forgiveness of sins," and the latter was accomplished through the one taking the place of the many. If we were to summarize what Mark has now told us, in both this passage (though we have not had time to follow it through) and his gospel as a whole, we might just as well say that "the Messiah died for our sins in accordance with the Bible."

This, of course, points us to Paul, where we find that summary both stated and expounded. But, before we get there, some final reflections are in order on the death of Jesus in the gospels.

First, it is vital to see that Matthew, Mark, Luke, and John are not simply telling us in descriptive language something that "really" belongs as a dogmatic formula. It is the other way around. The formula is a portable narrative, a folded-up story. The story is the reality—because it is the story *of* reality, historical reality, flesh-and-blood reality, Israel's reality, life-and-death reality. The Platonizing tendency in Christian theology, because of which the *goal* of "atonement" has been seen not as God's kingdom coming on earth as in heaven, but as God's people being rescued from earth and taken to heaven instead, has also taught us by implication to shrink the meaning of the gospel narratives so that they become mere vehicles for displaying something else, *illustrations* of the "truth" rather than *expositions* of it, of the way in which, in John's version, "the Word became flesh."

As far as the four evangelists are concerned, then, the meaning of Jesus's death is not a theological theme to be abstracted from this narrative or superimposed upon it. The meaning of Jesus's death is not a "heavenly" truth for which this "earthly" story is simply a distant analogy or "type." Nor is the actual historical story merely the backdrop against which a "supernatural" or nonhistorical drama is acted out. The marginalization of the four gospels within much normal "atonement" theology is not simply an accident. It is the direct, long-term result of the way in which "atonement" has been seen as a transaction taking place, as it were, in midair, with results that likewise are only tangentially related to actual human life, to the ongoing human story.

The "goal" has been seen as the distant one of "going to heaven," and since the gospels are not basically talking about that (though they are of course aware of the ultimate postmortem future), but about the kingdom of God coming on earth as in heaven, they have been set aside, being only occasionally mined for the odd saying that, taken out of context, appears to serve the goal that later theology has had in view. The result, as we have seen, has been the moralization of the human vocation and the paganizing of atonement theology. A sentence like Mark 10:45, with its allusion to Isaiah 53, has been taken out of context and made to serve the "works contract" rather than the "covenant of vocation," in which, right across the Bible, sins are dealt with so that humans can be set free to become image-bearers, part of the larger purposes of the creator God. The vision of the cross in all four gospels does not allow us to rest content with a detached, ahistorical understanding of either the kingdom or atonement.

Second, therefore, even before we get to Paul, we find the challenge of the cross reaching us in quite new ways. It is indeed revolutionary. Nothing is lost. We do not (of course!) have to give up the idea of Jesus "dying for our sins." Indeed, that remains at the very center. But that idea is refocused, recontextualized, placed within a narrative not of divine petulance, but of unbreakable divine covenant love, embodied in the actual person, life, actions, and teaching of Jesus himself. This means that in order to appropriate this for ourselves, to benefit from this story, it is not simply a matter of believing a particular abstract doctrine, this or that theory of how "atonement" might be thought to "work." No doubt that can help, though with the abstractions can come distortions, as we have seen.

No, the gospels invite us to *make this story our own,* to live within the narrative in all its twists and turns, to see ourselves among the crowds following Jesus and witnessing his kingdom-bringing work, to see ourselves also in the long-range continuation of that narrative that we call, in fear and trembling (because we know its deep ambiguities), the life of the church. In particular, as followers of Jesus from the very beginning have known, we are to make the story our own by the repeated meals in which the Last Supper is brought to life once more. If that was how Jesus wanted his followers not only to understand, but also to appropriate for themselves the meaning of the death he was to die, there is every reason to take it seriously as the sign and foretaste of the eventual kingdom, carrying within it the assurance that we too are those who share in the "forgiveness of sins." And, with that, the gospels give to those who read them the energy and the sense of direction to be Beatitude people for the world, knowing that the victory was indeed won on the cross, that Jesus is indeed already installed as the world's rightful ruler, and that his way of peace and reconciliation has been shown to be more powerful than all the powers of the world.

There is one particular moment in the gospel stories as told by Matthew and Mark to which we must return, because only in the light of the fuller picture can we begin to address it in all its complexity. This is the so-called cry of dereliction in Matthew 27:46 and Mark 15:34: "My God, my God, why did you abandon me?" I have stressed that all four evangelists saw Jesus as the living embodiment of YHWH himself, Israel's God, and that they saw his kingdom-bringing achievement, up to and climactically including his death on the cross, as the achievement of the one God himself. This was not about a human being trying to twist God's arm, as in the famous illustration (used by Albert Schweitzer) of Jesus throwing himself on the wheel of history and making it turn in the opposite direction. It was about the Lord of history coming in person, in the person who represented the promise-bearing people, to do what had to be done. How then can this embodied God cry out to "my God" that he has been abandoned? When we return to this question we will, I believe, be able not only to answer it, but to show how that answer works its way out into the life and work of the followers of Jesus in the often dark realities and challenges of the world.

# 11

---

# Paul and the Cross
# (Apart from Romans)

WHEN PEOPLE WONDER about the meaning of Jesus's death and go to the New Testament for clues, they normally turn to Paul. And Paul has plenty to offer them—too much, one might think. Hardly a page goes by in Paul without some reference to Jesus's death. A quick glance through his letters produces a bewildering range of imagery: the Messiah as the Passover lamb; as the sin offering; as the curse-bearer; as the one who "loved me and gave himself for me"; as the one who was "made to be sin for us"; as the one who "was rich, yet because of [us] . . . became poor"; as the glorious victor over the "rulers and authorities"; as the "place of mercy" (if that is the right translation of *hilastērion* in Rom. 3:25); and much more. If only, we sigh, he had said it just once and said it clearly. Or if only he had said it several times and always in just the same way.

Of course, it is possible to pull Paul into shape—our shape, all too often. We can set up a single scheme, as often as not the great penal substitution scheme beloved of those who embrace the "works contract." Just the other day I received a long e-mail from a man previously unknown to me, setting out in great detail an entire theological scheme based on the idea of "imputation," in which our sin is "imputed" to Jesus and his righteousness is "imputed" to us. The theory was laid out with copious references to learned writers from the nineteenth and early twentieth centuries and one or two of their more recent exponents as well. Within such a scheme more or less everything can be made to work, much as in a politician's speech, where all the awkward bits of evidence that don't quite support the party line can be either twisted into shape or quietly swept to one side. Thus sacrificial language (it is usually assumed) can be about "penal substitution," since, it is thought, the animal would be killed as punishment for the sins of the worshipper. Victory over the powers can be a dramatic way of saying that we are freed from the power as well as the guilt and penalty of our sins. And so on. But, like an intelligent audience at a political rally, careful readers of Paul may well conclude that in this scheme we have been told only one story, and that this story, though it may contain a powerful truth, is being distorted by not being displayed in relation to all the other stories with which it belongs and in relation to which it gains its true meaning.

What I want to do in this chapter is not, of course, to expound every single one of Paul's dozens of references to the cross. That would take a whole book in itself. Debating with rival interpretations of such passages would take at least another one after that. I shall try, instead, to show from some central passages that Paul, like Jesus himself, like the gospels themselves, was saying from a number of different angles and in a variety of different contexts the two things that together comprise the larger picture the early Christians had grasped.

First, Paul shared the early Christian vision of the *goal* of redemption. Humans were to be saved not for "heaven" (Paul never mentions that as the goal) or simply "to be with God forever" (that, though no doubt true, was not the point), but for the new creation. They were to share in the royal and priestly human work within both the present world and the world that was to be. Great wrath would come upon the present world; those who belonged to Jesus would be rescued from it for the new creation that would be born (Rom. 5:9; 1 Thess. 1:10).

Second, that goal would be attained *by means of* the death of Jesus, through which the powers of sin and death were defeated. That defeat was accomplished through the dying "for sins" of Jesus, Israel's Messiah: Jesus, representing Israel and the world, took upon himself the full force of the divine condemnation of Sin itself, so that all those "in him" would not suffer it themselves.

These two points are, I think, utterly secure. And, like any exposition of Paul, this one will fail unless it looks beyond the normal "goal" ("escaping hell" or "going to heaven") to the goal that Paul himself had in mind: that in the "covenant of vocation" humans who found salvation in Jesus the Messiah would become active participants, free from the lure and drag of the dark forces that had previously prevented this, within the work of new creation here and now. For Paul, the death of Jesus had emphatic *past* consequences, but those who realized that and who celebrated it as the ultimate revelation of divine love would by that very realization find themselves renewed and summoned to the life of holiness and unity, suffering and mission, that was at the heart of the vocation of the church in the first century as it is today.

We begin, though, with the various Pauline formulas that draw together the larger narrative into its pocket-size version. We have several times repeated 1 Corinthians 15:3 and pointed out that when you put that slogan into its first-century context, it appears in quite a different light from the ways in which it is commonly read today: "The Messiah died for our sins in accordance with the Bible." The natural first port of call in understanding this phrase is the biblical account of the "sins" of Israel through which the nation, supposedly bearing the promises and purposes of the creator God for his whole creation, had gone into exile, an exile that had continued, in the sense the prophets had articulated it, to the first century. The larger context of 1 Corinthians 15 makes it clear that the achievement of the cross, "dying for sins in accordance with the Bible," was then to be seen as the kingdom-establishing event, winning the initial decisive victory, which would be complete at the resurrection. And this summary is reflected in other one-line statements within longer arguments: one thinks of 1 Thessalonians 5:10 ("He died for us, so that whether we stay awake or go to sleep we should live together with him") or Romans 14:8–9 ("Whether we live or whether we die, we belong to the Lord. That is why the Messiah died and came back to life, so that he might be Lord of both the dead and the living"). Paul can appeal to the same point within a complex argument: "And so, you see, the weak person—a brother or sister for whom the Messiah died!—is then destroyed by your 'knowledge'" (1 Cor. 8:11). Paul can take for granted that all the people to whom he writes have the belief in the Messiah's death "for them" as part of their basic Christian identity.

There are other brief formulations that spell out the basic point a bit more. The opening summaries of letters often provide a strong clue as to the argument to come, and Galatians is no exception. In Galatians 1:4 Paul declares that Jesus, the Messiah, our Lord, "gave himself for our sins, to rescue us from the present evil age, according to the will of God our father." Or, to put it in the language of the biblical narrative to which Paul will appeal frequently in Galatians, the new Passover (liberation from the enslaving powers) is accomplished through the rescue from exile ("for our sins"), and all has taken place in fulfillment of the age-old divine purpose ("according to the will of God").

We will return to Galatians presently. Before we do so, it is worth noting in the same connection the repeated references to the death of Jesus in the opening passages of 1 Corinthians. Nowhere here does Paul explain *why* or *how* the cross of the Messiah has the power it does, but he seems able to assume that and to incorporate this assumption into a rhetorically powerful appeal:

The word of the cross, you see, is madness to people
who are being destroyed. But to us—those who are
being saved—it is God's power. . . . Jews look for signs,
you see, and Greeks search for wisdom; but we announce
the crucified Messiah, a scandal to Jews and folly to Gentiles, but to those who are called, Jews and Greeks alike,
the Messiah—God's power and God's wisdom. God's
folly is wiser than humans, you see, and God's weakness
is stronger than humans. (1:18, 22–25)

This then undergirds the otherwise curious and almost inexpli-
cable reference, in the next chapter, to the assumed victory of the
cross over the powers of the world:

We do, however, speak wisdom among the mature. But
this isn't a wisdom of this present world, or of the rulers
of this present world—those same rulers who are being
done away with. No: we speak God's hidden wisdom
in a mystery. This is the wisdom God prepared ahead of
time, before the world began, for our glory.

None of the rulers of this present age knew about this
wisdom. If they had, you see, they wouldn't have crucified the Lord of glory. (2:6–8)

Paul's implication here, though he does not explain it, is
that the crucifixion of Jesus of Nazareth somehow overthrew
the power of the "rulers," echoing perhaps the second stage of
Galatians 1:4 ("to rescue us from the present evil age") and
certainly anticipating the dense statement of Colossians 2:15
("God . . . stripped the rulers and authorities of their armor, and
displayed them contemptuously to public view, celebrating his
triumph over them in [Jesus]"). The main point to note from
these brief references is that Paul can assume that all those to
whom he writes are familiar with the very early traditions in
which such ideas have crystallized and that presumably he or

his colleagues have explained to the early converts, at least to some extent.

In particular, we must assume that for Paul it was certainly not a matter of ransacking his biblically stocked memory or his culturally aware mind for miscellaneous images, metaphors, and models to which he could refer more or less at random. Doubtless he was aware of the non-Jewish meanings of someone "dying for" someone else or for some cause, and doubtless he was aware of the dangers of saying what had to be said in such a way as to give credence to the idea of a detached, capricious, or malevolent divinity demanding blood, longing to kill someone, and happening to light upon a convenient innocent victim. That he could nonetheless go on saying that "the Messiah died for our sins" has a lot to do with the qualifying phrase "in accordance with the Bible," and as we expounded the possible meanings and implications of this earlier, we need say no more about it here. But for Paul it was crucial.

The vital nature of this biblical background was also highlighted in Paul's repeated insistence that the one who died was Israel's Messiah. The Messiahship of Jesus has not been a major theme in Pauline studies over the last century or two, and this state of affairs has meant a failure to grasp a central feature. Such an omission goes with the downplaying of the overall Jewish and biblically oriented way Paul's mind worked, the way he saw the larger storyline of Adam and Abraham, of Moses and the monarchy and the extended exile. Of course, within modern Western expectations, such things are largely irrelevant, just so many "noises-off" that might distract us from the supposed central task of explaining how the punishment of our sins was heaped onto the innocent victim, so that his successful performance of the "works of the law" might be "imputed" to us—the standard "works contract," which needs neither the actual biblical covenant theology nor the actual narrative in which that theology was so often expressed in Paul's world.

If we refuse to see Paul's Jesus as Israel's Messiah, we shall never understand what Paul understands to have taken place in his death. But once we grasp this point, all sorts of things that otherwise jar and jangle against one another can come together in a new and coherent whole—and can challenge us, even now, with the large-scale and worldwide implications of what Paul was actually talking about, as opposed to what the church has so often imagined he was talking about. This is revolutionary theology indeed. Paul was not merely offering a miscellany of metaphors as a way of saying that Jesus really did die for our sins. He was offering the dramatic and shocking resolution of biblical narrative, generating a new world in which those who are grasped by Jesus's death have a whole new set of tasks lying open before them.

Among those tasks—to quote the last of the short formulas I want to put on the table from the start—is the vexed challenge of the unity of all who follow Jesus. It is noticeable that where, in the last four hundred years or so, Christians have shrunk the meaning of Jesus's death to the level of a formula for how sinners can go to heaven, less and less weight has been put on what for Paul mattered vitally:

> The Messiah became a servant of the circumcised people
> in order to demonstrate the truthfulness of God—that is,
> to confirm the promises to the patriarchs, and to bring
> the nations to praise God for his mercy. As the Bible says,
> "That is why I will praise you among the nations, and
> will sing to your name." (Rom. 15:8–9)

That introduces other themes again. The Messiah as "servant" remains the clue. He has brought to its appointed goal the destiny of Abraham's people not so that they could escape the world and go to heaven, but so that they could be part of a worldwide people of praise. United worship here and now, rather than disunited church life in the present and a distant "heaven" after death, was always, as far as Paul was concerned, the divinely intended goal of the Messiah's death.

## Galatians

The theme of unity is nowhere more clearly displayed than in the much-misunderstood Letter to the Galatians. Despite the repeated assumptions of students, professors, and church people alike, Galatians is not about "salvation": neither that word, nor "save," nor "savior" is found in the letter. The idea of "salvation" is, of course, assumed, as we see through the many parallels with Romans, where "salvation" is a major theme and the words for it occur regularly. But the central argument of Galatians has nothing to do with "how to get saved." To assume that it does—let alone to assume that the normal "works contract" is the proper framework for answering that question—is to miss the whole point of the letter, to force Paul's language to say what it does not say and therefore (equally importantly) to prevent it from saying what it *does* say.

The letter is about *unity:* the fact that in the Messiah, particularly through his death, the one God has done what he promised Abraham all along. He has given him *a single family in which believing Jews and believing Gentiles form one body.* What Paul says about the cross in Galatians is all aimed toward this end: because of the cross, all believers are on the same footing. And if that is the "goal" of the cross in Galatians, we will gain a much better idea of the "means." As elsewhere in this book, our task is to rescue the "goal" from Platonizing "going to heaven" interpretations and the "means" from paganizing "angry God punishing Jesus" interpretations—and so to transform the normal perception of what "atonement theology" might be from a dark and possibly unpleasant mystery to an energizing and highly relevant unveiling of truth.

"Unveiling of truth" is in fact what Galatians is all about. For Paul, the messianic events of Jesus's death and resurrection (though, like "salvation," the resurrection is scarcely mentioned here) are all about disclosing the victory that the one God won, through Jesus, over the "powers" that had kept the non-Jewish nations enslaved to their own pseudo-divinities and had likewise kept the Jews themselves enslaved under the power of sin. As always, when Paul and other biblical writers talk about people being set free from slavery, they are echoing the Passover story, the Exodus narrative. This is no exception. But before we get to that point, which is in fact the very center of the letter, we should look briefly at the beginning and end. It is clear that the death of the Messiah is driving the argument throughout.

First, to repeat, we have the opening statement:

> Grace to you and peace from God our father and Jesus the Messiah, our Lord, who gave himself for our sins, to rescue us from the present evil age, according to the will of God our father. (1:3–4)

This, as is often pointed out, draws together the two strands of meaning available in the great Jewish narratives as we set them out earlier. "For our sins" corresponds to the forgiveness and return from exile strand, which then drives the "new Passover" strand. And the "new Passover" is all about release not from political enslavement under pagan empires, as in the original Exodus, but from the ultimate enslavement under the force of Sin as a power; Sin here is, perhaps (as in Rom. 7), standing in for the ultimate enemy, the satan, the accuser. In any case, what Paul says in this brief opening belongs on the map of standard Jewish eschatology, in which time was divided into the "present age," in which the world was still out of joint, and the "age to come," in which God would deliver the world and his people from all the various evil entailments of the "present age." This, Paul declares, has happened through the death of Jesus, and it has happened because the death of Jesus was "for our sins."

Balancing this, at the end of the letter we have another statement that, like the opening one, joins together the deeply personal meaning and the worldwide meaning (which some have called "cosmic") of the cross. The whole letter has held these together, and now Paul sums them both up:

> As for me, God forbid that I should boast—except in
> the cross of our Lord Jesus the Messiah, through whom
> the world has been crucified to me and I to the world.
> Circumcision, you see, is nothing; neither is uncircumci-
> sion! What matters is new creation. Peace and mercy on
> everyone who lines up by that standard—yes, on God's
> Israel. (6:14–16)

All this only makes sense, of course, if in the resurrection the new age has clearly come to birth. Jesus's crucifixion by itself could never have carried meanings like this, as Paul explains in 1 Corinthians 15:17: unless the Messiah has been raised, "you are still in your sins," not just because "you personally" might not have experienced forgiveness, but because the world as a whole had not turned its long-awaited corner. This is the point underlying these opening and closing statements: that the new world has come to birth; that the death of Jesus, as Israel's Messiah, was the means of abolishing the power of the old world; and that those who belong to Jesus are now part of the "new creation," "God's Israel." (That latter phrase is controversial, since many readers have resisted the implication that Paul would use the word "Israel" to refer to the whole people of Israel's Messiah, whether they were Jewish or non-Jewish. But the interpretation I have given seems clearly in line with the thought of the letter as a whole.)

The whole argument of the letter—that Gentile Jesus believers are full members already in the single family promised to Abraham and that therefore they should in no circumstances think of getting circumcised—is held together within these bookends. Paul clearly has in mind a temporal scheme in which the Mosaic law was designed to serve its God-given purpose for a deliberately

limited time, a kind of long bracket between the original promise
to Abraham and the fulfillment of that promise in the messianic
creation of the single family. This temporary period, like Israel's
sojourn in Egypt, was a form of slavery shared by Israel and the
non-Israelite nations alike. But the center of the letter is a compressed Passover narrative designed exactly to deal with this situation of total human slavery. The divine initiative to send both
Jesus and the Spirit was the action that turned the corner, bringing the world as a whole and the Messiah's people in particular
into the new world in which the power of evil had been dealt a
fatal blow:

> When we were children, we were kept in "slavery"
> under the "elements of the world." But when the fullness
> of time arrived, God sent out his son, born of a woman,
> born under the law, so that he might redeem those under
> the law, so that we might receive adoption as sons.
>
> And, because you are sons, God sent out the spirit of
> his son into our hearts, calling out "Abba, Father!" So
> you are no longer a slave, but a son! And, if you're a son,
> you are an heir, through God. (4:3–7)

The cross is not mentioned specifically in this passage. But the
close analogies with other similar passages make it clear that when
Paul talks about the "son of God" "redeeming" those under the
law, we are right to hear this as a reference to the crucifixion. This
is the heart of the matter: that in a "new Exodus" (the passage is
full of Exodus overtones), God has brought his plan to its long-
promised fruition (the "fullness of time"), so that now all those
who were enslaved, Jew and Gentile alike, can be welcomed as
"sons" (Israel as "son of God" is another Exodus allusion).

One more Exodus note: this action involves the fresh revelation of God himself, now to be seen as the God who sends the
Son and the Spirit of the Son. Therefore, Paul asks, "Now that
you've come to know God—or, better, to be known *by* God—

how can you turn back again to that weak and poverty-stricken lineup of elements that you want to serve all over again?" (4:9). In other words, those who have come to faith in Jesus the Messiah have come into a full knowledge of the one true God through seeing his revelation in action in his Son and his Spirit. But if they then get circumcised, they will be denying that this new revelation has happened; they will be pretending that the new age has not been inaugurated, and they will merely be wanting to find a slightly different way of continuing to live in the same old age they were in before. And the point for our purposes is that the cross of the Messiah has made all the difference. That is how the old age has been "crucified," and they to it, as Paul says of himself in 6:14—and, as we shall see, in 2:19–20.

But how has this "new Passover" come about? The answer, as we might have expected from someone steeped in the scriptural narratives, is "through God's dealing with the problem of ongoing exile." As we have seen all along in the present book, these two strands run together in the messianic events concerning Jesus. Passover takes precedence—it was, after all, the ultimate divine rescue operation and the ultimate revelation of God in action—but, granted the exilic state of Israel, "forgiveness of sins" needed to happen for this new Passover to take effect. And that is exactly what has happened:

> Those who belong to the "works-of-the-law" camp are
> under a curse! Yes, that's what the Bible says: "Cursed
> is everyone who doesn't stick fast by everything written
> in the book of the law, to perform it." . . . The Messiah
> redeemed us from the curse of the law, by becoming a
> curse on our behalf, as the Bible says: "Cursed is every-
> one who hangs on a tree." This was so that the blessing
> of Abraham could flow through to the nations in King
> Jesus—and so that we might receive the promise of the
> spirit, through faith." (3:10, 13–14)

Paul's exposition here is dense and allusive (and would be even more so if we included vv. 11–12), but the clue is found in the quotations cited here. They come from Deuteronomy 27. That is the passage in which Moses sets out the covenant stipulations before the people of Israel enter the promised land—and the stipulations turn into warnings, which turn into prophecies. Deuteronomy isn't thinking simply of individuals who do bad things and so incur punishment. Nor is the book proposing a regular cycle that goes around and around from curse to forgiveness and blessing and back to curse again, though no doubt such cycles are visible in scripture, for instance in the book of Judges. Deuteronomy, on the contrary, envisages a single narrative, and the book was read in that way in the first century. Israel *as a whole* will rebel, will disobey, will worship idols; and Israel as a whole will therefore incur the ultimate curse—of exile from the land, the long-range biblical equivalent to Adam and Eve's expulsion from the garden. Then, eventually, there will be restoration. But how will it come about, and what will it look like?

The problem this generates is not simply a problem for Israel itself. It was bad enough for the Israelites, as the psalmists complained: "How could we sing YHWH's song in a foreign land?" (Ps. 137:4). But Deuteronomy came of course at the close of the Pentateuch, the foundation charter for Israel; and the opening of Israel's history, the call of Abraham, had always envisaged a glorious future not just for Israel, but for the whole world. What then would happen to the blessing held out for all the nations from Genesis onwards? It is as though the delivery van, commissioned to take an urgent message to a town far away, had become stuck in a snowdrift through the driver's own culpable negligence. The point is not just that the van is stuck and the driver isolated and helpless; the problem is that the message is not getting through.

This explains what Paul means when he says that the reason that the "curse" fell on Jesus and was therefore exhausted was "so that the blessing of Abraham could flow through to the nations in King Jesus." He does not say, as many have said in expounding this passage, either that the law was wrong to pronounce the "curse" or that the purpose of Jesus's bearing the "curse" was that people in general could now be forgiven their individual sin. That, he would have said, is of course important, but it is not the point being made in this argument, which is about the single family God promised to Abraham and the way in which that family has now been created.

The passage, then, declares that the "exile" is over—because the "curse" has fallen on the Messiah himself, the single representative of Israel, and has thereby been exhausted. To use traditional language for a moment, this is undoubtedly "penal" (you can't get more "penal" than the Deuteronomic curse), and it is undoubtedly "substitutionary" (the Messiah's accursed death means that others are no longer under the curse). But this form of "penal substitution" has little or nothing to do with the narrative in which that theory is normally found. *That* narrative says the oblique language of the scripture passages being quoted is just a roundabout way of saying, "We sinned, God punished Jesus, and we are all right again." *That* narrative says that in Deuteronomy Israel is a mere example of humans being given a moral challenge, failing it, and needing to be rescued. Those are just attempts to smuggle a "works contract" into this passage—and doing so results in distortion of every line. *This* passage is about the "covenant of vocation," here specifically *Israel's* vocation, the seed-of-Abraham vocation, to be the means of blessing for the world. The curse has been borne; the blessing can now flow to the nations; and Jews themselves, the "we" at the end of the verse, can now receive the sure sign of covenant renewal, the down payment on the full "inheritance," namely, the Spirit.

Galatians 3:1–14 thus focuses on the achievement of the cross in undoing the Deuteronomic "curse of exile." This passage makes it clear that this happens through the *representative* work of the Messiah, who, because he *is* Israel's representative, can therefore appropriately act as *substitute*. Again, I use the traditional language in case the point is not clear; but what matters far more, I think, is the way in which this passage, in which the death of Jesus solves the problem of "exile," relates directly to the larger theme of the new Passover in 4:1–11. It is exactly as given in the summary of 1:4: the Messiah "gave himself for our sins" (corresponding to 3:10–14) "to deliver us from the present evil age" (corresponding to 4:1–11). The two go precisely together. The one is the means to the other.

The *goal*, over against the Platonizing distortions, is the fulfillment of the promise to Abraham to give the worldwide inheritance (see Rom. 4:13) to his entire single family. The *problem* is not the general problem of human sin or indeed of the death that it incurs. The problem is that God made promises not only to Abraham but through Abraham to the world, and if the promise-bearing people fall under the Deuteronomic curse, as Deuteronomy itself insists that they will, the promises cannot get out to the wider world. The *means* is then that Jesus, as Israel's Messiah, bears Israel's curse in order to undo the consequences of sin and "exile" and so to break the power of the "present evil age" once and for all. When sins are forgiven, the "powers" are robbed of their power. Once we understand how the biblical narrative actually works, so as to see the full force of saying that "the Messiah died for our sins in accordance with the Bible," the admittedly complex passage can be seen to be fully coherent.

Paul has already summed all this up in one of his most memorable statements of the effect of Jesus's death in chapter 2. The long autobiographical opening to the letter (much of chaps. 1–2 is Paul's own story, highlighting the points of special relevance to the urgent problem in Galatia) reaches its climax with the confrontation in Antioch, where Paul opposed Peter for his church-dividing behavior. Peter, anxious about the impression given to visitors from Jerusalem when they saw him eating alongside Messiah-believing but uncircumcised non-Jews, had separated himself from the Gentiles. We must, it seems, assume that this resulted in the Jewish believers eating at one table (or perhaps in one room) and the non-Jewish believers eating somewhere else. Since the unity of the church has not until comparatively recently been a topic of apparent urgency in modern Western Christianity, this passage has been read as though it is about something else, perhaps about the mechanism of "salvation." But Paul's emphasis is on the fact that the Messiah has one family, not two, and that to deny this is to deny the gospel itself, to suggest that the Messiah did not need to be crucified.

To make this point, Paul takes himself as the example of what happens when someone comes to be "in the Messiah." He is not describing "his own experience" as though it was special or as though it set a standard of "spiritual experience" that others ought to imitate. He is describing what is true of himself, as a Jew who has come to believe that Jesus is Israel's Messiah, in order to make it clear to Peter and anyone else listening, and now also to the Galatians as they hear this letter, that the Messiah's death and resurrection have the effect of putting to death *all* earlier identities as belonging to the "present evil age" and of creating a new identity in which all previous identities are left behind:

> Through the law I died to the law, so that I might live to God. I have been crucified with the Messiah. I am, however, alive—but it isn't me any longer; it's the Messiah who lives in me. And the life I do still live in the flesh, I live within the faithfulness of the son of God, who loved me and gave himself for me. (2:19–20)

We should not miss the strong resonance in the final decisive and climactic phrase of the first phrase of Galatians 1:4: "who gave himself for our sins." Nor should we miss the equally emphatic sequel: if one could belong to God's people simply by observing the Jewish law—as Peter was implying by his behavior and as the Galatians would be implying if they were to get circumcised—then the Messiah would not have needed to die (2:21). Paul's whole logic is working outward from the central messianic events. If Jesus has been raised from the dead, then he really is God's Messiah (Rom. 1:3–4); but if he really was and is God's Messiah, then his death was not simply a shameful tragedy, but rather a saving triumph, or rather *the* ultimate saving triumph. And if, with that death, exile was over, "forgiveness of sins" was a new reality etched into the cosmos itself, and the ancient enslaving "powers" had been defeated once and for all in the "new Passover"—why, then, the important thing was to live within and celebrate that new world, not go rushing back to the old one where sin and death still held sway and where Jews and Gentiles ate at separate tables.

Here we see, in particular, how for Paul the Messiah's death was intimately linked to the main thrust of the letter, namely, the inclusion of non-Jews in the family promised to Abraham without their needing to get circumcised. We can note the three main points once more. First, the event has occurred by which God has declared the "present evil age" null and void and has launched the "age to come," so that the powers of the "present evil age," *which are the powers that had previously held people captive,* have no longer any right to keep them prisoner. The new Passover means that all slaves are now offered freedom.

Second, the means by which this goal is attained is precisely the "forgiveness of sins." If, as Paul implies in 2:15, the objection of Jews (or Jewish Messiah believers) to the inclusion of Gentiles is that they are "Gentile sinners," then this objection is overturned precisely because the Messiah "gave himself for our sins." Anyone, Jew or non-Jew, who is "in the Messiah" cannot therefore any longer be categorized as a "sinner," and objections to their inclusion in the family on such grounds must be overruled.

Third, for a Jew (and Paul himself is the archetypal devout and zealous Jew, as he says in 1:13–14) to recognize Jesus as Israel's Messiah and come into the Messiah's family is to declare that "the son of God loved me and gave himself for me": and with that the Jew too is given a radically new identity, the ultimate Israel identity, the messianic identity: "It isn't me any longer; it's the Messiah who lives in me." Thus at every point the Messiah's crucifixion, interpreted through the Messiah's representative position vis-à-vis Israel and the divine purposes for Abraham's family, means the creation and maintenance of a single covenantal family, the one sin-forgiven people of God, the people already celebrating the life of the "age to come."

That is the main argument of Galatians. But there is more. The older readings, in which Paul is opposing something called "legalism" or the human attempt to earn "righteousness" by "good works," always had trouble with Galatians 5, in which Paul suddenly turns around and tells his audience to stop fighting and squabbling and to behave themselves. Are they then to do "good works" after all? But every move that this reading makes reveals just how much it has missed the point Paul is making. Once we recall the two main steps in his view of the cross, it all comes clear.

First, the new Passover has occurred; therefore you are now living in the Spirit-driven "age to come" and must, of course, behave appropriately. The "works of the flesh" belong in the "present evil age," so they must be left behind. The Spirit-inspired moral effort required to do this has nothing whatever to do with the earlier argument about "works of the law." (This problem only arises when such "works" and their elimination by the gospel are interpreted as the normal moralizing view of the human vocation and the "works contract" view of salvation it encourages.) The moral effort to which Paul refers has everything to do with recognizing what has actually happened in coming to belong to the Messiah's family. As Paul said in 2:19–20, it meant being cocrucified with Jesus: "Those who belong to the Messiah . . . crucified the flesh with its passions and desires" (5:24). A gospel-driven holiness is mandatory for the crucified and risen people of the Messiah. The world has been crucified to them, and they to the world. Because of the cross, they are part of the new creation. This is what happens once we leave behind the old "works contract" and, as new-Passover people, embrace the biblical "covenant of vocation."

Second, as in Galatians 1:4, this new Passover, the victory over the powers of darkness and of the "present evil age," has been accomplished because the Messiah "gave himself for our sins." The victory over the powers has been won because their iron grip on the human race, and thereby on the world, owed its strength to the idolatry and sin whereby humans in general, and in Paul's reading of scripture Israel in particular, had handed to the powers the authority that was properly theirs. The Messiah's death "for sins" under the right and proper curse of the law was therefore the necessary means whereby victory could be won. These two steps—Passover as the divine victory, the Messiah's death for sins as the means of that victory—undergird everything in the letter.

This, then, is how the meaning of the cross, set out in a short, sharp letter to a small group in south-central Turkey nearly two millennia ago, can leap across the barriers of time and space and pose an equivalent set of urgent, indeed revolutionary, challenges to the churches of today. We too are easily fooled into allowing distinctions of ethnic origin to determine the boundaries of our fellowship in the Messiah. We are easily fooled into supposing that because we believe in faith, not works, in grace, not law, the absolute moral challenge of the gospel can be quietly set aside. Paul's message of the cross leaves us no choice. Unity and holiness and the suffering that will accompany both are rooted in the Messiah's death. To regard them as inessential is to pretend that the Messiah did not need to die. It is to imply that the "present evil age" is still in untroubled control of the world, that the Gentiles are still under the unbroken rule of the "powers." It is to suppose that the ultimate revelation of divine identity—more, of divine *love* (as in 2:20)—has not happened. It is to deny the gospel.

## Corinthians

There are many passages in Paul's correspondence with Corinth in which he draws on the meaning of the cross of Jesus to ground the basic points he is making. At no point does he offer anything like a complete exposition of either what the cross achieved or why or how it achieved it. We have already noted the way in which, in 1 Corinthians 1–2, he seems to revel in the fact that the message of a crucified Messiah is scandalous to Jews and sheer madness to non-Jews—and that when the "rulers of this age" went ahead and "crucified the Lord of glory" they were, by implication, signing their own death warrant. Here and in many other places, we wish Paul had taken a couple more lines to spell out exactly what he meant and, not least, why and how *this* death had had *this* effect. At various points he draws on Passover imagery, particularly the need to get rid of "leaven" and the idea of being "redeemed" at a price, to insist that the Messiah's people are required to leave behind the patterns of life belonging to their former slavery. This implies that his audience were already reasonably familiar with the Exodus story and could make the connections:

> It's Passover-time, you see, and the Passover lamb—the Messiah, I mean—has already been sacrificed! What we now have to do is to keep the festival properly: none of the yeast of the old life, and none of the yeast of depravity and wickedness, either. What we need is yeast-free bread, and that means sincerity and truth. . . .
>
> Don't you know that your body is a temple of the holy spirit within you, the spirit God gave you, so that you don't belong to yourselves? You were quite an expensive purchase! So glorify God in your body. (5:7–8; 6:19–20).

He returns to the Passover theme again in chapter 10 in order this time to point out that the original Exodus narrative was full of times when the people rebelled, misbehaved, and were punished. He cautions the Corinthians not to be like that, saying, "These things happened to them as a pattern, and they were written for our instruction, since it's upon us that the ends of the ages have now come" (10:11). In other words, we are the ultimate Passover people and must understand the challenges facing us in the light of the original generation. Passover too is of course the context for the Lord's Supper, and like the original Passover that meal looks both backward and forward: "Whenever you eat this bread and drink the cup, you are announcing the Lord's death until he comes" (11:26). In other words, they are claiming the once-for-all death of the Messiah as their basic identity and they must therefore live appropriately.

All this, it seems, is once again in the service of what we often think of as "ethical" imperatives, but that are perhaps better seen as "eschatological" instructions. Now that the "ends of the ages" have converged upon them, now (in other words) that the "present evil age" has been condemned and the "age to come" has been inaugurated, they must learn what it means to live in the latter rather than the former. My point here is not to trace out all the implications of this for detailed behavior, the new social and cultural patterns that the believers in Corinth and elsewhere are to discern and put into practice. My point is the extent to which, in a letter that covers several quite different issues and is written to a church most of which, we may safely say, was not Jewish by birth, Passover is never far from Paul's mind and comes naturally into his arguments again and again. Nowhere here does Paul say explicitly what the *goal* of the Messiah's death really was or by what *means* that death achieved that goal. But everywhere he assumes that Passover is the context within which that death would find its ultimate meaning.

That point gives color and depth to the final great argument in 1 Corinthians, the discussion of resurrection in chapter 15. Here the underlying theme is victory: "But thank God! He gives us the victory, through our Lord Jesus the Messiah" (15:57). Paul assumes that Jesus is *already* ruling the world: "He has to go on ruling, you see, until 'he has put all his enemies under his feet'" (15:25, quoting Ps. 110:1). In order to argue for the future resurrection of believers, Paul thus explains the significance of the one-off resurrection of Jesus ahead of all the others. This was the victory, the "cosmic" triumph, that will result in the end in the utter abolition of death itself (this, of course, is what "resurrection" is all about). And the reason that death can be defeated—and was defeated in principle when Jesus rose again—is that on the cross Jesus dealt with sins.

The substance of the chapter is about the final victory, but the start of the chapter, repeating the early gospel summary, explains how that comes about: "The Messiah died for our sins in accordance with the Bible." Thus, in a verse we have had occasion to quote before: "If the Messiah wasn't raised, your faith is pointless, and you are still in your sins" (15:17). The Corinthians would be "still in their sins" not because they were not really converted, not because their faith was not strong enough, not because they showed no evidence of a changed life, but because that would be the case if the Messiah had not been raised. When the Messiah was raised, *death was conquered, which meant that sin had been dealt with.* That is the link. That is why, in accordance with the Bible, the message of freedom from all "powers" (the Passover message) is directly connected to the message of "forgiveness of sins" (the message of the end of exile).

The Second Letter to the Corinthians is utterly different from the first not only in mood, but also in literary style. This appears to be because, as he says in the first chapter, Paul had been utterly crushed by events in Ephesus. He doesn't say what had happened, but it seems to have been a major threat to life and limb and equally important to the balance of his mind and heart. On top of it all—whatever it was—he has clearly received a message or messages from the church in Corinth of which the tone as well as the content has disturbed him greatly. There seems to be a rival group of teachers there now, and they have poured scorn on Paul and his ministry, his style, his methods, and particularly his suffering. If only he were a real apostle, as they are, none of this would have happened to him! We only see this, of course, through Paul's response, but it seems from what he says and from how he says it that they were undermining him in particular because he was bringing shame on the church. How could they look up to someone who had been ill-treated in the way he had been?

Paul's answer is to explain to them the way in which his own ministry is shaped by the message of the Messiah and his cross. The letter has many twists and turns—there are jerky passages that look as if Paul was dictating it in bits, perhaps while on the road around northern Greece—but at its heart we find this message: that the true signs of apostolic ministry are to be found in the things that show that the apostle is formed by the Messiah himself, the Messiah whose death overturned all cultural expectations as well as all forms of power. Here we see, as it were, the large-scale exposition of Galatians 2:19–20. Paul has been crucified with the Messiah, and the life he now lives is the Messiah's own crucified and risen, suffering and glorious life. It is one thing to say, "We don't proclaim ourselves, but Jesus the Messiah as Lord, and ourselves as your servants because of Jesus" (4:5). Anyone might assent to that in theory, but it is quite another thing to find the meaning of that claim etched painfully into real life:

> We have this treasure in earthenware pots, so that the extraordinary quality of the power may belong to God, not to us. We are under all kinds of pressure, but we are not crushed completely; we are at a loss, but not at our wits' end; we are persecuted, but not abandoned; we are cast down, but not destroyed. We always carry the dead-

ness of Jesus about in the body, so that the life of Jesus
may be revealed in our body. Although we are still alive,
you see, we are always being given over to death because
of Jesus, so that the life of Jesus may be revealed in our
mortal humanity. So this is how it is: death is at work in
us—but life in you! (4:7–12)

And with even more rhetorical emphasis he expounds the true
apostolic life of suffering and shame as the very thing that ought
to recommend itself, not as something to be ashamed of:

We recommend ourselves as God's servants: with much
patience, with sufferings, difficulties, hardships, beatings,
imprisonments, riots, hard work, sleepless nights, going
without food, with purity, knowledge, great-heartedness,
kindness, the holy spirit, genuine love, by speaking the
truth, by God's power, with weapons for God's faithful work in left and right hand alike, through glory and
shame, through slander and praise; as deceivers, and
yet true; as unknown, yet very well known; as dying,
and look—we are alive; as punished, yet not killed; as
sad, yet always celebrating; as poor, yet bringing riches
to many; as having nothing, yet possessing everything.
(6:4–10)

Then even more dramatically, and now deliberately teasing his
audience, he lists all his "achievements"—only they are all the
wrong sort of thing, *the things that show his weakness* (11:21–12:7).
The Lord himself had said to him, "My grace is enough for you;
my power comes to perfection in weakness" (12:9). So he says:

I will be all the more pleased to boast of my weaknesses,
so that the Messiah's power may rest upon me. So I'm
delighted when I'm weak, insulted, in difficulties, persecuted, and facing disasters, for the Messiah's sake. When
I'm weak, you see, then I am strong. (12:9–10)

The point throughout is that the crucifixion of the Messiah is not just an event in the past that changed the world once and for all, though it certainly is that. It is not just the "mechanism" of salvation, though if we must use that language we can do so without inaccuracy. The Messiah's crucifixion was not a strange, one-off deal through which God played a trick on sin and death, after which normal operations were resumed, power went back to being what it always was, and the normal human lifestyles of honor and shame, boasting and prestige, social climbing and pretension could be picked up again where they had left off. Precisely because the Messiah's crucifixion unveiled the very nature of God himself at work in generous self-giving love to overthrow all power structures by dealing with the sin that had given them their power, that same divine nature would now be at work through the ministry of the gospel not only through what was said, but through the character and the circumstances of the people who were saying it.

That is Paul's central argument in 2 Corinthians. Though for the most part he is not talking about the effect of the cross with regard to its one-off dealing with sin and liberating the world from its grasp, he has discovered and discerned that the victory that was *won* through the cross has to be *implemented* through the cross—in particular, through the cruciform life and ministry of the apostles. Though Paul would no doubt say the same of all Christians in their varied callings, much of the letter is explicitly an explanation and defense of the nature of true apostleship, and it is in that light that I think we should read the central passage around which everything else revolves.

Here we see, again and again, the specific application of the "covenant of vocation." The purpose of the cross is not simply "so that we can go to heaven" (though the larger postmortem future is very present to Paul, especially at the beginning of chapter 5) or so that we can "be with God forever," though no doubt Paul believes that as well. Rather, as in Revelation 1, 5, and 20, the result of the Messiah's death is that humans, in this case those who exercise apostolic ministry, are called and equipped for that work. We glanced at this passage before, but it bears repeating here, so central is it to Paul's understanding of both the cross and the vocation that results from it:

> The Messiah's love makes us press on. We have come to the conviction that one died for all, and therefore all died. And he died for all in order that those who live should live no longer for themselves, but for him who died and was raised on their behalf. . . .
>
> It all comes from God. He reconciled us to himself through the Messiah, and he gave us the ministry of reconciliation. This is how it came about: God was reconciling the world to himself in the Messiah, not counting their transgressions against them, and entrusting us with the message of reconciliation. So we are ambassadors, speaking on behalf of the Messiah, as though God were making his appeal through us. We implore people on the Messiah's behalf to be reconciled to God. The Messiah did not know sin, but God made him to be sin on our behalf, so that in him we might embody God's faithfulness to the covenant.
>
> So, as we work together with God, we appeal to you in particular: when you accept God's grace, don't let it go to waste! This is what he says: "I listened to you when the time was right; I came to your aid on the day of salvation." Look! The right time is now! Look! The day of salvation is here! (5:14–6:2)

He says it again and again, developing the thought each time. The Messiah died (to reconcile us and the world to God); and God gave us this ministry (the ministry of reconciliation). The whole passage, like most of the letter, is about this ministry, this Messiah-shaped, cruciform, covenant-fulfilling ministry.

Many traditions, misled by the normal translation of 5:21b as "that in him we might become 'the righteousness of God,'" have imagined that in this verse we have a statement of what is called "double imputation": our sins are "imputed" to Jesus and his righteousness is "imputed" to us. But that is specifically not what Paul says. Indeed, that whole way of approaching things often owes more to the normal "works contract," at least at a popular level, than to anything deep in the New Testament. It implies that Paul's theology revolves around the moralistic "righteousness" that consists of "good behavior" in one shape or form—and that the merits of Jesus's good behavior can be credited to our account despite our bad behavior. That is a slimmed-down and distorted version of what Paul actually says. His point is that the cross has liberated people from sin, so that they can be God-reflecting, image-bearing, working models of divine covenant faithfulness in action. That is actually what 2 Corinthians as a whole is all about.

The first half of 5:21 does indeed make it clear, however, that at the heart of the gospel is the innocent Jesus dying the death of the guilty. Here we drill down to bedrock once more. "The Messiah did not know sin, but God made him to be sin on our behalf" (5:21a). At this point we are very close to Galatians 3:13 and indeed to the entire theme we observed in the narrative of Luke. Jesus was innocent, yet he died the death of the guilty. But notice what overall narrative frames this statement. It is not the quasi-pagan narrative of an angry or capricious divinity and an accidental victim. It is the story of love, covenant love, faithful love, reconciling love. Messianic love. It is the story of the victory of that love, because that self-giving love turns out to have a power of a totally different sort from any other power known in the world (which is why Paul is happy to say that he is strong when he is weak).

But here at last we begin to discover *why* it has that all-conquering power. If the enslaving powers are to be overthrown, they must be robbed of their power base; and their power base is, as we saw, the fact that humans hand over power to them by worshipping them instead of worshipping the Creator, by the idolatry and consequent distortion of life that can be lumped together as "sin." Once that sin has been dealt with, the power of the idols is broken; once the Messiah has been "made sin for us," the way is open for the ministry of reconciliation to fan out in all directions. Inside the Passover-like victory over the powers is the end-of-exile dealing with sin; and the way sin is dealt with is by the appropriate *substitution* of the one who alone is the true *representative*. The one bore the sin of the many. The innocent died in the place of the guilty. This only makes sense within the narrative of love, of new Exodus, of end of exile—of Jesus. Put it into another narrative, and it becomes a dark, pagan horror. Put it back where it belongs, and it speaks of a compelling love. "The Messiah's love makes us press on." That is the radical application of the cross to the apostolic life.

## Philippians

A passage from one of the letters Paul wrote from prison, Philippians, may be brought in at this point. The famous poem in Philippians 2 pivots on the crucifixion: each of the two halves of the poem consists of three three-line stanzas, and the line in the middle, as it were, holds its arms out in both directions, making shocking and revolutionary sense:

> *Who, though in God's form, did not*
> *Regard his equality with God*
> *As something he ought to exploit.*
>
> *Instead, he emptied himself,*
> *And received the form of a slave,*
> *Being born in the likeness of humans.*

> *And then, having human appearance,*
> *He humbled himself, and became*
> *Obedient even to death,*
>
> > *Yes, even the death of the cross.*
>
> > *And so God has greatly exalted him,*
> > *And to him in his favor has given*
> > *The name which is over all names:*
>
> *That now at the name of Jesus*
> *Every knee within heaven shall bow—*
> *On earth, too, and under the earth:*
>
> *And every tongue shall confess*
> *That Jesus, Messiah, is Lord,*
> *To the glory of God, the father. (2:6–11)*

Whole books have been written about this passage. My only purpose here is to draw attention to three things of special relevance for the themes of this book. First, the poem is clearly telling the story of Jesus with the cross at its center. That alone is worth comment. But in its multiple resonances with various biblical passages, such as Genesis and Isaiah, the poem is also telling the story of both the human race and Israel, with both of them focused now on Jesus as the Messiah, Israel's representative, who is also the quintessential human being. The cross stands at the center of the story of Jesus, Israel, the human race, the creator God, and his world. This is where the biblical narrative finds its heart.

Second, the cross here is the means of *victory* over all the powers of the world. At the name of Jesus, declares the poem, every knee shall bow. The poem provides no explanation for why this is so, at least not in traditional terms (such as "he died for our sins"). But in fact the whole of the first half of the poem offers itself as an explanation that fits remarkably well with themes we have seen elsewhere in the New Testament, for instance, in Mark

10. The first half of the poem describes Jesus's refusal to do what normal worldly power would do, namely, to exploit a status for one's own benefit. In Paul's day, and in the world well known in Philippi (a Roman colony), the contrast is stark: everyone knew how worldly emperors behaved, and Jesus did the opposite. His self-emptying, his humility, his obedience to the divine plan even though it meant his own cruel and shameful death—all this is the complete opposite of normal human behavior, normal imperial behavior. The result is that *the cross establishes the kingdom of God through the agency of Jesus.* That is what the last three stanzas of the poem are celebrating. We are here exactly on the same page as the four gospels.

Third, the poem in its present context is setting out the pattern of life that is both the foundation and the model for the way Jesus's followers ought to behave in relation to one another. The first four verses of the chapter stress the shared life of the community, mutual love and partnership in the spirit, heartfelt affection, and sympathy. On this basis Paul instructs the church:

> Hold on to the same love; bring your innermost lives
> into harmony; fix your minds on the same object. Never
> act out of selfish ambition or vanity; instead, regard
> everybody else as your superior. Look after each other's
> best interests, not your own. (2:2–4)

The poem then sets out the story of Jesus himself not only as the example of how to do this but as, so to speak, the *place where* this kind of life is to be found. The "place" is the Messiah himself, "in whom" his people find their identity: "This is how you should think among yourselves—with the mind that you have because you belong to the Messiah, Jesus" (2:5). They already belong to him and this is how his "mind" worked, so theirs should work in the same way not only because they are copying him, but because his "mind" is at work in theirs.

But this provides a clue to how Paul at least sees the logic of the cross underneath the surface of the poem. The Messiah was lord of all, yet became a slave. He was all-powerful, but became weak. He was equal with the Father, yet refused to take advantage of this status. Add to this the echoes throughout this passage from Isaiah 40–55, particularly the "servant" poems, and we can go one step farther: he was innocent, yet he died the death of the guilty. *This is how the cross establishes God's kingdom: by bearing and so removing the weight of sin and death.* The kingdom of God is established by destroying the power of idolatry, and idols get their power because humans, in sinning, give it to them. Deal with sin, and the idols are reduced to a tawdry heap of rubble. Deal with sin, and the world will glorify God.

There are many remarkable things about this poem, but we should note one in particular. Paul wrote this letter in the mid-50s of the first century, that is, less than thirty years after Jesus's execution. Either he wrote this poem for use in this letter, which is quite possible, or he was quoting a poem that either he or somebody else had already written. The poem is a masterpiece of compressed biblical theology. One can only stand in awe at the combination of insight and expression that could encapsulate so much in a mere seventy-six Greek words. What this tells me is that already in the very early church it was common coin, first, that Jesus's death established God's kingdom; second, that this came about because of his servant-shaped identification with sinful humanity, sharing their death and so bearing their sin; and third, that this action was not something Jesus did *despite* the fact that he was "in God's form" and "equal with God," but rather something that he did *because* he was those things. In whatever way the New Testament tells the story of the cross, it is always the story of self-giving divine love.

This is why I have said that the real danger in expounding the meaning of Jesus's death is to collapse it into a kind of pagan scenario in which an angry God is pacified by taking out his wrath on Jesus. The first Christians did not use the language of

"Trinity," but at the heart of what they believed about Jesus and his death, they affirmed, explained, insisted on, and turned into brilliant poetry the insight that what happened on the cross was the self-expression of the love that made the world.

## Colossians

A passage from another "prison letter" that is vital for our purposes is Colossians 2:13–15:

> In the same way, though you were dead in legal offenses, and in the uncircumcision of your flesh, God made you alive together with Jesus, forgiving us all our offenses. He blotted out the handwriting that was against us, opposing us with its legal demands. He took it right out of the way, by nailing it to the cross. He stripped the rulers and authorities of their armor, and displayed them contemptuously to public view, celebrating his triumph over them in him.

This is of course deliberately ironic. What seemed to be happening as Jesus of Nazareth hung in agony on the cross was that the "rulers and authorities" were celebrating their triumph over *him,* having stripped him of his clothes and held him up to public contempt. No, insists Paul, once you learn the meaning of the gospel, you have to see everything inside out.

We already heard the cryptic hint in 1 Corinthians 2:8, where the "rulers" wouldn't have executed Jesus if they had understood who he was and what the result would be. Here the point is spelled out far more graphically. If we ask Paul what had happened when Jesus died—if we bring to him our question of what had changed by six o'clock on that evening, what was different about the world, what was now true that hadn't been true twenty-four hours earlier—I think this is one of the primary things he would have said, that the rulers, the powers, had been defeated. When Paul speaks of the "rulers and authorities," he means both the visible rulers, the Herods, the Caesars, the governors, and the priests, and the "invisible" rulers, the dark powers that stand behind them and operate through them. By the time Jesus's body was taken down from the cross, Paul believed, these "rulers and authorities" had been stripped, shamed, and defeated.

Even at the time—especially at the time!—this must have sounded completely crazy. (Well, Paul did say that the "word of the cross" looked like madness.) One of the Caesars was still on the throne. His local officials around the world were still running the show with brutal efficiency. The chief priests were still in charge of the Temple in Jerusalem. Paul himself was in prison! So is this statement about God's overthrowing the rulers and authorities in the cross of Jesus simply a bit of over-the-top bravado, whistling in the wind, shaking an apostolic fist at the cosmos? No doubt the rhetoric is deliberately designed to sound a bit like that, but underneath there is a logic that is crystal in its clarity and compelling in its conviction. The power of the rulers has been broken—the new Passover, to use our earlier language, has now taken place for certain—because in the messianic events "God made us alive together with Jesus, forgiving us all our offenses." Victory over the powers, once more, is accomplished through the forgiveness of sins.

Paul adds a note about God "blotting out the handwriting that was against us," referring obliquely to the Jewish law, which had kept non-Jews out of the reckoning and had pronounced condemnation for disobedience on the Jews themselves. That has been done away with. It has been nailed to the cross. (Remember Gal. 2:19: "Through the law I died to the law, so that I might live to God"? This is a very similar point.) Once again, it is because of this victory that the Gentile mission was even thinkable. The "powers" that had held the nations captive had been defeated. The slaves could now walk free.

So how does "forgiveness" result in "victory over the powers"? Here we go back to our earlier analysis of sin and idolatry. The idols—and that includes human rulers when they are idolized, whether formally (as in the Roman Empire) or informally—gain their power because humans give it to them. Humans are designed to worship God and exercise responsibility in his world. But when humans worship idols instead, so that their image-bearing humanness corrupts itself into sin, missing the mark of the human vocation, they hand over their power to those same idols. The idols then use this power to tyrannize and ultimately to destroy their devotees and the wider world. *But when sins are forgiven, the idols lose their power.*

The reason Paul can be so triumphantly certain that by six o'clock on Good Friday the "rulers and authorities" had lost their power was that he knew, because of the resurrection of Jesus, that sin itself had been defeated. And one of the ways in which he knew in practice that this had happened was because, when he announced Jesus as Lord around the non-Jewish world, people believed it and gladly gave their allegiance to this new Master. The liberating power of the gospel was itself a demonstration of the truth it proclaimed.

As with the poetry of Philippians 2, so with the dense and polemical argument of Colossians 2: the fact that its message can be compressed into a few sentences, complete with rhetorical flourishes, must mean that this line of thought was already a frequent theme in the early church. When Jesus was crucified, the "powers" lost their power, because sin itself had been defeated and sinners forgiven. Once Jesus had chosen to do what he did at Passover time, joining the idea of a new or ultimate "Exodus" together with the idea that this was the time for the real "return from exile," the forgiveness of sins, and linking them together via passages like Isaiah 52 and 53, the stage was set. The new Exodus was accomplished through the forgiveness of sins, and forgiveness of sins was accomplished by the Messiah as the living and dying embodiment of the one true God, standing in the place of sinners and taking the full weight of their plight upon himself. Paul has already said as much in the poem earlier in the letter:

> *In him all the Fullness was glad to dwell*
> *And through him to reconcile all to himself,*
> *Making peace by the blood of his cross.* (1:19–20)

He repeats the point in 2:9: "In him . . . all the full measure of divinity has taken up bodily residence." This is in fact Temple language, but the point for our present purposes is that all that Paul ascribes to Jesus and his death in 2:13–15 is to be seen as the work of the one God himself. Here again the implicitly trinitarian structure of early Christian thought is all-important. Take that away, and the slide back toward some kind of pagan formulation has begun.

★ ★ ★

There are many other things one might say about the death of Jesus in the letters of Paul. I have argued elsewhere, for instance, that the little Letter to Philemon, though it does not mention the death of Jesus specifically, exemplifies its meaning, which for Paul focused on the "ministry of reconciliation." Paul extends one arm to Philemon and the other to Onesimus and brings them together within his own love for them both, insisting to Philemon that if Onesimus has wronged him in any way he, Paul, will make it good. That looks to me like a practical application of the cross.

Philemon functions as a small signpost to Paul's largest and most important letter, one that has always featured prominently in any discussion of the meaning of Jesus's death: the Letter to the Romans. This demands a deep breath and a fresh start.

# 12

---

# The Death of Jesus in Paul's Letter to the Romans

## *The New Exodus*

A T ONE POINT in *The Voyage of the Dawn Treader,* one of C. S. Lewis's Narnia stories, Lucy, the younger of the two heroines, finds herself in a magician's house. There she browses through an extraordinary book full of magic spells and comes upon a wonderful story. Lucy reads it with excitement and delight, but then finds that she can't quite remember it all—and when she tries to turn back the page to refresh her memory, she finds it's impossible. As the memory fades, all she can cling to is that "it was about a cup and a sword and a tree and a green hill"; and ever afterward what Lucy meant by "a good story" was a story that reminded her of the one she had read in the magic book.

I suspect—from conversations with many readers over the years—that plenty of people who read the Bible have that sort of feeling about Paul's Letter to the Romans. It's about righteousness and faith and love and wrath and God and Jesus and the Holy

Spirit and Adam and Abraham and Moses and Israel. At times it sweeps you along on a tide of extraordinary writing and glorious hope, while at other times it plunges you not only into gloom, but into serious puzzles, knotty intellectual problems, and arguments that will make you wonder whether St. Paul is losing his balance or whether, perhaps, you are the one losing your balance—which would hardly be surprising with all that complexity. And yet at the heart of it, particularly in chapters 5–8, Romans sums up in a few sentences what the early Christians wanted to say about the death of Jesus:

> Jesus our Lord . . . was handed over because of our trespasses and raised because of our justification. (4:24–25)

> This is how God demonstrates his own love for us: the Messiah died for us while we were still sinners. (5:8)

> You too died to the law through the body of the Messiah, so that you could belong to someone else—to the one who was raised from the dead, in fact—so that we could bear fruit for God. (7:4)

And then in more detail:

> God sent his own son in the likeness of sinful flesh, and as a sin-offering; and, right there in the flesh, he condemned sin. This was in order that the right and proper verdict of the law could be fulfilled in us, as we live not according to the flesh but according to the spirit. (8:3–4)

And in a glorious climax:

> If God is for us, who is against us? God, after all, did not spare his own son; he gave him up for us all! How then will he not, with him, freely give all things to us? . . . I am persuaded . . . that neither death nor life, nor angels nor rulers, nor the present, nor the future, nor powers,

nor height, nor depth, nor any other creature will be
able to separate us from the love of God in King Jesus
our Lord. (8:31–32, 38–39)

There is of course another passage that has been cited thousands, probably millions, of times as Paul's central statement about
Jesus's death, but it is more complex again, and the setting is often
misunderstood. In chapter 3 Paul describes the "redemption
which is found in the Messiah, Jesus" by saying:

God put Jesus forth as the place of mercy, through
faithfulness, by means of his blood. He did this to demonstrate his covenant justice, because of the passing over
(in divine forbearance) of sins committed beforehand.
This was to demonstrate his covenant justice in the present time; that is, that he himself is in the right, and that
he declares to be in the right everyone who trusts in the
faithfulness of Jesus. (3:25–26)

Almost every word in this dense statement has been given different interpretations at different times in the history of the church,
not least in the last two or three generations. There is a particular
reason for this, which we must face right away, because it relates
to the central concern of this book.

The first four chapters of Romans have for many years been
read as though they were a statement of our old friend the "works
contract." Humans were supposed to behave themselves; they
didn't. God had to punish them, but Jesus stood in the way, so
God forgave them after all (provided they believed in Jesus).
Rather than going to hell, they can now go to heaven instead.
That, with small variations, is how Romans 1–4 has been read.
It is frequently referred to as the "Romans road." When people
in churches preach and teach the kind of view that I have been
warning against throughout this book, it is to Romans that they
go to "prove" what they are saying.

And I am convinced that this is mistaken. That is why we need, in this chapter and the following one, to look at Romans in much more detail. At this point we cannot avoid getting our hands dirty with some detailed reading of the text. I have suggested in the previous chapters that the four gospels are far more important than has usually been supposed for understanding the early Christian view of what Jesus's death achieved. But sooner or later we must come back to Romans. Debates about the meaning of Jesus's death in the New Testament tend to stand or fall right here.

## The Puzzles of Romans

Three initial points set the scene for what needs to be said. First, Romans is an extremely subtle and careful composition in which the four sections (chapters 1–4, 5–8, 9–11, and 12–16) work together like the movements of a symphony. The sections each have their own inner coherence, style, mood, and flavor. They are, in all sorts of ways, quite unlike one another. But at the same time there is a larger thematic coherence, an overall flow, a significant number of threads that run through all the sections and tie the whole letter tightly together despite the obvious breaks and changes of pace. Each section is what it is because of where it is located in the overall picture. That means—among many other things—that we should beware of isolating any single section and treating it by itself as a statement of the "gospel." What Paul says about Jesus's death at any point is part of the larger argument he is mounting in that section.

Second, the reading of Romans has suffered from being regarded as the Bible's version of a handbook of systematic theology. This is not to say that it was only an "occasional" treatise, dashed off in a hurry for a particular purpose and so not suitable for larger theological formation. Far from it. But the danger has been that the topics that people wanted to discuss at certain points in church history—in particular, the doctrine of "justification" in the six-teenth century and thereafter—have been superimposed on the letter. The result has been that ideas that later dogmatic schemes reckoned "ought" to be discussed at certain points have been as-sumed to be present even when the evidence suggests otherwise. It is as though a child, having longed to visit the zoo in order to see the elephants, were to arrive on a day when the elephant house was closed for repair and, desperate to avoid disappointment, somehow convinced herself that the rhinoceroses was a strange kind of el-ephant after all. Conversely, ideas that the letter is in fact expound-ing, but that have no place in the dogmatic framework are simply ignored. A rhinoceros is worth looking at for its own sake.

An example of the former point concerns the labels that have often been put on the different sections of Romans. For many years it was assumed that Romans 1–4 was an exposition of "jus-tification" and that Romans 5–8 was therefore about "sanctifica-tion." There is some surface evidence for this in chapter 6, but to make chapters 5–8 a treatise about "how to live the Christian life," however helpful in some ways, is to miss its main point. Our determination to see elephants is ruining our capacity to see other animals that are also large, also gray, and also dangerous, but sig-nificantly different.

An example of the latter point is the way in which a great deal of exegesis has routinely ignored the climax of Romans 5–8, which is the renewal of all creation in 8:18–25. We came looking for elephants (in this case, the question of "how Christians end up in heaven") and so couldn't see the rhinoceros that was right in front of us.

Third, picking up from that theme of creation's renewal, the Letter to the Romans in fact offers a remarkable vision of what in the present book I have called the *goal* of God's rescue operation. Paul does not say that Jesus dies "so that we can go to heaven." "Heaven" is mentioned twice in Romans: in 1:18, where the di-vine wrath is revealed "from heaven," and in 10:6, where Paul quotes Deuteronomy to say that we do not need to "go up to heaven" to bring the Messiah down. For Paul, exactly in line with Revelation and other early writings, the result of Jesus's achievement is *a new creation,* a new heaven-and-earth world in which humans can resume their genuinely human vocation as the "kingdom of priests," the "royal priesthood." This needs a little further explanation.

The primary human problem that Paul notes in Romans 1:18 is not "sin," but "ungodliness." It is a failure not primarily of behavior (though that follows), but of *worship.* Worship the wrong divinity, and instead of reflecting God's wise order into the world you will reflect and then produce a distortion: something out of joint, something "unjust." That is the problem, says Paul: "ungodliness" produces "out-of-jointness," "injustice." Since this out-of-jointness clashes with the way things actually are, humans then suppress the truth as well, including ultimately the truth about God himself, and so the vicious circle continues; people continue to worship that which is not divine and swap the truth for a lie (1:18–26).

One can of course sum up all the consequent distortions and fracturings of human life with the word "sin." But to jump straight there without recognizing the careful analysis Paul has offered is itself to "miss the mark" in understanding what he is saying. "Sin" is not just "doing things God has forbidden." It is, as we saw, the failure to be fully functioning, God-reflecting human beings. That is what Paul sums up in 3:23: all sinned and fell short of God's glory. He is referring to the glory that, as true humans, they should have possessed. This is the "glory" spoken of in Psalm 8: the status and responsibility of looking after God's world on his behalf. This status and this activity are sustained by true worship of the true God. This is the royal vocation, undergirded by the priestly vocation.

That true worship, contrasting with the failure seen in 1:18–26, is what Paul sees Abraham offering in 4:18–22. The result, for those who share Abraham's faith, is expressed in cultic terms: "We have been allowed to approach, by faith, into this grace in which we stand; and we celebrate the hope of the glory of God" (5:2)—the "hope of God's glory" being, in the Jewish world of the time, the hope for the divine Glory to return at last to the Temple. That is part of the meaning of Romans 8, where the indwelling Spirit means that the Messiah's people not only share his "rule" over the new creation (8:18–25, picking up from 5:17), but also share his priestly intercession for the world (8:26–27, looking forward to 8:34). This then sets Paul up for the prayer theme, which holds together chapters 9–11, starting with lament (9:1–5), continuing with intercession (10:1), and ending in praise (11:33–36). This framework means that Paul is exemplifying and embodying the idea of a renewed priesthood standing between God and his people. It should be no surprise that chapter 12 begins with an equally "priestly" theme:

> So, my dear family, this is my appeal to you by the mercies of God: offer your bodies as a living sacrifice, holy and pleasing to God. Worship like this brings your mind into line with God's. (12:1)

Here again the section that is introduced with this "cultic" appeal concludes with a similar call to worship: the point of the whole gospel is to fulfill the promises to the patriarchs and to bring the nations to praise God for his mercy (15:8–9). Nor should we then be surprised (though some readers have been) when Paul moves into the concluding section of the letter by describing how he has been called to work "in the priestly service of God's good news, so that the offering of the nations may be acceptable, sanctified in the holy spirit" (15:16). All of this could be considerably expanded. This summary may be enough to alert us to the fact that, in Paul's presentation of salvation, the *goal* is for humans to share the "royal" and "priestly" ministry of the Messiah himself.

If that is the goal, how is that goal attained? This is the particular puzzle that Romans presents to our present topic. Granted all this framework, what does Paul say about the way in which the death of Jesus has dealt with this problem (idolatry and sin) and brought about this result?

## Romans 5–8 and the New Exodus

### Romans 5: Jesus's Death and the Coming of the Kingdom

At this point the normal route would be to say, "Look at Romans 3:21–26; you will find it all there." But actually Romans 3, important though it is, is part of a different argument. This is the heart of Paul's argument about God's "righteousness"—that is, his faithfulness to the covenant. The covenant in question is the covenant made with Abraham, which Paul expounds in Romans 4. As far as Paul is concerned from reading the ancient texts, this covenant is not just *with* Abraham, but is the promise that *through Abraham and his family* God would bless all the nations. In case there is any doubt on this point (which there often is), we can cite once again Paul's closing summary of the whole message in 15:8–9:

> The Messiah became a servant of the circumcised people
> in order to demonstrate the truthfulness of God—that is,
> to confirm the promises to the patriarchs, and to bring
> the nations to praise God for his mercy.

That is Paul's own summary of his own message. We should beware of trying to summarize it in other terms that ignore most of the elements he has so carefully expounded.

That, however, is what has happened with the traditional interpretation of Romans 1–4, which has relied on a "works contract" reading of the text. In this reading—you can see it in one commentary after another and hear it in one sermon after another—the promises to Abraham will always be played down. The patriarch will be seen as simply an advance example of someone who was "justified by faith." But this does no justice to what Paul actually says or indeed to the biblical meaning of the phrase often rendered the "righteousness of God" in 1:17; 3:5; 3:21; and 3:25–26. Romans 3:21–26 is in fact a compressed statement about the "redemption which is found in the Messiah, Jesus," and this compressed statement is designed not as a full statement of "atonement theology," but rather as a summary, with particular reference to God's covenant faithfulness, of the "new Exodus" that was achieved on the cross. (The word "redemption" is almost a technical term for "Exodus"; it of course awakens echoes of slave markets, but the primary biblical slave market was the Egypt from which God freed the descendants of Abraham.) Through this "new Exodus," despite the failure of Israel (2:17–3:9), God has brought his long-awaited plan to fruition. This will be the subject of our next chapter.

For the moment, though, we look toward the passage where Paul spells out this "new Exodus" more fully, taking his time to explain how it all "works." The passage in question is the next section of the letter: Romans 5–8. You might not guess this from those many treatments, both of Paul and of systematic theology, that assume that the letter divides at this point, with the first four chapters explaining the "problem of sin" and "how God has dealt with it" and the next four going on to other topics that follow from this but do not themselves constitute the heart of what Paul thinks about the saving work of Jesus. In fact, as the selection of quotations above indicates, there are more references to the death of Jesus and its meaning in chapters 5–8 than anywhere else in Romans (and indeed than anywhere else in Paul). We do well to note what these chapters are actually about. All the signs are that Paul sees this as a large-scale exposition of the "new Exodus": the rescue of humans from the slavery not of Egypt, but of "Sin," and their journey to the promised land not of Canaan, but of the renewed creation.

We need to approach this step by step. If Romans as a whole is a carefully composed set piece, chapters 5–8 are even more so. That doesn't mean (as some have suggested) that this section was originally written for a different purpose. It means, rather, that we can see several signs that Paul was designing his overall argument with structural and thematic care. Chapters 5–8 belong exactly here in the argument of the letter as a whole. Several lines of thought flow from chapters 1–4 into 5–8, and several others flow out of 5–8 into 9–11. Of these things we cannot now speak in detail.

In particular, chapters 6–8 form an extended exposition of the new Passover and Exodus within which Paul has woven a sustained discussion of the long and troublesome story of Israel under the Mosaic law. As we have seen throughout our discussions, in the Second Temple period the expectation of a "new Exodus" was fused with the longing for a real "return from exile," a ransom from the Deuteronomic "curse of the law." And this ransom would involve, centrally, the "forgiveness of sins," which as we saw in Galatians would liberate Israel from bondage and also enable the "Gentile sinners" to enter the people of God. This is more or less exactly what Paul expounds in these chapters.

First, though, the outer framework. The opening paragraph (5:1–5) announces the overall theme: those who are "justified by faith" (summing up 3:21–4:25) are given hope—hope of the "glory of God," because of the gift of the Spirit. The line from justification to hope is explained in more detail in 5:6–11, which anticipates the final celebration of 8:31–39: if the Messiah died for us when we were weak, ungodly sinners, then it must follow that through him we will be saved in the end. That is the logic of hope. And also the logic of love: the divine love displayed in 5:6–11 is gloriously celebrated in 8:31–39.

As Paul's arguments go, this one is relatively straightforward. Here, as often, he is simply declaring *that* the Messiah "died for us," *that* his death "reconciled us to God" (5:10); he is not explaining *how* these deceptively simple statements "work." However, in the middle of the sequence Paul says something that is often ignored, but may offer a fresh clue as to how to read 3:21–26, on the one hand, and 8:1–4, on the other:

> How much more, in that case—since we have been
> declared to be in the right by his blood—are we going to
> be saved by him from God's coming anger! (5:9)

The "coming anger" (or "wrath") of God was mentioned by Paul as the primary threat hanging over the human race in 1:18. This was reaffirmed in 2:5 ("You are building up a store of anger for yourself on the day of anger, the day when God's just judgment will be unveiled"). Most people, reading 3:24–26, have assumed and then tried to demonstrate that Paul is saying that this "wrath" falls on Jesus instead of on his people, that God put Jesus forth as a "propitiation," a means of turning away wrath. That is the position I have myself taken in commentaries and books. But there is a problem with this reading. Here, in Romans 5:9, Paul refers back to "being justified by his blood," which is a clear summary of 3:21–26, and then says that as a result of this "justification" believers *will* be saved by Jesus from the wrath or anger *that is still to come.* This doesn't seem to fit. If the wrath had been dealt with in 3:24–26—in other words, through Jesus's death, appropriated in present "justification"—then why would Paul speak of it in chapter 5 as still future? The answer, I think, is given in 8:1–4, to which we shall shortly come.

In any case, with hope secured because of the Messiah's death, Paul can stand back and survey the entire biblical narrative from Adam to the Messiah (5:12–21). If God's call to Abraham and the covenant that he made with him were designed to rescue the world from its plight, this purpose has now been accomplished in the Messiah, only more so: the Messiah has inaugurated the new creation, not simply a return to the original one. Hence the "how much more" of vv. 15 and 17. Hence too the promise that those who receive the abundance of divine grace will "reign in life" (v. 17). Here again is the *goal* of salvation, the restoration of the truly human destiny, of the covenant of vocation in which humans are called as the royal priesthood. The passage is dense, but when we take it slowly it all makes sense—within this framework. The Adam project, for humans to share in God's rule over creation, is back on track.

In and through it all, Jesus's death is referred to in several overlapping ways. It is "the gift in grace through the one person Jesus the Messiah" (v. 15), "the free gift" (v. 16), "the abundance of grace" (v. 17), the "upright act" (v. 18), and the "obedience" (v. 19)—the last of these echoing "obedient even to death" in Philippians 2:8. All this is seen as the work of "God's faithful covenant justice," an English phrase that is struggling to translate and unpack the dense language Paul uses in v. 21. And all, in particular, is about the inauguration of the *reign* of God or of "grace" (5:21). The idea of the "reign of grace" is a shorthand for *God's* reign, that is, God's kingdom, seen as the reign of divine grace.

This is all, in other words, kingdom-of-God language. This is how God has inaugurated his sovereign rule on earth as in heaven. That is how he has rescued human beings to be part of that new reality, to be active participants, not merely beneficiaries. Once liberated from sin, they can play their proper part again—a point of considerable significance when we consider how this "revolution" works out in and through Jesus's followers in our own day. All this, however, declares *that* God has rescued humanity through the death of Jesus, seen from several different but complementary angles. It does not yet explain *how* that is done. We glimpse the *goal* but not the *means*. That is still to come.

Paul has built into this narrative of Adam and the Messiah the darker theme of the Jewish law: "The law came in alongside, so that the trespass might be filled out to its full extent" (5:20). What does *that* mean? Older theologies, including the "works contract" as often understood, saw the Jewish law as the equivalent of the original commands given to Adam and Eve. It was, so people thought, the moral standard Israel was expected to keep in order to be God's people. It was the high moral bar that people in general, and Israel in particular, had to clear in order to be ruled "all right" in God's sight. Then, in this same works-contract analysis, it became clear that Israel could not keep the law. The "law" was then seen as a negative, dangerous, perhaps even demonic power. According to some, God gave the law in order to terrify people with the prospect of judgment, so that they would run to the gospel for relief. That appears to make some sense, provided you approach the whole thing from the works-contract point of view. But this is not, however, the sense Paul has in mind.

What Paul has in mind is a longer and more complex story, which he will unfold in chapter 7. This story is about the strange, unexpected divine purpose in giving the law, and this is what he has woven, as a foretaste, into the Adam-and-Messiah story of chapter 5. "The law," he says, "came in alongside, *so that* the trespass might be filled out to its full extent." The phrase "so that," italicized here, is vital. Paul is hinting that the often dark and sad history of Israel, the long descent into the "curse" of Deuteronomy, was not itself outside the divine purpose. *That descent under the law was to be the means by which redemption would come.* Even the exile itself, the long sojourn under the law's curse, was part of the eventual saving purpose. The "so that" indicates that this was *God's* intention. It was not an accident. Nor was it a demonic intrusion into the divine purpose.

We note in particular at the end of Romans 5 that Paul in his distinctive way has done exactly what we saw in the four gospels. He has told the story of "how God became king" in such a way as to demonstrate that the death of Jesus was the clue to that result. At this point we seem to be very close to a central and more or less universal early Christian perception of what the gospel was all about and how its power was unleashed. If that is so, we should be less than surprised that Paul, like the gospels in describing Jesus's last days, discerns the meaning of those days as the new Passover, the new Exodus.

### Romans 6–8: The New Exodus

As we read Romans 6–8, the first thing to get straight is that this is *not* Paul's "description of the Christian life." Yes, it often feels like that. We begin with the exciting moment of baptism (chap. 6), resulting in the bracing challenge not to let sin reign in our mortal bodies. We continue by puzzling over the description, in chapter 7, of the struggle with sin ("I don't do the good thing I want to do, but I end up doing the evil thing I don't want to do," 7:19). We learn to rely on God and to follow him into holiness, through suffering, and to glory (chap. 8). That is how many Christians have been taught to read these chapters, with local variations on the confusing bit in the middle. (Does Romans 7 describe the "normal Christian life," the pre-Christian life, or what?)

And, to a considerable extent, this reading "works." We can learn a lot and be fortified in our faith by approaching the chapters that way. We can even learn some important theology—just as you could learn quite a lot of English grammar by listening to Bob Dylan's songs, though that isn't why the songs were written, and there are many lines that don't work if you try to use them in that way. It's the same with Romans 6–8. These three chapters, in fact, are the full exposition of what Paul meant in Romans 3:24 when he described the unveiling of God's saving purpose as "the *redemption* which is found in the Messiah, Jesus." Romans 3:24–26, to be discussed in our next chapter, seems to be a shorthand summary of this "redemption." Paul has waited until this point to provide his much fuller account of what he there summarized in advance.

"Redemption," as we saw, is an Exodus term. These three chapters, like Galatians 4:1–11 only much more fully, constitute an Exodus narrative. Why would Paul want to write an Exodus narrative at this point? *Because Jesus chose Passover* as the explanatory setting for what he had to do. The early church from then on, as we have seen, used Passover as the basic route toward understanding why he died. Paul picks this up and celebrates it. Passover, as we have seen, had to do with the overthrow of the powers of evil, the rescue of God's people as they passed through the waters of the Red Sea, the giving of the law, and above all the strange and dangerous Presence of God himself, fulfilling his promises, coming to dwell in the tabernacle, and leading the people on the long, difficult journey through the wilderness to their promised inheritance. *All of these themes find their home in Romans 6–8* within the narrative of Messiah and Spirit. At their heart, again and again, is the Messiah's death.

Romans 6:2–11 is all about the death of the Messiah and about the fact that those who are baptized into him must "reckon" that they too have died. This death was like the passing of the Israelites through the Red Sea: those who pass through the waters of baptism are reminded that they have left behind the old world of slavery ("Egypt") and are on the way home to their inheritance. Like Israel in the desert (Paul draws out this implication in 1 Cor. 10 too), they must learn to live in God's new world, not slide back into their old ways. But this still only declares *that* Jesus's death has effected the "new Passover," not *how* it did so—though when Paul says in 6:10, "The death he died . . . he died to sin, once and once only," we can see him bringing together the two strands of the Jewish narrative, the Passover strand and the end-of-exile/dealing-with-sin strand. The result is that "Sin"—sin with a capital S—is personified, drawing on the same feature in 5:12–21. "Sin" in this sense is more than simply individual "sins." It is the slave master, the jailer, the Pharaoh from whose grip one is freed by coming through the water. That is what Jesus's death has achieved.

Romans 7:4 then summarizes and reemphasizes the point at the start of the next stage of the argument. When the Messiah died, "you"—anyone who belongs to the Messiah, anyone who is a member of his "body"—died at the same time. This looks forward through the developing argument, and Romans 8: 3–4 provides the climactic statement: when the Messiah died, God was condemning sin in his flesh. And the Messiah's death remains the sheet anchor of Christian assurance, all the way through the final glorious paragraph (8:31–39). Clearly, Romans 7 and 8 are crucial for Paul's understanding of Jesus's death.

But what does it all *mean*? How does it work? How does the death of Jesus, seen in this way, turn out to be the instrument by which God is accomplishing those long-term ends? How do these passages *explain* what happened when Jesus died? How do they help us answer our question about what was different by six in the evening on the first Good Friday? And, not least, how do they help us understand how the revolution that began on that day can sweep us off our own feet two thousand years later and then enlist us in its onward movement?

As we read Romans 6 carefully we discover that Paul is steadily unpacking the dense opening statement of 5:12–21. That passage, as we saw, was all about the sovereign, rescuing rule of God—in other words, the "kingdom of God." Just as in Philippians 2:6–11, the obedient death of Jesus is the way in which the new kind of power is unleashed into the world, the power of sovereign re-deeming love. A new reality has come to birth, just as it did when God overthrew the oppressors in Egypt and rescued his people from slavery. We saw just now that Paul could use the crossing of the Red Sea as an obvious image for baptism. It is highly likely that John the Baptist had had the same thing in mind when he launched his own movement. The kingdom movement had all along been a new-Exodus movement. And all this "works" because Jesus is Israel's Messiah, representing his people, so that what is true of him is true of them. He died, therefore they died—even if that seems counterintuitive. The Messiah's new life, risen from the dead, is indeed the inauguration of the "age to come," bursting in upon the "present evil age." Those who belong to him are to believe and to live by the belief that they died and rose again with him, so that they are no longer under any slavish obligation to obey the old master.

This, then, is ultimately kingdom-of-God language; it is Passover language; it has to do with the defeat of the powers of the "present evil age" that have held people captive, as Pharaoh had held ancient Israel captive in Egypt. The theme of the defeat of the "powers" remains vital throughout chapters 5–8, and Paul returns to it at the close, declaring that "neither death nor life, nor angels nor rulers, nor the present, nor the future, nor powers, nor height, nor depth, nor any other creature will be able to separate us from the love of God in King Jesus our Lord" (8:38–39). Victory over hostile powers and the rescue of people from their deadly grip is clearly the "big picture"—the Passover picture, the kingdom-of-God picture. So how is this accomplished?

Elsewhere in the New Testament, as we have seen, this large-scale achievement is said to have taken place through Jesus's death "for our sins." In Galatians 1:4, he "gave himself for our sins, to rescue us from the present evil age, according to the will of God"—the three elements that Paul and the other early writers hold in careful balance. As we have seen, the "dying for sins" element represents a retrieval of the other great narrative of ancient Israel: Israel's sins had resulted in exile, exile had been prolonged, a new "slavery" had been the result—so that the new Passover would need to be effected *through sins being forgiven*. And sins are forgiven, as we have seen in the gospels and in Paul's other letters, through the representative and substitutionary death of Jesus. But in Romans Paul goes one dramatic and decisive, unique and vital step farther.

In Romans 5 Paul moves quietly from talking about "sins," plural, to "Sin," singular. In 5:12 he talks of "sin" entering the world, bringing death in its train. "Sin" is being treated as an active power, more than simply the sum total of all human wrongdoing. This accords, of course, with the analysis I have given earlier of how "sin" is actually the result of idolatry, in which humans hand over their God-given powers to other "forces," which then enslave them. There is therefore no conflict (as some have supposed) between his language about "sin" and his language about "Sin." The two go together. Indeed, Romans 5:12 ("Sin came into the world through one human being, and death through sin, and in that way death spread to all humans, in that all sinned") functions as a short summary of the whole section 1:18–2:16. But in Romans 5:12–8:4—the sequence stops rather abruptly at 8:4, for reasons we shall discover—Paul speaks of Sin, the enslaving power. And this will enable him to give his fullest and clearest statement of how "Sin" and therefore "sins" are ultimately dealt with, so that, with the "exile" of death itself being over, the "age to come" of resurrection life can at last begin.

None of this, of course, reduces very tidily into easy dogmatic formulas. As usual, it is best to regard shorthand summaries such as Galatians 1:4 as just that, shorthand summaries, which gain their proper meaning from the fuller narratives that they are summing up. And what we now find in Romans 7:1–8:11 is just such a fuller narrative.

This central passage, in fact, is one possible expansion of the official formula to which we have often alluded: "The Messiah died for our sins in accordance with the Bible" (1 Cor. 15:3). As we have seen, the phrase "in accordance with the Bible" has little to do with isolated proof-texts and everything to do with the meaning of the long, dark, puzzling narrative of Israel ending with the question mark at the end of the books of Malachi and Chronicles. "Exile" was still in operation. The first Christians saw the message and accomplishment of Jesus as the long-awaited arrival of God's kingdom, the final dealing-with-sin that would undo the powers of darkness and break through to the "age to come." The whole point, as in Galatians 3, was that Israel's long and sad story was not just a rambling muddle, an accumulation of irrelevant but damaging mistakes of generations that had more or less lost the plot. Paul never saw Israel's past history like that, though many readers of Paul have assumed that he did.

Rather, like so many other Second Temple Jews, Paul saw Israel's history standing under the rubric of Deuteronomy 26–32. The covenant always envisaged blessings and curses, and the curses, the result of disobedience, ended in exile. One of the regular words for that "exile" or "captivity" when Israel's scriptures were translated into Greek was the word that Paul uses in his dramatic summary of Israel's plight under the law in Romans 7:23: *aichmalōtizonta,* "taking captive." Only after that would there come the great divine act of liberation and transformation through which the covenant would be renewed. Only then would the divine plan for the whole creation—the covenant plan *through* Israel for the world—be put into effect. Paul, as we see at many points, has wrestled long and hard with this story, and here we see what is arguably the most important result of that struggle.

For most of Christian history it has been quietly assumed that the long, complex prophetic sequence envisaged in Deuteronomy—so well known to Jews of Jesus's day, so little known to the followers of Jesus after the first few generations—was basically irrelevant to the Christian story. One could leap straight from Isaiah 53 and Daniel 7 into the gospels and proceed as though all was well. But every step away from the Jewish narrative, in this case the Jewish narrative as reaching its focal point in Israel's Messiah, is a step toward paganism. So it has proved in the long term, as the de-Judaized story had to find another narrative framework and eventually came up with the "works contract," in which the history of Israel was merely an example of people getting things wrong, even though it also contained a few detached promises pointing into the long-distant future.

So what was the divine purpose hidden within that long story of Israel under Mosaic law? In Romans 7 Paul comes up with a striking answer, which leads directly to his fullest and clearest statement of the *means* by which the *goal* was attained. The law was given, he argues boldly, in order to draw "Sin" on to one point, *so that it could be condemned there once and for all.* The story of "Israel under the Torah" was designed, he says, in order to accumulate sin, to heap it up into one place—and simultaneously to lead to Israel's representative, the Messiah. The double narrative we see in "twin" passages like Psalms 105 and 106—the resonant and hopeful story of election, rescue, and promise and the dark and sorry story of rebellion, failure, and exile—would run together at last, as the Messiah, the focal point of hope and promise, met the Sin that the law had heaped up. His death would then be the means by which "Sin," accumulated precisely through the Torah, would finally be dealt with. If we want to understand what the early Christians meant by "he died for our sins," this passage will offer us the fullest account.

Many Christians who are used to telling the story in the normal way will find this a complex distraction. Isn't it enough, they will say, to know "*that* he died for our sins"? Why do we have to drag the long and tortuous story of Israel into the picture? It has been all too easy to skip over that long story, to marginalize the real point of Israel's scriptures, and to hurry on past, stopping only to scoop up one or two proof-texts for future reference. But the "main point"—the end and goal of Jesus's public career—*means what it means because of the whole story.* The Messiah died for our sins *in accordance with the Bible,* not in accordance with some other scheme into which a few fragments of the Bible can be made to fit.

All this comes to clear expression in Romans 7:13. The whole chapter expands at length on the hint Paul gave in 5:20: "The law came in alongside" (alongside, that is, the Adam–Messiah sequence), "*so that* the trespass might be filled out to its full extent. But where sin increased, grace increased all the more." As we noted before, the "so that" was deliberate and important. This, Paul is saying, was the divine purpose in giving the law. But why would God want to do something that would *increase* the trespass? Doesn't that sound odd? Romans 7 explains. The "so that" (or "in order that") of 5:20 is repeated twice in 7:13:

> Was it that good thing [the law], then, that brought death to me? Certainly not! On the contrary, it was Sin, *in order that* it might appear as Sin, working through the good thing and producing death in me. This was *in order that* Sin might become very sinful indeed, through the commandment.

Who is the "me" here? The "I" and "me" of Romans 7 is a literary device through which Paul is telling *the life story of Israel under the Torah*. He doesn't want to speak of Israel as "they," as though he were dealing with "others," people distant from himself. This is his own story not in the sense of straight autobiography, but in the sense that he, Paul, a loyal Jew, is part of that same Israel "according to the flesh." (That, of course, increases the tension in Romans 9, but that is for another day.) His analysis here is *the subsequent reflection of one who has come to believe that the crucified Jesus is Israel's Messiah.* Only in the light of Jesus can Israel's story be told in this way. Only in the light of Jesus can he look back and see not only that the God-given Torah *had the effect* of increasing "Sin," but that *this was the divine intention all along.* Hence the "so that" in 5:20 and the doubled "in order that" in 7:13.

So what was the hidden divine purpose in this seemingly strange story? As we saw, from Romans 5:12 on Paul has referred to "Sin" in the singular, "Sin" as a force or power that is let loose in the world and that ultimately rules the world ("Sin reigned in death," 5:21). "Sin" here seems to be the accumulation not just of human wrongdoings, but of the powers unleashed by idolatry and wickedness—the powers that humans were supposed to have, but that, through idolatry, they had handed over to nongods. Paul then uses the word "Sin" as a personification for all this. Sometimes it seems as though, in 7:7–12 at least, Paul says "Sin" where he might have said "the satan," or at least the serpent in Genesis 3. In any case, in Romans 7 Paul is telling two stories, the story of Adam and the story of Israel, weaving them together to show—as in much Jewish tradition—just how closely that they resonated with one another. His main point is that, through the Torah, *Israel recapitulated the sin of Adam.*

Paul was unaware of Mark Twain's *bon mot*, "History never repeats itself, but sometimes it rhymes," but what he says here makes that point nicely. (As we saw in Part Two, this putting together of Genesis 1–3 and the later story of Israel was a fairly obvious move to make within the ancient Jewish world.) When the Torah arrived in Israel, Israel acted out on a grand scale the sin of Adam and Eve in the garden. Perhaps that "grand scale" contributes to the reason why, in 5:12–8:4, Paul refers to "Sin" as a power: it is Sin on steroids, "Sin" turned into a force, Sin grown up and doing its worst. The commandment was given: in the garden it was, "You shall not eat of the tree"; in the Torah it was, "You shall not covet." In each case, Sin seized on the commandment as its golden opportunity. "It deceived me," says Paul in 7:11, "and, through it, killed me."

This then leads to the crucial move in 7:13. As in 5:20, the "purpose" here is the divine purpose. If we were to say, "God gave the law in order to deal with Sin," we might assume that this meant, "God gave the law in order to teach people what Sin was and how to avoid it." But Paul has a quite different meaning in mind. God gave the law *so that . . .* So that what? What was the point of showing up Sin for what it was and allowing it to become "very sinful indeed"? The answer, as in 5:20, is because of what God was going to do next. But first Paul explains the strange double life that results for those who—like his own former self—are living "under the law," delighting in it as God's law, but finding that it accuses them:

> We know, you see, that the law is spiritual. I, however, am made of flesh, sold as a slave under Sin's authority. I don't understand what I do. I don't do what I want, you see, but I do what I hate. So if I do what I don't want to do, I am agreeing that the law is good.
>
> But now it is no longer I that do it; it's Sin, living within me. I know, you see, that no good thing lives in me, that is, in my human flesh. For I can will the good, but I can't perform it. For I don't do the good thing I want to do, but I end up doing the evil thing I don't want to do. So if I do what I don't want to do, it's no longer "I" doing it; it's Sin, living inside me. (7:14–20)

Doubtless, this passage has multiple resonances in the experience of anyone who has ever tried to keep any serious moral code. Doubtless too it is framed in such a way as to resonate with the non-Jewish moralistic tradition. But the main purpose of the passage does not lie in either of those areas. Paul is not attempting to describe either the normal Christian life or the normal pre-Christian life. He is not saying of any particular stage of spiritual experience, "This is what it feels like at the time," true though that might be. He is highlighting *the outworking of the divine purpose in the deeply ambiguous nature of Israel under the Torah.* Israel rightly embraced the law as the divinely given covenant charter, but found that all the law could do was to show "Sin" up and actually cause it to swell to its full extent. It may at first glance seem astonishing. But Paul is affirming that this was what God had intended all along when giving the law to a people who, as Israel's own scriptures testified repeatedly, were themselves rebellious, idolatrous, and sinful.

Why? What was the point?

When we read this passage in the light of our other investigations into the early Christian understandings of the "end of exile" and the "forgiveness of sins," we get a clue as to what Paul is saying. Israel's long "enslavement," the "continuing exile" of Daniel 9 and many other texts, was not just a long, dreary process of waiting. It was the time in which the strange power called "Sin," the dark force unleashed by human idolatry, was doing its worst precisely in the people of God. God's people were captive, enslaved, to Babylon and its successors and to the dark powers that stood behind them. What God was doing through the Torah, in Israel, was to gather "Sin" together into one place, *so that it could then be condemned.* If anywhere in the whole New Testament teaches an explicit doctrine of "penal substitution," this is it—but it falls within the narrative not of a "works contract," not of an angry God determined to punish someone, not of "going to heaven," but of God's vocational covenant with Israel and through Israel, the vocation that focused on the Messiah himself and then opened out at last into a genuinely human existence:

> So, therefore, there is no condemnation for those in the
> Messiah, Jesus! Why not? Because the law of the spirit
> of life in the Messiah, Jesus, released you from the law of
> sin and death.
> For God has done what the law (being weak because
> of human flesh) was incapable of doing. God sent his
> own son in the likeness of sinful flesh, and as a sin-
> offering; and, right there in the flesh, he condemned Sin.
> This was in order that the right and proper verdict of the
> law could be fulfilled in us, as we live not according to
> the flesh but according to the spirit. (8:1–4)

This statement looks back at last to Romans 2:1–11, where Paul had warned about the "condemnation" that would fall on evildoers. He has already said that those "in the Messiah" have the verdict pronounced over them—the verdict, that is, of "righteous" or "in the right." He has already promised that those who are thus "declared to be in the right by his blood" (5:9) will be rescued from the wrath that is still to come. Now we see what he means.

"There is no condemnation for those in the Messiah . . . because God . . . condemned Sin right there in the flesh." The punishment has been meted out. But the punishment is on Sin itself, the combined, accumulated, and personified force that has wreaked such havoc in the world and in human lives.

Here is a point that must be noted most carefully. Paul does not say that God punished Jesus. He declares that God punished Sin *in the flesh* of Jesus. Now, to be sure, the crucifixion was no less terrible an event because, with theological hindsight, the apostle could see that what was being punished was Sin itself rather than Jesus himself. The physical, mental, and spiritual agony that Jesus went through on that terrible day was not alleviated in any way. But theologically speaking—and with regard to the implications that run through many aspects of church life, teaching, and practice—it makes all the difference.

The death of Jesus, seen in this light, is certainly *penal*. It has to do with the punishment on Sin—not, to say it again, on Jesus—but it is punishment nonetheless. Equally, it is certainly *substitutionary:* God condemned Sin (in the flesh of the Messiah), and therefore sinners who are "in the Messiah" are not condemned. The one dies, and the many do not. All those narrative fragments we saw in Luke and John come into their own. "This man has done nothing wrong." "Let one man die for the people, rather than the whole nation being wiped out." But this substitution finds its true meaning not within the normal "works contract," but within the God-and-Israel narrative, the vocational narrative, the story *in accordance with the Bible*. Once we rescue this substitution from its pagan captivity, it can resume its rightful place at the heart of the Jewish and then the messianic narrative, the story through which—in 8:4 as elsewhere—humans are rescued not so they can "go to heaven," but so that "the right and proper verdict of the law could be fulfilled in us, as we live not according to the flesh but according to the spirit." Humans are rescued in order to be "glorified," that is, so that they may resume the genuine human existence, bearing the divine image, reflecting God's wisdom and love into the world.

What Paul has done is to locate the dealing-with-Sin within the larger kingdom-of-God narrative—just as, in their own way, the gospels did. The new Passover (rescue from the enslaving power) is accomplished by dealing with sins; only now, with "sins" growing to their full extent as "Sin," the two stories finally fuse together into one. To put it another way, Paul has told the long, sad story of Israel and arrived at last at the "slavery" of "exile" as in Deuteronomy 28. Israel needed a fresh start, such as is described in Deuteronomy 30, which Paul quotes in exactly this sense in Romans 10. But for that, as the prophets insisted, Israel's sins needed to be dealt with so that "exile" could be undone. Paul has now shown, through the complex but carefully consistent narrative he has told, how this joins up with the larger expectation of the "new Exodus." At the heart of this conjoined double story, he has told the story of the Messiah, the one who represents Israel and who therefore becomes the "place" where Sin does its worst. Again, this resonates with the narrative of the four gospels, in which, as we saw, evil of every sort was building up like a thunderstorm as Jesus went about announcing the kingdom. It gathered itself together and finally unleashed its full fury upon him. That is the story the gospels were telling. It is the story behind the use of Psalm 2 in Acts 4:23–31. It is the story Paul has now encapsulated in this powerful and crucial little statement.

In telling the story this way, Paul has resolutely located the deepest meaning of the cross within Israel's narrative. That is where it should remain. Take it out of that story, as I have argued already, and we will tell instead a quasi-pagan story, separating the death of Jesus from the love of the creator God. That has happened often enough, despite the fact that here Paul explicitly rules it out. It was, he insists, *God's* purpose to allow the Torah to heap up Sin in this way; it was *God's son,* his own second self, who was sent in the likeness of sinful flesh. It was *God's* love that was demonstrated in action, as Paul insisted in 5:8 and reaffirms in 8:31–39. It is, after all, no demonstration of love if I send someone else to do the necessary but horrible task in my place. That would demonstrate, if anything, a callous or even cynical manipulation. For the death of Jesus to be an expression—the ultimate expression—of the divine love, that covenant love that as we saw lay at the heart of so many ancient Israelite expressions of hope for covenant rescue and renewal, we would need to say, and Paul does say, that in the sending of the son the creator and covenant God is sending his own very self.

Ultimately we have to choose between a proto-trinitarian framework for understanding Paul's view of Jesus's death and a quasi-pagan one. The church has often found itself lapsing into the latter. Romans brings us back sharply to the former. Even when theologians and preachers have seen this danger and have insisted that what was achieved on the cross was the direct result of the Father's love, when the goal is Platonized ("going to heaven") and the human role is moralized ("good and bad behavior"), the structure of the implicit story will still run in the wrong direction.

Two other elements of this passage make their distinctive contributions. First, Paul describes Jesus's death as "a sin offering." This may seem strange. Why mention this particular sacrifice, one of many different sacrifices in Leviticus and Numbers, at this moment? It would be a mistake, as I hinted earlier, to think that the animal presented as a sin offering was being punished for the sins of the worshipper. That is not the point. The point is that in the Bible the "sin offering" is, again and again, the particular sacrifice that has to do with sins that the Israelite performed either unwillingly (not intending to do them) or unwittingly (intending to do them but not realizing that they were sinful). And Paul has analyzed the actions of the "I" in 7:13–20 in such a way as to place Israel under the Torah in exactly that position. "I don't understand what I do" (v. 15) is literally, "I do not know what I am doing"; this is *unwitting* sin, the sin of ignorance. "I end up doing the evil thing I don't want to do" (v. 20); this is the *unwilling* sin. The remedy is suited exactly to the problem. The forgiveness of sins, the major return-from-exile theme in Isaiah, Jeremiah, and Ezekiel, is now available. The exile is over. The slave master's power is broken. The covenant is renewed in and through Israel's Messiah. With that there is the assurance that the powers themselves are defeated, because Sin, the very foundation of their power, has been condemned.

That is why, second, the result is not that sinners are free to "go to heaven," but that they are free for the true human vocation, the royal priesthood in all its variations. It is when humans take up their proper vocation, redeemed by the Messiah and indwelt by the Spirit, that the "powers" find they are starved of their oxygen. That is what much of the rest of Romans 8 is about, starting with the end of v. 4: "as we live not according to the flesh but according to the spirit." This points ahead to the resurrection itself (8:9–11), to the life of taking responsibility for one's own body and its actions (8:12–16), and to the vocation to suffer and so to share the "glory" of the Messiah (8:17–25), that is, his strange, suffering, but powerful rule over the world. This leads to the ultimate new creation, when the present creation, groaning in travail, will be set free from its slavery to corruption and decay, "to enjoy the freedom that comes when God's children are glorified" (8:23). That is the ultimate "glory," the "royal" role for which humans were made and for which, as in 5:17, they are redeemed. They are "justified" in order to be "justice bringers." This is the result of the revolution accomplished on the cross. The work of the cross is not designed to rescue humans *from* creation, but to rescue them *for* creation. If we told the story that way, all kinds of problems would either be solved or at least appear in a new light.

The point then extends also to the "priestly" work of intercession. Humans who are redeemed through the Messiah and indwelt by the Spirit discover that, in the pain of ignorance about what to pray for, "that same spirit pleads on our behalf, with groanings too deep for words" (8:26). But God, the "Searcher of Hearts," knows what the Spirit is thinking, because the Spirit is pleading for God's people according to God's will (8:27). And so it goes on, to the final statement of assurance: nothing can separate us from the love of God revealed in the death of the Messiah.

I have stressed that here as elsewhere the picture only makes sense if we take the view that all the early Christians shared, that the living God of Israel was personally present in and as Jesus himself. This poses for later thinkers an obvious problem: How could God, as it were, be split into two? The first Christians do not seem to have seen it like that. Nor did they worry particularly about how to say what had to be said. They drew on various Jewish models already in use to talk about how the one God, utterly beyond and above the world he had made, was nevertheless present and active within it. This, after all, is how Israel's scriptures speak of Israel's God.

For Israel, of course, this way of thinking about God was focused in the Temple in particular and also in Torah itself. Discussions of Jesus and his identity have returned in our own day to the ancient Jewish Temple theology to discover all kinds of possibilities that had remained opaque when the discussion was stuck in non-Jewish categories. The Temple was, after all, the place where heaven and earth met. Why not say that one particular person might be the ultimate example of the same phenomenon, a person equally at home in both dimensions? The Torah was the revealed will of the transcendent God for his covenant people. Why not say that one particular person might finally embody the divine will? In some Jewish thought, these beliefs were already combined in the idea of "wisdom," the divine blueprint for humankind, of which David's son Solomon was seen as the primary exponent. When Paul speaks of God "sending" the Son (8:3; also Gal. 4:4), he is bringing together two strands of Jewish thought in particular: first, the idea of God "sending" the divine "wisdom" into the world, and specifically into the Temple; second, the idea of the "Father" and the "Son," which goes back to the language used of the Davidic Messiah in 2 Samuel 7, Psalm 2, and elsewhere.

As the argument of Romans 8 develops, all these concepts are firmly in play. It is the messianic identity and "glory" of Jesus that is shared with his followers in 8:17–25. When Paul speaks about the Spirit being present with Jesus's people, indwelling them, and leading them to their promised inheritance (8:12–16), the language he uses and the implicit story he is telling remind us of the pillar of cloud and fire in the original Exodus. There is a deep incipient trinitarian thought here, firmly rooted in the traditions of Israel. That larger conception of Israel's God provides the context within which everything Paul wants to say about the death of Jesus can be said clearly and without pagan distortion.

This opens up a possibility—to look back to the gospels for a moment—for understanding one of the most perplexing moments in the whole New Testament portrayal of Jesus's death: the cry of dereliction on the cross. The more strongly we affirm the doctrine of the Trinity (both Mark and Matthew, who report the cry, clearly believe that Jesus is the living embodiment of Israel's God), the harder it all seems to become. But the picture of God that emerges from Romans 8 suggests another way of seeing things.

Paul's remarkable description of prayer in Romans 8:26–27 indicates that there are times when "we don't know what to pray for as we ought to; but that same spirit pleads on our behalf, with groanings too deep for words." At that point, as we noted a moment ago, Paul declares that God, the "Searcher of Hearts," knows what the Spirit is thinking. The Spirit, as we just saw, is taking the role in this passage that in the Exodus narrative belongs to the glorious divine Presence. There is, in other words, no question that for Paul the Spirit is (in later language) fully divine. We thus have here a conversation going on between the Spirit, groaning with sighs too deep for words, and the Heart Searcher himself; the two are deeply in tune with one another, but the Spirit is groaning like a woman in labor. Does this mean a split within the Trinity? Certainly not. And if Paul can say that about the Father and the Spirit, through whose dialogue the church is conformed to the image of the Son (8:29), why should Matthew and Mark not say something very similar about the Father and the Son?

I suspect, in fact, that we have been misled by the easy assumption that while the Son and perhaps the Spirit are out and about on their various tasks, the Father is, as it were, waiting back at the office, calmly in charge of the world. In a sense that may be true. But if the Christology of the New Testament means anything, it means that we only learn the deepest truths about God himself by looking at Jesus. In Philippians 2 we discover that the life of self-abandonment and humility to which the Son devoted himself was not undertaken *despite* the fact that he was "in the form of God," but precisely *because* he was in the form of God. In Colossians 1:15 the Messiah is the "image of the invisible God"; in John 1:18 he is the one who makes known the God who cannot otherwise be seen. In Mark 10 Jesus insists that the power that overcomes the powers is the power of self-giving love. All these, it seems, converge in the actual events.

So what if it were true after all? What if the Creator, all along, had made the world out of overflowing, generous love, so that the overflowing, self-sacrificial love of the Son going to the cross was indeed the accurate and precise self-expression of the love of God for a world radically out of joint? Would it not then make sense to say that, just as the wordless groanings of the Spirit in Romans 8:26–27 are part of what it means to be God—to be both present in the depths of the world's pain and transcendent over it but searching all hearts—so the cry of dereliction was itself part of what it meant to be God, to be the God of generous love? Might that not enable us to give an account of the Trinity as overflowing, creative love? No doubt this, like all attempts to speak wisely and truly about God, will fall short of the reality. But once we allow Paul's view of the divine Presence and action in the world to help us shape our larger view, I think the possibility is at least open. If reading the gospels for all they're worth can help us with our reading of Paul (and this is what I have tried to make happen in this book), perhaps at this point at least Paul can help us with our reading of one of the hardest sayings in the gospels.

But all of this points back, within Romans itself, to the passage which for many interpreters is the very center of a Christian view of Jesus's death. What is Paul saying in Romans 3?

# 13

---

# The Death of Jesus in Paul's Letter to the Romans

*Passover and Atonement*

W E MUST NOW move back at last to the passage where most interpreters of Paul have tried to discern an "atonement" theology and where much debate has focused. The dense little paragraph we know as Romans 3:21–26 is arguably the beating heart of Romans 1–4 as a whole. Ask any preachers or biblical teachers to explain the meaning of the cross, and sooner or later they will come to this passage. It is a difficult passage, partly because Paul has crammed so much into a short space and partly because every phrase, almost every word, has been controversial down the years. But there is no escape: we must keep our nerve and work at it steadily.

Since my own translation will inevitably be seen as biased, I here quote the New Revised Standard Version. (Many other translations are available, of course, but at this point the NRSV is among the least problematic.) I highlight vv. 24–26, in which the crucial phrases occur:

But now, apart from law, the righteousness of God has
been disclosed, and is attested by the law and the prophets, the righteousness of God through faith in Jesus
Christ for all who believe. For there is no distinction,
since all have sinned and fall short of the glory of God;
*they are now justified by his grace as a gift, through the redemp-*
*tion that is in Christ Jesus, whom God put forward as a sacrifice*
*of atonement by his blood, effective through faith. He did this to*
*show his righteousness, because in his divine forbearance he had*
*passed over the sins previously committed; it was to prove at the*
*present time that he himself is righteous and that he justifies the*
*one who has faith in Jesus.*

Despite the difficulties this passage presents, I believe we are
in a good position, granted the argument of this book so far, to
get some fresh clarity on what Paul is saying here. Two things in
particular encourage me to think this.

First, the case I have presented so far feeds directly into this
present passage. I have argued that the early Christian view of
Jesus's death was focused on Passover and hence on the Exodus
story, now to be experienced as the new liberating event that was
also the great one-off "sin-forgiving" event. Though the language
here is unique to this passage, the outline meaning—Passover and
atonement, in fulfillment of the covenant and to forgive sins and
cleanse from impurity—is the same. This helps us to understand
not only what Paul is here saying so densely, but also how such a
formulation could already exist so early in the Christian movement. The passage may be unique, but it summarizes in its own
particular way an interpretation of Jesus's death that was widely
characteristic of the first generation.

Second, there are fresh and compelling ways of reading Romans 1–4 as a whole that can provide real help in getting a grip
on this passage, which seems from a structural point of view to
be intended as the dense heart of the whole argument. The pas-

sage has regularly been read as the vital move *in the wrong story*—
the story, once again, of a "works contract" in which, to put it
crudely, humans sin, God punishes Jesus, and humans are let off.
This omits elements that were vital for Paul and that he sets out
in detail in 1:18–3:20 and chapter 4, the large passages that flank
this short one. Once we understand the larger overall story Paul is
telling rather than the story that some parts of Christian tradition
have hoped he was telling, these vital verses spring into new life.

For a start, there is the *covenantal* element. Israel's vocation, on
the one hand (2:17–20), and the divine promises to Abraham,
on the other (chapter 4), come together in the accomplishment
of Israel's Messiah. The Messiah is thus the means *both* of God's
faithfulness to Israel *and* of the answering faithfulness of Israel
to God. One central biblical term to refer both to the divine
covenant faithfulness and to the status of the covenant member
is *tsedaqah*, in Greek *dikaiosynē*, regularly (if potentially mislead-
ingly) translated into English as "righteousness" or "justice." This
word, in one form or another, occurs no fewer than seven times
in Romans 3:21–26, more than any other word (including "God"
and "Jesus") except for the definite article.

Further, there is the *cultic* element. The primary failure of the
human race was *idolatry,* a failure of worship. This is emphasized
in 1:18–23, prior to any mention of actual sin. Humans in general
"swapped the glory of the immortal God for the likeness of the
image of mortal humans—and of birds, animals, and reptiles"
(1:23). Israel, in particular, did this when making and worshipping the golden calf when they should have been preparing to
receive the glorious divine Presence in the tabernacle; Paul here
echoes Psalm 106:20, which recalls that incident. Abraham, by
contrast, gave God the glory, believing his apparently impossible
promises (4:20–21). This failure as well as the culpable sin it produces are directly addressed at the heart of the passage.

These two, covenant and cult, go naturally together. God's
covenant with Abraham and his family, coming into vivid op-

eration in the Passover and the Exodus, led directly to the construction of the tabernacle and, eventually, to the Temple that replaced it. The central cult object was the "ark of the covenant," on whose lid God would meet with his people, having provided, through the "blood of the covenant," the appropriate cleansing, so that his sacred Presence could dwell with his people and their representative, the high priest, could actually enter his holy Presence. This was to be repeated on each Day of Atonement. The Greek word for the lid of the ark is *hilastērion,* which is perhaps the central word in this whole passage, closely associated with "blood," in this case that of Jesus. All this we will explore in more detail presently.

It should be clear from this that the question of sin and forgiveness, which is usually made the focus of this passage, is not sidelined as people sometimes imagine, but is actually highlighted within this "covenantal" reading. God's covenant with Abraham and through Israel for the world was there precisely in order to deal with sin, as "the Jew" in 2:17–20 knows and claims. The cult was there so that, despite persistent idolatry and sin, Israel could remain God's covenant people; he could dwell in their midst, and they with him. All this, as we saw in Part Two, acquired new focus and urgency in the Second Temple period, when many Jews longed for a new Passover that, in liberating Israel from pagan enemies, would constitute the "forgiveness of sins," the real "return from exile." At the heart of this would be the long-promised return of YHWH himself, as in Isaiah 40–55, Ezekiel 43, and Malachi 3. In first-century Jewish rereadings of scripture "forgiveness of sins" went closely with these other themes, all of which, as we shall see, feature in the present passage.

All these themes, in fact, come rushing together in Romans 3:21–26, much as a million telephone conversations and Internet downloads can somehow be contained in a cable the width of your little finger. No wonder the passage is so dense. But—to change the metaphor—if we listen carefully we will be able to hear, one by one and then in a rich harmony, all the instruments of the Pauline orchestra playing their own line within the equal music of the gospel.

This is not, however, how Romans 3 has usually been understood.

## The Usual Reading of Romans 3— and Its Problems

The usual way of reading Romans 1–4, sometimes (as we have seen) called the "Romans road," is the straightforward "works contract." God requires perfect obedience; all fail, and sin; all must die; Jesus dies in our place; we are forgiven and assured of going to heaven. In this reading, the word "righteousness" in this passage is assumed to refer to "goodness" or "good moral standing." We have no goodness ("righteousness") of our own, but God conveys, reckons, or otherwise grants to believers a different "righteousness," a status that comes from God himself ("a righteousness from God"), perhaps even consisting of God's own moral status (the "righteousness of God" in that sense), or even, though Paul never says this, the "righteousness of Christ." Theories differ at this point, but in one way or another this "righteousness" consists of the moral status, the utter goodness or worth that belongs to God or to Christ, focused on the death of Jesus in place of sinners. He takes their sin; they take his "righteousness." In some versions of the theory, the "righteousness of Christ" also includes his perfect obedience, his keeping of the law, which is then "reckoned" to believers. Some translations, notably the New International Version, have rendered Romans 1:16–17 and 3:21–26 in such a way as to compel readers toward this kind of sense and to make it difficult to hear anything else. This too is how 2 Corinthians 5:21 is normally read, though I have argued in chapter 11 of this book and more fully elsewhere that this is not what Paul means.

At the heart of this usual reading of Romans 3 stands a particular interpretation of the rare word *hilastērion* in v. 25, namely, the "place or means of 'propitiation.'" This would mean that the "wrath of God" spoken of in 1:18–2:16 has been meted out on Jesus, so that those who trust in him may escape that wrath; so that, with divine justice "satisfied" by Jesus's death, God can justify people justly, as in v. 26. (In some versions the "righteousness" of God is taken to include God's punitive justice, so that the phrase also points to an interpretation in which God punishes sins on the cross.)

This way of understanding *hilastērion* sometimes claims support from the use of the term in a Jewish writing roughly contemporary with Paul's, the book called 4 Maccabees. Toward the end of that book, summarizing the effect of the martyrdoms suffered under the Syrian persecution of the second century BC, the writer says that the martyrs had become, "as it were, a ransom for the sin of our nation," since "through the blood of these devout ones and their death as an atoning sacrifice, divine Providence preserved Israel that previously had been mistreated" (17:21–22). The word for "atoning sacrifice" here is *hilastērion,* and, though the passage is not entirely clear, the sense has often been taken to be that the deaths of the martyrs somehow propitiated the divine wrath that was otherwise hanging over the nation. We shall return to this later.

Coming back to Romans 3, the usual reading is that through this "propitiation" those who trust in what Jesus did on the cross can be declared to be "in the right." This event of "reckoning of righteousness" is called "justification" (confusingly, the English words "righteous" and "just" translate the same Greek root, *dikaios*). The present passage is normally seen as central to this doctrine. In this usual narrative of "justification," humans start off with no moral credit, nothing to qualify them to escape hell and go to heaven; but God's action in Christ gives them the credit, the "righteousness," they need. They are therefore "justified."

There are several different ways of explaining this reading of Romans 3 in theory and of arguing for it exegetically. I have here given the stripped-down, bargain-basement version. Whatever sophistication may be introduced by theologians, expositors, and preachers, this is what people normally "hear" when the "Romans road" is being expounded. But, as I shall now argue, it is not what Paul is saying.

Problems in this usual reading meet us at every turn. This can seem a little technical. But since those who expound Romans in the traditional way are usually committed to regarding scripture, including Paul's letters, as divine revelation, it must be permissible—indeed, mandatory!—to probe and see what actually happens to the text as a whole when we take this line.

For a start, this understanding of 3:21–26 leaves vv. 27–31 stranded. It appears to change the subject, from "how you acquire this 'righteousness'" to "how Jews and Gentiles come together into a single faith family." That, indeed, is what many writers and preachers have imagined.

So too chapter 4 becomes seriously undervalued. Many who expound Romans regard Abraham in this chapter merely as an "example" of "someone in scripture who was justified by faith." Sometimes the chapter is simply labeled as a "proof from scripture" of the "doctrine" that Paul has supposedly been expounding in chapter 3. But this misses the whole point.

This reading also ignores the plain meaning of 2:17–20. It flattens out Paul's careful statement of the vocation of "the Jew" (to be the light of the world) into simply another aspect of the general truth that "all have sinned." This in turn leaves 3:1–9 high and dry, or at least very difficult. This short passage consists of a rapid-fire series of questions and answers that make excellent sense if we read 2:17–29 in the way I am suggesting, but very little sense any other way. Again, many commentators and preachers have noticed this; some very careful and "conservative" expositors declare that the passage is too complex and puzzling to be much help. This in turn results in a failure to see what Paul is getting at in 3:21–26.

Finally, the "problem" Paul is addressing is assumed to be simply human wrongdoing ("sin"). However, in Romans 1:18–23 and in the summary of that passage in 3:23 we find a deeper element as well. "Sin" is rooted in idolatry, the swapping of the divine Glory for images. Here Paul is exactly on the map of Second Temple Jewish writings. But many today, eager to talk about "sin," have forgotten that it is the second-order problem. The root cause of the trouble is the worship of idols.

These exegetical problems point to the underlying theological difficulties with the usual reading. This usual reading is all about how we get "right with God" in order to "go to heaven"; but Paul never mentions "going to heaven," here or elsewhere in Romans, and the idea of being "right with God," though related to Paul's theme, is usually taken out of the specific context he intends. Ironically, the usual reading takes "going to heaven" (or some near equivalent) for granted and then complains if, instead, someone tries to reintroduce into these chapters the themes that Paul demonstrably *is* expounding. It all becomes so complicated, people grumble—when what they really mean is, "I am so used to reading this passage one way that I find it hard to switch and consider other options."

Further, the usual reading assumes that the problem Paul is facing is divine wrath and that in 3:24–26, and in particular with the key term *hilastērion,* he is explaining how this wrath is somehow dealt with. This is lexically possible, but there are four problems with it. First, as we shall see in a moment, the word in context is far more likely to refer to the "mercy seat," the place in the tabernacle or Temple where God promises, as the focus of his covenant, to meet with his people and to that end provides cleansing for both the people and the sanctuary so that the meeting can take place. Second, it is simply a mistake to assume, as the "usual" reading has done, that a reference to the Bible's sacrificial system indicates that a sacrificial animal is being killed in the place of the worshipper. Third, when Paul sums up the effect of the present passage in 5:9, he says that if we have been "justified by his blood," we *shall* be saved from the future wrath. He cannot therefore intend the phrase "justified by his blood"— the summary of 3:24–26—to mean "being saved from wrath," or 5:9 would be a tautology ("being saved from wrath, we shall be saved from wrath"). Fourth, at the heart of this passage Paul says that God has passed over former sins in his forbearance. This is the very opposite of "punishment." It could be of course (and many have suggested this) that God had previously "passed over" sins in order to save up the punishment until it could be vented on Jesus. But there is no indication that this is what Paul has in mind.

These problems are bad enough. But there are more.

Looming over all these difficulties, the phrase "God's righteousness," which dominates the present passage, does not mean "a righteous status that God conveys to people." It is clear at the end of the passage, in vv. 25–26, that it refers to God's *own* "righteousness." God displays his "righteousness" in that he himself is "righteous"; when he "justifies" people, he does so justly. If that is the conclusion of the argument, stated with unusual emphasis, it is highly likely that the opening of the paragraph, the unveiling of "God's righteousness," refers to the same point. But what then is this "righteousness of God"?

In Israel's scriptures, to which Paul explicitly appeals in 3:21b ("the law and the prophets bore witness to it"), God's "righteousness" is not simply God's status of being morally upright. It is, more specifically, *God's faithfulness to the covenant*—the covenant not only *with* Abraham and Israel, but *through* Israel to the wider world. The actual phrase "God's righteousness" itself is rare in the Old Testament, but there are plenty of occurrences of "my righteousness," "his righteousness," or "your righteousness" and statements about God doing what is right or being in the right, which point this way, however much they are sometimes obscured by different translations—a problem for which there is no space here. A careful reading through the Psalms and Isaiah 40–55 will make the point. Again and again the meaning of "righteousness" is not simply that God does what is right (though that is of course true as well), but that, as one focused example of this, he is *faithful to his covenanted promises,* utterly reliable in following through what he said he would do, specifically in relation to the covenant that he made with Israel and through Israel for the world. Of course, in Deuteronomy and the prophets this "faithfulness" can mean, and often does, that God will punish his people if they commit idolatry: the covenant stipulated that this would happen, and when it does (particularly in the exile, seen in Deut. 28–29 as the ultimate consequence of idolatry), it is a sign not of God's unfaithfulness, but of his faithfulness. Perhaps the most obvious example of all this is Daniel 9, where the divine righteousness is seen at work in both the covenantal punishment of Israel's sins by exile (vv. 4–14) and then the promised and prayed-for covenant restoration (vv. 15–19).

This idea of God being faithful to the covenant clearly seems to be Paul's meaning here in Romans 3. Within the larger unit of chapters 1–4 as a whole, 3:21–26 is framed more particularly between the argument that starts at 2:17 and the exposition of Genesis 15 in chapter 4. A preliminary glance at both (we will fill in the details presently) will make the point.

Romans 2:17–3:9 is concerned, first, with the worldwide purpose of Israel's divine vocation (2:17–20); second, with Israel's covenantal failure (2:21–24; 3:2–4); and third, with the problem that this poses for God's *dikaiosynē,* his "righteousness" (3:5). How is God to be faithful to the covenant—to rescue and bless the world through the Jews—if Israel is faithless? Romans 4 is then all about God's covenant with Abraham, its worldwide purpose, and the way in which, through the gospel, God has now been faithful to that covenant. These two (Israel's vocation to rescue the world;

God's covenant promises to Abraham to give him a worldwide family) obviously go together. The divine purpose *through Israel for the world* is the subject of the passages both before and after 3:21–26. There is every reason, therefore, for taking "God's righteousness" in 3:21 in its normal biblical sense of "covenant faithfulness." There is every reason too to understand the display of that "righteousness" as connected with God's somehow rescuing the world from idolatry and sin, *through Israel,* in order to create a single worldwide family for Abraham. The actual arguments Paul advances on either side of our passage, in other words, strongly support a reading of *dikaiosynē theou* and cognate ideas in 3:21–26 as "covenant faithfulness." This fits with what we just saw about the passage itself, which ends with an emphatic reference to God himself being "righteous," rather than to "God's righteousness" as a moral status or quality that God credits to others.

Paul is not, then, talking about God's moral uprightness in general. He is referring more particularly to his faithfulness to his covenant purposes, enacted through the faithful Messiah, Jesus, through which he brings his putting-right purposes (his "justice") to the world. That is why, in my own translation, I have rendered the relevant phrases as God's "covenant justice," though it is impossible, without descending into barbarism, to render every use of the *dikaios* root in the same way:

> But now, quite apart from the law (though the law and the prophets bore witness to it), *God's covenant justice* [*dikaiosynē*] has been displayed. *God's covenant justice* comes into operation through the faithfulness of Jesus the Messiah, for the benefit of all who have faith. For there is no distinction: all sinned, and fell short of God's glory—and by God's grace they are freely declared to be in the right [*dikaioumenoi*], to be members of the covenant, through the redemption which is found in the Messiah, Jesus.

God put Jesus forth as the place of mercy, through faithfulness, by means of his blood. He did this to demonstrate *his covenant justice* [*dikaiosynē*], because of the passing over (in divine forbearance) of sins committed beforehand. This was to demonstrate *his covenant justice* [*dikaiosynē*] in the present time: that is, that he himself is in the right [*dikaios*], and that he declares to be in the right [*dikaioutai*] everyone who trusts in the faithfulness of Jesus.

Even those who follow the traditional line through this passage, in fact, will usually agree that vv. 25–26 really do seem to be talking about God's faithfulness to the covenant. This should be taken as a solid fixed point.

Some who recognize this have tried to ward off the implications for the larger passage by proposing that perhaps Paul is here quoting and radically modifying a pre-Pauline formula from an earlier "Jewish Christian" circle for whom this notion of "covenant faithfulness" was still important—while for Paul, these interpreters assume, such a notion was irrelevant. That is another telltale sign of what is going on in such reconstructions. A Western tradition of reading has broken away from the Jewish roots of the gospel and has thereby taken a significant step toward an entirely different understanding, so that, like those eighteenth-century critics who didn't like the rich density of Shakespeare, it can only see a mere "pre-Pauline Jewish Christian formula" where Paul is saying something central to his entire argument.

Such readings then suggest that Paul has taken this original shorthand formula about God's faithfulness to his covenant with Israel, still visible in vv. 24–26, and has modified it so that now it speaks, *instead,* about *something different,* namely, Jesus's death as the remedy for human sins. This can then be fitted into one version or another of the usual "works contract," as though sin, punishment, and forgiveness were the only things Paul was really interested in at this point. (Any attempt to suggest that the "covenant" is somehow Paul's leading theme at this point is then regarded with suspicion, as though it means taking sin, punishment, and salvation less seriously—a suggestion whose absurdity has not prevented its frequent repetition.) But this is not a wise way to read any piece of writing. Particularly when a writer produces a dense little passage like this, it is greatly preferable to assume that the words are there because they say what the author intended. The traditions of reading against which I am arguing have done their best to exclude the idea of the covenant with Israel from Paul's thought at this key point. It can't be done.

In particular, it can't be done because Romans 3:21–26 (and the whole passage to the end of chapter 4) is designed—as we might expect—to be the answer to the questions raised in the previous section. This is where we need to pull the camera back a little and survey in more detail the passages we glanced at earlier, on either side of the central one.

The usual "Romans road" reading of the letter assumes that the *only* point Paul is making between 1:18 and 3:20 is that "all humans are sinful." This then leads us into the "works contract": we are moral failures; we need to get "right with God" if we're going to get to heaven; Jesus dies in our place; the job is done. And at one level this is better than nothing. The glass may be one-third full. But something vital has been left out, like a cocktail without the all-important shot of bourbon. You can still drink it. Some important flavors are really there. But the intended meaning, the real "kick" to Paul's argument, is missing.

Actually, there are two missing meanings. First, the usual reading ignores the implicit Temple theme, evident in the second half of Romans 3:23: "All sinned, *and fell short of God's glory.*" This is not a coded way of saying "they failed to qualify for the 'glory' of 'heaven.'" It refers back, rather, to 1:21–23: "They knew God, but didn't honor him as God" (literally, "They did not *glorify* him as God"), and "they swapped the *glory* of the immortal God for the likeness of the image of mortal humans." This echo (via Ps. 106:20) of the story of the golden calf indicates that, as we see in 1:18–32 as a whole, *behind "sin" itself there lies idolatry*. Humans have turned away from the creator God and have worshipped and served created things instead. They have even created for themselves second-order images of created things, thus worshipping objects twice removed from the creator God and thereby abusing their own God-given human powers for a purpose that reverses and undercuts their genuine human vocation. Human skill and ingenuity were designed to work for God's purposes in the world, not to generate alternate gods for people to worship instead. "Sin," then, is not simply the breaking of God's rules. *It is the outflowing of idolatry.*

That is the primary problem of Romans 1. It is the problem to which Paul refers in the second half of 3:23. And it is the problem that is then addressed directly in 3:24–26, where Jesus himself is put forward by the creator God as the place and the means of the fresh meeting between the true God and his human creatures. That is why, when describing Abraham's faith, Paul indicates that the patriarch reversed the idolatry: "He grew strong in faith and gave glory to God" (4:20). And that is why, immediately after the end of the whole argument, Paul sums up to the point he has reached in the cultic language of 5:1–2, where those who are justified have "access" to the divine grace and celebrate the "hope of the glory of God." The first thing that is missing from the usual line of thought, then, is any attempt to show how Paul deals not just with "sin" itself, but with the idolatry that lies behind it and the ensuing loss of "glory."

The second thing missing from the usual account is any attempt to show how 3:21–26 fits with the line of thought Paul introduced in 2:17–24. (Here I develop further the point I mentioned briefly a moment ago.) This passage too has been squashed out of shape, in this case by readers assuming that Paul is here simply talking about "the Jew" as a special case within the "works contract." In this "usual" reading, Paul is merely rubbing in the point that all humans are sinful. Jews may think they are morally superior to Gentiles, but in fact they are not. It is of course true that in 3:19–20 Paul does indeed conclude that nobody, whether Jew or Gentile, can be "in the right before God." The Torah itself makes this clear. Paul then hammers the same point home again in 3:23: "All sinned, and fell short of God's glory." But this overall argument (that all human beings are sinful, and that Jews are no exception) cannot be allowed to nullify the specific *and different* point that 2:17–3:9 is actually making. This too is vital if we are to understand the inner dynamic of 3:21–26.

Here, once again, we see the difference between the "works contract" and the "covenant of vocation." It has been assumed that Paul, addressing "the Jew" in 2:17, is talking about a works contract; but in fact he is clearly speaking of Israel's vocational covenant. The Jew against whom Paul is arguing—his own former self, we may suppose—is not saying, "I am an exception to the rule of universal sin." The Jew against whom he is arguing is saying, "Yes, the world is indeed in a mess; but we Jewish people, armed with the Torah, are God's chosen solution to this problem. We have been given the divine vocation of sorting out this mess, of putting the world right." And Paul basically agrees with this. This has been so unexpected in many traditions of reading that Paul's plain words have been overlooked.

He does not dispute that "the Jew" really does have a particular status and equipment:

> But supposing you call yourself a "Jew." Supposing you rest your hope in the law. Supposing you celebrate the fact that God is your God, and that you know what he wants, and that by the law's instruction you can make appropriate moral distinctions. (2:17–18)

He agrees—indeed, he would insist on the point—that these privileges are given so that Israel may be the light to the nations:

> Supposing you believe yourself to be a guide to the
> blind, a light to people in darkness, a teacher of the
> foolish, an instructor for children—all because, in the
> law, you possess the outline of knowledge and truth.
> (2:19–20)

This is a classic statement of the well-known Jewish belief—variously expressed, but common across many traditions—that *God's call of Abraham and his family was designed to put right what was wrong with the world.* Paul is *not* saying, as some commentators have imagined, "You are a bigot, imagining yourself to be morally superior." He is saying, "You believe that God has called you—has called Israel as a whole—to be the light of the world." And Paul affirms that belief. "The Jew" whom he is addressing is quite correct. This is indeed what the scriptures say. This is the vocation of Israel.

The problem, however, was pointed out long before by Israel's own scriptures, on page after page. The prophets said it repeatedly: Israel's vocation didn't work out the way it might have, because Israel went wrong. This is not a new charge. Paul is not making it all up on the basis of his newfound belief in Jesus. He is not "rejecting Judaism" because he has found something different, something he considers "better." (When Paul confronts his own former self as a Jew who did not believe Jesus to be the Messiah, he is not engaging in what we today might think of as "comparative religion," setting one "system" over against another and contrasting their relative merits and demerits. His larger position is what we might call *messianic eschatology*: if Jesus is Israel's Messiah, then Israel's God is regrouping his people around Jesus, just as other first-century messianic movements tried to corral loyal Jews around their central figure. But he does not base 2:21–24 on this. He simply repeats the scriptural charges.) As many Jews in our own day have insisted, Israel has a long and noble tradition of *critique from within* going back to scripture itself, and Paul is simply continuing the practice. The prayers of penitence in Ezra 9, Nehemiah 9, and Daniel 9 said it all. The "curse" of Deuteronomy had come into force: Israel had been exiled. In 2:24 Paul quotes Isaiah 52:5, which also echoes also Ezekiel 36:20: "Because of you, God's name is blasphemed among the nations." The non-Jewish nations were supposed to look at Israel and *praise* Israel's God. Instead, they looked at Israel and blasphemed his name. The vocation had turned sour.

Paul then sharpens the critique by supposing for a moment (2:25–29) that God can and will summon Gentiles into his family, making them a people who really do keep the law. What he means by this is not our present concern. But it highlights the question that is already on the table from 2:17–24: If this was the divine plan, what has become of it? If God called and commissioned Israel to be the light to the nations, how will that plan now go forward? If God established his covenant through Abraham as the means by which the world would be made right, but if the covenant people have let him down, is God now going to abandon the covenant, forget Israel, and do things by a different route?

At this point the usual reading of Romans—reflecting the traditional view of the church—has answered: yes! God has parked his broken-down car in a side road somewhere and has completed the journey on foot. He has jettisoned the covenant with Israel and has instead intervened in person, in Jesus. This is how the "gospel" is presented by many Christians today, including those who use the "Romans road." As we have seen, that explanation simply goes like this: we sinned, God sent Jesus to die for us, we are saved. No mention of Israel. But when you leave out Israel, your shortened story will easily tip over into a non-Jewish way of thinking, into, as we have seen, a platonic view of the ultimate goal ("heaven"), a moralistic view of the human vocation ("good behavior"), and a downright pagan view of salvation (an innocent death placating an angry deity).

And at some point this non-Jewish story all too often turns into an anti-Jewish story. That was a risk in Paul's day too. That is why he wrote Romans 9–11—which was only partially successful, as we can see from the rise of the anti-Jewish teacher Marcion in second-century Rome. But my point here is simply that if we imagine that Paul is pushing the vocation of Israel to one side and replacing it with something else, we will never be able to understand the intricate details of Romans 3.

The usual reading means that, in theological language, "incarnation" takes the place of "election." This mistake is all the easier to make in that Paul does indeed believe in incarnation, and it is indeed one of the vital elements in this whole argument. But for him the incarnate Son *is also Israel's Messiah*. Incarnation does not cancel election; it brings it to its climax. The living God comes into his world in the person of Israel's representative, to do for Israel and the world what they could not do for themselves, to be the place of meeting between the Creator and his human creatures. That explosive fusion of roles forms the heart of Paul's theological vision, here and elsewhere. But this is to get ahead of ourselves. The usual reading of Romans—incorporating some version of the "works contract"—imagines that, for Paul, God has indeed put the covenant with Israel to one side and has accomplished salvation by a different route. But Paul's answer to the question directly and precisely contradicts this move. No, he says, God has not abandoned the covenant: "Let God be true, and every human being false!" (3:4). Or, in more detail:

> The Jews were entrusted with God's oracles. What follows from that? If some of them were unfaithful to their commission, does their unfaithfulness nullify God's faithfulness? Certainly not! (3:2b–4a)

*God has not given up on his plan to bring light to the world through Israel.* Moreover, God's "faithfulness" to that plan (as opposed to some other plan) *is exactly what is meant by "God's righteousness,"* as

3:5 makes clear. Literally translated, the beginning of that verse reads, "But if our unrighteousness establishes God's righteousness . . ." This sets the tone. Paul thus arrives at the conclusion of the first major section of Romans (1:18–3:20) with a complex set of problems to solve. If God is to unveil his "righteousness," these problems must be directly addressed.

First, there is the underlying issue of idolatry, injustice, and plain old "sin." That is clear. It hasn't gone away. It hasn't, as some suppose, been displaced by all this talk of the covenant, of Israel's vocation. Nor, however, should we forget that the problem with "sin" was not just the breaking of moral laws, but idolatry and the consequent failure to grasp the truly human vocation and reflect God's glory into the world: "All sinned, *and fell short of God's glory*" (3:23). Sin matters; so, behind it, does idolatry. All this must be dealt with if God is to put the world right.

But, second, there is the problem of God's faithfulness to the covenant. Faced with the problem of idolatry and sin (1:18–2:16), God called Israel to be the light of the world (2:17–24), having established by his covenant with Abraham that he would give him a worldwide family (4:1–25). It would be very strange if God made solemn promises to rescue the world through Israel, through Abraham's family, and then responded to Israel's faithlessness by himself being faithless to those promises. Romans 4 is all about the covenant that God made with Abraham in Genesis 15. It is not a detached statement about someone in the ancient scriptures who was "justified by faith." It is not simply a "proof from scripture" of the "doctrine" that Paul has stated in Romans 3. Abraham is not simply an "example" of either the way God's grace operates or the way some humans have faith.

When Paul quotes Genesis 15:6 in Romans 4:3 ("Abraham believed God, and it was calculated in his favor, putting him in the right"), he invokes the entire chapter, as his frequent references and quotations make clear. To be sure, Paul insists that Abraham's faith (in the God who raises the dead) is in its essence the same as Christian faith (that God raised *Jesus* from the dead). But this takes place within the larger covenantal context. Genesis 15, after all, is where God establishes with Abraham the covenant: he will give him a family of many nations, which involves not just the single "promised land," but *the whole world*. That is what Paul says in Romans 4:13, implying that he is reading Genesis in the light of psalms such as Psalms 2 and 72, where the "inheritance" is extended under the Messiah's rule from a single piece of territory to the entire creation. And this in turn depends, as he says in 4:5, on taking the Abrahamic promise to mean that God would "justify the ungodly," in other words, that God would take "sinners" from throughout the world and bring them, forgiven, into his family. (The vital note of forgiveness of sins is emphasized in the quote from Ps. 32 in 4:6–8.) The family in question, he makes clear in 4:17–22, is the family that shares with Abraham the true worship of God (i.e., "faith[fullness]"). Abraham, unlike those spoken of in 1:18–23, "grew strong in faith and gave glory to God, being fully convinced that God had the power to accomplish what he had promised" (4:20–21).

*The question Paul faces in 3:21–26 is then the double problem of human sin and idolatry, on the one hand, and the divine faithfulness, on the other.* This central passage is flanked on either side by passages that speak of the divine faithfulness to the covenant with Abraham and his family as the means by which this human plight will be resolved.

All this means a vital shift from the usual reading of Romans to a truly Pauline one. Paul is not saying, "God will justify sinners by faith so that they can go to heaven, and Abraham is an advance example of this." He is saying, "God covenanted with Abraham to give him a worldwide family of forgiven sinners turned faithful worshippers, and the death of Jesus is the means by which this happens." This joins up with the clear implication of 2:17–20: God called Israel to be the light of the world, the answer to the problem of human idolatry and sin.

The usual reading of Romans 3:21–26 is therefore outflanked. It is a shallow reduction of what Paul is actually saying. Sin and God's dealing with sin in the death of Jesus are undoubtedly central, but these are set within the larger questions of both idolatry (and therefore of true worship) and God's commitment to rescue the world *through Abraham's family, Israel.* Neither Romans 1:18– 3:20 nor Romans 4 is simply concerned with "sin" and "justification," as in the normal reading. They are indeed concerned with both, but they frame both within the question of *cult* and the question of *covenant.* If there are signs that Romans 3:21–26 is also about cult and covenant, we should assume that this is what Paul thinks he is talking about.

We can come even closer. Romans 3:27–31, the bridge between our key passage and chapter 4, is all about the coming together of Jew and Gentile, circumcised and uncircumcised, on the basis of *pistis,* "faith"—which looks like an additional fulfillment of the hints Paul dropped in 2:25–29. And the heart of Romans 3:27–31 is the firm declaration that the God in whom both Jew and Gentile must believe is the One God of Israel: Jewish-style monotheism is at the heart of the justification by which Gentile and Jew alike are declared to be within the sin-forgiven family. *The whole passage, from 2:17 to 4:25, is all about God's covenant with Israel and through Israel for the world and about the true worship at the heart of this covenant, the worship of the one true God, which replaces the idolatry of 1:18–23 and thus undoes the sin of 1:24–32.*

Thus, before we probe into any specific details of the passage, it is clear that the usual reading of 3:21–26 has screened out these larger contexts of meaning. It is always possible, of course, that Paul has jumped from one topic to a different one and then back again. Some have tried to read the text that way. But in a tight, interwoven piece of writing like this the high probability is that the author intends the opaque bit in the middle (opaque to us, presumably not to him!) to be the explicit bridge between what went before and what comes after. What has happened in the usual reading, instead, is that a particular meaning has been assumed for 3:21–26 and the passages on either side have been read in the light of this assumed meaning, distorting both.

When, therefore, we note that 3:25–26, at least, seems to be speaking of the divine covenant faithfulness, the *dikaiosynē theou*, we ought to assume not that Paul is quoting earlier "Jewish Christian" formulations, which he is then anxiously modifying, but that this is indeed his central topic. *God's faithfulness to the covenant with Israel, even granted the large-scale failure of Israel as a whole, will result in the rescue of the whole sinful world.* This is what we ought to assume the passage will be about.

Likewise, when we note that the central statement of the passage, that God "put forth Jesus as the place of mercy," uses the word *hilastērion,* which in the scriptures refers to the covering of the "ark of the covenant," the place where God cleanses Israel from sins so that he and his people can meet, we ought to assume that he is speaking of the way in which true worship is being restored in place of idolatry. Paul is not simply invoking a "cultic metaphor" alongside a "law court" metaphor, on the one hand, and a "slave market" metaphor, on the other. He is thinking of the restoration of true cult, true worship: the one God cleansing people from defilement so that the true meeting, the heart of the covenant, may take place at last.

These assumptions will not let us down. The covenant is indeed the context; the restoration of true worship is indeed the goal. The passage is indeed about God's dealing with sin. But the way God does this is, first, by fulfilling his ancient covenant promises and, second, by thereby addressing idolatry, the underlying problem of all human faithlessness. In other words, God is unveiling his "righteousness" through the faithfulness to death of Israel's Messiah, Jesus. To try to understand God's dealing with sin in this passage without placing the covenant and the cult at the center is to opt for a shallow and ultimately misleading understanding. We must put Paul's train of thought back together again if we are to understand its central point, the death of Jesus as the means of dealing with sin.

All this is reinforced if we glance at the passage that immediately follows the great single argument of 1:18–4:25. In 5:1–2 Paul states the result of God's faithfulness as the restoration of "access" to "grace" and of the hope of "glory." And, as 5:6–11 makes clear, everything that Paul has now said is grounded in the unbreakable covenant love of the one God: "God demonstrates his own love for us" in 5:8 is the further dimension, still in covenantal language, of "God's covenant justice has been displayed" in 3:21. This looks forward to the final scene in Romans 1–8, where in 8:31–39 we find justification rooted in the death of Jesus as the effective expression of the divine love. In that passage, the renewed cult is focused on Jesus himself, at God's right hand, interceding on behalf of his people: the king, in other words, acting as the priest (8:34). There is no space here to develop this further, but it increases the strong sense that in 3:21–26, which on anyone's account must be seen as the vital turn in the argument, we are dealing not simply with a "works contract" as imagined in the usual "Romans road," but with the covenant and the cult as the ways by which the one God deals with sins and so creates a forgiven and worshipping worldwide people.

With this introduction, then, we take a deep breath and plunge into the difficult detail of the passage.

# Redemption Reimagined

### *God's Covenant Faithfulness*

Romans 3:21–26 states its own theme with such heavy emphasis that we cannot miss it: the *dikaiosynē theou,* the "righteousness of God." Paul highlights this in vv. 21–22 and then again in vv. 25–26:

> But now, quite apart from the law (though the law and the prophets bore witness to it), *God's covenant justice* [*dikaiosynē*] has been displayed. *God's covenant justice* [*dikaiosynē*] comes into operation through the faithfulness of Jesus the Messiah, for the benefit of all who have faith. (3:21–22)

> He did this to demonstrate *his covenant justice* [*dikaiosynē*], because of the passing over (in divine forbearance) of sins committed beforehand. This was to demonstrate *his covenant justice* [*dikaiosynē*] in the present time: that is, that he himself is in the right [*dikaios*], and that he declares to be in the right [*dikaioutai*] everyone who trusts in the faithfulness of Jesus. (3:25b–26)

One does not normally accuse Paul of heavy-handed repetition. Usually, we have the opposite problem: he is going so fast that his arguments skip over steps that are obvious to him, but that we have to fill in for ourselves, panting along behind him and trying to keep up. When he labors the point like this, then, we should sit up and take extra notice. Since the occurrences of the key terminology in vv. 25–26 clearly refer to God's *own* "righteousness," and since the larger context of 2:17–3:9 and chapter 4 demand a reference to God's faithfulness to his covenant promises and purposes, there is an overwhelming case for taking vv. 21–22 in the same sense. The main thing Paul wants to say in this paragraph is that *God has done, in and through Jesus, what he promised and purposed all along.* According to chapter 4, God promised to give Abraham a worldwide family, dealing with sin so that this large "ungodly" family could be "justified." According to chapter 2, what God purposed was that Israel would be the light of the world, the means of dealing with the problem of 1:18–2:16. The statement that in the gospel events God has unveiled and displayed his *dikaiosynē* is most naturally to be taken as the statement that the promise has been fulfilled and the purpose accomplished. (Paul summarizes his argument in similar terms in Romans 15:8–9.)

Paul is at pains to stress that this unveiling of God's covenant justice is an act of free grace: those who believe are "by God's grace . . . freely declared to be in the right" (3:24a). God is under no obligation to do this. God is in nobody's debt. This too is covenant language: the "grace" of God in Paul looks back to similar language in scripture, indicating both that God has made promises out of his own loving purpose, not out of constraint, and that when he keeps them it is out of pure mercy—a point that Paul emphasizes when he sums up the whole argument in 12:1. And this mercy involves God's being true to himself, his own character, purposes, and promises.

But throughout the Second Temple period the divine covenant faithfulness was seen in a double light. This was summarized in Daniel 9, but it goes back, through many generations, texts, and traditions, to Deuteronomy 27–32, a passage to which Paul returns not least in the later exposition of the divine faithfulness in Romans 9–11. Faced with Israel's idolatry, God's covenant faithfulness would require him to let Israel reap the consequences, which would mean exile. But that same divine faithfulness would then mean restoration. And this coming restoration, the liberation from oppressive pagan powers, would be the new Exodus. The original Exodus was the fulfillment of God's promises to Abraham (Gen. 15:13–16), so the renewal of the covenant would mean the newer, greater Exodus, this time involving the forgiveness of sins. That, famously, is the emphasis of Jeremiah 31:31–34, and also of Isaiah 40–55, to which we shall presently return.

The framework for these six crucial verses is therefore set. The events concerning Jesus unveil and display the covenant faithfulness of Israel's God. The scriptures themselves and the surrounding context in Romans indicate that this will mean God's dealing with idolatry and sin and fulfilling his Israel-shaped purpose for the world. This, in outline, is what Paul thinks he is saying in this passage.

### The Messiah's Faithfulness to God's Purpose for Israel

The Israel-shaped purpose, to which Israel itself had been faithless, has been fulfilled in the Messiah himself. That is the point of Romans 3:22, and this is why I take the contested phrase *pistis Christou* here (and often elsewhere) in the sense of the "Messiah's faithfulness." Thus I read v. 22 as saying, "God's covenant justice comes into operation *through the faithfulness of Jesus the Messiah* for the benefit of all who have faith." This answers exactly to the sequence of thought in 3:1–5. Israel's privilege was to be *entrusted* with the divine oracles; that is a way of summing up the vocation spelled out in 2:19–20. But Israel had been "faithless" *to that commission,* putting in question the divine "faithfulness" (3:3) and the divine "truthfulness" (3:4); but God will be seen to be *dikaios,* true to his covenant justice, despite it all (3:4b–5). God will not change his plan. The Messiah, Israel's representative, will complete Israel's role. This is one reason, perhaps the most important one, why the badge of membership in the new covenant family is *pistis,* "faith" or "faithfulness": it is the sign of Messiah people. (We should note that in Paul's world the word *pistis* regularly carried associations of "fidelity," "loyalty," and similar ideas. For him it clearly included "belief" in the sense of both trusting in God and believing *that* God raised Jesus from the dead [4:24–25; 10:9]. But we should not let that sharp focus screen out the wider meanings.)

The point about the Messiah's death, then, is that it demonstrates in action the faithfulness of God to his covenant plan—the plan to rescue the world through Israel, to renew the whole world by giving Abraham a vast, uncountable sin-forgiven family. It was not a matter of Jesus's persuading God to do something he might not otherwise have done. The Messiah's death accomplishes what God himself planned to do and said he would do. Somehow, the Messiah's faithful death *constitutes* the fulfillment of the Israel-shaped plan. Or, to put it another way (since Paul, like all the early Christians, had thought everything through again in the light of the resurrection), when God called Abraham, he had the Messiah's cross in mind all along.

One place in Israel's scriptures where that divine plan comes into sharp focus is in Isaiah 53. When Paul sums up his whole train of thought in 4:24–25, he alludes to that chapter. We would therefore be right to assume that that statement of Israel faithfulness, of servant faithfulness, of crucified Messiah faithfulness is in mind throughout chapter 3 as well, and we will presently explore the effect this has on our interpretation. When Paul describes Jesus's death in 3:24–25, then, we are to see this as the accomplishment of the Israel-shaped purpose—a strange idea, to be sure, but one for which Isaiah 40–55 provides a dark but important advance signpost.

As we advance cautiously toward the heart of this little passage, several things are coming into focus. God is faithful to the covenant; and, since the covenant focused on the purpose and promise to rescue the world through Israel, this is what has happened in and through the Messiah, who has offered to God the Israel-shaped obedience, the "faithfulness," that was previously lacking.

### Justified by Faith

Before we get to our main purpose in looking at this passage—to understand what Paul is saying about the death of Jesus—we must look briefly at the result of this display of divine covenant faithfulness. All who believe, Paul declares, are "justified." The double context we have noted all along (as in "God's *covenant justice*") provides the closely intertwined double meaning of this famous though difficult notion. On the one hand, all who believe are declared to be members of Abraham's family, just as, for instance, in

Galatians 3:29. "Justification" is the *covenant declaration,* establishing in a single family all who share the messianic *pistis.* Equally, on the other hand, justification means that this believing family is declared to be *in the right.* The first of these answers particularly to Romans 2:17–29, which ends with the quizzical note about God redefining his people. The second answers to the larger issue of 2:1–16: the final judgment is coming, and people will be either "condemned" or "justified." The latter meaning, in fact, is bound to be near the surface of alert readers' minds because of the blatant and repeated law-court imagery of 3:19–20: every mouth will be stopped, and the whole world held accountable before God; the Torah itself will be unable to rescue anyone and can only point out sin.

The point we must grasp is that these two contexts of meaning are not to be played off against one another. They dovetail together. God chose Abraham to reverse the sin of Adam; God gave Israel the task of bringing light to the world. The covenant promise and the covenant purpose were always intended to deal with sin. God would not deal with sin any other way; that is part of the point of 3:1–5. And God would not be faithful to the covenant if he did not deal with sin; the whole narrative of Genesis rebels against the idea. That is why, as he is expounding Genesis 15 in Romans 4, Paul highlights the note of forgiveness (4:6–8). As usual, we must not separate what Paul (following scripture!) has held firmly together.

This "justification" takes place *in the present time,* as Paul says up front ("but now," 3:21) and then spells out (in v. 26). The verdict of the *future,* as in 2:1–16 and 8:31–39, has already been announced in the *present.* This provides the particular dynamic of Paul's famous justification theology and is the direct result of what has happened in the Messiah. When God raised Jesus from the dead, he not only declared that Jesus really was his "son" (1:3–4), the one he had "sent" into the world to undertake his purpose (8:3–4); he also *vindicated* him against the charges of being a false

Messiah, declaring him to be in the right. This could then be seen as a legal verdict, with the same two meanings (covenantal and forensic) as before: Jesus really was Israel's representative, the Messiah, fulfilling God's covenant purposes; and Jesus was "in the right," despite the verdict of the court that had sent him to his death.

And with that verdict, announced in Jesus's resurrection, God also declared the same verdict over those who would be "in the Messiah": "They are freely declared to be in the right, to be members of the covenant, through the redemption which is found in the Messiah, Jesus" (3:24). Justification takes place "in the Messiah." What God said of Jesus in his resurrection God says of all who are "in him." People sometimes play the language of "justification" off against the language of "incorporation," but this is clearly a mistake. We see the same point (being justified *in the Messiah*) in Galatians 2:17, or for that matter Philippians 3:9.

This is why, summing up the argument in 4:24–25, he says that Jesus was "handed over because of our trespasses *and raised because of our justification.*" It isn't that the resurrection of Jesus *causes* that "justification." Rather, it is the sign that *this justification has in principle taken place on the cross.* As Paul says in Romans 5:9, we are justified "by his blood"; and, as he declares in 1 Corinthians 15:17, "If the Messiah wasn't raised, . . . you are still in your sins"—a throwaway remark, and all the more important because of it. Here we are near the heart of Paul's theology, and indeed of this present book: *on the cross the real revolution took place,* and the resurrection is the first sign that it has happened. Among many results of this revolution, justification takes its vital place, partly because of the assurance of sins forgiven, but also because of the assurance of membership in Abraham's family (again, as in Gal. 3). Behind both of these, there is for Paul the sense that with the victory of the cross the powers that have ruled the world, the idols that have kept the human race in their grip, have been overthrown. As in John 12:30–32, this is the necessary step before the peoples of the world can be set free from their present "rulers" and drawn to Israel's Messiah.

In any case, the point of justification "in the present time" is that it *anticipates* the verdict that will be announced on the final day. This final verdict, whether of "condemnation" or of "justification," was described in 2:1–16, and Paul looks ahead to that moment in 8:31–39—but with the knowledge that "there is no condemnation for those in the Messiah, Jesus" (8:1), because God has already condemned sin itself (8:3). The point Paul is making in Romans 3 is that this verdict *is already known* when someone "believes in the one who raised from the dead Jesus our Lord" (4:24). One of the themes of Romans 5–8 is the explanation of how the verdict issued in the present corresponds to the verdict that will be issued in the future (in the form, as with Jesus himself, of people being raised from the dead). But this is not our present concern.

So far, then, we have seen that 3:21–26 announces the unveiling in action of the covenant justice of God, fulfilling the promises to Abraham and the purpose of Israel. We have seen that this has been effected through Jesus, Israel's Messiah, taking upon himself the vocation to which Israel as a whole had been unfaithful. We have seen that this results in the covenantal declaration of "justification," in the present time, for all who believe. We must now move cautiously inward, to see what Paul says about how this complex covenantal revelation has taken place.

### New Passover, New Exodus

Granted the covenantal context of the whole passage, both in its wider framing in Romans 2 and 4 and in the central emphases we have just studied, we should not be surprised that the heart of the passage also has a covenantal focus. This has to do with what God has done in Jesus the Messiah. Here the key words are *apolytrōsis,* "redemption," and *hilastērion,* "place of mercy":

> All sinned, and fell short of God's glory—and by God's
> grace they are freely declared to be in the right, to
> be members of the covenant, through the *redemption*
> [*apolytrōsis*] which is found in the Messiah, Jesus. God
> put Jesus forth as the place of mercy [*hilastērion*], through
> faithfulness, by means of his blood. (3:23–25a)

When Paul says that God's covenant justice has been unveiled "through the *redemption* which is found in the Messiah," he uses the word *apolytrōsis,* the word you might use for "redeeming" a slave from a slave market: you pay the slave owner, and you set the slave free. But this is no miscellaneous metaphor, any more than the reference to the "place of mercy" is simply a random metaphor borrowed from the sacrificial cult, or "justification" simply an idea plucked from an otherwise unrelated law-court setting. The word regularly carried one particular set of meanings for Jews of Paul's day. Israel had been enslaved in Egypt; God's great act of liberation, overcoming Pharaoh and the Egyptian gods and rescuing his people, was the *apolytrōsis,* the great "redemption" at the heart of Israel's covenant story. Like so many other early Christians and in line with Jesus himself, Paul interprets the cross in relation to Passover: a new Passover, a new Exodus.

As anyone who has attended a Passover celebration will recall—and as Jews both ancient and modern know in their bones—Passover is a complex event. Its narrative positively bristles with different elements: bricks without straw, the call of Moses, the revelation of the divine name, the plagues in Egypt, the Passover meal itself, the slaughter of the firstborn, the crossing of the Red Sea, the pillar of cloud and fire, the grumbling of the people, the arrival at Mt. Sinai, the construction of the tabernacle. Each one subdivides, so that, for the uninitiated, the writings of Jews of Paul's day appear to be peppered with disjointed references to plagues, unleavened bread, angels giving the Torah, or items of tabernacle furniture. These, however, are not in fact disjointed.

The links are there in the great narrative so widely known, so easily summoned to mind, in that world if not in ours. And we do not have to go very far in the story to see that when Paul says *apolytrōsis,* he has this entire picture very much in mind.

The original Exodus was the moment when God fulfilled his promises to the patriarchs (Exod. 2:24) and established his covenant with the whole people (19:5; 24:3–8). When Jeremiah spoke of a "new covenant" (31:31–34), he was looking back to this original moment in order to look ahead to the even greater deliverance that God would one day accomplish, and this was central to the early Christian perception of what had been accomplished in Jesus. The new Passover was modeled on the old one. This time, however, it would not mean simply liberation from an enslaving human power. It would mean liberation from sin, the sin that had caused the enslavement of exile. That is why, as we have seen, the reimagining of Passover in the Second Temple period needed to include the idea of atonement or forgiveness.

But liberation from slavery, of whatever sort, was only the negative side of Passover. The positive purpose of the Exodus was to set Israel free to worship the covenant God (Exod. 3:12, 18; 4:23; 5:1; 8:1, 20, 27; 9:1, 13; 10:3, 7–11, 24–26). Why this was impossible in Egypt is not made clear, but there may have been a sense that, with the local Egyptian gods holding sway, worshipping YHWH, at least in the way intended, would have been impossible. (Something similar may be said of Isaiah's "new Exodus" in chapter 52: the exiles have to leave Babylon and come home to Zion, where the divine Glory will come to dwell with them once more.) When, therefore, the people have been brought out and given the Torah as the covenant charter, the covenant is then ratified with the sacrificial blood sprinkled on the people (the "blood of the covenant," as in Exod. 24:8). They are now God's people indeed.

And they were then to construct the tabernacle as the place where God would meet with his people, where the covenant, as a kind of marriage, could be solemnized (an idea familiar from the prophets; Jer. 2:2 is one possible reference among many). The covenant *event* (the rescue from Egypt) was designed to lead to the covenant *meeting* (YHWH and Israel coming together in solemn mutual relation). If we find this event and this meeting together like this in a narrative sequence purporting to explain how God has been faithful to the covenant, we are on solid ground in saying that the Exodus narrative stands behind the whole thing and, conversely, that the difficult and dense parts of Paul's statement must be interpreted in that light.

### Mercy Seat and Meeting Place

The specific place of this meeting, in the most holy place within the tabernacle, was at the "ark of the covenant." This was the acacia-wood box, overlaid with gold, that contained the tablets of the Torah, the covenant documentation (Exod. 25:10–16). More precisely, the location for this meeting was the lid of the ark, the *kappōreth* (25:10–22). This was where, at the end of the book of Exodus, the divine Glory appeared in the cloud to meet with the people (40:20–21, 34–35). Precisely what was understood by this term remains a matter of debate. The older interpretations suggested "covering." But recent research has challenged this, connecting the Hebrew word with the root *kippēr,* meaning "cleanse" or "purge." The *kappōreth* was where purification would be made, so that God and his people could safely meet; the blood of the sin offering was to act as a ritual detergent to purify the sanctuary, so that the place on earth where the divine Glory came to dwell, as in Exodus 40, might be kept pure, maintaining not only the covenantal link between God and Israel, but also the very fabric of the cosmos, the joining of heaven and earth. This is where the Passover event was heading all along: to the establishment of the unbreakable bond between God and his people and to the symbolic recreation of Eden, where heaven and earth had been in easy commerce one with the other. The event led to the meeting;

God's covenant with Abraham resulted in the establishment of the covenant with Abraham's family. Paul in Romans 3 is tracking exactly with this sequence of thought.

The Hebrew word *kappōreth* was rendered in the Greek translations of scripture as *hilastērion*. This posed quite a problem when English translations of scripture were being produced. One could hardly say that God put forth Jesus as a "lid" or even as a "covering." That is why some translations made the innovation of rendering the word as "mercy seat," though the lid of the ark was not a "seat" in the modern sense except perhaps in the sense we use when we describe the heart as the "seat of the emotions" (hence, perhaps, Tyndale's rendering as "seat of mercy," the place from which mercy flows, where it is to be found). Strictly speaking, the "lid" was not the place of "mercy" as such, but the place of both "meeting" and "cleansing." This was where God *met* with his people; and, in order for this to take place, it was where the priest *cleansed* the sanctuary from the defiling effects of the past sins of Israel with the sprinkled blood of the sacrifice.

These are not categories that come naturally to modern Western readers of Paul, but if we are to understand him, we must enter his world, where such things were second nature, rather than dragging him forward too quickly into our own (picking up, perhaps, some medieval meanings en route!). He has just said in 3:23 that human sin meant a falling short from God's glory, echoing the fuller statement of how humans turned away from the divine Glory in 1:21–23. This is cultic language; it has to do with human worship and particularly Jewish worship. That was the primary point where humans had failed, worshipping idols instead; the primary answer to this problem is given right here, in 3:24–26. No surprises, then that Paul draws on this combination of Passover and Day of Atonement, focused on the *hilastērion,* as the central point of his statement about the divine covenant faithfulness manifested in the death of Israel's Messiah. But there seems to be both less and more in this than has usually met the eye.

First, there is less, because this context, in and of itself, says nothing about *punishment,* which has been a very common interpretation of the passage. As we saw earlier, the killing of the sacrificial animals was not, in ancient Israel, the important part of the ritual. The killing did not take place on the altar (an important difference from much pagan ritual). Cutting the animal's throat was simply the prelude to the release of blood, symbolizing the animal's life, which was then used as the all-important agent for purging or cleansing the worshippers and also the sacred place and its furniture, thus enabling the all-holy God to meet with his people without disastrous results. And that meeting took place precisely on the *kappōreth,* the place of cleansing or purgation. There is nothing here about punishment. Neither the older meaning of "covering" nor the recent scholarly consensus concerning "purgation" carries that implication.

The only time in Leviticus when an animal has sins confessed over its head, the animal in question—the "scapegoat"—is precisely *not* sacrificed. It is, after all, impure, and would not be suitable as an offering. It is driven out into the wilderness. Even though later traditions indicate that the person leading the goat into the wilderness would then kill it by pushing it over a cliff (presumably lest it find its way back and so pollute the people or the sanctuary again), such killing, even supposing it took place, had to do with symbolically removing the sins, not with punishing the goat on behalf of the people.

What is more, the goat that *was* killed on that day and the other animals used as sin offerings made regularly throughout the year were likewise not being "punished" in the place of the people. Sin offerings were a sign of penitence for accidental sins: acts you knew were sinful but had not intended to commit or acts you committed without realizing they were sinful. (According to the legislation, if you did know and did intend to do them, no sacrifice could be offered. Such high-handed offending was to be punished, not forgiven.) So when Paul writes in Romans 3:25 that

God put Jesus forth as a *hilastērion,* he does not mean that God was punishing Jesus for the sins of Israel or the world. Had he wanted to say that, he would not have echoed the language of the Day of Atonement. That was not what it was about.

This conclusion is borne out by two additional considerations. First, we have already noted, on the basis of Romans 5:9, that Paul does *not* intend this passage as a statement of how the punishment deserved by sinners—the "wrath" of 1:18–2:16—was meted out on Jesus instead. In 5:9, as in 1 Thessalonians 1:10 and 5:9, the "wrath" is still in the future, and those in the Messiah will indeed be rescued from it; but what is going on in 3:21–26 is "in the present time" (note "but now" in v. 21 and "in the present time" in v. 26). When Paul speaks in 5:9 of being "declared to be in the right by his blood," he is indicating the *prerequisite* for "being saved from wrath," not the idea that such a rescue has already taken place. When he looks ahead to the *future* day in 8:3–4, he speaks of God's condemning sin in the Messiah's flesh, so that there is "no condemnation." That is speaking of the *final* day of judgment. This penal substitution, framed carefully as we saw by Paul by the long story of Israel and the strange work of the law, is the truth toward which, I believe, the "propitiation" readings of 3:24–26 are straining. But reading it back into the present passage distorts both the passage and the doctrine.

There is another indication in 3:25–26 that Paul does not think he is here talking about God's punishing Jesus on behalf of people's sins. He declares that God had "passed over" former sins, in his *anochē,* his "forbearance." (If there is a reference here to "Passover" it is very oblique. "Passing over" and "Passover" are close in English, but there is no such link in Greek.) In the normal "works contract" approach, interpreters have looked at this passage for an account of how sins were *punished.* But the whole point of *anochē* is that sins are *not* punished. In Romans 2:4, Paul asks his imaginary interlocutor whether, in his arrogance, he is despising the "riches of God's kindness, forbearance (*anochē*) and patience," which were supposed to lead one to repentance. Punishment is what would happen later, if this opportunity were missed: "By your hard, unrepentant heart you are building up a store of anger for yourself on the day of anger" (2:5). What we have in the present passage, though, is not a statement of how that punishment fell on Jesus, but rather a statement of how the sins that had been building up were "passed over." God has drawn a veil over the past, as Paul said in Athens (Acts 17:30).

Paul is not here saying, then, that God has *punished* former sins, whether of Israel or the Gentiles, certainly not that he has punished them in Jesus. There is no mention here of such a punishment then exhausting the divine wrath. That, as we saw, would leave 5:9 looking very odd. Paul says, rather, that God has chosen to overlook the "former sins." Nor could one say—though this is a frequent line of interpretation, to which I myself have been drawn in the past—that the "forbearance" of God means that punishment for earlier sins has been merely delayed and is then meted out on Jesus. The assumption here must be, I think, that Paul is referring to Israel's former sins. God is faithful in the Messiah to the covenant *through Israel for the world,* and to that end he has pushed the "former sins" to one side.

Second, if there is less here than we have normally imagined—the *hilastērion* does not denote a "propitiatory sacrifice," in which Jesus is punished for the sins of others—there is also more. Once we have put that older suggestion to one side, a quite different set of meanings comes into view. Paul, who is here after all referring to ancient Israelite sacrificial ritual, is using language from Jewish Temple theology. For us this seems a leap into a different world; for him it was second nature. Though we commonly think of the Letter to the Hebrews as the central place in the New Testament where the Temple (or in that case the wilderness tabernacle) was explored for Christian significance, there is more Temple theology in Romans than is usually recognized, and I think this passage is part of that. In his world the Temple (and before that, the tabernacle) was supposed to be where heaven and earth over-lapped; the problem was that such an overlap was extremely dangerous. The idea of the *kappōreth,* the *hilastērion,* as the meeting place and the cleansing place, answers exactly to this purpose and this problem.

What Paul says about this *hilastērion* in 3:25 is that God has supplied it, has "put it forth"—or rather, has put *him* forth, since the *hilastērion* is of course Jesus himself. This corresponds closely to the later statements about God demonstrating his love through the Messiah's death (5:8), about God sending his own son in the likeness of sinful flesh and as a sin offering (8:3), and about God not sparing his own son, but giving him up for us all (8:32). The reestablishment of a meeting place between God and humans is the result of divine initiative, "by God's grace . . . freely" (3:24). And this, as we shall see presently, is the surprising, usually un-noticed heart of the passage. The answer to human idolatry, the root of sin, is the fresh revelation of the one true God. God has supplanted the idols worshipped by Israel and the nations alike with a fresh revelation of himself. This fresh unveiling-in-action of the one God will call all peoples to leave their idols and worship him. That is how Paul summarizes the main thrust of his gospel in 1 Thessalonians 1:9. That, I think, is at the heart also of this dense statement of that same gospel.

For the moment, though, we must return to the question of how what Paul says in Romans 3:24–26 addresses the problem of human sin. As we have seen, in the Second Temple period, the hope for a final great act of divine deliverance, a new Passover, included the hope for the ultimate "forgiveness of sins." Passover was not itself an "atoning" festival. Conversely, the Day of Atonement, by itself, was not about rescue from slavery, the overthrowing of hostile powers. But the particular situation of Israel, from Babylon to the time of Jesus and indeed beyond, demanded that the hope of Israel should somehow bring these two together. The way to national liberation would be *through* the forgiveness of sins:

as we have seen repeatedly in this book, sin is the grip that the "powers," working through idols, have clamped on those who worship them, so that dealing with sin and breaking the power of the "powers" are two sides of the same coin. And this is where the narrative of Israel has arrived. It is no longer simply a matter of coming out of Egypt and constructing the tabernacle as the place of meeting, the new Eden where heaven and earth may come together. It is about a much darker place: Israel has committed idolatry, has sinned, and has ultimately gone into exile. At the heart of the new Passover, therefore, there would be a new kind of atonement: God purifies his people in and through the shed blood of Jesus, so that the covenant may be renewed, and not just renewed, but now effective for the whole world. (Something like this seems to be the meaning of 1 John 2:2.) At the heart of new *apolytrōsis* would stand the new *hilastērion*. And this would display the covenant faithfulness of Israel's God, calling the whole world to worship.

The *hilastērion* would therefore be the place of cleansing. When mortal humans come into the Presence of the living God, they bring with them pollution, particularly the ultimate pollution of death and anything to do with it. Sin matters because it is the telltale symptom of idolatry. (How can you come into God's Temple if you have been surreptitiously worshipping other gods?) Idolatry, turning away from the source of life, results in sin, which already breathes the musty air of death. And death is the ultimate denial of the goodness of God's creation—the very thing that the Temple, holding together heaven and earth, was supposed to affirm. How, then, can the Temple be cleansed so that humans, with the polluting smell of death upon them, can nevertheless come into God's Presence? The answer supplied by the levitical rituals is that the sacrificial blood is the sign of God-given life, a life more powerful than death, a life therefore that purifies both sanctuary and worshipper. Cleansing thus enables meeting. The *hilastērion* points to both. That is why Paul can sum up the effect of Romans 1–4 by saying at the start of chapter 5 that we have "peace with God" and "access" by faith to his Presence. This is Temple language. Paul believes that it results directly from what he has said in chapter 3.

### The Servant Vocation

Our exposition of Romans 3:21–26 has introduced us to a combination of themes that strike a complex chord with what is, arguably, the greatest part of Israel's greatest prophetic book. Isaiah 40–55, taken as a whole, is all about the unveiling of divine covenant faithfulness in overthrowing the gods of Babylon and liberating God's people from the pagan enemy. It anticipates, in other words, a new Exodus. But this poem is also, from start to finish, about the way in which this act will involve the ultimate forgiveness of Israel's sins and how this will be done through the faithful obedience of a strange figure who at one level *is* Israel ("You are my servant, Israel, in whom I will be glorified," Isa. 49:3) and at another level stands over against Israel, representing the people and doing for them what they cannot do for themselves. Within the sustained drama of the poem, all these trains of thought come together in the announcement of YHWH's kingdom in 52:7–12 and in the fourth and final Servant Song, 52:13–53:12. If exile is the "punishment" for Israel's sin, that punishment now falls on the "servant" alone. He represents Israel; his faithful obedience is offered in place of Israel's unfaithful disobedience. And if exile is the result of Israel's idolatry, the "servant" unveils, in action, the "arm of YHWH," revealing Israel's God before the nations at last, so that all may now be called to worship:

> *YHWH has bared his holy arm*
> *before the eyes of all the nations;*
> *and all the ends of the earth shall see*
> *the salvation of our God. . . .*

> So shall he startle many nations;
>   kings shall shut their mouths because of him;
> for that which had not been told them they shall see,
>   and that which they had not heard they shall contemplate.
> Who has believed what we have heard?
>   And to whom has the Arm of YHWH been revealed? (Isa.
>     52:10, 15; 53:1)

All of these themes resonate so strongly with what Paul writes in Romans 3:21–26 that we are not surprised, as the larger argument comes to its close at the end of chapter 4, that Paul echoes this passage in Isaiah. In 4:24–25, pulling together the threads of his argument with a sharp tug, he aligns the story of Abraham with the story of the "servant" and focuses both on Jesus. This is where the Israel vocation, outlined in 2:19–20, had been going all along. This is the vocation to which Israel as a whole had been faithless (3:2), but to which Jesus, as Israel's representative Messiah, has been faithful (3:22). Paul has just quoted Genesis 15:6 one last time: Abraham believed God, "and it was calculated to him in terms of covenant justice." But, he says:

> It wasn't written for him alone that "it was calculated to
> him." It was written for us as well! It will be calculated
> to us, too, since we believe in the one who raised from
> the dead Jesus our Lord, who was handed over because
> of our trespasses and raised because of our justification.
> (4:23–25)

This is not, to be sure, a straightforward quotation from Isaiah 53, though there are several verbal echoes. Nobody who knew Isaiah 53, especially in the Greek version, would miss the resonance. Though Paul has put the point in a fresh way, this conclusion succeeds in summarizing the larger argument and claiming powerfully and evocatively that what has happened in Jesus fulfills not only the Torah, as witnessed in the exposition of Genesis

15 in Romans 4 as a whole, but the Prophets as well. That is what Paul claimed in 3:21, and he has now demonstrated it.

But this resolution of the ultimate problem, this "punishment that made us whole" (Isa. 53:5), means what it means and makes the sense it makes not within the moralistic works contract, an abstract scheme of sin and punishment, but within the covenant of vocation, the image-bearing, glory-sharing covenant. The human vocation, Israel's vocation, Jesus's vocation. *God's* vocation. Incarnation is indeed at the heart of Romans 3. But incarnation here is not the alternative to election, to the purposes of God for Abraham's people. Jesus in himself, and in his death, is the place where the one God meets with his world, bringing heaven and earth together at last, removing by his sacrificial blood the pollutions of sin and death that would have made such a meeting impossible. "While we were enemies," writes Paul in Romans 5:10, summing up the present argument once more, "we were reconciled to God through the death of his son." Quite so. It isn't all about "works," whether done or not done. And it isn't all about "punishment." It is about vocation, and about Temple. And about love.

Love (another great Isaianic theme) is, after all, the deepest meaning behind Paul's language of "covenant justice." The covenant is after all the *marriage* of God and Israel. Paul picks up that language in many passages where he speaks about the Messiah himself and his people—a sure sign that he sees in Jesus the human embodiment of Israel's God. (I am sometimes taken to task for using the word "embodiment" in this context, as though I am shy of saying "incarnation." I am not, as the previous paragraphs indicate. It's just that I regularly prefer English terms to Latin—particularly when the Latin terms have worn so smooth with use that not all their proper features are visible.) It is to that marriage and to its purpose that God has been faithful. This is why in Romans 5–8, drawing out the fuller meaning of what has been said in chapters 3–4, Paul can speak unambiguously of the divine love, *agapē,* and indeed of the Messiah's love as well

(8:31–39). Chapter 8 as a whole is the glorious heaven-and-earth celebration, itself replete with Temple language, that follows precisely from the "meeting" of heaven and earth in the covenant-fulfilling "putting forth" of Jesus in chapter 3.

What then does this say as we look back to Romans 3:21–26? It insists that we read what Paul says here about the death of Jesus in the light of the larger covenantal narrative from Abraham through the Exodus story and on to the exile and the question of the ultimate "forgiveness" that would undo that exile and so fulfill the original covenant purposes. And at the heart of that we find not an arbitrary and abstract "punishment" meted out upon an innocent victim, but the living God himself coming incognito ("To whom has the arm of YHWH been revealed?"—in other words, "Who would have thought that *he* was YHWH in person, in power?"), coming to take upon himself the *consequence* of Israel's idolatry, sin, and exile, which itself brought into focus the idolatry, sin, and exile of the whole human race. Expelled from Eden, the human race ended up with Babel. Expelled from Canaan, Israel ended up in Babylon. After Babel, God called Abraham and made covenant promises to him; after Babylon, those promises were made good.

Here we see a clue to an important distinction. Exile was not an arbitrary punishment. If Israel worshipped gods other than YHWH, it was impossible to remain in the land—and it was impossible for the glorious Presence of YHWH to remain there either. By worshipping other gods, God's people effectively sold themselves as slaves. The slavery of exile was thus the *consequence* of what Israel had done. It can of course be seen as "punishment," and that is the image Isaiah 53 uses again and again ("He was wounded for our transgressions, . . . upon him was the punishment that made us whole, . . . YHWH has laid upon him the iniquity of us all," 53:5–6). But Isaiah has framed this sharp-edged description of the "servant's" death within the long poem about God's faithfulness to the covenant, his victory over the idols, his dealing with exile, renewing the covenant (chap. 54), and so renewing creation itself (chap. 55). Our study of Romans indicates that Paul has exactly this larger narrative in mind as well rather than the truncated works contract in which "punishment" is the central theme.

*This means that the language of "punishment" must be used with great care.* It would be easy at this point to lose our balance, to tip back once more into the "works contract." "Oh well," someone might say, "so Paul really was referring to Isaiah 53, so he did believe in penal substitutionary atonement, so we can go on telling the story as we always have." Not so fast, Paul would respond. Isaiah's language and Paul's language mean what they mean within the larger story of God and Israel, of God's covenant purposes through Israel for the world. You cannot take the language out of that context without making it mean something different. (Think what happened when the language of "ransom" was taken out of its biblical context and made to stand by itself, generating wrongheaded questions about who the ransom price would be paid to.)

The idea of "punishment" is in reality a sharp metaphor for the *consequence* that is writ large across the history of Israel—just as, when Paul is talking about sin and its results in Romans 1, he repeats three times that "God gave them up." The corrupting and corrosive lifestyles he describes are not arbitrary, but rather the *result,* the *consequence,* of the original idolatry. This doesn't mean that God is not involved in those consequences. God, as Creator, hates the idolatry and dehumanization that deface and damage his beautiful world and his image-bearing creatures. Unless that is so, God is not a good God, but a careless, faceless bureaucrat.

*But if we take the "punishment" metaphor and make it central, a very different narrative emerges*—just as if we take a phrase like the "righteousness of God" and turn it into a medieval formula about the moral standing that we need, that God possesses, and that God then grants to his people—we transform the first-century meaning into something that, as we have seen, distorts the whole of

Romans 1–4 and causes much of Paul's subtle nuance to be lost. The normal reading of Romans 3 as the "works contract" and the "punishment" that falls on Jesus so that it may not fall on us is just such a distortion. It takes Isaiah's metaphor and rebuilds a different narrative around it. It is as if one were to take Paul's vivid metaphor about the whole of creation groaning in travail and make it into the central feature of Romans 8, insisting then on reading the rest of that chapter with reference to an actual woman going into labor. One would only do that, of course, if the meaning of the rest of the chapter had dropped out of sight; and that is precisely what has happened in the Christian tradition as the story of Israel has been sidelined and other themes have come in to take its place.

If Paul is hinting at "punishment" in this passage, it can only mean what it means in Isaiah, which has to do with the "servant" fulfilling Israel's vocation—and simultaneously with the "servant's" embodying YHWH himself, the powerful "arm of YHWH," to take upon himself the consequence of Israel's rebellion, idolatry, and sin, so that Israel and the world may be rescued. He will draw onto himself the actual results of Israel's sin—the pagan hostility against God's people—in order to exhaust it and so make a way through.

But if the "servant" is indeed the "arm of YHWH" under the guise of a suffering, bruised, and unrecognizable Israelite, then a new possibility emerges at the heart of Romans 3:21–26. The primary fault of the human race, according to Romans 1, is idolatry. The primary response, from the one God himself, is to "put forth" the Messiah as the place of meeting, the ultimate revelation of the divine righteousness and love.

### The Fresh Revelation of God

In the original Exodus narrative, Israel's God reveals his name to Moses and then, toward the end of the story, his Glory (Exod. 3:13–15; 33:17–34:9). This divine Glory, which finally comes to dwell in the tabernacle (40:34–38), resting (we assume) on the *kappōreth,* is what the tabernacle was made for, the reality for which the golden calf of Exodus 32 was a horrible substitute. In Paul's revised Exodus narrative too I suggest that we are meant to see Jesus, "put forth" by God as the *hilastērion,* as the revelation of God's personal presence. This then forms the divine answer to the problem that, with universal sin, the human race had fallen short of God's glory. The aspect of God's character that is highlighted in the present passage is of course his *dikaiosynē,* his covenant justice; but this is seen precisely *in Jesus,* not as a general truth that might be inferred from his death. He is the place where heaven and earth meet.

This is the point at which the mystery of incarnation, the fresh and personal divine initiative, meets the mystery of election, the vocational purpose of Israel. This is the context within which the *hilastērion* means what it means: the place where God and his people come together. That place is Jesus himself. And Jesus himself, the focus of belief, invoked in prayer, loved in answer to his own love, is the ultimate answer to the problem of idolatry. "He is the image of God, the invisible one" (Col. 1:15), the reality of which all other "images" are at best distorted parodies. The vocation of Israel turns out to have been, all along, a plan designed for God's own personal use. *God put Jesus forth,* Paul seems to be saying, *as the place where heaven and earth overlapped, the place where the loving Presence of the one God and the faithful obedience of the true human being would meet and merge and be realized in space, time, and matter.* Jesus, as Israel's Messiah, represented Israel; Israel, called to be the light of the world, represented that wider world. In Jesus the vocation of Israel and of all humans was summed up in faithful obedience. Many readers of Paul have imagined that he did not articulate a fully "incarnational" Christology. If I am right, this passage shows that he did; but it was rooted in Jewish views of the Temple and already woven securely into tight formulas such as the present passage.

Paul has thus addressed the larger problem he had highlighted in Romans 1:18–23: the underlying cause of "sin" itself was idolatry. Now the one God has revealed himself, has manifested his covenant justice, to draw all peoples to his Presence. This points ahead at once to 3:27–31, in which Paul demonstrates that through the gospel Jew and Gentile alike are reckoned, on the basis of faith, to be members of the single family that worships the one true God. This is highlighted again when Paul, having insisted in the main argument of chapter 4 that Abraham's family was always intended to include both Gentiles and Jews, describes Abraham's faith as one of giving glory to God and trusting his power (4:20–21). And the argument then naturally emerges into the summary in 5:1–2, where those who are justified by faith have "peace with God" and "access to this grace in which we stand," celebrating the "hope of God's glory." The new Temple has been constructed; the "meeting" has taken place.

When, therefore, we follow through the theme of Israel's election rather than jettisoning it to concentrate on Jesus, we find that it highlights the role and person of Jesus in a way usually ignored. "God put him forth as a *hilastērion*"; you could not get a "higher" view of Jesus than by seeing him, in this way, as the place where and the means by which the one God comes to dwell with his people. One might almost have thought that Paul had been reading John: "The Word became flesh, and tabernacled among us. We gazed upon his glory" (1:14). For John, the cross reveals God's glory; for Paul, God's "righteousness"; for both, God's love.

### Echoes of the Martyrs

Now at last I think we can see what may have been going on in the use of language similar to Paul's in 4 Maccabees 17, a passage often cited in the hope of proving the more usual reading, the truncated narrative of sin, punishment, and salvation. Fourth Maccabees in turn appears to depend on 2 Maccabees, whose chapter 7 also includes phrases that some have seen as pointers toward Paul's meaning. (The dates of these two books are quite uncertain; but even if, as some think, 4 Maccabees was written later than Paul, this does not rule out the possibility that the kind of thing it says was already known in Paul's Jewish world.) It is impossible to be certain about these things; the data is too limited, and the authorship unknown. But one possible line of thought may be proposed.

First, 2 Maccabees 7 tells the grisly story of the seven brothers and their mother who, following the example of the elderly Eleazar, allow themselves to be tortured and killed rather than submit to the vicious de-Judaizing policy of Antiochus Epiphanes, the Syrian king who was doing his best, in the 160s BC, to erase Jewish identity and so facilitate his takeover of the country. The passage contains some of the most striking pre-Christian affirmations of bodily resurrection. The martyrs, in the midst of their tortures, celebrate their allegiance to the one God, the Creator, and trust him to give them their bodies back again. But there is more. Twice the martyrs acknowledge that Israel as a whole is being punished because of the nation's sins (7:18, 38). But, declares the seventh brother, the suffering they are presently enduring should draw the nation's punishment to its close:

> I, like my brothers, give up body and life for the laws of our ancestors, appealing to God to show mercy soon to our nation and by trials and plagues to make you confess that he alone is God, and through me and my brothers to bring to an end the wrath of the Almighty that has justly fallen on our whole nation. (7:37–38)

The "trials and plagues" may be an allusion to the Exodus from Egypt. And the focus then is on the purpose of the martyrdoms. At the moment, the Jewish nation is suffering because of its own sins, and the fierce hostility of the Syrians is being interpreted as the outworking of the wrath of Israel's own God, as in Jeremiah and similar accounts of the exile. But the claim here is that the suffering of the martyrs themselves will somehow draw this "wrath" to one place, so that it may be exhausted. The writer of the book is in no doubt: the project (if we can call it that) was successful. Immediately after these martyrdoms, Judas Maccabeus starts his revolution against Antiochus Epiphanes; and "the Gentiles could not withstand him, for the wrath of the Lord had turned to mercy" (2 Macc. 8:5). For the writer, at least, a very practical atonement had been made. This was not at all about sin barring the way to an eternal "heaven." It was about sin bringing upon itself the wrath of Syria, which was interpreted (after the fashion of the exilic prophets interpreting the Babylonian conquest) as the wrath of Israel's God; and about the strange dispensation in which the martyrs could somehow draw that double "wrath" onto themselves, so that it would burn itself out and "mercy" would transpire instead.

If we look for an explanation of this line of thought, the obvious place to start would be Isaiah 40–55, and particularly the fourth Servant Song, which we looked at a moment ago. We have no way of knowing whether this kind of interpretation was widespread, or whether it was a momentary idea of either the martyrs themselves or their hagiographer. But we can get some idea of what happened in the subsequent tradition. The book called 4 Maccabees tells some of the same stories. But they have been carefully taken out of the specific context of fiercely stated Jewish-style monotheism, complete with the promise of bodily resurrection, and turned into moral tales about Jewish heroes whose souls are taken up to heaven. The book is written, so it seems, for a non-Jewish audience. It reminds us of the way in which Josephus, explaining the Jewish parties to his Roman audience, makes them sound very much like the schools of pagan philosophy. As a result, the martyrdoms become examples of "noble death," a well-known category in the pagan world. And where 2 Maccabees appeared to lean on Isaiah 53 to suggest that the martyrs might, by their deaths, have exhausted the divine wrath that was operating through the Syrian oppression, this writer turns the thought in a more pagan direction:

> Because of [the martyrs] our enemies did not rule over our nation, the tyrant was punished, and the homeland purified—they having become, as it were, a ransom for the sin of our nation. And through the blood of those devout ones and their death as an atoning sacrifice [*hilastērion*], divine Providence preserved Israel that previously had been mistreated. (4 Macc. 17:20–22)

Little sense is left in this book of the larger covenant story of God, Israel, and the world. The strong, and strongly Jewish, themes of God's good creation and of the promise of resurrection are pushed to one side. So are the themes in Isaiah that contextualize the fourth Servant Song, preventing it from lapsing into this kind of quasi-pagan narrative; and so are the themes in Romans that flank what Paul says in chapter 3. Certainty on a point like this is impossible. But what I think may have happened is that the author of 4 Maccabees was eager to present the Jewish martyrs to a pagan audience as dying a noble death on behalf of their country, while still distantly echoing some elements of Israel's scriptural heritage. He has therefore combined those two strands, producing a mixture neither fully scriptural nor completely pagan. We should not take his book as a sure guide to what might happen when someone like Paul, convinced that the Messiah has come and has embodied the divine covenant faithfulness, offers a fresh reading of the Torah and Prophets with a fresh Temple theology at its heart.

But I have argued throughout this book that something similar to the mistake of 4 Maccabees, only more so, has happened in more recent Western Christian tradition. We too have swapped the ancient Israelite vision of God and the world (focused on the Temple and thence the new creation and brought into expression in Passover and the other great gatherings, such as the Day of Atonement) for the assumed "goal" of a Platonized "heaven," the assumed human vocation of virtue or good behavior, and the dangerously paganized vision of how humans who have failed to attain that vocation might nevertheless gain that goal. Romans 1–4 has been read with little or no attention to the theme of the divine covenant with Israel and through Israel with the world. Other ideas, particularly the popular image of "God punishing Jesus," envisaged as a separate, noncovenantal abstract transaction, have come in to take the place of that all-important theme. Many distortions have resulted not only through that teaching but also, ironically, through teachings that, in reaction against the distorted view, have themselves proposed equally unsatisfactory alternatives.

### The New Covenant in Jesus's Blood

When we look back at the analysis offered here of Romans 3:21–26, there is one point that demands further comment. Even though this passage is unique among the early Christian writings, it appears after all suddenly familiar. We have approached it on strict exegetical grounds, coming cautiously into the passage from either end, where the emphasis, from 2:17 on and then again in chapter 4, has been on the divine covenant, the divine promises and purposes to and through Abraham and his family. Coming to the passage this way, we have then worked inward, to find the notions of a new Passover combined with a new sin-forgiving act accomplished through the blood of Jesus. Though the emphasis of the whole passage fits, of course, with the specific argument of Romans, this combination of themes is so strikingly similar to the combination we find in the various accounts of the Last Supper that it is hard to suppose this to be accidental.

This is not the place to ponder the question of how these various traditions came to be as they are. That would in any case be a matter of speculation. But it seems to me striking that in summarizing the meaning of Jesus's death for the purposes of his own present argument, Paul finds himself in the same territory as the gospel writers—and in the same combination of themes as he himself deployed when writing 1 Corinthians 11:23–26. It looks as though we are here in touch with some of the very earliest Christian reflections on the cross, rooted in the intentions, teaching, and dramatic actions of Jesus himself. And here, as there, we come back once again to the point. In this event, all the early Christians tell us, the living God was revealed in human form, in utter self-giving love, to be the focus of grateful worship, worship that would replace the idols and would therefore generate a new, truly human existence in which the deadly grip of sin had been broken forever.

## Conclusion: Redemption Accomplished, Revolution Launched

Now at last we see how the difficult detail of Romans 3:24–26 makes exactly the point that is needed *granted the argument that runs from 2:17 through chapter 4.* Israel had been faithless to the divine vocation to bring blessing to the nations; but Israel's failure is dealt with in the proper way, by the reality to which the Day of Atonement had always pointed. The Messiah, in his faithful death, had very specifically accomplished the purpose for which Israel had been called. The covenant purposes of God *for* Israel, and *through* Israel for the world, were at last established, with Jesus's own blood as the blood of the new covenant. In other words, *Jesus, as Israel's Messiah, is the place where and the means by which God's covenant purposes and Israel's covenant faithfulness meet, merge, and achieve their original object.*

And with that the true God was shockingly unveiled to the world as the true focus of worship, displacing the idolatries that had lain at the heart of sin. Israel's past sins, the faithlessness that had apparently thrown the covenant into jeopardy, had been passed over, while the purpose of the covenant was gloriously fulfilled in the creation of a worldwide justified people. The "covenant of vocation"—Israel's vocation to be the light of the world—was fulfilled. As a result, God and Israel "met" in Jesus. In Jesus, as Israel's representative, God and Israel, God and the human race, God and the world met and were reconciled. "God was reconciling the world to himself in the Messiah" (2 Cor. 5:19). The Messiah is, in Paul's mind, the unique place where Israel's God really does meet with his people. He embodies Israel as the king who sums up his people in himself and whose faithfulness stands in for their faithlessness. He embodies Israel's God himself come to rescue his people. The divine rescuing purposes and Israel's vocation come rushing together in the same human being, the same event. That is what Paul is saying here.

This passage does not, then, focus on the point that most of us, including myself in earlier writings, have assumed. Paul is not simply offering a roundabout way of saying, "We sinned; God punished Jesus; we are forgiven." He is saying, "We all committed idolatry, and sinned; God promised Abraham to save the world through Israel; Israel was faithless to that commission; but God has put forth the faithful Messiah, his own self-revelation, whose death has been our Exodus from slavery." That larger context is vital and nonnegotiable. If it seems suddenly complex for readers today, that is our problem; at least its complexities are biblical complexities rather than the endless ramifications of theory that seem to be required with every step that different traditions take away from that biblical home base. If we take what Paul says out of its Jewish context—and ultimately out of its Jewish eschatological context, replacing that with a Platonized vision of the "goal"—then we will end up with a moralized vision of the human vocation and a paganized view of the means of redemption. That has happened again and again. It is time to put things back as they should be.

So what, in the light of all this, would Paul say had actually happened by six o'clock on the first Good Friday evening? If Romans 3:21–26 was all we had to go on, what might we conclude?

First, he would say that the age-old covenant plan of the Creator, to rescue humanity and the world from sin and death, had been accomplished. The new Passover had taken place, in fulfillment of God's promises to Abraham. Second, he would say that this had been accomplished by God himself, in his act of covenant faithfulness (for which the shorthand is "love," though Paul does not use that word until chapters 5 and 8), drawing together Israel's vocation and his own deepest purposes in the faithful death of the Messiah. Third, as befits a "Passover" moment, he would say that people of all sorts—Jews and Gentiles alike—were now free, free from past sins, free to come into the single covenant family. They were "freely declared to be in the right," to be within God's justified people, able to look ahead to the final day without fear of condemnation (5:9; 8:1; 8:31–39). Fourth, as we have seen in all the other early Christian strands of thought we have studied, Paul saw the new Passover also as the "dealing with sins" through which exile was undone. This is where Passover and the "Day of Atonement" meet and merge. Fifth, and at the heart of it all, Paul saw Israel's representative Messiah "handed over because of our trespasses," in the sense intended in Isaiah 53. Dealing with sins robs the "powers" of their power; and this, as we have seen, is the key that unlocks all the other doors.

The death of Jesus, in this passage, must not be shrunk to the small scale of the usual formula of, "We sinned; God punished Jesus; we're all right again." No, the history matters; Israel was the place where the weight of the world's sin lay heavy, where the exile of Adam and Eve from the garden was acted out by the waters of Babylon. History matters then, because salvation in the New Testament is not seen as an escape from the world of space, time, and matter, but rather as its redemption. The death of Jesus was the moment when the great gate of human history, bolted with iron bars and overgrown with toxic weeds, burst open so that the Creator's project of reconciliation between heaven and earth could at last be set in powerful motion. The myrtle will at last replace the brier, and the cypress the thorn.

Nothing vital in traditional Western understandings has been lost through this approach. What has been lost is the paganized vision of an angry God looming over the world and bent upon blood. What Paul gives us instead, here and throughout his writings, is the Jewish vision of the loving, generous creator God, who gives his own very self for the life of the world. Much traditional theology has of course insisted on this very point. But the frameworks within which this central truth has been set have often allowed a very different underlying meaning to be "heard." No doubt this is partly because of the hard hearts of the hearers. But I think it is also because the full biblical story has been set aside in favor of a truncated narrative. "The Messiah died for our sins *in accordance with the Bible" and its own great narrative.* We are not at liberty to replace this with narratives of our own.

We must, as always, remind ourselves that Romans is not a "systematic theology" in which all the basic theological topics are laid out in summary form. Nor is Romans 3:24–26 an attempt to say everything one might want to say—even everything *Paul* might want to say—about the "atonement." As with every other time when Paul mentions Jesus's death, these verses do the job he wants them to do within their larger context. The larger context here is the faithfulness of God to his covenant with Abraham and Israel. That faithfulness, through which the Israel purpose is fulfilled and the world-saving purpose accomplished, has now been unveiled in action. Once we liberate Romans 3:21–26 from the burden of trying to say "everything about the cross," it too experiences its Exodus. It is free to make its own point in its own way and thereby to contribute vitally to the larger argument of the letter as a whole.

## Beyond the Gospels and Paul

I have not tried, in this book, to provide a complete account of what the New Testament says about the death of Jesus. I have looked mainly at the four gospels, Acts, and Paul with a glance or two at the book of Revelation. For a full account I would naturally want to add the relevant material from two other early Christian letters, the Letter to the Hebrews and the First Letter of Peter. They offer other angles of vision, though for what it's worth I think they complement the picture I've been sketching. Hebrews, in particular, explores what it means to think of Jesus as simultaneously the ultimate high priest and the ultimate sacrifice. First Peter addresses a situation where followers of Jesus are facing fierce persecution and interprets the cross both as the once-for-all achievement of Jesus and as the model set for his followers by that achievement. It would be interesting to pursue these further in relation to the way we have approached the central New Testament writings, but that must be a task for another time, and perhaps another pen.

What we can say beyond any doubt is that within the first generation of the church there was an explosion of revolutionary beliefs about what had been accomplished on the day Jesus died, but that the revolution had a definite shape that remained constant across different traditions and widely different styles of expression. The early "official" summary remained the gold standard: the Messiah "died for our sins in accordance with the Bible." Those who expounded this belief did so with a robust understanding of each element. The great narratives of scripture, it was assumed, had finally arrived at their divinely intended goal. This was naturally controversial then, and it has been controversial ever since, just as every messianic claim was controversial in early Judaism, meaning as it did that other claims about where Israel's history might be going were to be set aside. The early Christians stuck to the basic belief. Jesus had been raised from the dead; therefore, he really was Israel's Messiah; therefore his death really was the new Passover; his death really had dealt with the sins that had caused "exile" in the first place; and this had been accomplished by Jesus's sharing and bearing the full weight of evil, and doing so alone. In his suffering and death, "Sin" was condemned. The darkest of dark powers was defeated, and its captives were set free.

Despite his repeated hints, none of Jesus's followers initially regarded his death as anything other than a complete disaster. Nobody knew, on the evening of the first Good Friday, that any of this sequence of thought, from victory over the "powers" to dealing with sins, might even be thinkable. But once Jesus had been raised from the dead, and once his followers had thought their way through the great scriptural stories that alone could make sense of such a thing, they knew that the revolution really had begun. And, in knowing that, they knew that the same revolution had caught them up in its wake. What Jesus had decisively launched they must determinedly continue. And that brings us, in conclusion, to ourselves. Where do we fit into this story?

# PART FOUR

# The Revolution Continues

# 14

—

# Passover People

I HAVE ARGUED in this book that, according to the earliest Christians, *when Jesus died, something happened as a result of which the world was a different place.* By six o'clock on the evening of the first Good Friday, the world had changed. A revolution had begun.

The first sign of the difference came on the third day, when Jesus was raised from the dead. Without that, his followers would have concluded with shame and sorrow that he was just another failed Messiah. But his resurrection was not simply a surprise happy ending to the story. It was, and was bound to be seen as, a glorious *beginning*. It meant that the darkest and strongest power in the world, the power of death itself, had been defeated. If that was true, then a new power, a different *sort* of power from all others, had been unleashed into the world.

How had this happened? As the early Christians looked back with Easter eyes at Jesus's kingdom-launching public career and his bizarrely "royal" death (with "King of the Jews" above his head), they soon reached the conclusion that his death itself had been the ultimate victory. That is what we have been exploring in this book. But that victory seemed to have been won not at the very end of the "present age," but right in the middle of it, with suffering and wickedness still rampant all around. This could only mean that the victory was coming in two stages.

Jesus's followers themselves were to be given a new kind of task. The Great Jailer had been overpowered; now someone had to go and unlock the prison doors. Forgiveness of sins had been accomplished, robbing the idols of their power; someone had to go and announce the amnesty to "sinners" far and wide. And this had to be done by means of the new sort of power: the cross–resurrection–Spirit kind of power. The power of suffering love. It was quite a struggle for the first Christians to learn what that meant: to work for the kingdom of God in a world that neither wanted nor expected any such thing. It is that work, the work we sometimes call "mission," that we must now consider. If Jesus's death really did launch a revolution, what does it look like, and how do we join in?

Here we run into a problem. I have been arguing in this book against one particular way of looking at the cross of Jesus. Millions of Christians in many parts of the world still think the cross means "Jesus died for my sins so that I can go to heaven." The "mission" of the church, then, becomes a matter of explaining to more and more people that he died for them too and urging them to believe this, so that they too can go to heaven. I have taken part in many events that have had that as their aim, some of which were explicitly called "missions." True, in recent years several thinkers have made a distinction between "mission" (the broadest view of the church's task in the world) and "evangelism" (the more specific task of telling people about Jesus's death and resurrection and what it means for them); but the word "mission" is still used in the narrower sense as well, often referring to specific events such as a weeklong "evangelistic rally."

Part of my aim in this book has been to widen the scope of the "mission" based on what Jesus did on the cross without losing its central and personal focus. I hope it is clear, in fact, that this task of telling people about Jesus remains vital. But I have also been arguing that the early Christian message is not well summarized by saying that Jesus died so that we can go to heaven. That way of looking at the gospel and mission both shrinks and distorts what the Bible actually teaches. It ignores Jesus's claim to be launching God's kingdom "on earth as in heaven" and to be bringing that work to its climax precisely on the cross. It ignores the New Testament's emphasis on the true human vocation, to be "image-bearers," reflecting God's glory into the world and the praises of creation back to God. Fortunately, a great many Christians live up to all this in practice even though they may only believe the shrunken theory.

But that's not a good place to be. The practice is far more likely to be sustained over time if those engaged in it and the leaders and teachers in their churches understand the biblical and theological basis for what they are doing. Many other Christians, convinced of the "going to heaven" theory, have come to regard any talk of working for God's kingdom in the present world as a dangerous distraction. We ought (so they think) to see ourselves as "citizens of heaven" and therefore have nothing much to do with "earth." Sometimes this view is backed up by the belief that God will actually destroy the present world. Why, then, would we bother with it? Why plant a tree if the garden is going to be dug up tomorrow?

I have argued against this view elsewhere, particularly in *Surprised by Hope* and *Surprised by Scripture*. Indeed, the reason for that double "surprise" is partly that the New Testament view of God's new creation still comes as a shock to many in our world, both Christian and non-Christian. But in the present book I want to go deeper than before into the difference between the "usual" view of "mission" I have mentioned—the idea of "mission" as "saving souls for heaven"—and the "mission" that I believe flows from the extraordinary, indeed revolutionary, vision of the achievement of Jesus in his death.

*Christian mission means implementing the victory that Jesus won on the cross.* Everything else follows from this.

The point is that this victory—the victory over all the powers, ultimately over death itself—was won *through* the representative and substitutionary death of Jesus, as Israel's Messiah, who died so that sins could be forgiven. To suggest, as many have done, that we have to choose between "victory" and "substitution" is to miss the point, whichever we then choose. The New Testament affirms both *and indicates, as we have tried to map out, the relationship between them.* The "powers" gained their power because idolatrous humans sinned; when God deals with sins on the cross, he takes back from the powers their usurped authority. The question now is: What does it look like when this integrated vision of the death of Jesus is turned into mission? Answering that question—or at least beginning to answer it—is the purpose of this final part of the book.

★ ★ ★

For the sake of clarity, I have spoken here of two versions of "mission," though I am naturally aware that things are more complicated than that, in both church history and current practice. It may help, though, to explain very briefly, at the risk of considerable oversimplification, how we got to our present position. The recent "backstory" of these two versions looks like this.

For many protestant Christians in Europe and America in the seventeenth and eighteenth centuries the mood was one of optimism. New things were happening, and the gospel was going forward, changing lives and communities. As Europeans traveled the globe, they had a sense of spreading what they saw as Christian civilization in areas previously unknown. This, they believed, was how the kingdom of God would indeed come on earth as in heaven. This was one outflowing of the solidly this-worldly focus of some Reformation theology. It led to what has been called the "Puritan hope": the vision that the kingdoms of the world would become the kingdom of God, as it says in Revelation 11:15. When Georg Frideric Handel set scripture passages to music in his oratorio *Messiah,* this text from Revelation was used in his "Hallelujah Chorus," a powerful celebration of the kingdom of God on earth as in heaven.

But my point is not just this chorus itself. What matters even more is where the chorus comes in the work as a whole. The selection and arrangement of texts were not random. The oratorio divides into three parts: first, the hope for the Messiah, and his birth and public career; second, his death and resurrection and the worldwide preaching of the gospel; third, the resurrection of the dead and the joy of the new creation. The "Hallelujah Chorus" celebrates the fact that the true God now reigns over the whole world, so that their kingdoms have become his; and it is placed not at the end of the third and final part, but at the end of the *second* part.

This reflects closely the view of mission held by many in the seventeenth and eighteenth centuries (the first performance of *Messiah* was in 1742). First would come the worldwide kingdom, achieved through the preaching of the gospel; then, and only then, the final resurrection. The aim of "mission" was therefore then to bring the nations into submission to God the Creator and to his Son, Jesus the Messiah. That is, after all, what Psalm 2 had indicated as the divine purpose. And Psalm 2, speaking of the dramatic divine victory over all enemies, was the text set immediately before the "Hallelujah Chorus." It was quite clear what view of "mission" was being advocated.

By the late eighteenth century, however, a very different mood began to prevail. Many Christians in Europe and America continued to pour energy into social and cultural reform. But many others saw this as a distraction from "preaching the gospel," by which they meant "saving souls for heaven." Had the texts of *Messiah* been selected a hundred years later, in the 1840s, one might imagine that the "Hallelujah Chorus" would have been placed at the very end, celebrating the worship of heaven—though the text from Revelation about the world's kingdoms now belonging to the one God and his Messiah might then have looked strange, since the new mood insisted that the world's kingdoms were irrelevant. Had not Jesus said, "My kingdom is not of this world"? (No, actually. What he said in John 18:36 was that his kingdom was not *from* this world, but the text, in its misleading King James Version, was quoted endlessly to show the folly of any kind of social, cultural, or political "mission.") New mood, new mission: now the mission would try to snatch souls from the world, not to bring the kingdom of God into the world.

This second mood contributed to the cultural movement that called itself the "Enlightenment." With many Christians bent on escaping the present world, leaving it to its own devices and desires, the world channeled the optimistic energy of the earlier Christian mission into "secularism," the development of the world and society as though God was either remote or nonexistent. Having banished God to a distant "heaven," earth was free to move under its own steam and in its own chosen direction. This split-level world, a modern version of the ancient philosophy called Epicureanism, is still widely assumed as the norm. The Enlightenment was, in effect, trying to get the fruits of the older Christian culture while ignoring the roots.

Most modern Western countries emphasize education, medicine, and the care of the poor; these were all concerns of the church from the earliest times. It is an open question whether such concerns can be sustained in a just and peaceful society in a world from which God has been banished. Of course, part of the Enlightenment rhetoric is to point out that many wars and injustices had been committed by the churches themselves or by people claiming to act in God's name. This cannot be denied. The charge must be faced with penitence and shame. But it remains the case that social concern beyond one's own family, faith, or nation, more or less unknown in the ancient world, was part of the church's life from its earliest days. The second mood I have been describing has often been as quick to disown that tradition as the secular world has been to dismiss it.

Dividing history into "periods" or "movements" is always tricky, but these two stand out. In part, the second was a reaction against the overoptimism of the first. It too bred a reaction, as new "social gospel" movements arose in the early twentieth century, insisting that the emphasis on "going to heaven" wasn't the point and that following the Jesus of the gospels meant working to help the poor and the sick here and now. Many churches today are shaped through traditions that go back to one or another of these movements, and many debates in church councils, synods, and the like reflect the unresolved issues in question.

Many Christians grew up reading the Bible in the light of this or that version, often without realizing that these traditions of reading scripture were themselves shaped by cultural forces that distorted some elements of biblical teaching and screened out others altogether. None of us can escape that problem. But what I have tried to do in this book is to outline a way of understanding the New Testament's vision of Jesus's death, particularly that in the gospels and Paul, a vision that, by giving attention to various strands often ignored and by sketching a way of combining things that have often been played off against one another, will relaunch something more like the first movement than the second. Such a missional vision will need serious reshaping. There were problems (to put it mildly) with that earlier optimism. But I believe we can and must make the attempt. This is already happening, in fact. Many contemporary mission organizations are well aware of the need to advance a holistic mission without losing the cutting edge of personal evangelism. My hope is that a fresh appraisal of what the cross achieved will undergird this new vision and give it biblical and theological depth and stability.

## Rethinking Mission

The case I have been putting forward in this book is not just a thinker's puzzle for theologians to argue over in dusty seminar rooms. It is immediately and urgently practical. The "victory" is achieved *because* Jesus "gave himself for our sins," rescuing and forgiving humans and so breaking the deadly grip of the powers they had been worshipping. A mission based on a supposed "victory" that does not have "forgiveness of sins" at its heart will go seriously wrong in one direction. That was the danger of the first view I outlined: triumphalism without forgiveness at its core. A mission based on "forgiveness of sins" where we see things only in terms of "saving souls for heaven" will go wrong in the other direction. That was the danger of the second view: a message of forgiveness that left the powers to rule the world unchallenged. The New Testament insists on both and in their proper relation. That has been my case. When we get this right, the church's true vocation emerges once more.

Notice what then happens. When we see the victory of Jesus in relation to the biblical Passover tradition, reshaped through the Jewish longing for the "forgiveness of sins" *as a liberating event within history,* we see the early Christian movement not as a "religion" in the modern sense at all, but as a complete new way of being human in the world and for the world. People talk glibly of the "rise of Christianity" or even of Jesus as the "founder of Christianity" without realizing that to give Jesus's movement a name like that (an "-ity" alongside all the "-isms") is at once to diminish it, to make it one example of a category, one species within a genus. That is not how it appeared to Jesus's contemporaries. To think of his revolutionary movement in that way is at once to distort its sense of mission.

Of course, many now hear the word "Christianity" within the echo chamber of a weary and cynical Western modernism, for which the "church" is simply a large organization full of arcane rituals and bland platitudes, with fingers in other people's pies, acting as a triumphal and imperial force in the world and providing guilt trips and the fear of hell for any who get in its way. A caricature, of course, but church must bear its share of blame for it. That is why a fresh vision of the cross ought to challenge standard views of what Jesus's followers are called to do and be—*if they are to be true to the original revolution.*

According to that original revolution, rescued humans are set free to be what they were made to be. "Forgiveness," achieved through God's Son's "giving himself for our sins," is the key to the liberating victory. Sin matters, and forgiveness of sins matters, but they matter because sin, flowing from idolatry, corrupts, distorts, and disables the image-bearing vocation, which is much more than simply "getting ready for heaven." An overconcentration on "sin" and how God deals with it means that we see things only with regard to "works," even if we confess that we have no "works" of our own and that we have to rely on Jesus to supply them for us. (Equally, an underemphasis on "sin" and how God deals with it is an attempt to claim some kind of victory without seeing the heart of the problem.) The biblical vision of what it means to be human, the "royal priesthood" vocation, is more multidimensional than either of the regular alternatives. To reflect the divine image means standing between heaven and earth, even in the present time, adoring the Creator and bringing his purposes into reality on earth, ahead of the time when God completes the task and makes all things new. The "royal priesthood" is the company of rescued humans who, being part of "earth," worship the God of heaven and are thereby equipped, with the breath of heaven in their renewed lungs, to work for his kingdom on earth. The revolution of the cross sets us free to be in-between people, caught up in the rhythm of worship and mission.

Expressing the missional vocation in this way and basing it like this on the revolutionary victory of the cross help us to avoid some obvious dangers. Without the sense of the victory being already won, we might easily lurch from arrogance (thinking that we had to win that victory ourselves) to fear (thinking that the world was too powerful and that we should escape it or at least hunker down and wait for Jesus to return and sort everything out himself). The initial victory gives us the platform for work that is both confident and humble. However, without the sense that the victory is won *through* the forgiveness of sins, "mission" could easily detach itself from the calling to be people who themselves have been rescued from the grip of the powers, people who themselves know what it means to live as grateful forgiven sinners.

No doubt there are checks and balances here within the church as a whole and within individual lives. We need one another, and we need pastoral care and direction within the church. Sometimes we need, for our own sake and the sake of the work in which we are engaged, to sense afresh just how dark and deep the power of sin really is and to know afresh what it means to be delivered from it. At other times, focusing on sin all the time might actually become neurotic or even self-indulgent, when we should instead be looking outward, working to bring healing and hope to the world. All Christian pilgrimage is a matter of rhythm and balance. This will vary according to different personalities, different churches, and different social and cultural situations. We need one another's help to attain that rhythm and balance and keep them fresh. But within the Body of Christ as a whole we need to keep our eyes fixed on the larger picture and discern our individual vocations, replete as they will be with healing possibilities for us as well, within that.

What matters is that we are constantly brought back in touch with the center of the faith: that Jesus "gave himself for our sins, to rescue us from the present evil age, according to the will of God our father" (Gal. 1:4). Each element of that is vital; each informs and undergirds the others. The loving purpose of God, working through the sin-forgiving death of Jesus, frees us from the power of the "present evil age," so that we may be part of God's new age, his new creation, launched already when Jesus rose from the dead, awaiting its final completion when he returns, *but active now through the work of the rescued rescuers,* the redeemed human beings called to bring redeeming love into the world—the justified justice-bringers, the reconciled reconcilers, the Passover People.

Many Western Christians have discovered that if we try to act on this basis, bringing God into the public square, working as explicit Christians for justice and peace in the world, we run into problems. Partly this is because the non-Christian Western world, shrill in its zealous secularism, would like to see the church shrink, huddle into a corner, and ultimately disappear altogether. Statistics that appear to point in this direction are seized upon eagerly. Likewise, any sign of a renewed mission will meet howls of protest and charges of "triumphalism" or worse. In part this is quite justified. We can all recite the litany of the church's follies and failings: crusades, inquisitions, and so on. The modern world, no less than that of several centuries ago, has seen major mistakes made in the name of the gospel. Very often, when Christian people have set out to "make the world a better place," they have sadly left the world a worse place instead. Their tangled motives and flawed schemes have become simply another variation on the world's normal power games.

This should not put us off. A world full of people who read and pray the Sermon on the Mount, or even a world with only a few such people in it, will always be a better place than a world without such people. Church history reminds us of the radical difference that can be made, that has been made, and that please God will be made. But the point is that once the revolution was launched on Good Friday, the vital work was already done. We do not have to win that essential victory all over again. What we have to do is to respond to the love poured out on the cross with love of our own: love for the one who died, yes, but also love for those around us, especially those in particular need. And part of the challenge of putting that into practice is that the powers, in whatever form, will be angry. They want to keep the world in their own grip. They will fight back.

The New Testament shows again and again what this means in practice. The book of Acts, in particular, shows the church facing danger at every turn. I once saw a commentary on the book of Acts that was entitled "The Church Marches In." That is a risky way of looking at it, implying an easily won military invasion. The church's mission was from the start neither easy nor military. Nor was it an "invasion," for that matter. The whole point was that the creator of the world was reclaiming his rightful possession from usurping powers. Acts is a book of cheerful (and sometimes not so cheerful) muddle and puzzle, as Jesus's first followers blunder around trying to find out what they are supposed to be doing, nudged this way and pushed that way by the Spirit, facing sharp disagreement and potential division inside the movement and even sharper hostility from outside. Acts has plenty of martyrs, riots, and frustrating failures. The powers are fighting back. And yet Acts ends with Paul in Rome, under Caesar's nose, announcing God as King and Jesus as Lord.

Paul's own interpretation of this strange phenomenon is worth quoting in full, because it opens up the point that must be made at the center of any account of Christian mission: *the victory of the cross will be implemented through the means of the cross.* One of the dangers of saying too easily that "the Messiah died for our sins" is to imagine that thereafter there would be no more dying to do, no more suffering to undergo. The same problem comes when we too eagerly celebrate the one-off victory as though there would be no more follow-up victories to be won. The opposite is the case, as Jesus himself had always warned. The victory was indeed won, the revolution was indeed launched, through the suffering of Jesus; it is now implemented, put into effective operation, by the suffering of his people. This is why Paul could write:

> We recommend ourselves as God's servants: with much
> patience, with suffering, difficulties, hardships, beatings,
> imprisonments, riots, hard work, sleepless nights, going
> without food, with purity, knowledge, great-heartedness,
> kindness, the holy spirit, genuine love, by speaking the
> truth, by God's power, with weapons for God's faith-
> ful work in left and right hand alike, through glory and
> shame, through slander and praise; as deceivers, and
> yet true; as unknown, yet very well known; as dying,
> and look—we are alive; as punished, yet not killed; as
> sad, yet always celebrating; as poor, yet bringing riches
> to many; as having nothing, yet possessing everything.
> (2 Cor. 6:4–10)

It was hard for Paul's audience to understand this. They lived, as we do, in a competitive society where everyone was eager to look good, to be successful, to impress the neighbors. The beaten, bedraggled figure of Paul was hardly that of a leader one might to be proud of. Yet Paul rubs their noses in the point that this is the Messiah pattern, the cross pattern. This is how the victory was won. Jesus himself went to the place of shame and degradation. This is how the revolution was launched; this is how it makes its way in the world. And this is why, for every one person today who reads Seneca, Plutarch, or Epictetus (among the greatest philosophers of Paul's day), there are thousands who read Paul and find his message life-giving. This is why too for every theologian who puzzles over abstract definitions of "atonement," there are thousands who will say, with Paul, "The son of God loved me and gave himself for me"—and who will then get on with the job of radiating that same love out into the world.

I suspect that this message about the necessity of suffering has not been fully understood in today's church, especially in the comfortable Western churches to which I and many of my readers belong. We all know in theory that the Christian life will involve suffering. Yet those who are eager for "bringing the kingdom," for social and cultural renewal in our day, can easily forget that the revolution that began on the cross only works through the cross. And those who are eager to "save souls for heaven" are likely to regard suffering simply as something through which most of us some of the time and some of us most of the time will have to pass, rather than as something *by means of which* the rescuing love of God is poured out into the world. The latter is closer to the mark. "The blood of the martyrs is the seed of the church." This well-known quotation from the African theologian Tertullian, writing around AD 200, reflects the early Christian perception that suffering or dying for the faith is not simply a necessary evil, the inevitable concomitant of following a way that the world sees as dangerously subversive. Suffering and dying is *the way by which the world is changed*. This is how the revolution continues.

This is etched into the New Testament at point after point. We return once again to Acts, this time to chapter 12. The fact that the victory had already been won when Jesus died did not mean that Herod wouldn't kill James, but it did mean that Peter was then wonderfully rescued from jail. Acts offers no explicit interpretation of this strange combination of events. Had I been James's mother or wife, I think I would have chafed at the strange providence that worked its victories in such apparently random fashion, and I would only partly have been comforted by reflecting how Jesus's own mother had felt at the foot of the cross. Or take Acts 16. The fact that the victory had already been won didn't mean that Paul and Silas wouldn't be beaten (illegally, as it happens) by the authorities in Philippi, but it did mean that when they then sang hymns at midnight, the prison doors were shaken open by an earthquake and they found themselves converting the jailer and demanding—and receiving—a public apology from the magistrates. Or go to Acts 27–28. The victory achieved by Jesus didn't stop Paul from being shipwrecked, but it did mean that when he got to Rome to announce God as king and Jesus as Lord, he would know that he came with the scent of victory already in his nostrils. The God who defeated death through Jesus and rescued Paul from the depths of the sea would enable him to look worldly emperors in the face without flinching.

At each point we have the sense that these things are not coincidental. Those who follow Jesus are precisely *not* to suppose that there will be no suffering along the way or that, if there is, it means they must have sinned or rebelled to have deserved such a thing. (They may, of course, but that isn't the point, as Paul emphasizes in 2 Corinthians.) On the contrary. The suffering of Jesus's followers—of the whole Body of Christ, now in one member, now in another—brings the victory of the cross into fresh reality, so that fresh outflowings of that victory may emerge.

That seems to be what Paul has in mind when he says in Colossians 1:24 that he is celebrating his sufferings, which are for the benefit of the young church. He is completing in his own flesh, he says, "what is presently lacking in the king's afflictions on behalf of his body, which is the church." This is a striking claim. It seems to mean that part of Paul's apostolic vocation is to go ahead of the young churches scattered around the Mediterranean world, like a brave commander on the battlefield drawing the enemy fire away from those more vulnerable, to take upon himself the suffering that might otherwise come their way. There is no sense here of Paul trying to add to the once-for-all achievement of Jesus. He elsewhere emphasizes that, for instance in Romans 6:10. But his claim here goes closely with what he says in more discursive mode in Romans 5:3–5 and then at length in 8:17–25. It is worth looking briefly at both.

In the first of these passages Paul explores the inner dynamic of suffering. This is how it works, so to speak, inside the person concerned:

We also celebrate in our sufferings, because we know that suffering produces patience, patience produces a well-formed character, and a character like that produces hope. Hope, in its turn, does not make us ashamed, because the love of God has been poured out in our hearts through the holy spirit who has been given to us. (5:3–5)

But then, in the other passage, he explains that sharing the Messiah's sufferings is the means by which, already in the present and then ultimately in the future, those who belong to him will share his rule in the new creation:

If we're children, we are also heirs: heirs of God, and fellow heirs with the Messiah, as long as we suffer with him so that we may also be glorified with him. This is how I work it out. The sufferings we go through in the present time are not worth putting in the scale alongside the glory that is going to be unveiled for us. Yes: creation itself is on tiptoe with expectation, eagerly awaiting the moment when God's children will be revealed. Creation, you see, was subjected to pointless futility, not of its own volition, but because of the one who placed it in this subjection, in the hope that creation itself would be freed from its slavery to decay, to enjoy the freedom that comes when God's children are glorified.

Let me explain. We know that the entire creation is groaning together, and going through labor pains together, up until the present time. Not only so: we too, we who have the first fruits of the spirit's life within us, are groaning within ourselves, as we eagerly await our adoption, the redemption of our body. We were saved, you see, in hope. But hope isn't hope if you can see it! Who hopes for what they can see? But if we hope for what we don't see, we wait for it eagerly—but also patiently. (8:17–25)

This rich, vivid portrayal of the present time—with creation groaning in expectation like a pregnant woman about to give birth, and with the Messiah's people groaning within themselves as they long for their new resurrection bodies—is perhaps the finest description in the New Testament not only of what it means to share the Messiah's sufferings, but also of why that is necessary. When Paul speaks of the Messiah being glorified and of his rule over the whole creation, he has several psalms in mind, notably Psalm 2, which speaks of the Messiah's worldwide rule, and Psalm 8, which speaks of the "glory and honor" proper to human beings who are called to exercise delegated authority over God's world. What we have here, as a result, is a dynamic fusion of messianic hope and human vocation, reshaped around the suffering of Jesus and refocused on the suffering of his followers. Paul has thus filled out the "inner dynamic" described in chapter 5 with a vision of the wider purpose of this suffering.

This is how it works. The Messiah suffered and won the victory over the powers of evil. The church, the Messiah's people, must suffer in the present, because they share the Messiah's life, his raised-from-the-dead life, and this is the way to implement the Messiah's victory. This is part of what it means to share in his "glory," his splendid rule over the world, which at present is exercised through the Spirit-led work and suffering of his people.

And through their prayer. Paul joins all these themes together in a unique passage, Romans 8:26–27, that brings the inner personal dynamic of suffering together with the larger world-redeeming purpose. This time he is alluding to Psalm 44, which speaks of God searching the hearts of his people (v. 21) and whose next verse, which Paul quotes a little later, refers to God's people "being like sheep destined for slaughter." The world-changing task of God's people in the present, rooted in the Messiah's victorious suffering, has its ultimate depth in prayer, particularly the prayer that comes from the indescribable depths of a sorrow-laden heart:

> In the same way, too, the spirit comes alongside and
> helps us in our weakness. We don't know what to pray
> for as we ought to; but that same spirit pleads on our
> behalf, with groanings too deep for words. And the
> Searcher of Hearts knows what the spirit is thinking,
> because the spirit pleads for God's people according to
> God's will. (8:26–27)

We should not forget, as we contemplate the depth of pain in this passage, that ten verses later Paul is declaring, in a shout of praise, that the Messiah's people are "completely victorious." As in the Psalms themselves, these things belong together.

As we saw in an earlier chapter, Romans 8:26–27 is the passage that supplies a vital clue to the otherwise shocking question of how Jesus, the living embodiment of Israel's God, could cry out, "My God, my God, why did you abandon me?" Here we have the Holy Spirit, who in Romans 8 is clearly the powerful presence of Israel's God himself, groaning inarticulately from the heart of creation. And the Father—the Searcher of Hearts—is listening. This is the extraordinary "conversation" in which the suffering church is caught up. And because it was always the will of the Creator to work in his world *through* human beings, this human role of intercession—of patient, puzzled, agonized, labor-pain intercession—becomes one of the key focal points in the divine plan, not just to put into effect this or that smaller goal, but to rescue the whole creation from its slavery to corruption, to bring about the new creation at last. Paul has a great deal to say about suffering elsewhere in his writings, but I think this passage goes to the heart of it all. It clarifies for us the way the revolution of the cross is worked out in the present time. Suffering was the means of the victory. Suffering is also the means of its implementation.

A word of caution is required at this point. When I was quite young, I was told by a senior church official responsible for the training of ordination candidates that it was good for us junior folk to have a tough time in college—to live in a damp apartment, to be constantly pulled away from our young families, and so on. This suffering would toughen us up and prepare us for real life in active ministry. Now, although there is no doubt a grain of truth in that—especially in that in active ministry seniors may sometimes bind heavy burdens on their subordinates while not lifting them themselves!—the church has a poor track record in the way it has approached such things. The idea that "suffering is good for you, therefore you need to put up with the conditions we are laying upon you" is at best callous and patronizing. At worst it is unpardonable and abusive. Jesus himself, warning that suffering was bound to come, pronounced a solemn woe on the person through whom it came (Matt. 18:7). Life will throw quite enough problems at us without the church adding more while telling us sanctimoniously that it's good for us. If we hadn't recognized this problem already, we would have been reminded by the fully justified protests of many in the feminist movements, who have rightly pointed out that the message about necessary suffering has often been preached by men to women, indicating that the women have to put up with whatever life throws at them while the men organize things to their own advantage.

But suffering, nevertheless, is still the means by which the work goes forward. First Peter explains this in considerable detail, perhaps because the audience of that sparkling little letter had somehow imagined that the Messiah had done all the suffering, so that there was no more for them to face. The book of Revelation emphasizes the same point in its own ways. At one level all this continues to be perplexing, especially when we ourselves are facing that suffering (in other words, when the problem ceases to be merely theoretical and becomes urgent and personal). But when we pause for a moment we can, I think, glimpse something of why all this should be necessary. It has to do with Jesus's own sense of vocation and with the redefinition of power itself which he modeled, embodied, and exemplified.

Jesus was not the kind of revolutionary who would call for twelve legions of angels, sweep all his enemies away in a moment, and leave nothing to do thereafter. As we have seen throughout this book, the revolution he accomplished was the victory of a strange new power, the power of covenant love, a covenant love winning its victory not *over* suffering, but *through* suffering. This meant, inevitably, that the victory would have to be implemented in the same way, proceeding by the slow road of love rather than the quick road of sudden conquest. That is part of what the Sermon on the Mount was all about.

Did we really imagine that, while Jesus would win his victory by suffering, self-giving love, we would implement that same victory by arrogant, self-aggrandizing force of arms? (Perhaps we did. After all, James and John, as close to Jesus as anyone, made exactly this mistake in Luke 9:54 and again in Mark 10:35–40. Perhaps even Jesus's mother thought the same way; her great Magnificat, in Luke 1:46–55, sounds quite like a battle hymn.) Once you understand the kind of revolution Jesus was accomplishing, you understand why it would then go on being necessary for it to be implemented step by step, not all at one single sweep, and why those steps have to be, every one of them, steps of the same generous love that took Jesus to the cross. Love will always suffer. If the church tries to win victories either all in a rush or by steps taken in some other spirit, it may appear to succeed for a while. Think of the pomp and "glory" of the late medieval church. But the "victory" will be hollow and will leave all kinds of problems in its wake.

I think many, if not most, Christians understand this instinctively, without needing to see the theological or biblical underpinnings. Such people do not need a book like this to explain it all to them. One might as well give someone a flashlight to go and see if the sun had risen. It is after all generous love, Jesus-shaped love, that draws people into the Christian family in the first place, not the complex crossword puzzles of subtle theologians. But what a book like this may be able to do is to explain to such people and to confused onlookers how the larger picture fits together, so as to avoid the risk that love itself may be subverted by other influences. In particular, it may explain how the mission of the church is organically and intimately related to the great events at the heart of the faith.

The truth of all this was brought home to many in my generation as we learned about Dietrich Bonhoeffer. He was one of the most brilliant young men of his generation and one of the finest theological minds of the century. When World War II broke out, he found himself in the comparative safety of the United States, but he believed firmly that God was calling him to return to his native Germany. Working as a pastor and teacher at a time of terrible ambiguities and uncertainties, with many friends regarding him as "a bit extreme" but with his conscience urging him on, he joined the campaign against Hitler, knowing well where it might lead. His *Letters and Papers from Prison* tells its own story of profound reflection and prayer as he faced the hangman's noose not long before the end of the war. Who can say what wonderful works he might have written, had he survived? But who can tell what impact his faithful life and witness have had precisely through his martyrdom?

This points all the way back to earlier examples of similar victories. In AD 177 a pagan mob in the city of Lyons, in southern France, killed several of the leading Christians in the area. The result was that Irenaeus came to Lyons as the new bishop (the previous bishop was among the martyrs) and was able, from that post, to teach and write vigorously on the subversive, world-changing truths of incarnation and resurrection against those, like the early Gnostics, who wanted to settle for a quieter life with the sharp edges of the gospel smoothed out. The blood of the martyrs was, in this case, the seed of some life-changing and gospel-enhancing theological teaching, which has served the church well ever since.

Come forward from there a century or more. The initial victory of Jesus on the cross did not spare the church at the end of the third century from vicious and violent persecution under the emperor Diocletian. But the victory showed itself in a different way. Far from being stamped out, the church continued to grow at such a rate, not least because of the witness of those who had faced death for their faith, that the Roman Empire was forced to admit defeat. Nobody had known that people could live like that or face death like that. This was something new. They recognized the Jesus followers as a strange new presence in their midst, neither a "religion" nor a "political power," but a whole *new kind of life,* a new way of being human.

That, of course, brought new challenges. Victories always do. That moment when the church was first permitted and then authorized as the official religion of the state was indeed difficult, and brought the church into a potentially compromised situation. Nobody ever suggested the church would face no challenges to its integrity, or that Jesus's followers would never have difficulty working out what following him would mean in new situations. But it did mean that many brave and wise teachers and leaders navigated and negotiated their way through the new challenges, and that what at the time were clearly "Christian values"—an emphasis on education, medicine, and looking after the poor as well as on avoiding idolatry and immorality—ceased to be the strange, unnatural concerns of a minority and became instead the way of life that an increasing number recognized, not just as a new way to be human, but as a far better way.

Sometimes things are not so clear-cut. In our own day the harrowing novel *Silence* by the Japanese writer Shusaku Endo tells of the sustained and vicious persecution of the small Japanese church a few hundred years ago and of the appalling dilemmas faced by those who wanted to stay loyal to their faith. As I write, the novel is being made into a film by the director Martin Scorsese. The Japanese Christian artist Mako Fujimura (with Philip Yancey) has written about it in a moving book entitled *Silence and Beauty*. As Fujimura brings out, even when God seems silent—as in the novel—there is still a message to be heard. Light is present in the darkness. Sometimes even silence can speak with hidden beauty and truth. These are uncomfortable messages for comfortable Western Christians to hear, and they are all the more important for that.

But we don't have to look to novels or to distant history. While I have been working on this book, Christians have been beheaded in public on a beach in North Africa. Others have been shot, raped, and tortured. On the day I am revising this chapter, a message comes from the struggling Christian community in Ethiopia, which is facing a massive refugee crisis and with it increased tensions between tribal as well as religious groups. Those of us for whom a visit to the dentist is about as much pain as we normally experience in a month and who confidently expect to worship and study scripture without any threats from either the authorities or hostile local groups find it almost impossible to imagine being in such a position. But these are our sisters and brothers. They are, quite literally, "martyrs"; the word means "witnesses." Some of those who were beheaded on that beach shouted out "Jesus!" in their last moments. They knew him, loved him, and were ready to die for him, as he had died for them. We cannot tell what effect their witness will have in the days to come, but history suggests it will be powerful.

For every story that makes the news headlines, there are a million others. Again and again Jesus's followers find that when they are weak, then they are strong; that the monsters that loom so large and that can indeed do serious damage from time to time are hollow inside. The idolatry and sin that gave them their energy and puffed them up with pride has been cut off at the root with the forgiveness of sins. As became apparent with the fall of Eastern European Communism, many societies had been in the grip of what had seemed massive, powerful, invincible forces. But once their bluff was called, they collapsed like a bunch of pricked balloons. There is, no doubt, a certain pragmatic wisdom in the advice that one should not "poke the dragon." But in the Bible the dragons have already been conquered, and even though they may lash their tails angrily, they are in fact a defeated, mangy old bunch.

Believing this and living on this basis can be exhilarating as well as dangerous. Part of the skill lies in discernment, in knowing which dragons to challenge, when, and on what grounds. But when there are forces at work in our world dealing in death and destruction, propagating dangerous ideologies without regard for those in the way, or forces that squash the poor to the ground and allow a tiny number to heap up wealth and power, we know we are dealing with Pharaoh once more. Idols are being worshipped, and they are demanding human sacrifices. But we know that on the cross the ultimate Pharaoh was defeated. And so we go to our work, not indeed with some kind of slogan-driven social agenda to keep the chattering classes happy, nor with the arrogance that expects to "build the kingdom" by our own efforts, but in prayer and faith, with the sacramental ministry and prayer of the church around and behind us and with the knowledge that the victory won on the cross will one day have its full effect. We expect to suffer, but we know already that we are victorious.

The sacramental life, in particular, can have a power that is sometimes overlooked by those who, afraid of the wrong use of baptism or the Eucharist, have downplayed them within their central teaching. That wasn't Paul's line. As far as he was concerned, as he explains in Romans 6, someone who had been baptized into the Messiah had already died, been buried, and been raised to new life. That had happened to Jesus, and what was true of him was true of his people. That is why (for instance) Martin Luther, the great German Reformer, could say, *Baptizatus sum,* "I have been baptized!" as his ultimate protection against the power of evil. He had been brought into the protection of Jesus's victory.

That doesn't mean of course that no harm can come to baptized persons or that they can no longer fall into grievous sin. Part of Paul's point in that same chapter, Romans 6, is that those who have come into the Messiah's family must constantly make it real, in thought and deed: "Calculate yourselves as being dead to sin, and alive to God in the Messiah, Jesus," and "Don't allow sin to rule in your mortal body" (6:11, 12). A similar warning is given in 1 Corinthians 10:12: "Anyone who reckons they are standing upright should watch out in case they fall over"! Like the Israelites leaving Egypt, just because you have escaped the life of total slavery, that doesn't mean you won't have to work hard to translate your newfound freedom into actual life.

This brings us to the other major sacrament, the "breaking of bread," the Lord's Supper, the Eucharist, or the Mass. (The fact that the church has developed different names for this event is an indication that we all know it's important and are anxious to interpret it appropriately, but that, like everything to do with Jesus's death, it remains contested territory.) Paul seems to be aware of the point we made earlier, that Jesus used his final meal with his followers not only as a way of explaining what his forthcoming death would mean, but as a way of enabling them to share in that death, making it quite literally part of their life through eating the bread and drinking the wine. Paul addresses the situation in Corinth, where, as he says in 1 Corinthians 8:5, there were "many gods and many lords," all doing their best to lure the young Christians away from Jesus. "Whenever you eat this bread and drink this cup," he says, "you are announcing the Lord's death until he comes" (11:26). He doesn't mean that the ceremony of the Lord's Supper is a good occasion for a sermon on the meaning of Jesus's death, though no doubt that will sometimes be true as well. He means that *doing it declares it.*

Think how this works. The actual event—the breaking of bread, the pouring of wine, and the sharing of both all in Jesus's name, which recall his last meal before his death—effectively makes a public announcement. This may have seemed odd to the Corinthians, who were used to sharing the bread and the wine in private, not in front of their pagan neighbors or the wider world. But the word Paul uses for "announce" (*katangellō*) is a word regularly used in his culture to describe the announcement of a public decree. If a message came from Rome with a new imperial decree to be read out in the public forum in Corinth with all citizens paying attention, *katangellō* might well be the word you'd use to describe what was going on.

So what does Paul mean here? *Doing it declares it:* breaking the bread and sharing the cup in Jesus's name *declares* his victory to the principalities and powers. It states the new, authorized Fact about the world. It confronts the shadowy forces that usurp control over God's good creation and over human lives with the news of their defeat. It shames the dark powers that stand in the wings, waiting for people to give them even a small bit of worship so that they can use that power, sucking it out of the humans who ought to have been exercising it themselves, to enslave people and render them powerless to resist the temptations that the powers have within their repertoire. The bread-breaking meal, the Jesus feast, announces to the forces of evil like a public decree read out by a herald in the marketplace that Jesus is Lord, that he has faced the powers of sin and death and beaten them, and that he has been raised again to launch the new world in which death itself will have no authority.

I know that for some readers this sort of talk seems dangerous. Am I not encouraging a kind of magic in which robed priests try to manipulate created elements to produce special effects? Isn't that the kind of thing that the Protestant Reformers protested against? Yes, the Reformers did protest against what they saw as a kind of magic, but that didn't stop them developing their own rich and serious sacramental theology. The abuse doesn't take away the proper use. Magic is, in fact, a parody of the truly human vocation. Image-bearing humans, obedient to the Creator, are meant to exercise delegated authority in the world in order that life can flourish. Magic is the attempt to gain power over the Creator's world without paying the price of self-giving obedience to the Creator himself. But the sacraments are the very opposite of this. They are the celebration that *Jesus* has paid the price and that *he* has all power on earth and in heaven. They are the powerful announcement of his victory. They can and should be used, as part of a wise Christian spirituality, to announce to the threatening powers that on the cross Jesus has already won the victory.

All this talk of "victory" means what it means because, as we have seen, on the cross Jesus died *for our sins;* the blood of the new covenant was shed *for the forgiveness of sins.* Sins, to say it once more, were the chains by which the dark powers had enslaved the humans who had worshipped them. Once sins were forgiven on the cross, the chains were snapped; victory was won. This opens up several vistas on the church's mission. For this we need one last chapter.

# 15

---

# The Powers and the
# Power of Love

WHEN THE RISEN Jesus met the frightened disciples in the upper room in Jerusalem, he commissioned them for a worldwide mission. In John's gospel this comes out with lapidary simplicity: "As the Father has sent me, so I'm sending you" (20:21). This will mean, he says, "If you forgive anyone's sins, they are forgiven," and "If you retain anyone's sins, they are retained" (20:23). For this awesome task they are given the gift of the Holy Spirit. In the next chapter, as this commission is focused for a moment on Peter's rehabilitation, it comes with an explicit warning: this will mean suffering. "When you are old, you'll stretch out your hands, and someone else will dress you up and take you where you don't want to go" (21:18)—a reference, it seems, to Peter's own forthcoming crucifixion. Then Jesus says familiar words, but they are now full of new meaning: "Follow me!"

In Luke's gospel things are put slightly differently, but with the same overall effect:

"This is what is written," he said. "The Messiah must
suffer and rise from the dead on the third day, and in
his name repentance, for the forgiveness of sins, must be
announced to all the nations, beginning from Jerusalem.
You are the witnesses for all this. Now look: I'm sending upon you what my father has promised. But stay in
the city until you are clothed with power from on high."
(24:46–49)

It is all too easy for us, in our individualized Western world, to
jump at once to the "personal" meaning of this and ignore the
larger whole. "Repentance" and "forgiveness": yes, we think, I
have repented of my sins, and I have been granted forgiveness.
That, to be sure, is vital. But if we go there too soon, we may
miss the breathtaking sweep of what is being said. Jesus's followers
are to go out into the world equipped with the power of his own
Spirit to announce *that a new reality has come to birth,* that its name
is "forgiveness," and that it is to be had by turning away from
idolatry ("repentance").

Something has happened, clearly, that has unleashed this new
kind of power into the world. That something is the chain-breaking,
idol-smashing, sin-abandoning power called "forgiveness," called
"utter gracious love," called *Jesus.* It isn't that first you have to repent and then, as a result, God may decide not to press charges on
this occasion. It isn't that somehow you thereby gain "forgiveness"
as a kind of private transaction unrelated to the truth about the
wider world. It is, rather, that forgiveness is the new reality. It is the
way the new creation actually is. All it requires to belong to that
new creation, with that banner over its doorway, is that you should
turn from the idols whose power (did you but know it) has already
been broken and join in the celebration of Jesus's victory.

This is why, by the way, "believing in Jesus's resurrection" isn't
simply a matter of giving acknowledgment to the fact that on the
third day he rose again from the dead, though of course it includes

that. To say yes to Jesus's resurrection is, by that very thought and deed, to say yes to the new world of forgiveness that was won on the cross, the world that was then launched into heaven-and-earth reality on Easter morning. It is not a matter first of convincing oneself that perhaps "miracles" may happen after all, then that Jesus's resurrection might be one of them, and then that the evidence really does seem to point this way. Resurrection and forgiveness are not strange things that might perhaps happen in the old creation. They are the hallmarks, the telltale signs, the characteristic marks of the new creation. Believing in them is a matter of glimpsing and clinging to the reality of that new creation itself.

Believing in Jesus's resurrection is hard not merely because it's difficult to get our minds around the idea of a person going through death and out into a new sort of bodily existence the other side, though that does indeed challenge our imaginations at the deepest level. It's hard because we are asked to grasp or be grasped by the fact that a new reality, a new mode of existence, has been introduced to the world. This is at the heart of the ongoing revolution: that *a new way of being human* has been launched, a way that starts with forgiveness (God's forgiveness of those who turn from their now defeated idols) and continues with forgiveness (the forgiveness offered by Jesus's followers in his name and by his Spirit to all who have wronged them). This is why forgiveness, in both senses, looms large in the prayer Jesus taught his followers. This is what it looks like, sounds like, and feels like when heaven comes to earth, when God's kingdom comes and his will is done in the world of humans as it is in the world of the angels. Forgiveness is the new reality. It is the power of the revolution. Praying the Lord's prayer and believing in Jesus's resurrection turn out ultimately to be all about the same thing.

We can see this in some graphic recent examples. In many cultures and countries in the world "forgiveness" is seen as a sign of weakness. If someone has wronged you, you should get even! Justice has not been done! You have been robbed of your rights!

I have seen people eaten up by that philosophy. It pervades every aspect of their lives. Every thought turns into a grudge, and every grudge clamors for revenge. And I have seen people who have given up that philosophy and discovered the healing power of forgiveness. It can and does happen. This always catches us by surprise, perhaps because it is the true and sure sign of the world still waiting to be fully birthed.

When, in June 2015, relatives of the murder victims in Charleston, South Carolina, came face-to-face with the killer, several of them told him at once that they forgave him. Something similar happened after the Amish school shooting in October 2006. These incidents, widely reported, strike secular journalists and their readers as strange to the point of being almost incredible. Do these people really mean it? It is clear that they do. The forgiveness was unforced. It wasn't said through clenched teeth, in outward conformity to a moral standard, while the heart remained bitter. Forgiveness was already a way of life in these communities. They were merely exemplifying and extending, in horrific circumstances, the character they had already learned and practiced.

In fact, once again, the incredulity of many who heard those stories matches the incredulity of people in the first century, as well as in our own, when hearing the story of Jesus's resurrection. And for the same reason. In both cases we are witnessing a new world coming to birth. Resurrection and forgiveness belong together. Both are the direct result of the victory won on the cross, because the victory won on the cross was won by dealing with sin and hence with death. Resurrection is the result of death's defeat; forgiveness, the result of sin's defeat. Those who learn to forgive discover that they are not only offering healing to others. They are receiving it in themselves. Resurrection is happening inside them. The wrong done to them is not permitted to twist their lives out of shape. Forgiveness isn't weakness. It was and is a great strength.

Resurrection and forgiveness together are vital for understanding the extraordinary and large-scale result of the victory won on the cross. The nations of the world were now set free to worship the one true God.

## Freedom

One of the greatest achievements of the cross is routinely overlooked by modern Christians. We tend to think of the early mission to the wider non-Jewish world as simply a good piece of news to be shared as widely as possible: "Jesus died so you can go to heaven—seize the chance while you can!" But even when we have revised that formulation to focus on new creation rather than "heaven," we are missing something deep that stands behind and underneath it. Because of the cross, *the world as a whole is free to give allegiance to the God who made it.*

Up to the time of Jesus the people in the countries and cultures surrounding Israel had gone their own ways. They had worshiped idols and served them. That, at least, was the normal Jewish perception, and the records, both written and archaeological, back it up. To be sure, in many nations and at many times people had reacted against the pagan systems that surrounded them. Fine moralists and subtle thinkers dreamed of a better world. As Paul noted in Athens, the pagan poets themselves pointed to a larger truth. But the nations as a whole were in the grip of dark, unforgiving systems of thought and practice. And the victory of Jesus on the cross meant that now at last that power was broken.

We saw this earlier in our brief study of John's gospel. Some Greeks had come to Jerusalem for Passover, and they wanted to see Jesus. Instead of going to meet them, however (perhaps he did, but John does not say so), Jesus made a comment that implied that he saw their request as a sign that it was time for the great victory to be won, the victory through which non-Jews would be set free from the dark power that had hitherto enslaved them, free to worship the one true God. "This is the moment," he says, "for the son of man to be glorified. . . . Unless a grain of wheat falls into the earth and dies, it remains all by itself. If it dies, though, it will produce lots of fruit" (12:23–24).

And then, after another interruption, he explains the point:

> Now comes the judgment of this world! Now this world's ruler is going to be thrown out! And when I've been lifted up from the earth, I will draw all people to myself. (12:31–32)

In other words, Jesus will die on the cross; this will be the way in which his glory is fully revealed (a major theme in the gospel); and it will also be the victory over "this world's ruler," the dark power that has held the nations captive. This is Jesus's answer to the arrival of the Greeks. Once he has died on the cross, "all people" will be free to come to him and so discover the living and true God.

This is the secret of the "Gentile mission," which began with Peter's visit to Cornelius in Acts 10 and continued spectacularly, in practice and also in theory, in the work of Paul. People have often imagined that Paul's mission to the non-Jewish world was undertaken simply because, finding his Jewish contemporaries unwilling to stomach such an odd message, he was desperate to win a few followers, so he went to non-Jews instead, offering them a less demanding message. That demeaning analysis misses the point. The Gentile mission was neither a pragmatic reaction to supposed Jewish intransigence nor a mere opportunistic attempt to boost recruitment for a strange new sect. From the earliest writings we have, it was seen as the direct and necessary result of the creator God overthrowing on the cross the powers that had kept the nations captive. Up to now the nations had been enslaved; the cross had opened the gates to freedom.

This is what Paul says in his speech before Herod Agrippa II, a great-grandson of Herod the Great. He tells of meeting Jesus on the road to Damascus and of the very specific commission Jesus gave him:

I am going to establish you as a servant, as a witness both
of the things you have already seen and of the occasions
I will appear to you in the future. I will rescue you from
the people, and from the nations to whom I am going to
send you so that you can open their eyes to enable them
to turn from darkness to light, and from the power of
the satan to God—so that they can have forgiveness of
sins, and an inheritance among those who are made holy
by their faith in me. (Acts 26:16–18)

Now at last the satan's power has been broken, so that forgiveness
of sins and membership in a new family is open to all! This fits
exactly with what Paul says when he reminds the Thessalonians
of the message he had proclaimed to them from the beginning.
People all over Greece, he says, are telling how the Thessalonians

turned to God from idols, to serve a living and true
God, and to wait for his son from heaven, whom he
raised from the dead—Jesus, who delivers us from the
coming fury. (1 Thess. 1:9–10)

This is the message we hear also in two of the best-known
speeches of Paul in Acts, first to the puzzled crowds in Lystra,
urging them to turn away from foolish idols to the living God
(14:15–17) and then to the court of the Areopagus in Athens
(17:22–31). In the latter Paul speaks of the one true creator God.
The pagan world gave plenty of indications, including poems
and the haunting inscription "To an unknown god," that people
were aware of this true God. But the truth was badly distorted
by the normal temples and what went on inside them. The Creator, however, was now introducing a new dispensation. He had
drawn a veil over the past and was commanding everyone, everywhere, to turn away from these follies, warning of a coming day
of reckoning at which the man he had raised from the dead would
be the judge of all.

This message was, of course, foolishness to the Greeks. Paul says as much elsewhere (1 Cor. 1:23). But the message retained power: the power of forgiveness, of a new world, a new creation, a new start. A new God? New to them, perhaps, but in fact this was the God who had made the world and looked after it all along, but of whom most peoples had been ignorant. And though Paul does not mention the crucifixion of Jesus in the two speeches just outlined, when we study his mature reflection in the letters, we can see what is going on. As we saw earlier, his vision of the death of Jesus included the fact that all pagan divinities had been defeated. Paul, like most Jews of his day and many subsequently, believed that in God's good purposes world history was divided into the "present age" (the time when the powers were still ruling) and the "age to come," when God would assume his rightful power at last. The dark powers invoked in paganism had held the world captive in the "present evil age," but now something new had happened:

> The Messiah . . . gave himself for our sins, to rescue us from the present evil age. . . .
>
> We were kept in "slavery" under the "elements of the world." But when the fullness of time arrived, God sent out his son, born of a woman, born under the law, so that he might redeem those under the law, so that we might receive adoption as sons. . . .
>
> However, at that stage you didn't know God, and so you were enslaved to beings that, in the proper nature, are not gods. But now that you've come to know God—or, better, to be known *by* God—how can you turn back again to that weak and poverty-stricken lineup of elements that you want to serve all over again? (Gal. 1:3–4; 4:3–5, 8–9)

> We speak wisdom among the mature. But this isn't a wisdom of this present world or of the rulers of this present world—those same rulers who are being done away with.

No, we speak God's hidden wisdom in a mystery. This is
the wisdom God prepared ahead of time, before the world
began, for our glory. None of the rulers of this present
age knew about this wisdom. If they had, you see, they
wouldn't have crucified the Lord of glory. (1 Cor. 2:6-8)

God blotted out the handwriting that was against us, opposing us with its legal demands. He took it right out of
the way, by nailing it to the cross. He stripped the rulers
and authorities of their armor, and displayed them contemptuously to public view, celebrating his triumph over
them in him. (Col. 2:14–15)

It should be clear from the casual way in which Paul introduces
most of these points that this is a regular and vital feature of his
thought. He is not exploring or expounding a new idea. It is
basic. When Jesus died, the "powers" lost their power. They can
still rage and shout, but the power of Jesus is stronger. And it is
the power—to say it again—of *forgiveness*. The past is blotted out.
A new world has begun. A *revolution* has begun, in which power
itself is redefined as the power of love. Paul had discovered in
towns and cities, in private houses and public streets, in formal
and informal settings, that the news of Jesus, crucified, risen, and
reigning, was "God's power, bringing salvation to everyone who
believes" (Rom. 1:16). The reign of the crucified Jesus only had
to be announced for it to become effective. The powers that had
held people captive were powerless to stop them believing, to prevent them from becoming part of God's new creation. The gospel
was—and is—the powerful announcement that the world has a
new lord and the summons to give him believing allegiance. The
reason the gospel carries this power is that it's true: on the cross
Jesus really did defeat the powers that had held people captive.
For the early Christians, the revolution *had happened* on the first
Good Friday. The "rulers and authorities" really had been dealt

their death blow. This didn't mean, "So we can escape this world and go to heaven," but "Jesus is now Lord of this world, and we must live under his lordship and announce his kingdom." The revolution had begun. It had to continue. Jesus's followers were not simply its beneficiaries. They were to be its agents.

What might it mean for the church today to live by the same belief? It would mean recognizing, for a start, that the "powers," though defeated on the cross, are still capable of enslaving millions. When we in the Western world think of forces that enslave millions we tend to think of the ideologies of the twentieth century, not least Communism, which until 1989 had half the world in its grip and still controls the lives of millions. Many in southern Africa think back to the terrible days of *apartheid* and remember with a shudder how racial segregation and the denial of basic freedoms to much of the nonwhite population were given an apparent Christian justification. Similar reflections continue to be appropriate in parts of the United States, where the victories won by the civil rights movement in the 1960s still sometimes appear more precarious than people had thought.

It is worth pointing out that in each case the Christian church had a key role to play in the downfall of these different systems. The Polish protests in the early 1980s, led by devout Catholics, slowly but surely began the process of shaking the Eastern European house of cards. The old *apartheid* system was broken not simply through protests and boycotts from secular moralists in the rest of the world, but through the tireless and costly work and prayer of Desmond Tutu and many other Christians, some working in public view and many under the radar. Those of us who remember the 1970s will recall that commentators predicted, as a matter of certainty, a major civil war in South Africa. That this did not happen was largely due to that patient, prayerful struggle. Similar things might be said about the work of Martin Luther King, Jr., and many others in America, speaking with a powerful Christian voice that refused to be drowned out by the Ku Klux

Klan, on the one hand, or the militant Black Power activists, on the other. These things have happened in my lifetime, and they are neither to be discounted nor explained away as the inevitable progress of enlightened liberal values in the modern world. As we should know, there is nothing inevitable about such things. What we witnessed was the power of the cross to snatch power from the enslaving idols.

It is comparatively easy to name yesterday's idolatrous systems. It is much harder to point to the equivalents in today's and tomorrow's world. Here the church needs the wisdom of the serpent as well as the innocence of the dove, and both often seem to be in short supply. But when Christians in non-Western countries look at Europe and America, they see, behind our own much-vaunted "freedoms," another set of idolatries and enslavements. The familiar trio of money, sex, and power are enthroned as securely as ever. A sign in my local charity shop tells me that a quarter of the world's wealth is owned by so few people that they could all fit on an ordinary bus, while millions of desperately poor people save up what little they have to pay people smugglers to ferry them dangerously across the Mediterranean, where, if they make it across the sea, barbed wire and refugee camps await them and local politicians agonize over how to cope.

You don't have to hold a doctorate in global economics to know that something is radically wrong with whatever "systems" we have, or don't have, in place. Western politicians clearly have no ready answers, bent as they are on solving yesterday's problems with pragmatic short-term solutions. We don't have a narrative that could make sense of the problem, let alone one that might solve it. And with a newly militant branch of Islam (disowned, of course, by the vast majority of the world's Muslims) ready to advance its own cause by exploiting the plight of others, we are all aware that things could get worse.

Faced with this situation, churches of all kinds in all countries need the gift of discernment to see where idolatry has resulted in slavery and to understand what it would mean to announce, in those places, the forgiveness of sins and the consequent breaking of the enslaving powers. This will be complicated, contested, and controversial. These things always are. But the attempt must be made. Clearly money is a major factor, and the nations that for centuries have profited from their "enlightened" cultural, technological, and economic status must look at themselves in the mirror and ask the kinds of questions that white South Africans had to face in the 1980s. Clearly too the way in which the Enlightenment had defined "religion" so as to separate it from the rest of real life has turned out to be an apparent luxury whose price is only now being revealed. The principalities and powers have been quite happy to have that discreet veil cast over their steady advance, and it is time for them to be unmasked.

The victory of the cross needs to be announced over that usurped power, so that the millions whose lives have been squashed out of shape can once again have hope—real hope, not simply the "hope" of arriving in an increasingly unwelcoming northern Europe. How to make that victory known is all the more difficult in view of the fact that so many churches have colluded with the privatization and spiritualization of "salvation" on the model I outlined earlier. But the attempt must be made—not simply to return to the seventeenth-century optimism, which as we saw could easily lead to some form of triumphalism, but to hold together the *whole* truth of the gospel, the forgiveness of sins through which the dark power is broken, and to find every way possible, through symbol and action as well as through words and reason, by which it may be announced and applied. The task may seem impossible, but that's what they said about the resurrection.

If money is one obvious problem, another is sex. We are all now aware of the way in which vulnerable people have been and are being sexually exploited on a grand scale. What was until recently behind a screen has increasingly come to light. We wring our hands and wonder what we can do, as our children and grandchildren are exposed to graphic pornography, tricked into "sexting," and encouraged to regard as "normal" various practices that most of my generation had never even heard of. But the problem, I believe, goes farther back and has come to light in my country at least through the high-profile revelations of sexual malpractice on the part of well-known public figures. They were able to get away with it in the 1960s and 1970s, it seems, because the climate of the times was all in favor of "liberation" and all against any form of "repression." It was fashionable, and still often is, to sneer at marriage, virginity, abstinence, and self-control. Any who wanted to argue for, let alone practice, the sexual ethic that until recently had been assumed by Jews, Christians, and Muslims alike were laughed out of court, mocked for being "repressed" or "killjoys," and invited to "become more grown up" and to "live in the modern world."

The fruits of this are all around. Celebrities have been able to indulge their sexual appetites more and more openly, relying on the popular mood, especially in the media, not to be "judgmental," but instead to be "tolerant" and even "supportive." As we now know, many clergy have joined in, citing to themselves and quite often to others the biblical warnings about not judging "lest you be judged" and about living not by law, but by love. The fact that these biblical teachings sat side by side in scripture with a robust no-nonsense sexual ethic was quietly forgotten. The church has faced, and still faces, one lawsuit after another brought by the innocent victims whose mental health was, again and again, irreparably damaged in the process. We know all this, but still in public discourse the Western world finds it unthinkable to tell any adults that their sexual desires must be resisted. The exception to this is of course pedophilia, and for that remaining taboo we may be grateful. But the shrillness of denunciation there shows up the absence of wise thinking on most other related topics.

What might it mean for the gospel to confront the power of Aphrodite, the goddess of erotic love, in our own day? It will mean, for a start, moving beyond the low-grade thirdhand Freudianism in which different groups accuse one another of psychological instability. It will mean a clear reaffirmation of the early Christian teaching, especially for those who hold office within the church. The misunderstandings here are so widespread and the muddled thinking so confused that one might be tempted to despair. But if we believe that on the cross Jesus won the victory over all the powers that hold people captive, we must take courage and proceed. In particular, we must reaffirm that the heart of that victory is the forgiveness of sins. This too can be misunderstood. "Don't you believe in forgiveness?" people will ask when someone is caught in bad behavior—as though "forgiveness" meant "tolerance" or the declaration of a general "anything goes" kind of amnesty. It does not. In the New Testament, "forgiveness" goes closely with "repentance"; and "repentance" doesn't just mean feeling sorry (perhaps because one has been caught!), but is an active turning away from the idols one had been worshipping. Just as in the world of business and high finance, and also in the world of lotteries and gambling, Mammon is available for worship on every street corner and every computer screen, so in the world of human relations Aphrodite can be summoned up on the iPad, the iPhone, or any of a number of other clever devices.

The other false deity regularly seen in our contemporary world is of course "power" itself, particularly power in the sense of military might and force. Here, alongside Mammon and Aphrodite, we face Mars, the ancient god of war. Many in recent years, mindful of centenaries connected with World War I, have been pondering the causes of that terrible conflict. Among other reflections it has been fascinating to see how, once various initial preparations had been put in position "just in case," it was almost impossible to prevent war breaking out: a massive buildup of troops here, a total breakdown of trust there. As with Mammon and Aphrodite, once people hand over their human responsibility to the dark forces of military violence, something seems to take over whose consequences cannot be foreseen, let alone controlled. Shakespeare's warning, "Cry

'Havoc!' and let slip the dogs of war," comes true again and again, as previously hidden lusts and drives, let off the normally restraining moral leash, wreak all kinds of violent wickedness, producing a chaos that only exhaustion, human or financial, can stop. As long as societies do with Mars what we seem to have done with Mammon and Aphrodite, giving them unquestioning worship and obedience, this pattern will continue, and the human disaster that results—millions of refugees, orphans, ruined cities—will be seen simply as another "problem" to be solved by politicians rather than as the telltale signs of an idolatry of which we should repent. Part of believing in Jesus's victory on the cross is believing that he there overcame those idols, so that it is now possible—despite what many say and most believe—to resist them and find radically different ways of addressing global difficulties. Not for nothing did Jesus invoke God's blessing on the peacemakers.

These idolatries will not be avoided and their power will not be broken by moral effort alone. In the New Testament moral effort—which is enjoined on all Jesus followers—takes place in the context of the initial victory won on the cross. Moral effort needs mental effort, and the mental effort needs to be focused on that victory and turned into prayer for the victory to be applied today and tomorrow. The sacraments will help here, but spiritual guidance and counsel will help a great deal too.

So too moral failure needs to be seen for what it is. Nobody imagined that Christians would be perfect, just like that! When a Christian sins, in this or any area of life, what is happening is a radical inconsistency, like a musician playing music from the wrong symphony or a host at a dinner party pouring out vinegar instead of wine. This relates to the problem I highlighted earlier: if we see the human vocation simply as the "works contract," then we are likely to regard moral failures as merely the breaking of particular rules. They are much more than that. They are a refusal to follow the script for the great new drama in which we have been given our parts to learn. A sinning Christian is like someone

walking on stage and reciting the lines that belonged in yesterday's play. We have been given new lines for the new play, the
great drama in which the royal priesthood takes up its new duties,
including of course the renewed vision of holiness, but going far
beyond into the life of worship and witness where the "rules" are
a small, if still vital, element in a much larger vocation. And part
of that vocation is precisely to celebrate Jesus as Lord *on the territory where other gods have been worshipped.*

When it comes to Mammon, we need to know how to use
money, particularly how to give it away. When it comes to Aphrodite, we need to know how to celebrate and sustain marriage,
how to celebrate and sustain celibacy, and how to counsel and
comfort those who, in either state, find themselves overwhelmed
with conflicting and contrary desires. We are not, after all, defined by whatever longings and aspirations come out of our hearts,
despite the remarkable rhetoric of our times. In the area of human
well-being, that is the road to radical instability; in the area of
theological beliefs, it leads to Gnosticism (where you try to discern the hidden divine spark within yourself and then be true to
it). Jesus himself was quite clear, following in the prophetic tradition: the human heart is deceitful, and out of it come all kinds of
things that defile people, that is, that make them unable to function as genuine human beings, as the royal priesthood they were
called to be. The gospel Jesus announced was not about getting
in touch with your deepest feelings or accepting yourself as you
really are. It was about taking up your cross and following him.
That is tough, and it doesn't stop being tough when you've done
it for a year, or a decade, or a lifetime. The victory won through
suffering on the cross is implemented, here as elsewhere, through
the suffering of Jesus's followers, most of whom will continue to
be troubled from time to time by temptation in relation to money
and sex and many other things beside.

Including, of course, power. At the heart of the gospel is a redefinition of power. That is one of the central ways in which the

early Christians interpreted the death of Jesus. The reason the cross carried such life-changing power, and carries it still, is because it embodied, expressed, and symbolized the true power of which all earthly power is either an imitation or a corrupt parody. It isn't the case that power as we know it in the "real" world is the "norm" and the Christian subversion of it is a kind of bizarre twist that might just work even though we don't see how. The gospel of Jesus summons us to believe that the power of self-giving love unveiled on the cross is the real thing, the power that made the world in the first place and is now in the business of remaking it; and that the other forms of "power," the corrupt and self-serving ways in which the world is so often run, from global empires and multimillion businesses down to classrooms, families, and gangs, are the distortion.

Please note, I am not suggesting (as some have done) that power itself is a bad thing. As I have insisted throughout this book and elsewhere, the creator God wants his world to flourish and be fruitful under human direction, and this applies to communities and human organizations as much as to farms, fields, and gardens. The Bible knows nothing of anarchy, except as the state that results when tyranny collapses under its own weight, leaving a dangerous vacuum behind.

Part of the trouble with power in today's Western world is that because many Western countries got rid of tyrants a century or two ago—or we thought we did—we are no longer in a good position to name tyranny when it stares us in the face. The triumph of liberal democracy has meant that we all assume two things as basic (granted that we may modify them here and there in practice). First, we assume that being elected gives officials a mandate to run things the way they want for the next few years. Second, we assume that the way to stop a bad government is to vote for a better one next time. A few moments of reflection, let alone a few minutes of remembering what elected Western governments have done over the last few generations, ought to make us realize that this (to say the least) is not enough. In the ancient democracies of Greece and Rome, such as they were, elected officials were frequently put on trial for mismanagement and corruption after their term of office, something we seem strangely reluctant even to imagine. And in any case the early Jews and Christians were not particularly interested in *how* someone attained office, but they were very interested in *what they did once they were there.* This is where the vocation of prophecy comes in alongside that of the royal priesthood. Another word about this may help.

Power, after all, is frequently held and wielded not by elected officials and politicians, but by well-positioned lobbying groups, on the one hand, and the media, on the other. They will say in their defense that their mandate—sometimes given theoretical justification, more often just quietly assumed—is to hold the elected officials to account (the media) and to remind them of the real needs and interests of their constituents (the lobbyists). There is no doubt a grain of truth in that, but it is almost completely hidden under a ton of unscrutinized agendas. Official oppositions sometimes provide genuine critique, but often they don't. Journalists sometimes do, but often simply reflect their own equally distorted agendas. We should not assume that our systems are automatically the best we could possibly have. This is where those who believe in the victory of the cross have something to say—quite literally. As Christians, our role in society is not to wring our hands at the corruption of power or simply to pick a candidate that supports one or another supposedly Christian policy. The Christian role, as part of naming the name of the crucified and risen Jesus on territory presently occupied by idols, is to *speak the truth to power* and especially to speak up for those with no power at all.

I have seen this again and again, mostly in cases that never made the newspapers but significantly transformed actual communities. I saw it when friends working in the prison system, some of them as chaplains, were able to go to the prison governors and point out ways in which the system was failing to protect many highly vulnerable young people in their care. I saw it when a small group managed to protest successfully on behalf of a man who had fled for his life from another country at a time when the government was keen to boost its statistics for keeping such people out. I saw it when young people from a church went to a back street in a poor neighborhood where drug dealers and others had been openly plying their trade. The young people swept the street, repainted the backs of the houses, and planted flowers all the way along, which encouraged the residents to take control of their own environment instead of handing it over to bullies. And I have seen it in the cheerful campaigning of large groups of churches for the dropping of the unpayable debt in Africa and elsewhere; nobody else was making a noise about this, and the bankers (soon to face their own unpayable debts, which were then written off!) were eager to stifle such a protest. But the churches persisted, pointing out the realities of the present situation and the highly beneficial results of debt remission. In some cases, not all as yet, the debts were remitted.

All this can happen and often does. Sometimes it gets the church into trouble. "Keep out of things you don't understand!" we are told. "Teach people how to pray and don't meddle in public affairs!" But followers of Jesus have no choice. A central part of our vocation is, prayerfully and thoughtfully, to remind people with power, both official (government ministers) and unofficial (backstreet bullies), that there is a different way to be human. A true way. The Jesus way. This doesn't mean "electing into office someone who shares our particular agenda"; that might or might not be appropriate. It means being prepared, whoever the current officials are, to do what Jesus did with Pontius Pilate: confront them with a different vision of kingdom, truth, and power.

The Jesus way, launched in his public career, won through his sin-forgiving death on the cross and bursting upon the wider world in his resurrection, resonates with the ancient prophecies of scripture, including the glorious vision of how power was meant to be exercised. This is one expression among many of the standard we must never tire of repeating:

> *Give the king your justice, O God,*
>     *and your righteousness to a king's son.*
> *May he judge your people with righteousness,*
>     *and your poor with justice. . . .*
> *May he defend the cause of the poor of the people,*
>     *give deliverance to the needy,*
>     *and crush the oppressor. . . .*
> *May all kings fall down before him,*
>     *all nations give him service.*
> *For he delivers the needy when they call,*
>     *the poor and those who have no helper.*
> *He has pity on the weak and the needy,*
>     *and saves the lives of the needy.*
> *From oppression and violence he redeems their life;*
>     *and precious is their blood in his sight. (Ps. 72:1–2, 4, 11–14)*

We are not at liberty to strike texts like these out of the Bible, though some might like to do so—whether because this ancient vision of restorative justice looks too dangerously left-wing for those in power or whether because "we Christians ought to focus on spiritual matters, not earthly ones." Nor will it do to think to ourselves that we will try to practice justice and mercy in our private lives, while letting the rest of the world do its own thing unchecked. Like many of the great Christian social reformers of an earlier day, we need to be bold in season and out of season in speaking up for the needs of the poor. (There is a popular parody of this just now, in which everybody wants to be a "victim" in order to claim sympathy and perhaps "rights." Little good will come of this, least of all for the many genuine victims.)

The gospel will not allow us to retreat into the private "Christian" space imagined by those for whom the death of Jesus does little except forgive our sins so we can go to heaven. The forgiveness of sins, as we have seen, breaks the grip of the "powers," and the followers of Jesus must make that point again and again and work to bring it to reality. It has happened before—literally, with the ending of the slave trade and the subsequent freeing of the slaves—and it needs to happen again. And happen it will, because the victory of the cross is real, and the power of the Spirit to implement that victory is real as well. But those who are called to this particular royal and priestly ministry, to worship the Jesus who reasserted the power of love and to bring that powerful love to bear upon the enslaved world, will suffer in some way or other as they do so. That, as we have seen, is the norm. And those who stand behind them, praying for their work in the spirit of Romans 8:26–27, will groan in the Spirit as they find themselves faced with apparently insuperable challenges. But victory is already won. Nothing in all creation can stop this all-powerful love.

I have spoken of the most obvious places where idols are worshipped in our time and where forgiveness and freedom from slavery must be announced and implemented by the followers of Jesus. But precisely because our vocation as Jesus followers is to be renewed humans, the "royal priesthood" who worship the true God and work for his kingdom in the world, our own lives must be subject to the same critique, the same vocation. There is no place for people who want to go charging off to implement some social, cultural, or political agenda but who think that this absolves them from the challenge to personal holiness. There is always a danger of using large public issues to stop our ears against the nagging problems within—just as there is an opposite danger, of being so obsessed with our own struggles for sanctity that we fail to notice the plight of the poor. Holiness is multidimensional.

And holiness will always be shaped by the cross. Paul speaks of "putting to death" the impulses and deeds that bubble up from within us and distort our genuine human vocation. His letters are full of sharp practical counsel of this sort. Financial corruption, sexual immorality, evil and malicious speaking—all must be killed off (see, for instance, Col. 3:1–11). Easier said than done, of course, but once more the victory of the cross is central. And note carefully: this is not a matter of saying, "Now that you're a Christian, you must follow the rules." Rules matter, but they matter because they are one of the guardrails within the much larger vocation, to worship the true God and work for his kingdom. Every time you are tempted to sin, you are being asked to hand over to some alien force a little bit of your own God-given power, which is supposed to be exercised over yourself, your life, and the parts of the world you touch. You are being drawn into the sphere in which some "power" is at work, under the control of the satan. At that moment you are also being called (did you but know it) to exercise your true power as a genuine human being, to practice your vocation as part of the royal priesthood. Sin is a distraction from our true tasks, a distortion (at best) of our true vocation. It keeps the powers in power. Resisting it—especially when we have allowed habit to take us effortlessly in that direction—will be difficult, sometimes painful, sometimes profoundly depressing. That is part of taking up the cross.

When you or I, faced with a major miscarriage of justice or mercy in our world or a major crisis in global politics or in the life of our own community, can praise the God we know in Jesus as the one who has already won the victory over all the powers of evil, we are able to go to our work, in whatever sphere it is, in a totally different spirit from the one full of fear and frustration that might otherwise accompany us. The combined ministry of intercession and "glory," of which Paul speaks in Romans 8, is ours for the taking, given in the gift of the Spirit, though always—Paul warns us explicitly—in the context of suffering. We cannot assume (though sadly some Western Christians have) that we are now mandated to live the Christian version of a modern Western "good life." Things were not meant to be like that: not that we seek suffering, but that, if we are acting as image-bearers, as the royal priesthood, there will be many times when we exercise this ministry, celebrating the victory of Jesus through tears and tiredness, through grief and the groaning of the Spirit. This work of intercession and stewardship extends outward into all areas of life. It calls some to a life of contemplation and quiet intercession, others to move onto a rough housing estate to work with homeless kids and drug addicts, others to study (whether the Bible or modern textbooks of economics, land management, and so on) and to work at the highest levels to bring fresh wisdom into God's world. The revolution of the cross sets us free to be the royal priesthood, and the only thing stopping us is our lack of vision and our failure to realize that this was why the Messiah died in the first place.

For this reason we must not only reaffirm the traditional teaching about the impact of the cross upon our personal lives. We must go farther. It isn't just that "now that we are forgiven, we ought not to return to the sins of which we have formerly repented," though that is true and is reaffirmed many times in scripture (see, for instance, 2 Cor. 12:19–21). It is, rather, that we have a vocation to pursue a calling that is far richer than simply telling other people to repent and believe in Jesus, so that they can go to heaven, and trying to behave ourselves while we do it. Telling people to believe in Jesus is always good, of course, whatever the deficiencies of the way we do it, but such words will mean what they are meant to mean when they are heard within the context of the church's overall royal and priestly vocation to be working for signs of new creation in the wider world, signs that the victory of the cross and the forgiveness of sins are a reality.

That is why I argued in *Surprised by Hope* that evangelism needs to be flanked with new-creation work in the realms of justice and beauty. If we are talking about the victory over evil and the launch of new creation, it won't make much sense unless we are working for those very things in the lives of the poorest of the poor. If we are talking about Jesus winning the victory over the dark powers and thereby starting the long-awaited revolution, it will be much easier for people to believe it if we are working to show what we mean in art and music, in song and story. The great philosopher Ludwig Wittgenstein said, "It is love that believes the resurrection," and hearts can be wooed by glorious or poignant music, art, dance, or drama into believing for a moment that a different world might after all be possible, a world in which resurrection, forgiveness, healing, and hope abound. Gifts that stir the imagination can frequently unblock channels of understanding that had remained stubbornly clogged when addressed by reasoned words.

And those who are working for justice and beauty, just like those who are working to bring a fresh new articulation of the good news so that people may believe, must themselves have the same things etched, perhaps nailed, into their own lives. It will be painful. That is part of the point, not that we seek the pain, but that we seek to follow Jesus. Holiness and mission are two sides of the same coin. Both involve bringing the reign of Jesus to bear in places where up to now the powers have held sway. The powers will not give in without a fight. But, exactly as with Jesus himself and exactly as he told his first followers, the fight itself and the suffering it involves (of whatever sort) are not incidental. The insight at the heart of Jesus's own vocation was that suffering would not simply be the dark tunnel through which Israel would pass to God's future. It would somehow be the means by which that future would be achieved. Most Christians today do not see things like this. Once we realize that we are part of the revolutionary movement that began at the cross, it may become clear once again, as it was to the first generation of Jesus's followers.

## Cruciform Mission

The message of the cross, as I have outlined it in this book, thus challenges the normal ideas of *eschatology*. If we start with the idea simply of "going to heaven," what the New Testament says about the cross won't quite fit, but if we start instead with the new creation, it all makes sense. The same is true about the view of *humanity*. If we start, as millions of Christians have done, with the idea that humans are meant to behave themselves, to conform to God's standards, so that they can be good enough for fellowship with him here and hereafter, once again what the New Testament says about the cross won't quite work. But if we start instead with the idea of reflecting the divine image, of worshipping the true God and serving him in his world (the "royal priesthood"), then the message of the cross (with Jesus himself as the ultimate "royal priest") will make full sense. And the same is true about the view of *the cross itself*. If we imagine that we can have either half of Galatians 1:4 (the Messiah "gave himself for our sins, to rescue us from the present evil age") without the other, we will reduce and distort the full meaning. And, finally, this message challenges the usual views of *mission*. Mission, as seen from the New Testament perspective, is neither about "saving souls for heaven" nor about "building the kingdom on earth." It is the Spirit-driven, cross-shaped work of Jesus's followers as they worship the true God and, confronting idols with the news of Jesus's victory, work *for* the signs of his kingdom in human lives and institutions.

Notice that, in all these cases, the disagreement between the New Testament view I am expounding and the "usual" range of views is oblique. Nor am I suggesting that nobody has said all this before, only that the point of view I have been putting forward, rooted in the New Testament, is a long way from what most Western Christians, and Western non-Christians for that matter, imagine to be the meaning of the cross. I am not saying— the New Testament is not saying—that "life after death" doesn't matter or that human behavior doesn't matter. Nor am I saying that the cross has nothing to do with Jesus "dying for my sins" or that Christian mission is not about explaining this to people so that they may come to believe. Far from it. What I am saying, based on the revolutionary meaning of Jesus's crucifixion, is that "life after death" is a quite different thing from what most Western Christians have imagined, since the ultimate future is a life *after* "life after death," in other words, the life of the resurrection and the ultimate new creation; that "human behavior" from a biblical point of view is quite a different thing from the normal view of codes of either morality or self-discovery, because what matters is not "works" (whether ours or Jesus's), but *vocation,* the human calling to worship God and reflect him into his world. And I am therefore saying, in the present chapter, that through the cross Jesus won the Passover victory over the "powers," that he did this precisely by dying under the weight of the world's sin, and that Christian mission consists of putting this victory into practice using the same means.

All this brings us back once more to the heart and center of all Christian discipleship. The new Passover is the large, overarching reality. Jesus has defeated all the anti-God, anticreation powers. He has stripped them of their borrowed robes and robbed them of their hollow crowns. And he has done this by dealing with the sins, the human idolatries and injustices, that handed to the "powers" the authority and responsibility given to humans in the first place. But the way Jesus has done these two things, nesting inside one another as they do, is by coming as Israel's Messiah, as the messianic "Son of God" (who wears that title for the double reason that he is both David's rightful heir and the unique "only Son of the Father"), so that he could "love his own people in the world, and love them right through to the end" (John 13:1), demonstrating in action that "greater love" that would lay down its life for its friends. His loving *identification* with the idolaters, the unjust, the sinners, the weak, the foolish, seen in those endless parties in the gospels and then in his sharing of the fate of the brigands on Golgotha, is the context in which he can be their *substitute,* the one bearing the sins of the many. And that means what it means not because of a "works contract," a celestial mechanism for transferring sins onto Jesus so that he can be punished and we can escape, but because of the "covenant of vocation"—Israel's vocation, the human vocation, Jesus's own vocation—in which the overflowing love, the love that made the sun and the stars, overflowed in love yet more in the coming to be of the truly human one, the Word made flesh, and then overflowed finally "to the uttermost" as he was lifted up on the cross to draw all people to himself.

Though we can say and write words like that, words that obviously point beyond themselves into the bright shadow of reality, which, like the cloud on the Mount of Transfiguration, can sometimes enclose us as we contemplate their truth, we know that the reality itself goes far beyond even that. As we tell the story again, as we listen to the musical settings, as we contemplate some of the great works of art that help us to glimpse the way in which the horror and pain of the world and the powerful love of the creator God came rushing together on to one place; as we find ourselves battling an intransigent magistrate on behalf of someone suffering injustice or praying at a deathbed and feeling a soft hand squeeze at the name of Jesus; as we find ourselves singing "When I Survey the Wondrous Cross"; as we find ourselves stopped in our tracks once more by the forgiving love that won't let us go sneaking back to the place of slavery—on these occasions and on thousands more we know that we are in the presence of the Lover himself. Christian devotion today has everything to gain and nothing to lose by exploring what the early Christians meant when they said that the Messiah died for their sins "in accordance with the Bible," by understanding better how the great story fits together and how it all makes sense. Christian theology, undergirding that devotion, has everything to gain and nothing to lose by abandoning its Platonized eschatology, its moralized anthropology, and its paganized soteriology and embracing instead the vision of new heavens and new earth with renewed humans rescued from the power of sin and death to take their proper and responsible place, here and now and in the age to come, within that new world.

Yes, it will mean taking up our own cross. Jesus warned us of exactly that (Mark 8:34–38). It will mean denying ourselves—a phrase we used to hear in hymns and sermons, but for some reason don't hear quite so much today. How remarkable it is that the Western church so easily embraces self-discovery, self-fulfillment, and self-realization as though they were the heart of the "gospel"—as though Mark 8 didn't exist! Yes, following Jesus will mean disappointment, failure, frustration, muddle, misunderstanding, pain, and sorrow—and those are just the "first-world problems." As I have already said, some Christians, even while I have been working on this book, have been beheaded for their faith; others have seen their homes bombed, their livelihoods taken away, their health ruined. Their witness is extraordinary, and we in the comfortable West can only ponder the ways in which our own unseen compromises—perhaps because of our platonic eschatology—have shielded us from the worst things that are happening to our true family only a short plane ride away.

But the first generations of Christians, with the New Testament writers at their head, would remind us that these are not simply horrible things that may happen to us despite our belief in the victory of Jesus. They are things that may come, in different ways and at different times, because this is how the kingdom comes. We are always tempted to turn the kingdom of God into the instrument of our own worldly "success" or "comfort." Some in our own day have forgotten the warnings of 1 Timothy 6:5–10, warnings against attempting to use the gospel as a way to get rich. Many have ignored the fact that for every word of Jesus against sins of the body there are a dozen against sins of the bankbook. Yes, there are also promises of great blessings. There will be seasons of apparent "success" and times of great "comfort." But both those words get redefined by the gospel, redefined according to the revolutionary victory won on the cross. And this applies as much to ministry in the church as it does to individual lives. It is all too easy to equate "success" with increasing congregations and growing budgets. Church history teaches otherwise.

The revolution, in fact, is going forward, and we with it. Statistics tell us that church attendance is in fact shrinking in the Western world; some of the countries where the early church was most securely established (Turkey, North Africa) now have hardly any Christian presence at all, though many devout believers in countries unimagined by Chrystostom or Tertullian still learn from those great early teachers. However, as the cynical Western world sneers, millions elsewhere and a great many in the West itself are discovering the joy of faith and hope and the love that will not let them go. The revolutionary victory on the cross is making its way in the revolution of communities, even whole countries, and not least of individual lives. I do not think that the individual message is any *more* important than the larger, worldwide or cosmic message. But nor is it any less important. The revolution has happened through Jesus and is now a fact about the world; but it is a fact that has to be implemented *through* his followers, and for that to be the case it must also be a truth that happens *in* them. The revolution is cross-shaped at every point. That is what baptism is all about; attempts are sometimes made to pervert it into the idea that "God accepts me as I am," but baptism always meant dying, and still does. When Jesus "accepted" Zacchaeus "as he was" by going to lunch with him, Zacchaeus was utterly transformed by that encounter. The revolution is always shaped by the cross, which launched it in the first place.

All this is summed up and brought into sharp biblical focus in John's dramatic story of Jesus washing the disciples' feet (13:1–38). This is a vivid and moving scene that, like most biblical stories, has more dimensions than might appear at first glance.

John places the scene at the start of the long buildup to the cross. Jesus has come to Jerusalem for the last time. The way John has told the whole story so far indicates that this is the moment of confrontation, of victory, of the completion of Jesus's kingdom work. But Jesus, instead of marching into the Temple and facing up to the power brokers (he had done that already in chap. 2), takes his followers to the upper room and shares with them the secret of what is about to happen. Only he doesn't simply explain it in words. Words point to the reality, and the reality is about flesh and blood; so Jesus explains his meaning in symbolic action and in the parables, warnings, comfort, and instruction that it generates.

John's gospel has brought us back again and again to the Temple. But now, though Jesus and his followers are not in the Temple but in a private room, John wants us to understand that we are looking at the true Temple. Jesus and his followers are standing for a moment at the dangerous intersection between heaven and earth. And over it all, and all that is to come, John speaks of love: covenant love, the divine love that goes all the way to the end (13:1). There was nothing that love could do for them that love did not do for them. And this is how it works.

Jesus is enabling them to be there, in this new sacred space, by purifying them for God's Presence. They need to be washed to have a share in his life. The foot-washing story follows the pattern of the famous poem in Philippians 2, which says that Jesus does not regard his equality with God as something to exploit, but empties himself, dies the slave's death on the cross, and is then exalted. In this scene Jesus removes his outer garments and acts the part of the slave to cleanse the disciples. Then, after getting dressed again, he tells them he's given them an example to follow. The foot washing is an acted parable of what Jesus is about to accomplish through his incarnation and death. He has laid aside the garments of heaven to reveal his glory on the cross, cleansing his followers so that they can be part of God's new Temple, the microcosm of God's new creation.

But within the story of the foot washing we hear a dark and dangerous note. The satan, the accuser, has already put it into Judas's heart to betray Jesus (13:2). Judas will be the accuser's mouthpiece, embodying and enacting the great accusation, the anti-God, anticreation, antihuman force at large in the world. We recall how, at the start of Mark's gospel, as soon as Jesus begins to announce God's kingdom, there are demons shrieking at him in the synagogue (1:23–24). So here, as Jesus prepares for what is to come in this moment of deep intimacy, the satan is at work. The powers of evil are gathering for one last desperate attempt to thwart the divine rescue operation. This is John's way of saying what Luke has Jesus say in 22:53: this is their hour, the time when the power of darkness is doing its worst.

All this is part of the larger theme that runs throughout the second half of John's gospel. As we noticed before, in John 12 Jesus is faced with the Greeks at the feast, and he looks beyond them to the new moment in the divine plan, when the great victory is to be won that will enable the nations of the world to be freed from their slavery and to worship the true God. This sense of final confrontation, of the kingdom of God against the kingdom of the satan, increases through the Farewell Discourses (John 13–17), until we see Jesus confronting Pontius Pilate (the kingdom of God against the kingdom of Caesar) and arguing with him over kingdom, truth, and power, before, in the crowning irony of the gospel, Pilate loses the argument by sending Jesus to be crucified. As Paul said, if the rulers of this age had known what they were doing, they wouldn't have crucified the Lord of Glory (1 Cor. 2:8). They were signing their own death warrant. Jesus's kingdom is of a different sort, and it has the last word.

After the foot washing and after Judas has gone out into the dark (13:30), Jesus tells the disciples with a sense of excitement that God is going to be glorified at last and that they must love one another as he has loved them (13:31–35). Glory and love: two great Johannine (and indeed Pauline) themes. How is God glorified? Through the work of his Son, the true divine image, the genuinely human one. The Word had become flesh; in our midst he appeared like God's new dwelling place, God's true tabernacle; and we gazed upon his glory. That is what John told us at the start of his gospel (1:14). This, then, John is saying, is what it looks like when the glorious divine Presence returns to Jerusalem at last, when the watchmen shout with joy because God is becoming king. This is what it looks like when Babylon is overthrown, when Pharaoh's hosts are defeated, and the slaves are set free. This is what it looks like when the Servant is exalted and lifted up high so that kings will shut their mouths because of him. This is what it looks like when the scriptures are fulfilled.

And this is why, when John tells the story of the new Eden, the new creation, the day of resurrection (chaps. 20–21), there is no serpent to be seen. Mary is weeping, but Jesus tells her to dry her tears. The disciples are scared, but Jesus comes through the locked door and tells them not to be afraid. Thomas doubts and questions, and Jesus answers him and accepts his newfound faith and worship. *New creation can happen because the power of the satan, of Babylon, of Pharaoh has been broken.* That is how the story works. That is what is different by six o'clock on the evening of Good Friday, though Jesus's followers don't realize it until the third day, which is the first day of the new week, the start of the new world.

All this is framed, like so much of the New Testament, within the story of Passover (John 13:1). As we have seen throughout this book, the first Christians knew that Jesus had chosen Passover as the frame within which his death would mean what it was meant to mean. Judas, energized by the satan, is like hard-hearted Pharaoh, who won't let Israel go, so that when the victory comes it will be decisive and final. And the love, the "uttermost" love, that Jesus pours out is the sharply focused divine covenant love, which had made promises to Abraham, promises that his descendants would be freed from slavery and given their inheritance, promises that were fulfilled when this love came down to Egypt to rescue them. John is telling the story of the new Exodus, the new tabernacle, and of course the new Torah: "I am giving you a new commandment," says Jesus. "Love one another . . . just as I have loved you" (13:34). The people who are rescued by the cross and the love it reveals will then be shaped by the cross and the love it will reveal through them to the world: "This is how everybody will know that you are my disciples, if you have love for each other" (13:35). This is how we learn not only to *tell* the story of Jesus, but also to *live* the story of Jesus. There is a straight line from here to Jesus's commissioning of the disciples in John 20 and particularly to his recommissioning of Peter in John 21. This is the source, and the shape, of all Christian mission.

There is a poignant final passage in John 13. Peter realizes that Jesus is going to a place of great danger, and he declares that he will follow him and give his life for him (13:37). The reply is full of gentle, sad irony. Will *Peter* lay down *his* life for *Jesus*? Actually, in an hour or two Peter will find he is still part of the problem, not part of the solution. The complex musical lines of the story are brought together into the single great chord, dark and glorious, that heralds the unveiling of utter love.

So here, in a passage that is narrative and not dogma, we have all the elements of a Christian understanding of the cross. We have the cleansing from sin that allows access to the divine Presence. We have the ultimate defeat of evil: the satan has done its worst and has been overthrown. We have the example of self-giving love to be followed, so that the world may believe. And we have the sharply personal challenge: Will *you* do this for *me*? Look to yourself, and be thankful that *I* will do it for *you*.

And with all this we lift up our eyes and realize that when the New Testament tells us the meaning of the cross, it gives us not a system, but a story; not a theory, but a meal and an act of humble service; not a celestial mechanism for punishing sin and taking people to heaven, but an earthly story of a human Messiah who embodies and incarnates Israel's God and who unveils his glory in bringing his kingdom to earth as in heaven. The Western church—and we've all gone along with this—has been so concerned with getting to heaven, with sin as the problem blocking the way, and therefore with how to remove sin and its punishment, that it has jumped straight to passages in Paul that can be made to serve that purpose. It has forgotten that the gospels are replete with atonement theology, through and through—only they give it to us not as a neat little system, but as a powerful, sprawling, many-sided, richly revelatory narrative in which we are invited to find ourselves, or rather to lose ourselves and to be found again the other side. We have gone wading in the shallow and stagnant waters of medieval questions and answers, taking care to put on the right footwear and not lose our balance, when only a few yards away is the vast and dangerous ocean of the gospel story, inviting us to plunge in and let the wild waves of dark glory wash us, wash over us, wash us through and through, and land us on the shores of God's new creation.

The cross itself, in short, stands at the center of the Christian message, the Christian story, and the Christian life and mission. It has lost none of its revolutionary and transformative power down through the centuries. The cross is where the great story of God and creation, focused on the strange story of God and Israel and then focused still more sharply on the personal story of God and Jesus, came into terrible but life-giving clarity. The crucifixion of Jesus of Nazareth was a one-off event, the one on behalf of the many, the one *moment in history* on behalf of all others through which sins would be forgiven, the powers robbed of their power, and humans redeemed to take their place as worshippers and stewards, celebrating the powerful victory of God in his Messiah and so gaining the Spirit's power to make his kingdom effective in the world.

The message for us, then, is plain. Forget the "works contract," with its angry, legalistic divinity. Forget the false either/or that plays different "theories of atonement" against one another. Embrace the "covenant of vocation" or, rather, be embraced by it as the Creator calls you to a genuine humanness at last, calls and equips you to bear and reflect his image. Celebrate the revolution that happened once for all when the power of love overcame the love of power. And, in the power of that same love, join in the revolution here and now.

# ACKNOWLEDGMENTS

I have been writing about the cross on and off and in various places for many years. That is inevitable, granted that the focus of my academic work has been the New Testament and that the focus of my work as priest, preacher, and bishop has been the biblical, sacramental, and liturgical life of the church, which brings one back to the cross every day, or at least every week. But this is the first time I have tried to stand back and set out the whole picture of what the early Christians said about the death of Jesus. As I have done so, I have been surprised to see quite new elements emerging and new connections between them. The overall argument presented here is quite fresh; I have surprised myself with the lines of thought and interpretation I have found myself pursuing, including in some places saying significantly different things from what I have said in my earlier published work.

I hope this book will encourage followers of Jesus to think afresh about the central events of their faith. But I also hope it will explain to puzzled onlookers something of why we Christians regard the brutal liquidation of a young Jew two thousand years ago in the way we do. I also hope that, even though it lacks the bits and pieces of an "academic" study, it will encourage theologians, preachers, and teachers in the churches to return to their foundational texts and to see if there is perhaps more to be said about what we have called the "atonement" than we had previously realized. The early Christians believed that Jesus's death had launched the revolution. It had changed the world. I think they were right. This book is my attempt to explain why.

This is, of course, a "popular" book in the sense that I have not provided the detailed scholarly apparatus with which an argument like this might be supported. A fair amount of that is contained in my earlier works, particularly in the large series entitled *Christian Origins and the Question of God,* published in London by SPCK and in Minneapolis by Fortress Press. Within this, the scene is set in *The New Testament and the People of God* (1992); the material about Jesus and the gospels is explored in *Jesus and the Victory of God* (1996); and the material about Paul is expounded in *Paul and the Faithfulness of God* (2013), together with the articles reprinted in *Pauline Perspectives* (same publishers, 2013), particularly the more recent pieces on Romans. Other more popular works flank the present book, for instance, *Evil and the Justice of God* (London: SPCK; Downers Grove: InterVarsity, 2003), *Justification* (same publishers, 2009) and *Surprised by Hope* (London: SPCK; San Francisco: HarperOne, 2007). The heart of the present book is, however, substantially new, and represents a development and in some cases a significant revision of positions I have taken previously, for instance, in my commentary on Romans (in the *New Interpreters Bible,* vol. 10 [Nashville: Abingdon, 2002]).

The present book began as a series of extracurricular lectures at St. Mary's College, St. Andrews, organized by Dr. Andrew Torrance. I am grateful to him and to the audience of colleagues and students who came regularly, asked sharp and difficult questions, and continued to wrestle with the issues. I make special mention here of one student, Dr. Norio Yamaguchi from Japan, whose own probing of the first-century meanings of Passover, on the one hand, and the Day of Atonement, on the other, kick-started some of the trains of thought that I have tried to follow up here. Dr. Yamaguchi is not, of course, responsible for what I have done with these ideas, but I probably wouldn't have started to ask some of the key questions if he had not nudged me into doing so.

I also thank Bishop Robert Forsyth, from Sydney, Australia, for his help in the initial brainstorming for the lectures and cheerfully absolve him too from any responsibility for the ways in which my ideas have developed. The same is true also of my colleague Dr. David Moffitt, whose own work on the Letter to the Hebrews and on the understandings of sacrifice in the ancient Jewish world and in the New Testament have been extremely stimulating. Though they come from very different angles, Dr. Michael Horton, Dr. William Lane Craig, and Dr. Jack Levison have given me the benefit of their experience and insight, and even though we still disagree about many things, I hope we can still continue to learn from one another. The Reverend Peter Rodgers, continuing a scholarly friendship of nearly half a century, has been a constant encourager and a discerning critic. Special mention must be made of Dr. Jamie Davies and Max Botner, my research assistants at the start and finish of this project, who have helped in numerous ways, not least in thinking through the complex and interlocking questions I am dealing with.

The book formed the basis of the lectures and seminars I gave at Pepperdine University in Malibu, California, during a memorable week in May 2016, and I am especially grateful to Mike Cope and his colleagues, who organized that week, and to the university president, Dr. Andy Benton, and his colleagues for their warm welcome and hospitality. A similar set of lectures was given at Wycliffe Hall, Oxford, in June 2016, and I am very grateful to the principal, the Reverend Dr. Michael Lloyd, and his colleagues for their hospitality and encouragement.

I must also thank a much larger company from around the world who have supported this work in prayer, in e-mail messages, and sometimes by personal meetings and crucial discussions. Thinking and writing about the cross is difficult at several levels, and those who have upheld me through the process have earned my deep gratitude. My grateful thanks as ever to Mickey Maudlin at HarperOne and to Simon Kingston from SPCK for their wise and careful editorial advice and to their respective colleagues for seeing another of my books through the press. My family, and particularly my dear wife, have as usual sustained me throughout this work.

Speaking of family, Leo Valentine Wright was born on May 1, 2016, as his grandfather was arriving in California to give the Pepperdine Lectures. This book is dedicated to him in the hope and prayer that he may come to know for himself the truth and the love of which I have tried to write.

N. T. Wright
St. Andrews
July 2016

# SCRIPTURE INDEX

OLD TESTAMENT

*Genesis*
1–2, 89
1–12, 95
1:26–28, 79
2:2, 197
3, 104, 284
3:8, 107
3:22–24, 95
11, 97
12, 107
15, 304, 313, 314, 322, 335–36
15:6, 313, 335
15:13–16, 319

*Exodus*
2:24, 326
3:12, 18, 182, 326
3:13–15, 108, 339
4:23, 182, 326
5:1, 326
5:1–3, 182
6:2, 108
7:16, 182
8:1, 20, 27, 182, 326
9:1, 13, 182, 326
10:3, 7–11, 24–26, 182, 326
15:18, 117

19, 166
19:4–6, 89
19:5, 326
19:5–6, 78
19:6, 128
20, 108, 182
24, 188
24:3–8, 187, 326
24:8, 192, 326
25:10–16, 327
25:10–22, 327
25:17–22, 108
31:31–34, 326
32, 340
33:17–34:9, 339
40, 110, 112
40:20–21, 34–35, 327
40:34–38, 340

*Leviticus*
26, 104

*Numbers*
14:21, 95
21:4–9, 212

*Deuteronomy*
4:37, 133
7:6–7, 132
10:14–15, 21, 133
26–32, 281

27, 239
27–32, 319
28, 104, 288
28–29, 304
30, 151, 187, 288
30:2, 151
30:15–20, 95
32, 104

*2 Samuel*
7, 113, 200, 292
7:11–14, 109
23:17, 187

*1 Kings*
8, 110, 112
8:11, 110
8:46–53, 111

*2 Kings*
9:21–37, 57

*Ezra*
9, 311

*Nehemiah*
9, 311

*1 Maccabees*
2:1, 127

*2 Maccabees*
**6:12–16**, 129
**7**, 128, 129, 341–42
**7:18, 38**, 342
**7:32–33, 37–38**,
    126–27
**7:37–38**, 342
**8:5**, 343

*Psalms*
**2**, 110, 122, 200, 288,
    292, 314, 359, 371
**2:1–2**, 205–6
**2:7**, 190
**2:8**, 96
**8**, 268, 371
**22**, 122–23
**44:21**, 371
**46**, 116
**47:9**, 151
**72**, 79, 96, 110, 314
**72:1–2, 4, 11–14**, 402
**72:19**, 95, 110
**89**, 96, 110
**98**, 116
**105**, 202, 282
**106**, 202, 282
**106:20**, 297, 308
**110**, 122
**110:1**, 248
**132**, 110
**137:4**, 239

*Isaiah*
**2**, 81
**6:3**, 111
**9:2–7**, 139
**11**, 78, 96
**11:1–10**, 139
**11:9**, 95
**40–55**, 106, 111, 112,
    200, 257, 298, 304, 319,
    321, 334, 343
**40:1–2**, 114

**40:3–11**, 114
**40:10–11**, 134, 140
**41:8–10**, 134
**42:1**, 141, 190
**42:1–9**, 139
**42:6–7**, 135
**43:1, 3–4**, 133
**49**, 82, 166
**49:1–7**, 139
**49:3**, 125, 334
**49:6**, 154, 189
**49:8**, 82
**49:13–16**, 135–36
**50:4–9**, 139
**50:10**, 125–26
**51:3**, 136
**51:9–10**, 140
**52**, 65, 92, 111, 112, 117,
    157, 260, 326
**52:5**, 311
**52:7**, 116, 193
**52:7–12**, 180, 334
**52:8**, 112
**52:10**, 141
**52:10, 15**, 334–35
**52:13–53:12**, 114, 125,
    139, 189, 334
**53**, 111, 124–25, 126,
    127, 131, 157, 189, 197,
    215, 222, 224, 260, 281,
    321, 335, 337, 338, 343,
    348
**53:1**, 335
**53:1–2**, 141
**53:5**, 194, 336
**53:5–6**, 337
**53:12**, 215
**54–55**, 157, 338
**54:5–10**, 136–37
**55:1–3**, 135
**59:2**, 155
**59:15–16**, 141
**60:1–3**, 90
**61:1–4**, 139

**63:1–6**, 139
**63:5, 9**, 141–42
**63:8–9**, 133

*Jeremiah*
**2:2**, 327
**5:7**, 221
**25:15–17**, 221
**31**, 151
**31:3**, 133
**31:31**, 192
**31:31–34**, 64–65, 115,
    319
**49:**12, 221

*Lamentations*
**3:22–23**, 133
**4:21**, 221
**4:22**, 114

*Ezekiel*
**10–11**, 111
**36:20**, 311
**37**, 104
**43**, 92, 111, 112, 298

*Daniel*
**2**, 118, 209–10
**6:10**, 111
**7**, 209, 210, 281
**7:14**, 209
**9**, 64, 151, 184, 210, 286,
    304, 311, 319
**9:4–14**, 304
**9:15–19**, 304
**9:24**, 93, 118, 210
**9:26**, 210
**12:1**, 122

*Hosea*
**11:1**, 134

*Habakkuk*
**2:14**, 95

*Malachi*
3, 200, 298
3:3, 80

New Testament

*Matthew*
1, 202
1:21, 209
3:17, 190
4:3, 6, 206
4:9, 207
5:3–12, 217–18
5:13–16, 219
5:21–26, 219
5:27–32, 219
5:33–37, 219
5:38–48, 219
5:39, 40, 41, 45, 219
6:10, 218
10:28, 196
11:29, 201
12:24, 191
12:29, 206
18:7, 372
26:26, 185
26:28, 186
26:29, 183
26:67, 219
27:30–32, 35, 54, 219
27:40, 206
27:46, 225
28:18, 207, 218

*Mark*
1, 202
1:23–24, 412
1:24, 205
8:34–38, 409–10
10, 192, 255–56, 293
10:16, 21, 191
10:35–40, 374
10:35–45, 222

10:37, 220
10:38, 221
10:39, 221
10:40, 221
10:42–45, 222
10:45, 170, 171, 197, 215, 224
11:12–18, 181
13:1–31, 181
14:22, 185
14:24, 186
14:36, 221
15:34, 225

*Luke*
1–2, 202
1:35, 200
1:46–55, 374
1:68–75, 149
1:76–77, 149
2:30–32, 150
3, 202
3:3, 151
4:3, 9, 206
4:6, 207
9:54, 374
12:4–5, 196
12:5, 216
13:1–5, 215
13:34, 189, 216
19:42, 204
19:42–44, 216
19:44, 200
19:45–46, 216
20:9–19, 216
22:18, 161, 183
22:19, 185
22:20, 186
22:37, 215
22:40, 190
22:53, 207, 215, 413
23:2, 213
23:18–19, 24–25, 213
23:31, 189, 216

23:39–41, 213–14
23:41, 47, 174
23:42, 214
23:42–43, 214
23:47, 214–15
24:21, 145
24:26–27, 87, 145, 217
24:44–49, 150
24:46–49, 384

*John*
1, 202
1:14, 22, 112, 200, 341, 413
1:18, 200, 293
1:29, 36, 209
3:14–15, 212
3:16, 5, 13, 43, 171, 213
8, 212
11:50, 211
11:51–52, 211
12, 413
12:23–24, 387–88
12:30–32, 323
12:31–32, 207, 388
12:32, 211
13–17, 208, 413
13:1, 192, 202, 408, 412, 414
13:1–38, 411–12
13:2, 207, 412
13:30, 413
13:31–35, 413
13:34, 414
13:35, 414
13:37, 415
14:30, 207
15:13, 47, 193, 208
16:8–11, 208
17:4, 197
17:12, 212
18–19, 207
18:8, 212
18:18, 190

*John* (cont.)
**18:36**, 360
**19:30**, 197
**19:36**, 209
**20–21**, 414
**20:21**, 383
**20:23**, 383
**21:18**, 383

*Acts*
**1:6**, 155
**1:6–8**, 160
**1:9–11**, 155
**1:11**, 161
**2**, 162
**2:11**, 163
**2:23**, 199
**2:36**, 165
**2:38**, 151
**2:40**, 165
**2:41**, 165
**2:42**, 163
**2:46–47**, 163, 165
**3:18–26**, 152
**3:21**, 155
**3:31**, 161
**4:2**, 155
**4:4**, 165
**4:23–31**, 288
**4:24–31**, 163
**4:26**, 205–6
**4:27–28**, 199
**4:29–30**, 206
**5:14**, 165
**5:28**, 153
**5:30–32**, 153
**6–7**, 162, 165
**7:56–60**, 163
**8**, 164
**8:12**, 155
**10**, 164, 388
**10:41–42**, 154
**11:24**, 165
**12**, 164, 368

**13:38–39**, 154
**13:46–47**, 154
**14**, 162
**14:15–17**, 389
**16**, 368
**17–19**, 162
**17:22–31**, 389
**17:30**, 331
**17:31**, 154, 161
**19:8**, 155
**20:25**, 155
**20:28**, 194
**21:21**, 165
**21:28–29**, 162
**24:6**, 162
**24:15**, 21, 155
**25:8**, 162
**26:16–18**, 389
**26:23**, 155
**27–28**, 368
**28:23**, 155
**28:31**, 161, 165
**31**, 155

*Romans*
**1–2**, 85
**1:3–4**, 243, 322
**1:16**, 391
**1:16–17**, 299
**1:17**, 271
**1:18**, 267, 268, 273, 307
**1:18–23**, 297, 302, 314, 315, 341
**1:18–25**, 85
**1:18–26**, 268
**1:18–32**, 32, 308
**1:18–2:16**, 280, 300, 313, 318, 330
**1:18–3:20**, 297, 313, 315
**1:18–4:25**, 317
**1:21–23**, 307, 328
**1:23**, 85, 297
**1:24–32**, 315
**1:25**, 85

**1:32**, 85
**2:1–11**, 286
**2:1–16**, 85, 322, 324
**2:4**, 330
**2:5**, 273, 331
**2:17**, 304, 309, 315, 345, 346
**2:17–18**, 309
**2:17–19**, 322
**2:17–20**, 297, 298, 301, 304, 314
**2:17–24**, 308, 311, 313
**2:17–29**, 301
**2:17–3:9**, 271, 304, 309, 318
**2:19–20**, 310, 320, 335
**2:21–24**, 304, 310
**2:24**, 311
**2:25–29**, 311, 315
**3:1–5**, 320, 322
**3:1–9**, 301
**3:2**, 335
**3:2–4**, 304
**3:2b–4a**, 312
**3:3**, 320
**3:4**, 312
**3:4b–5**, 320
**3:5**, 271, 304, 313
**3:19–20**, 309, 322
**3:20**, 307
**3:21**, 271, 305, 317, 322, 330, 336
**3:21–22**, 318
**3:21b**, 303
**3:21–26**, 270, 271, 273, 295, 297, 298, 299, 301, 302, 304, 305, 307, 308, 309, 314, 315, 316, 317, 324, 330, 334, 335, 337, 339, 345, 348, 349
**3:21–4:24**, 272
**3:22**, 320, 335
**3:23**, 268, 302, 307, 308, 309, 313, 328

**3:23–25a**, 324–25
**3:24**, 276
**3:24–25**, 321, 323, 328, 332
**3:24–26**, 273, 276, 295–96, 302, 303, 306, 308, 316, 330, 332, 346, 349
**3:24a**, 319
**3:25**, 227, 300, 329, 332
**3:25–26**, 265, 271, 303, 306, 318, 330
**3:25b–26**, 318
**3:26**, 300, 322, 330
**3:27–31**, 301, 315, 341
**4:1–25**, 313
**4:3**, 313
**4:5**, 314
**4:6–8**, 314, 322
**4:13**, 241, 314
**4:17–22**, 314
**4:18–22**, 268
**4:20**, 308
**4:20–21**, 297, 314, 341
**4:23–25**, 335
**4:24**, 324
**4:24–25**, 264, 320, 323, 335
**4:25**, 315
**5**, 216
**5:1–2**, 308, 317, 341
**5:1–5**, 272
**5:2**, 269
**5:3–5**, 369, 370
**5:6–11**, 272, 317
**5:8**, 13, 129, 264, 289, 332
**5:9**, 229, 273, 286, 303, 323, 330, 331, 348
**5:10**, 273, 336
**5:12**, 279, 280, 283
**5:12–21**, 273–74, 276, 277, 278
**5:12–8:4**, 280, 284

**5:17**, 83–84, 269, 290
**5:20**, 275, 282, 283, 284
**5:21**, 84, 274, 283
**6:2–11**, 276, 277
**6:7**, 29
**6:10**, 31, 277, 369
**6:11, 12**, 379
**7**, 235
**7:1–8:11**, 280
**7:4**, 264, 278
**7:7–12**, 284
**7:13**, 282, 283, 284
**7:13–20**, 289–90
**7:14–20**, 285
**7:19**, 276
**7:23**, 281
**8**, 33, 69, 157, 221
**8:1**, 348
**8:1–4**, 273, 286
**8:3**, 291, 324, 332
**8:3–4**, 264, 278, 322, 330
**8:3–39**, 289
**8:4**, 280, 287, 290
**8:9–11**, 290
**8:12–16**, 290, 292
**8:13**, 29
**8:17–25**, 290, 292, 369, 370
**8:18–24**, 33
**8:18–25**, 267, 269
**8:23**, 290
**8:26**, 291
**8:26–27**, 269, 292, 293, 371, 372, 403
**8:27**, 291
**8:29**, 293
**8:31–32, 38–39**, 264–65
**8:31–39**, 272, 278, 317, 322, 324, 336–37, 348
**8:32**, 332
**8:34**, 269, 317
**8:38–39**, 13, 279
**9–11**, 319
**9:1–5**, 269

**10**, 288
**10:1**, 269
**10:6**, 267
**10:9**, 320
**11:33–36**, 269
**12:1**, 269, 319
**14:8–9**, 230
**15:8–9**, 233, 269, 270, 319
**15:16**, 269

*1 Corinthians*
**1–2**, 246
**1:15**, 103
**1:18**, 22, 231
**1:22–25**, 231
**1:23**, 390
**2:6–8**, 231
**2:8**, 164, 258, 391, 413
**5:7–8**, 246
**6:19–20**, 246
**8:5**, 379
**8:11**, 230
**10**, 246, 277
**10:11**, 247
**10:12**, 379
**11:23–26**, 346
**11:24**, 185
**11:25**, 186
**11:26**, 247, 379
**15**, 25, 230, 247
**15:3**, 5, 229, 280
**15:11**, 173
**15:17**, 157, 236, 248, 323
**15:25**, 155, 248
**15:57**, 248

*2 Corinthians*
**4:5**, 249
**4:7–12**, 249–50
**5:14–6:2**, 252
**5:18**, 81
**5:19**, 81, 156, 194, 347
**5:21**, 81, 82, 253, 299

*2 Corinthians (cont.)*
**5:21a**, 253
**5:21b**, 253
**6:2**, 82
**6:4–10**, 250, 367
**11:21–12:7**, 250
**12:9–10**, 250
**12:19–21**, 405

*Galatians*
**1:3–4**, 235, 390
**1:4**, 230, 231, 241, 242, 245, 279, 280, 361, 407
**1:13–14**, 243
**2:15**, 243
**2:17**, 323
**2:19**, 259
**2:19–20**, 238, 242, 244, 249
**2:20**, 5, 13, 192, 245
**2:21**, 243
**3**, 323
**3:1–14**, 240
**3:10, 13–14**, 238
**3:10–14**, 241
**3:13**, 82, 253
**3:14**, 83
**3:29**, 322
**4:1–11**, 241, 241, 276, 277
**4:3–5, 8–9**, 390
**4:3–7**, 237
**4:4**, 291
**4:9**, 238

**5**, 244
**5:24**, 244
**6:14, 15**, 238
**6:14–16**, 236

*Ephesians*
**1:10**, 33, 49, 157, 161

*Philippians*
**2**, 412
**2:2–4**, 256
**2:5**, 256
**2:6–11**, 67, 254–55, 278
**2:8**, 274
**2.8b**, 55
**3:9**, 323

*Colossians*
**1:15**, 293, 340
**1:24**, 32, 369
**2**, 221, 260
**2:9**, 261
**2:13–15**, 258, 261
**2:13–16**, 164
**2:14–15**, 391
**2:15**, 231
**3:1–11**, 403

*1 Thessalonians*
**1:9**, 332
**1:9–10**, 389
**1:10**, 32, 330
**5:9**, 32, 330
**5:10**, 230

*1 Peter*
**2:9**, 128

*2 Peter*
**3:13**, 146

*1 John (First Letter of John)*
**2:1–2**, 212
**2:2**, 333
**4:10–11**, 47–48

*Revelation*
**1**, 128, 165, 251
**1:5–6**, 78
**5**, 128, 165, 166, 251
**5:9–10**, 78, 159, 166
**11:15**, 359
**13:8**, 69
**20**, 128, 165, 251
**20:6**, 78, 128
**21–22**, 157

GREEK BIBLE

*4 Maccabees*
**1:10–11**, 129–20
**6:22**, 130
**12:17**, 130
**17**, 341
**17:20–22**, 130, 344
**17:21–22**, 300

# SUBJECT INDEX

Aaron, 95, 128

Abelard, 26–27

Abraham, 83, 91, 134, 202, 220, 232, 233, 238, 239, 264, 268–69, 322; covenant with/divine promises to, 94–95, 106, 107, 149, 152, 234, 236, 237, 240, 241, 243, 244, 270, 271, 273, 297–98, 303, 304–5, 310, 311, 313–14, 318, 319, 320–21, 328, 414; in Pauline writings, 268–69, 273, 297, 301, 304–5, 308, 311, 313–14, 318, 320–21, 335, 345

Acts of the Apostles, 149, 151–55, 159–65, 331, 205; Christian mission, 366–67; Gentile mission, 388; Paul's speeches, 389–90; suffering and, 368–69; when written, 177

Adam and Eve, 91, 94, 95, 96, 103, 105, 239, 275, 284, 322, 348

*Aeneid* (Virgil), 52

Alexander, Cecil Francis, 14, 14n

Alexander Janaeus, 58

Andrew, Saint, 221

Anglicanism (Church of England), 13–16

Anselm, Saint, 26, 27, 29

Antiochus Epiphanes, 126–27

*Apion* (Josephus), 58

Apostles' Creed, 25

ascension, 69, 155, 162, 166, 169, 178

Athanasius of Alexandria, 25

atonement, 26, 34, 36, 37, 45, 46, 82, 132, 169, 170, 367; gospels and, 172, 196–225; meaning of, 68–69; moral example theory, 26; new Passover and, 326, 333; Old Testament and, 93; paganism and, 62, 148, 185, 224; in Pauline writings, 295, 296, 349; punishment models, 45–46, 48, 62; representative substitution and, 210–25; satisfaction theory, 26–27; theologies of, 53, 152, 170, 171, 175, 176, 185, 193, 201, 223, 224, 263, 295, 415, 416. See also Day of Atonement

*Atonement, The* (Hengel), 62

Bach, John Sebastian, 9, 27

baptism, 151, 221, 276, 278, 378–79, 411

Barabbas, 213, 216

bar-Kochba, Simon, 201

Barnabas, 154

Barth, Karl, 28

Bible: analysis of human plight in, 86; Authorized (King James) Version, 13, 360; New International Version, 299; New Revised Standard Version, 295–96. See also New Testament; Old Testament; *specific books*

Body of Christ, 364, 369

Bonhoeffer, Dietrich, 375

Bracchiolini, Poggio, 30
British Museum, 8
Bunyan, John, 11, 11n

Caesar, Julius, 4, 61–62
Caesar Augustus, Emperor, 51–52,
    59–60
Caiaphas, 211
Calvin, John, 27, 33, 49, 76
Cato, 61–62
Christianity: center of the faith,
    364; cultural expectations about
    heaven, 146–47; culture of violence
    and death and, 41; dealing with
    evil and, 36–37; development of
    Jesus "died for our sins" idea, 24,
    25–27; diminishing of central gospel
    message, 115; downfall of oppressive
    systems and, 392, 399; Easter and,
    34; Eastern Church, 26, 27, 33;
    follies and failings, 365; fundamental
    truth, 23; good news of, 42, 43, 151;
    heaven as the goal, 74, 199, 415; idea
    of dying for someone else in, 61;
    in modern culture, 8; moral effort
    and, 397; paganism and, 62, 74, 147;
    paganism and salvation, 94, 113,
    142, 147, 345, 347, 409; paganism
    and the crucifixion, 34, 74, 96, 126,
    131, 132, 189, 193, 194, 224, 234,
    253, 254, 257, 261, 281, 287, 288,
    289, 292, 349; persecutions, 37–38,
    376, 377; Platonizing of, 148, 158,
    223, 224; Reformation and doctrine,
    28–37; as revolutionary movement,
    362; shrinking of, 410–11; sin as
    the problem, 74; social justice and,
    400–402, 404–5; suffering and the
    Christian life, 368–73, 404; theologies
    of atonement, 25, 53, 152, 170, 171,
    175, 176, 185, 193, 201, 223, 224,
    263, 295, 415, 416; Western church,
    158, 161, 199; Western modernism
    and, 362–63

Christianity (early Church): beliefs
    of, 166; critics of, 20; God present
    in Jesus, 291; good news of, 17, 18;
    meaning of crucifixion for, 5, 18, 20–
    21, 25–26, 39–40, 60–61, 65, 93–94,
    96, 99, 102, 117–18, 166–67, 169, 178,
    189, 264, 277, 296, 350–51; meaning
    of resurrection, 346, 351; scriptural
    heritage of, 68; world of, 65–66
Christian mission, 356; challenges of,
    409–10; commissioning the disciples
    and, 383–84, 415; contemporary
    organizations, 361; "cruciform
    mission," 406–16; evangelism vs.,
    356; forgiveness of sin and, 362; to
    free people from sin (dark powers),
    387–406; history of, 358–61; holiness
    and, 406; launching God's kingdom
    and, 357, 360; love and, 365–66;
    Passover People and, 365; Puritan
    hope, 358–59; rethinking, 362–81;
    saving souls for heaven, 356, 357, 359,
    360, 361, 362, 368, 407; social gospel
    movements, 361; suffering and, 368,
    373; what it is, 358
Chronicles, 91, 280
Chrystostom, 411
Cicero, 53–54
*Civil War* (Lucan), 61–62
*Civil Wars* (Appian), 57
Colossians, 231, 258–61, 293, 369
*Commentary on Matthew* (Origen), 54
Communism, 377–78, 392
Constantine, Holy Roman Emperor, 38
1 Corinthians, 173, 246–48, 277, 323,
    346, 379; "announce" (*katangellō*) and
    the Eucharist in, 379–80; opening
    passages, 230–31, 248
2 Corinthians, 81–82, 87, 248–54, 299,
    366–67, 369; central argument, 251
Cornelius, 164, 388
covenant: "blood of the covenant," 192;
    Deuteronomy 27 and, 239; faithfulness
    of God and, 119, 131–37, 185, 194,

297–98, 303, 304, 312–13, 314, 316, 333, 349; of God and Israel, 64, 126, 134, 149, 152, 270, 271, 273, 286, 289, 297–98, 309, 311, 312, 325, 328; in Pauline writings, 297–98, 301–7, 310–27, 345–49; renewal of, 119, 151, 157, 186, 188, 191, 192–93, 194, 222, 281, 304, 333, 381; of vocation, 76–87, 102, 224, 229, 245, 251, 274, 286, 309, 336, 347, 408, 416; of works (works contract), 74–76, 82, 83, 94, 147, 224, 227, 232, 234, 244, 245, 253, 265, 270, 275, 281, 312, 317, 338

covenant love, 374, 414

Cranmer, Thomas, 16

creation, 76–77, 102, 107; Adam project, 274; in Genesis, 91; God's plan to rescue and restore, 101, 197–225; human distortion of, 80, 100; human vocation and. 68, 76, 77, 79, 80, 84, 86, 95, 99, 100–101, 103, 105, 113, 148, 155, 159, 224; Israel's vocation and, 89–91, 159; new, 102, 148, 157, 162, 176, 229, 268, 274, 290, 333, 365, 370, 385, 414, 416; renewed in the promised land, 95–96; royal priesthood and, 77–80; as Temple, with divine "image" at heart of, 95

Cromwell, Oliver, 33

cross: advice of Justin Martyr about, 21, 21n; Jesus order to followers and, 58; made from shipwreck fragments, 8–9; reality of crucifixion and image, 54; as symbol of fear, 37–38; meditation or prayer and, 12; worn by Christians, 7. *See also* crucifixion of Jesus

Crossman, Samuel, 14n

crucifixion: early history of, 55–56; of followers of Spartacus, 57; horror of, 54, 59; as ignoble death, 59, 63; mocking a victim, 59; nails used, 56; purpose of, 55–57; Roman Empire's use of, 7, 10, 53–58, 173; for slaves and rebels, 19, 55, 56–57, 58, 59,

178; social, communal, and political meaning, 54–55, 60; symbolism, 60; theological or religious meaning, 60; whipping, scourging, and public humiliation with, 57

crucifixion of Jesus (the cross), 5, 6, 12, 19, 28–37, 287; as act of love, 16, 43, 47, 194, 222, 251, 253, 257, 293, 346, 399, 415; in art, music, and literature, 8–11, 15, 17; as central to Christianity, 21; centurion at, 174; in context of the Greco-Roman world, 51–63; in context of the Jewish world, 63–65; cry of dereliction, 225, 292, 372; date of, 58; depicted in hymns, 13–16, 38, 48; depicted in the New Testament, 13, 17, 27, 49, 67, 172–73, 174, 184; as divine act, 16, 194, 198, 199, 289; divine purpose for the world and, 83; in doctrine, 21–22, 25–27, 33; exposition by Athanasius, 25; first-century setting of, 51–69; in Gnostic gospels, 21; historical authenticity of, 178; human elements of the story, 10; "instruments of the Passion," 10; Jesus's last words, 197; "King of the Jews" notice, 178, 210, 221, 355; mocking by crowds, 198, 206; mocking by Pilate, 59; paganizing of, 34, 74, 96, 126, 131, 132, 189, 193, 194, 224, 234, 253, 254, 257, 261, 281, 287, 288, 289, 292, 349; Passover and, 64, 178–94; power of, 5–13, 18, 19, 185, 398–99; as revolution's beginning, 3–4, 5, 12, 18, 34, 35, 36, 40, 46–47, 69, 83, 84, 138, 146, 148, 169, 170, 174, 197, 278, 323, 349, 355, 365, 367, 391, 414; Roman soldiers and, 52; as scandalous, 19–20, 37, 59; suffering Messiah and, 174, 177, 180; theological meaning/study of, 170–71; theories about what it achieved, 73–74; two thieves being crucified and, 213–14, 216; as world-changing, 3, 69, 146, 156, 170, 251, 258, 278, 355, 368, 418

crucifixion of Jesus (meaning of):
according to early Christians, 5, 18,
20–21, 25–26, 39–40, 60–61, 65,
93–94, 96, 99, 102, 117–18, 166–67,
169, 178, 189, 264, 277, 296, 350–51;
according to the gospels, 196–225;
according to Jesus, 170, 171, 174, 183,
189; contemporary ideas, 233; divine
wrath satisfied by, 28–37, 42–47, 147,
185, 221, 234, 257, 263, 267, 273, 286,
300, 303, 330, 331; as dying for our
sins, 22, 192–93, 211–25, 229, 240–41,
245, 248, 287, 356, 358, 362, 363, 367,
381, 408, 409 (see also representative
substitution); forgiveness of sin as
purpose of, 7, 12, 64, 97, 106–19, 142,
149–58, 160, 163–64, 169, 211–25,
251, 260, 277, 279, 296, 337, 356,
362, 364, 381, 416; to fulfill scripture,
"in accordance with the Bible," 5, 13,
17, 22, 23, 66, 87, 94, 96, 97, 99, 103,
105, 119, 138, 142, 145, 148, 150,
152–53, 154, 158, 160, 163, 169, 173,
176, 177, 188, 223, 229, 230, 232, 241,
248, 255, 264, 273, 280, 282, 287, 349,
350, 366, 381; as global restoration
and, 106; heaven and earth uniting
and, 49, 78–79, 156; as a kingdom
event, 230; New Testament view,
415; Pauline ideas, 227–61, 263–349;
as penal substitution, 29–30, 31, 35,
38–39, 227–28, 240, 330; to redeem
all nations, 150, 151, 153; to renew
vocation, 79, 81–87, 89–91, 100, 148,
153; as a sacrifice, 67, 177, 186–87,
188, 197, 273, 289, 300, 330, 331; as
victory over evil (Christus Victor), 26,
39, 46, 119, 142, 148, 161, 165, 180,
183, 184, 192, 205, 209, 210, 215, 221,
222, 228–31, 235, 241, 243, 245, 248,
253–55, 259–60, 277, 279, 280, 290,
293, 319, 323, 332, 351, 355–56, 358,
362, 363, 364, 369, 381, 384, 386–87,
397, 403, 405, 408

Daniel, 64, 92–93, 111, 114, 118, 119,
151, 179, 184, 210, 304, 319
Dante, 28
David, 92, 109, 128, 140, 187, 203
Day of Atonement, 64, 138, 184, 298,
328, 330, 332, 346, 348
death: defeat of, 248, 355, 358, 386;
exile and, 97, 103, 104, 105, 111;
expulsion from the garden and, 95,
96, 103; idolatry and, 102; pagan
noble death, 61, 62, 63, 131, 137,
138–39, 343; sin and, 103, 283
Deism, 36
deliverance ministry, 12–13
De Rerum Natura (Lucretius), 30–31
Deuteronomy, 91, 95, 97, 114, 151, 239,
304; "curse of the law," 272, 275, 281,
311; in Pauline writings, 268, 281,
319; "Song of Moses," 104
devil/Satan, 101, 102, 207, 284, 389,
404, 412–13, 414
Diocletian, Emperor, 376
"double imputation," 253
Dream of Gerontius, The (Elgar), 15

Eleazar, 130, 342
election, 282, 312, 336, 340, 341
Elgar, Edward, 15
Endo, Shusaku, 376
Enlightenment, 35, 172, 360
Ephesians, 33, 49
Epictetus, 367
Epicureanism, 31, 35, 36, 162, 360
Epistle (Seneca), 55–56
eschatology, 28–29, 33, 34, 35; of
Ephesians, 33, 49; "Four Last Things,"
29; God's kingdom on earth, 35,
49; heaven-and-hell framework, 33,
35, 49, 74, 406; Jewish, 235, 347;
messianic, 310; paganized, 34, 147,
409; Platonized, 158–59, 347, 409,
410; resurrection of the body, 175
Eucharist, 13, 185–87, 379–80
Euripedes, 61, 125

evil (dark powers), 13, 46, 101, 180, 191,
192, 222, 259, 286, 351, 380, 381,
392–406; defeated by the Messiah,
205, 206; depicted in Luke, 216; in
Israel's scriptures, 202–3; "natural,"
36; opposition to Jesus and, 203–7;
personal sin vs., 36; political and
social, 36. *See also* sin

*Evil and the Justice of God* (Wright), 36

Exodus, 63, 78, 89, 91, 92, 95, 108, 180–
81, 326, 339–40; *kappōreth* in, 327;
narrative of, 182; new, in Romans,
263–94, 319, 324–27; new, of Isaiah,
326; new, of Jesus, 117, 127, 134, 138,
157, 182, 184, 188, 194, 237, 260,
347, 414; redemption and, 271

Ezekiel, 92, 104, 106, 111, 112, 184, 290

Ezra, 184

final judgment, 128–29, 154, 322, 330

forgiveness, 5, 36, 42, 104;
contemporary examples, 385–86;
crucifixion of Jesus and, 7, 12, 64, 97,
106–19, 142, 149–58, 160, 163–64,
169, 211–25, 251, 260, 277, 279, 296,
337, 356, 362, 364, 381, 416; Israel's
sins and, 138, 151; in the Lord's
Prayer, 385; "new covenant" for,
64–65; new Passover and, 326; power
of, 384, 391, 402; revolution of the
cross and, 385. *See also* sin

Francis, Pope, 8

Fujimura, Mako, 376–77

Galatians, 82–83, 231, 234–45, 259, 280,
281, 322, 323; Exodus narrative, 277;
main argument, 244; new Passover,
230, 235, 237, 238, 241, 243, 245,
246–47; opening, 230, 235; "The son
of God loved me and gave himself
for me" (2:19–20), 139, 192, 227, 242,
243–44, 367; unity theme, 234–35,
241, 243, 272

Galba, Emperor, 59

Galilee, 58

Genesis, 78, 79, 89, 94–95, 255, 335–36

Gibson, Mel, 53, 57

glory/God's glory, 180, 268, 269, 272,
287, 290, 317, 327, 339–40, 341, 404,
413

Gnosticism, 21, 172, 375, 398

God: Abraham and, 94–95, 106, 107,
149, 152, 234, 236, 237, 240, 241,
243, 244, 270, 271, 273, 297–98, 303,
304–5, 310, 311, 313–14, 318, 319,
320–21, 328, 414; "angry God," 30–
31, 32, 38–39, 43–44, 74, 132, 147,
234, 273, 311; covenant faithfulness,
119, 131–37, 185, 194, 297–98,
303, 304, 305–6, 312–13, 314, 316,
317–20, 333, 349; as Creator, 76, 77,
79, 80, 82, 86, 91, 93, 95, 97, 100, 110,
308, 338; divine love, 16, 17, 23, 24,
30, 46, 47, 119, 135; divine name, 108,
339–40; divine Presence, 95, 107–19,
160, 161, 162, 163, 222, 277, 333–34,
413, 415; as king, 79–80; meeting
his people at the lid of the ark, 108;
"new heavens and new earth" of,
34, 49, 68, 74, 78, 102, 105, 146, 157,
268, 409; rescue plan of, 4, 5, 22, 34,
82, 101, 104, 106, 111, 137, 152, 157,
158, 171, 180, 192, 267, 271, 287–88,
290, 320, 347, 372; self-giving love
of, 194, 222, 251, 253, 257, 293, 346,
399, 415. *See also* crucifixion of Jesus;
incarnation

*Gospel of Thomas*, 21, 172, 173

grace, 155, 216, 274, 282, 296, 317, 319,
332

Haggai, 92, 112

Handel, Georg Frideric, 359

*Harry Potter* (Rowling), 10

heaven, 28, 29, 33–34, 35, 38, 49, 94;
common view, 146–47, 162; defined,
162; "going to heaven" as goal, 36,
49, 68, 74, 78, 105, 146, 154–55, 166,

heaven *(cont.)*
171, 196, 199, 214, 223–24, 234,
251, 287, 290, 302, 345, 347, 356,
357, 361, 415; moral behavior and,
158–59; in Pauline writings, 267–68;
Platonized view, 113, 158, 171, 234,
289, 311, 345, 347; "Romans road"
and, 265, 299, 345; saving souls for,
356, 357, 359, 360, 361, 362, 368, 407
Hebrews, 69, 331, 350
hell, 38, 39, 78, 94, 113; Gehenna, 215
Hengel, Martin, 62
Herod Agrippa I, 164
Herod Agrippa II, 388
Herodotus, 55
Herod the Great, 58, 203, 206, 368
Hezekiah, Judas ben, 58, 203
Homer, 52, 125
Horace, 62
Hosea, 188
"How Great Thou Art" (hymn), 17, 17n

idolatry, 68, 74, 77, 85–86, 245;
crucifixion as overthrow of, 26, 46,
119, 142, 148, 161, 165, 180, 183,
184, 192, 205, 209, 210, 215, 220,
221, 222, 228–31, 235, 241, 243, 245,
248, 253–55, 259–60, 277, 279, 280,
290, 293, 319, 323, 332, 351; cultic
element in Romans, 297, 308, 313,
315, 316, 317, 334, 337–39, 341;
defined, 77; exile and, 103, 105, 114,
319, 333; God's punishment for, 304;
of Israel, 103, 105, 108, 114, 122, 308,
334; money, sex, power as, 77, 101,
378, 393–400; as sin, 100, 101, 102,
105, 257, 260, 270, 283, 286, 302,
308, 313, 333
*Iliad* (Homer), 52
incarnation, 13, 18, 46, 113, 139, 174,
192, 200, 219, 237, 242, 244, 289,
312, 322, 332, 339–41, 346, 367, 408,
415; in John 1:14, 22, 112, 200, 341,
413

intercession, 372, 404, 405
*In Verrem* (Cicero), 54
Irenaeus, 375
Isaac, 91
Isaiah, 89–90, 92, 104, 111, 112, 114,
116, 137, 139, 157, 179, 184, 255,
260, 290, 304, 319, 321; faithful
love theme, 131, 134–37, 336; new
Exodus of, 326; New Testament
references, 125–26; royal passage, 139;
Servant Songs, 114, 123–24, 139–40,
194, 257, 343, 344; Servant vocation,
333–39
Israel and the Jews: Babylonian
captivity, 91, 92, 97, 104, 111, 117,
138, 184; concept of heaven and hell
and, 113; covenant of, 64, 126, 134,
149, 152, 270, 271, 273, 286, 289,
297–98, 303, 325; crucifixion by the
Romans and, 55, 58; crucifixion of
Jesus in context of, 63–65; in Egypt,
91–92, 93, 127, 138, 180, 182; exile
and, 91–97, 104–6, 113, 117, 118,
121, 137, 138, 184, 222, 229–30,
241, 277, 281–83, 286, 311, 333, 334;
first century, festivals and holy days,
63–64; forgiveness of sins, 138; God's
purpose for, 99, 108; Hasmonean
priest-kings, 57–58, 127–28; idea of
dying for someone else, 61, 62; idea
of suffering for someone else, 125,
128, 129; idolatry and, 103, 105, 108,
114, 122, 297, 308, 334, 340; the
Messiah and, 65, 68, 97, 116, 117,
119, 121–22, 174, 281, 282, 283,
290, 312, 346; Mosaic law and, 272,
274–75, 289; "new covenant," 64;
Passover and, 63–64, 92, 117, 157;
persecution of, 37–38; postexilic
period prophets, 92, 112; redefining
hope of rescue, 146–60; redemption
and, 145; restoration, 106, 111, 113–
14, 115, 116, 117, 119, 122, 137, 160,
161, 165, 239, 272; revolt in Galilee,

58; ritual sacrifice, 67, 177–78, 187, 289; Roman conquest, 58, 184; scandal of a crucified Messiah, 19; Second Temple period, 112, 122, 137, 142, 201, 272, 281, 302, 319, 332; sins of, 184, 229, 331, 333, 334; suffering of, 122–24, 126–27, 128; Syrian invasion, 126–27, 128; twelve tribes, 180; vocation of, 89–91, 105, 159, 304, 309, 310, 311, 312, 322, 324, 335, 340, 347; Western Wall, 112. *See also* tabernacle; Temple; Torah (holy law)

Jacob, 91, 107–8, 202
James the Apostle, 220, 221, 368, 374
Jephthah, 41
Jeremiah, 64, 92–93, 104, 114, 151, 181, 184, 192–93, 290, 319, 326
Jesus Army, 6–7, 7n, 12
Jesus of Nazareth: action in the Temple, 181; awareness of crucifixion as punishment, 58; compassion and love, 47, 191–92, 193, 201, 202; death on the cross (*see* crucifixion of Jesus); as exorcist, 191, 205, 207; followers of, 13, 21, 23, 25, 26, 47, 51, 55, 58, 65, 67, 68, 93, 96, 105, 118, 156–57, 158, 161, 162, 164, 166, 173, 174, 175, 178, 182, 185, 186, 188, 190, 191, 193, 198–99, 200, 201, 208, 219, 220, 225, 256, 274, 281, 292, 350, 351, 355, 356, 363, 366, 369, 371, 376, 377, 379, 384, 385, 392, 397, 398, 402, 403, 406, 407, 411–12, 414; gospel accounts, 170–71; gospel portrait, 190–92, 201, 202; hostile forces and, 203–7; as Israel's God returning, 200–210; as king, 55, 119, 178, 199, 201, 256; kingdom of God and, 119, 170, 171, 178–79, 183, 191, 192, 199, 204, 211, 214, 256, 288, 355, 412–13; liberation of Israel and, 161; meaning of the cross

for, 61, 170, 171, 174, 182, 183, 189; as the Messiah, 163, 177, 210, 222, 232–33, 243, 255, 283, 312, 346, 408; new Exodus of, 117, 127, 134, 138, 157, 182, 188; as the new tabernacle, 113; Passover, use of by, 64, 169–94; priesthood of, 80; risen, appearances, 145, 383; as son of God, 13, 18, 38, 46, 110, 113, 139, 174, 192, 200, 219, 237, 242, 244, 289, 312, 322, 332, 339–41, 346, 367, 408, 415; suffering of, 48; twelve disciples, 180; vocation of, 179, 184, 189, 190, 194, 197, 199, 211, 219, 222, 324, 335, 373–74
*Jewish Antiquities* (Josephus), 58
*Jewish War* (Josephus), 54, 58
Jezebel, Queen, 57
Joffe, Roland, 10
1 John (First Letter of John), 47, 212, 333
John, Gospel of, 13, 113, 172, 193, 203, 287, 293, 323–24, 387; arrival of the Greeks, 387–88; commissioning the disciples, 383, 415; Farewell Discourses, 208, 413; glory and love themes, 413; idea of dying for someone else, 62; incarnation and, 22, 112, 200, 341, 413; interpretation of the crucifixion, 208, 341; Jesus as return of Israel's God, 200; Jesus as the Passover lamb, 209; Jesus claims authority in heaven and earth, 207; Jesus's love depicted in, 192; Jesus vs. Satan in, 412–13; Jesus washing the disciples' feet, 411–12; kingdom of God and, 360; new Exodus of, 414; passion narrative, 27, 189; Passover and, 414; portrayal of Jesus by, 202; representative substitution and, 211–13; the risen Christ in, 414; theology of the cross and, 113
John the Apostle, 5, 47–48, 205, 220, 221, 374
John the Baptist, 149, 200, 201, 278

Josephus, 53, 54, 56, 58, 104, 201, 209, 343

Joshua, 203

Josiah, King of Judah, 203

Judas, 10, 207, 412, 414

Judges, 41, 203

justification, 267, 272, 273, 300, 301, 315, 321–24

Justin Martyr, 21, 21n

King, Martin Luther, Jr., 392

kingdom movement, 278

kingdom of God, 18, 116–19, 155, 160–67, 171, 209; achievement by love, 374; Christian mission and, 357, 359, 360; crucifixion starting, 222, 230; distortion of, 410; as heaven on earth, 196, 197, 223–24; Jesus's death and, 183, 257, 280; Jesus's ministry and, 119, 170, 171, 178–79, 191, 192, 199, 204, 205, 214, 256, 288, 412–13; Jesus's redefining, 211; in Matthew, 217–19; in Pauline writings, 164–65, 270–76, 278, 288; reign of grace, 274

Lamentations, 114

Last Supper, 67, 161, 170, 182, 183, 185–87, 197, 225, 247, 345

*Letters and Papers from Prison* (Bonhoeffer), 375

Leviticus, 289, 329

Lewis, C. S., 263

Lord's Prayer, 218, 385

Lord's Supper. *See* Eucharist

Lucan, 61–62

Lucretius, 30–31

Luke, Gospel of, 13, 51, 145–46, 148–50, 154, 160, 172, 287; atonement theology, 189; birth narratives, 200; books of, 149; on the crucifixion, 171, 177; green tree and dry/one hen and chicks, 189; incident in the garden, 190; interpretation of the crucifixion, 215, 216; Jesus as return of Israel's God, 200; Jesus claims authority in heaven and earth, 207; Jesus's pointing to the scriptures in, 87, 105–6; on the kingdom of God, 161, 164, 165–66; meeting on the road to Emmaus, 145, 148, 156, 176; parable of the vineyard, 216; passion narrative, 172–74; release of Barabbas, 213; representative substitution and, 213–17; threats against Jesus, 203; two thieves crucified, 213–14, 216; vicarious suffering and, 189; when written, 152

Luther, Martin, 27, 28, 30, 33, 378

Maccabean writings, 125–27, 129–31, 138, 300, 341–44

magic, 380–81

Magnificat, 374

Malachi, 91, 92, 112, 280

Marcion, 312

Mark, Gospel of, 13, 172, 293; atonement theology and, 220; cry of dereliction, 225, 292; interpretation of the crucifixion in, 215; Jesus as return of Israel's God, 200; passion narrative, 172–73, 174; rebuke of the disciples, 191–92; representative substitution in, 220–25; threats against Jesus, 203

Mary, Mother of God, 374, 414

Matthew, Gospel of, 13, 172; the Beatitudes, 217–18, 220; cry of dereliction, 225, 292; genealogy of Israel, 219–20; interpretation of the crucifixion in, 217; Jesus as return of Israel's God, 200; Jesus claims authority in heaven and earth, 207; kingdom of God and, 217–19; Lord's Prayer, 218; passion narrative, 27, 172–73, 174; representative substitution and, 217–20

McGregor, Neil, 8

Messiah: Good Friday and, 194; Jesus as, 65, 68, 97, 116, 117, 119, 121–22,

174, 281, 282, 283, 290, 312, 346, 408; prophecies of, 210; redemption and, 290; as servant, 233; would-be, 201

*Messiah* (Handel), 359; "Hallelujah Chorus," 359

Michelangelo, 28

ministry of reconciliation, 252

*Mission, The* (film), 10

"moral example" theory, 26

Mosaic law, 75, 236, 272, 282

Moses, 181, 182, 202, 212, 239

"My Song Is Love Unknown" (hymn), 13–14, 14n

Nahum, 58

Nathan, 109

National Gallery, London, "Seeing Salvation" exhibition, 8, 37

Nehemiah, 184

Newman, John Henry, 15, 15n

New Testament: accounts of the crucifixion, 13, 17, 27, 49, 172–73, 174, 184 (see also crucifixion of Jesus); accounts of the Last Supper, 186; accounts of the resurrection, 175, 176; Christian mission and, 358, 366; Christology of, 293; crucifixion as ending of Israel's scriptures, 93; first fifty years of Christianity and, 65–69; gospel narratives, 66, 69, 196–225; Jesus died for our sins in accordance with the Bible as rule for, 66; letters of, 66; Pauline writings, 226–350; redefining Israel's hope of rescue, 146–60; Reformers and, 32–33; use of Israel's scriptures in, 66, 125–26, 151–52, 154, 155, 202; what it is about, 40. *See also specific books; specific concepts; specific events*

*New Testament and the People of God, The* (Wright), 63

Nicene-Constantinopolitan Creed, 25

Numbers, 289

*Odes* (Horace), 62

Old Testament, 87; arrangement of, 90; as book of moral examples, 41; coming Messiah as king and conqueror, 122; covenant in, 76; divine anger in, 132; evil in, 202–3; expulsion from the garden, 95; faithful love theme, 131–37; heaven and earth as together, 95; narrative of divine Presence, 107–19; narrative of vocation, 87, 89–91; Pentateuch, 91, 239; promised land, 95–96; prophecies of, 179; references to, early Christian writings, 66–67; righteousness in, 303–4; "sin offering" of, 289; suffering, 122–31. *See also specific books; specific persons*

Onesimus, 261

Origen, 54

pacifism, 45, 48

paganism: atonement and, 62, 148, 185, 224; defeat of divinities, 390; in 4 Maccabees, 344; interpretation of the crucifixion and, 34, 74, 96, 126, 131, 132, 189, 193, 194, 224, 234, 253, 254, 257, 261, 281, 287, 288, 289, 292, 349; noble death of, 63, 131, 137, 138, 343, 344; poets, 387; salvation and, 94, 113, 142, 147, 311, 345, 347, 409; suffering, 125, 126, 129, 131, 189, 194

*Passion of the Christ, The* (film), 53, 57

Passover, 63–64, 92, 117, 157, 209, 277; Jesus's use of, 64, 178–94, 208–9, 277, 414; as kingdom moment, 188, 193; meal, 185–86, 187 (see also Last Supper); narrative of, 325–26; new, of Jesus, 186, 187, 188, 194, 222, 230, 235, 237, 238, 241, 243, 245, 246–47, 259, 288, 326, 332, 351, 362, 408; in Pauline writings, 272, 276, 278–79, 288, 296, 324–27, 345, 348; as victory over powers of evil, 183, 188

Passover People, 365

Paul of Tarsus, Saint, 177, 193; "in accordance with the Bible" and, 280; on achieving holiness, 403; in Athens, 387, 389; atonement theology and, 295, 296; on baptism, 378, 379; clashes with temples, 162; covenant of vocation and, 83–84, 245, 251–52; the cross as a scandal, 19, 59, 246; on the crucifixion, 5, 173, 227–61, 263–94, 295–349; "curse of the law" and, 82–83; Deuteronomy 32 and, 104; *ephapax*, 26; at Ephesus, 248; familiarity with crucifixion, 59, 63; Gentiles and, 151, 154, 164, 236, 241–42, 243, 272, 309, 311, 348, 388–89; goal of redemption, 228–29; heaven and, 33–34; imprisonments, 368; incarnation and, 312; influence of, 367; Jesus as Messiah, 232–33, 243; Jesus's commandment to love and, 47; Jewish thought and, 291–92; in Lystra, 389; meaning of Jesus's death and resurrection, 103, 157, 194, 227–61, 263–94; the Messiah dying for our sins and, 87, 229, 232, 233, 235–36, 241, 242, 243, 245, 248; ministry of intercession and "glory," 404; nature of apostolic ministry and, 81–83; Pauline studies, 232, 233; representative substitution and, 223, 240–41, 254;; revolutionary theology of, 233; road to Damascus and, 388–89; in Rome, 161, 369; salvation and, 84; as Second Temple Jew, 281, 283, 302, 306, 347, 390; sermon in Pisidian Antioch, 154; speeches in Acts, 389–90; story of, in Acts, 164–65; suffering and, 32, 368–70; theological vision of, 312, 323; unity theme, 233, 234; warning to the church in Corinth, 22; what's wrong with the human race and, 84–85. *See also specific writings*

penal substitution, 29–30, 31, 35, 38–39, 227–28, 234, 240, 286, 287, 330

Pentecost, 163

Peter the Apostle, 10, 151, 153–54, 155, 164, 165, 205, 221, 241–42, 368, 373, 388, 415

Pharisees, 203

Philemon, 261

Philip, 164

Philippians, 55, 67, 254–58, 274, 293, 323, 412

Pilate, Pontius, 18, 52, 59, 198, 206, 208, 215, 401, 413

*Pilgrim's Progress* (Bunyan), 11, 11n

Plato, 34

Plutarch, 34, 367

Pompey, Gnaeus, 58, 61–62

Potok, Chaim, 9–10

"Praise to the Holiest in the Height" (hymn), 15, 15n

priesthood, 80. *See also* "royal priesthood"

Promenade Concerts, performance of Bach's *St. Matthew Passion*, 9

promised land (New Eden), 92, 95–96, 108, 109, 239, 272, 314

Protestantism, 75

Psalms, 109, 114, 116–17, 122–23, 137, 140, 151, 179, 304, 359, 371

purgatory, 28, 29, 30, 35

Puritan hope, 358–59

Q Gospel, 172–73, 188

Rahner, Karl, 30

Rattle, Sir Simon, 9

Ratzinger, Joseph, 30

redemption, 132, 137–42, 145; for all nations, 150, 151, 153–54; as *apolytrōsis*, 324–26, 333; complete, 138; Pauline writings and, 228–29, 265, 271, 276–77, 290–91, 323–27, 333, 348–49; as "saved souls going to heaven," 146, 229, 347; through suffering, 116, 119, 125, 131, 188–89

Rees, Timothy, 48n

Reformation, 25, 27, 28–37; theology, 358

representative substitution, 192–93, 211–25, 240–41, 254, 287, 358, 367, 381

resurrection, 4, 7, 20, 27, 60–61, 69, 104, 110, 146, 156, 157, 161, 169, 175–78, 230; archetypal forgiveness-of-sins moment, 156–57; belief in, 384–85; of the body, 28–29, 34, 175–76; coming together of heaven and earth, 161; early Christians and, 351; forgiveness with, 386; God's "new age" and, 175; as heart of salvation, 49; internal, 386; in Luke, 214; Pauline writings and, 234–35, 236, 247–48, 260, 323; "Puritan hope" and, 35; as sign of revolution, 4, 34, 36, 323, 355; ultimate, of the dead, 169, 359

Revelation, 5, 69, 79, 82, 157, 165–66, 373; Handel's *Messiah* and, 359, 360

revolution (of the cross): continuation of, 410–11; crucifixion as start of, 3–4, 5, 12, 18, 22, 34, 35, 36, 40, 46–47, 69, 83, 84, 138, 146, 169, 170, 278, 323, 349, 365, 367, 391, 414; forgiveness and, 391; God's kingdom coming on earth, 40, 161, 359; Jesus-based, 18, 68; Jesus's followers as agents of, 392; meaning of, to early Christians, 4–5; new commandment for, 414; new reality of, 157; as new way of being human, 385; overthrow of idolatry (powers) and, 26, 46, 119, 142, 148, 161, 165, 180, 183, 184, 192, 205, 209, 210, 215, 220, 221, 222, 228–31, 235, 241, 243, 245, 248, 253–54, 255, 259–60, 277, 279, 280, 290, 293, 319, 323, 391–92; Paul and, 82; as portrayed in the gospels, 220; power of love and, 222, 391, 398–99, 403, 408–9, 414; as reconciliation between heaven and earth, 78, 82, 146, 157, 349; rescuing humans for creation, 290; resurrection as sign of, 4, 34, 36, 323; what it is, 356, 363. *See also* kingdom of God

righteousness, 75, 81–82; *dikaiosynē* (covenant justice), 297, 304, 305–6, 318, 340; in the Old Testament, 303–4; in Romans, 263, 270, 271, 296, 299, 301, 303, 305, 312–13, 316, 317–20, 338

Roman Catholicism, 29, 30, 31, 35

Roman Empire (Greco-Roman world), 6–7, 45, 51–63; conquest of Palestine, 58; crucifixions in, 7, 10, 19, 53–58, 63, 173, 178; idea of dying for someone else in literature of, 61–62; persecutions by, 376; revolutionary movements against, 119, 201, 213; soldiers of, and prisoner abuse, 56; wrath and arms in, 52–53, 60

Roman-Jewish war, 119

Romans, 83–84, 157, 227–61, 263–94, 295–350; Adam-and-Messiah story, 274–75, 282; addressing "The Jew" in, 308–10; *aichmalōtizonta*, word used in, 281; as anti-Jewish, 312; atonement theology, 271, 349; baptism, 276, 278, 378; chapter 3, central statement, 265, 270, 294, 295–349; chapter 3, righteousness of God, 317–20; chapter 3, usual reading of, 299–317, 339; chapter 5 summary, 341; closing summary, 270; covenantal element, 297–98, 301–7, 310–27, 345–49; creation's renewal, 267; cultic element, 297, 302, 308, 313, 315–17, 328, 334, 337–39, 341, 346; description of prayer, 292; *dikaiosynē* (covenant justice) in, 297, 304, 305–6, 318, 340; divine love (*agapē*), 336; divine plan in the Messiah, 320–21; divine wrath and, 257, 263, 267, 273, 286,

Romans *(cont.)*
300, 302, 303, 330, 331; echoes of
the martyrs in, 341–45; exile and,
337; faithfulness of God and, 304,
312, 314–20; grace in, 317; heaven
in, 267–68; *hilasterion*, 300, 302, 316,
324–27, 331, 332, 333, 340, 341;
incarnation, 339–41, 346; inclusion
of Gentiles and, 315; interpretation
of the crucifixion, summary, 348–49l
Jesus's death and the coming of the
Kingdom, 270–76; Jewish law theme,
272, 274–75, 281; Jewish roots of,
306; justification theology, 267, 272,
273, 300, 301, 315, 321–24; kingdom
of God and, 278, 280, 288; language
of punishment in, 333–39; law court
imagery, 322–24; meaning of Jesus's
death in, 261, 263–94, 321; mercy
seat and meeting place, 302, 327–34;
the Messiah "died for us," 273, 282;
messianic eschatology, 310; Mosaic
law and, 281–83; narrative of Messiah
and Spirit, 277; new Passover, new
Exodus, 271, 272, 276–94, 324–27,
345, 348; overall theme, 272; Passover
allusions, 272, 276, 278–79, 288;
*pistis Christou*, 320–22; prayer theme,
269; puzzles of, 266–70; redemption
*(apolytrosis)*, 276–77, 323–27, 333;
reign of grace, 274; return-from-exile
theme, 290; righteousness in, 263,
270, 271, 297, 299, 301, 303–6, 312–
13, 316–20, 338; "Romans road,"
265, 299, 307, 311, 317; salvation,
269; sanctification and, 267; sections
of, 266; servant vocation, 333–39; sin
and forgiveness of sin, 268, 276–94,
298, 309, 313, 314, 315, 322, 330–31,
341, 379; Temple theme, 307–8,
333–34, 336, 337, 344; Temple
theology, 331–32; ungodliness and
failure of worship, 268; unity theme,
348; vocation of royal priesthood,

268, 269; works contract and, 75, 76,
265, 270, 281, 297, 299, 306, 307–9,
312, 317, 338; worship and, 268–69;
315, 316, 328, 333, 346
royal priesthood, 49, 68, 76, 77–80, 89,
99, 128, 159, 165, 166–67, 268, 269,
290, 363, 403, 404, 405, 407

sacramental life, 378–80
sacramental theology, 380–81
sacrifice: death of Jesus as, 67, 177, 186–
87, 188, 197, 289, 330; propitiatory,
273, 300, 330, 331; ritual of, 67,
177–78, 187–88, 289, 302–3, 329, 331
*St. John Passion* (Bach), 27
*St. Matthew Passion* (Bach), 9, 27
salvation, 5, 49, 84, 159, 171–72, 229,
234, 251; goal of, 274; National
Gallery exhibition, 8, 37; in New
Testament, 348; pagan view, 94,
113, 142, 147, 311, 345, 347, 409;
in Pauline writings, 269; Platonized
view, 94, 142, 156, 158, 234;
resurrection and, 49; soteriology and
missiology, 35, 147, 409
Sarah, 95
"satisfaction" theory, 26–27
Schweitzer, Albert, 121, 188, 190, 193,
194, 225
Scorsese, Martin, 376
Sellars, Peter, 9
Seneca, 55–56, 367
Sermon on the Mount, 365, 374
Shakespeare, William, 396–97
Silas, 368
*Silence* (Endo), 376
*Silence and Beauty* (Fujimura), 377
sin, 94, 245; of Adam and Eve, 284,
322, 348; in a Biblical framework,
97–103; Biblical words for, 99, 100;
Christian mission and, 387–406;
church today and, 392; concept of,
as "out-of-date," 37, 98–99; dark
powers and, 102, 117, 180, 222, 351,

380, 381, 392–406; death and, 86, 103; "double imputation" and, 253; exile and, 104–6, 114, 117, 118, 121, 138, 151, 184, 209, 222, 333, 334; forgiveness of, 104, 106, 107–19, 121, 137–42, 149–58, 160, 163–64, 187, 225, 272, 319, 362, 363, 364, 381, 386, 402–3; forgiveness of, ultimate, 119, 127, 188, 222–23, 280, 332, 334, 337, 356; idolatry and, 85–86, 100–101, 102, 105, 257, 260, 270, 283, 286, 302, 308, 313, 333; of Israel, 184; Jesus dying for our sins, 22, 37, 42, 94, 115, 119, 154, 173, 177, 199, 229, 232, 233, 240–41, 245, 248, 255, 282, 351, 366, 381; Lamentations and, 114; moral failures and, 397–98; in Pauline writings, 85, 86, 227–30, 232, 233, 235, 236, 238, 240–45, 248, 251–55, 257, 259–61, 268, 276–94, 313–15, 322, 330–31, 379; power of, 364; as preventing entering heaven, 36, 68; punishment of, 42, 44; rejecting the Messiah as, 153; rescue from and new Exodus, 271–72; ritual sacrifice and, 329–30; seen as the problem, 74; separating people from God, 155; as symptom, 86; today's false deities (money, sex, and power), 393–400; the Torah and the law and, 284–86; as vocational failure, 84, 103, 105; why humans sin, 101–2; "works contract" and, 75; wrathful God and, 38–39, 43–44, 132. *See also* atonement
social gospel movements, 361
Solomon, 109–10, 111, 203, 291
soul, 29, 74; saving souls for heaven, 356, 357, 359, 360, 361, 362, 368, 407
South African *apartheid*, 41, 392
*Spartacus* (film), 57
Spirit/Holy Spirit, 20, 157, 161, 162, 169, 290, 291, 292–93, 404–5
Stephen, the Martyr, Saint, 162, 163

suffering, 116, 119, 121–31, 171; apostolic life and, 164, 229, 250, 276, 398; Christian life and, 368–73, 404; idea of suffering for someone else, 125, 128, 189; love and, 374; 2 Maccabees and, 342–43; of martyrs, 126, 127, 128, 343, 368, 375, 377; of the Messiah, 141, 174, 177, 180, 194, 219, 221, 245, 249, 290, 351, 356, 370, 371, 398; "messianic woes," 122, 188, 190; in Old Testament, 122–31; pagan tradition and, 125, 126, 129, 131, 189, 194; Pauline writings and, 368–72; redemptive, 116, 119, 124, 125–27, 131, 145, 188–89, 368–71; Schweitzer's, 121, 122, 188, 193, 194
*Surprised by Hope* (Wright), 34, 157, 357, 405
*Surprised by Scripture* (Wright), 357

tabernacle, 64, 95, 108–10, 162, 182, 277, 297, 298, 325–27, 332, 340, 413; ark of the covenant, 108–9, 298, 327; Jesus as new tabernacle, 113; lid of the ark (Gr., *hilastērion*; Heb. *kappōreth*), 298, 316, 327–29, 330, 332, 340
Temple: cleansing of, 333; as creation-in-miniature, 95 ; heaven and earth meeting in, 291, 412; Jerusalem Temple, 161, 162; Jesus's action in, 216; Jesus's threat to destroy, 197–98; Jewish Temple theology, 67, 291–92, 331; John's gospel and, 412; "new temple," 156, 157, 412; Roman destruction of, 58, 112 ; Solomon's, 109, 110, 111, 119, 162; theme in Pauline writings, 307–8, 331, 333–34, 336, 337, 340, 344
Tertullian, 368, 411
"There Is a Green Hill Far Away" (hymn), 14, 14n
Thessalonians, 332
Thomas the Apostle, 414
Thucydides, 55

Tiberius, Emperor, 52, 174

Titus, Emperor, 58

Torah (holy law), 64, 146, 187, 203, 282, 283, 284, 285, 286, 288, 289, 291, 309, 322, 325, 326, 327, 335, 344; Jesus fulfills, 335–36; new, of Jesus, 414

Tower of Babel, 107, 202

Tree of Life, 95, 103, 104

Trinity, 25, 48, 257–58, 261, 289, 293–94

Tuccio, Francesco, 8–9

Tutu, Desmond, 392

Twain, Mark, 284

"utter gracious love," 384

Varus, governor of Syria, 58

Vespasian, Emperor, 58

Virgil, 52

*Virtue Reborn* or *After You Believe* (Wright), 159

vocation: covenant of, 76–87, 102, 224, 229, 245, 251, 274, 286, 309, 336, 347, 408, 416; "cup" imagery, 221; human, 187, 224, 268, 311; human, as "image-bearers," 68, 76, 77, 79, 80, 84, 86, 95, 99, 100–101, 103, 105, 113, 148, 155, 159, 224, 288, 357, 380–81, 404, 407; of Israel, 89–91, 105, 159, 304, 309, 310, 311, 312, 322, 324, 335, 340, 347; of Jesus, 179, 184, 189, 190, 194, 197, 199, 211, 219, 324, 335, 373–74; royal, of Psalm 2, 190; "royal priesthood" as, 268, 269, 290, 363; servant vocation, 333–39; of works (works contract), 297, 306, 307, 308–9, 416

Voltaire, 42

*Voyage of the Dawn Treader, The* (Lewis), 263

*W1A* (TV series), 195

wars, 45, 48, 52–53, 396–97

Watt, Isaac, 15, 16n

Westminster Confession, 74

"When I Survey the Wondrous Cross" (hymn) 15–16, 16n

wisdom, 291, 390–91

Wittgenstein, Ludwig, 405–6

works contract. *See* covenant of works

worship, 161–63, 166; life of faith, 169; new community and, 163; in Pauline writings, 268–69, 297, 315, 328, 333, 346; prayers of penitence, 311; ungodliness and failure of worship, 268, 297

Wright, N.T., boyhood experience, 13

Yancey, Philip, 376

Zacchaeus, 411

Zechariah, 92, 112, 149P